MUHAMMAD ALI

Through The Eyes Of The World

For more information on the Muhammad Ali Center,
visit: www.alicenter.org

For more information on **Muhammad Ali – Through The Eyes Of The World**,
visit: www.throughtheeyesoftheworld.com

Printed in the United Kingdom by MPG Books Ltd

Published by Sanctuary Publishing Limited, Sanctuary House, 45-53 Sinclair Road,
London W14 0NS, United Kingdom

www.sanctuarypublishing.com

ISBN: 1-86074-401-X

MUHAMMAD
ALI
Through
The
Eyes
Of
The
World

Foreword by Lennox Lewis

Compiled & Edited by Mark Collings

Acknowledgements

"The mission of the Muhammad Ali Center is to preserve and share the legacy and ideals of Muhammad Ali, to promote respect, hope and understanding and to inspire adults and children everywhere to be as great as they can be."
– Muhammad Ali Center Mission Statement

As a paper boy in 1950s Owensboro, Kentucky, a hundred or so miles from Muhammad Ali's birthplace of Louisville, I spent as much time reading the newspapers as I did delivering them. It was through this medium that I first learned of a potential Golden Gloves Champion – Cassius Marcellus Clay. Being a local boy, I followed his career and am still enthralled by Muhammad Ali's life. I've always had the feeling that we have been close friends since we were kids, although I've never met him. I don't need to – he's always around. And that closeness is the abiding message that comes through the many contributions in this book.

Muhammad Ali – Through The Eyes Of The World, together with the documentary of the same name, was conceived to provide revenue for the Ali Center in Louisville and to highlight the aspirations of Muhammad and the Center in their untiring efforts to help the socially disadvantaged and to inspire the need to promote conflict resolution throughout the world. Its method? Assemble a dazzling array of sportsmen, celebrities, family members and friends and ask, "What does Muhammad Ali mean to you, your generation and your world?" As the answers prove, everyone has their own story, their own take, their own recollections of how Muhammad has captivated, encouraged, cajoled and influenced them in so many ways – and continues to do so, day after day.

Alongside the people who have very kindly given their time to the *Muhammad Ali – Through The Eyes Of The World* book and documentary, the following deserve a special thank you for making the project happen: Caroline Warde, Stuart Watts, Sue Carls, Logan McCulloch, Gerald Davies, Rod Smallwood, Penny Braybrooke, Jeff Hudson, Dan Froude, Alan Heal, Michelle Knight, Chris Bradford, Martin Leake, Ivor Saunders, Paul Burgess, Mark Peacock, Mark Bowes, Jill Stempel and Clare Warde, who carried the box.

David Crowe
Through The Eyes Of The World
London 2001

Contents

Foreword - Lennox Lewis

Former Twice World Heavyweight Champion

The first Ali fight I saw was the "Thrilla In Manila", against Joe Frazier. Me and my mother watched it on TV. There was a lot of hype surrounding this fight so I was particularly excited. I just loved his showmanship, and I said to my mum that I was going to emulate him one day. And I'm trying to do that today.

It wasn't easy growing up a black kid in the East End of London, but Ali gave us a sense of pride. He was a black man and he was heavyweight champion of the world, and his success gave young, black kids, unfortunate kids, something to look up to, something to go for. It gave them hope, faith and strength.

He was all around, in the sense that he was involved with the kids, helping people. He started by winning the Olympic gold medal, which is a great achievement, and then he lost the title three times. But he was able to come back all three times, like he said he would, so he's a man of good ethics, a man of honour. He wants you to believe he can do whatever he says he can do, because *he* believes it.

I liked all of Muhammad Ali's fights, because they were all different. I liked his last couple, because those are the fights that really showed the spirit of a true champion, to be able to come back after being beaten like that. A lot of people come to his fights to see him lose, so it was great to see him come back and actually win, because a lot of people didn't think he could do that. The Leon Spinks fight was one of the favourite fights for me. He actually came back and beat him mentally, used his ring science to win, using the rope-a-dope in that fight and showing how effective it was. It was a different spin on the sports-science aspect of boxing. This was something new. Nothing that I would do! But it showed that Muhammad Ali had invented a new style of boxing that worked for him.

That was one of the things that really stood out for me, the sweet science of the sport. Sweet science to Muhammad Ali and me is hitting without being hit. That involves good movement; good, fast hands; and being able to not get hit. He was great for those things.

The first time I actually met Muhammad Ali, I was at the North American Games in Indianapolis and he actually came down to watch the American team – I was boxing for the Canadian team at that time – and he was watching at the ringside. I remember I just wanted to make a good fight of it. I wanted to show off the fact that my style is like his style. In the back of my mind, I was kind of emulating him. This man that I respect so much is at the ringside, so I wanted to do good. So I went out there and I won that fight. It felt great.

When I won Sports Personality Of The Year, I was standing beside Muhammad Ali, who won Sports Personality Of The Millennium. That was a great moment for me, because I'm there sitting with the man that I look up to, and we're both in front of the world with great awards.

Ali is a great icon. Somebody that has gone through trials and tribulations and achieved things through his whole career. He remained a character and remained himself and stayed true to his beliefs through all of this. He's a showman. He transcended his sport.

Introduction

Ali Goes Home by Mark Collings

"*When Ali comes into view, the dogs start barking, the kids start running and the windows are thrown up. Everybody runs into the street, and down the dusty road comes the figure, the person.*"
    – Tom Owen, Louisville community historian

24 FEBRUARY 2000

I'm heading towards the Seelbach Hotel, on the corner of Fourth Avenue and Muhammad Ali Boulevard, in Louisville, Kentucky. Louisville is a river city, built on the banks of the deep waters of the Ohio River. It is neat and compact and boasts a rich sporting tradition – the Kentucky Derby is held at Churchill Downs, three or four miles away.

There is a line from an article in the *Louisville Courier-Journal*, that describes Kentucky as "an attraction of opposites. Unimaginable wealth amid unspeakable poverty. Beauty and ugliness snuggling up to each other in uneasy intimacy. A place with mountains and bayous. A white state (92 per cent) whose most famous citizen is black."

The newly constructed shopping mall on the way to the hotel is filled with shops selling the usual garish designer outfits. In the corner, there is a group of young black kids shining shoes. A couple are on their knees, buffing the brogues of white office workers who sit reading their newspapers. A lean, young, black kid skips into my path and asks me if I want a shoe shine.

"No thanks. I'm looking for the Seelbach Hotel."

"Seelbach's just outside on the right."

"Thanks. Are any of you going to the Ali tribute tomorrow?"

The lean kid looks nonplussed, as do the rest of the group. "Ali tribute? Muhammad Ali? Don't know nothing about that." I explain to the group that their hometown is paying tribute to its most famous son.

"Ali? No, man. Can't take time off. We need the wages, man."

A small kid, wearing a Chicago Cubs vest, pipes up from the back of the group. "My man, here," he says, pointing to a stocky kid, flipping polish in the air, "he goin' to be the next Ali."

The next Ali can't supress a grin. "Sure am," he says.

"You a boxer?" I ask.

"Yeah, man, I box up this goddamn shoe polish every night."

The group laughs.

"What weight?" I ask him.

"Middleweight, man, but I'm goin' all the way up to heavyweight to whip that English boy's ass." The group fall about laughing and the young fighter keeps flipping the polish with a wide grin on his face. He is built more like Mike Tyson but he has Ali's lip.

"If I bump into Mr Lewis I'll tell him you're on your way."

"Today, football may have its Namaths and other stars; basketball has its Chamberlains, Birds and Jordans; baseball has its Babe Ruths. And boxing has Cassius Clay. But humanity has Muhammad Ali."
– Thomas Meeker President and CEO of Churchill Downs, Inc

An attraction of opposites. It's a good way to describe Ali. The Black Muslim champ, who spouted the white-hating rhetoric of the Nation of Islam but shared his glory years with an assortment of white advisors and friends. The man who preached separatism while living in luxury, in white, middle class suburbs. The champion of goodwill who often ruthlessly taunted his opponents. The warrior with the face of an angel.

Muhammad Ali Boulevard runs through the centre of the city. Everything that happens in Louisville seems to revolve around his name in one way or another. The shops, banks and hotels all sit on the edge of his Boulevard. Even his brother, Rahaman, has moved into an apartment there. "So Ali will know where to find me," he says.

Maybe the Ali magic has rubbed off on this small Southern city. There is a warmth and dignity about the place. Maybe they are reasons why Muhammad and his wife Lonnie are moving back, that and the chance to oversee the construction of the Muhammad Ali Center.

The Alis have been living in the small town of Berrien Springs, Michigan, for the past ten years – in a farmhouse once owned by Al Capone – but they are planning a move back to Louisville. Berrien Springs will miss them. It will miss the good work they have done in the community and it will miss Muhammad's spontaneous trips to McDonald's for a quarter-pounder with cheese and a joke with the locals. But there is work to be done in Louisville.

The Muhammad Ali Center has been a dream of Muhammad and Lonnie's for many years. Since Ali lit the Olympic flame in Atlanta in 1996 and the cogs of the Ali industry began to turn once again. The idea is to build the Center in downtown Louisville, overlooking the river. It will be a place, as Lonnie says, "where the values and virtues that Ali represents can come together, to continue the inspiration that his life has already given to multitudes of people."

It is an ambitious project – a museum, a conference centre, and a place to inspire young and old – and they need somewhere in the region of $80 million to set it up and complete it by the scheduled date of summer 2003. If anyone can pull it off, the Alis can.

It's unusually hot for a February – 75° – and I'm at the Seelbach Hotel bar waiting to meet the champ. I've been invited to a special reception in his honour. Louisville sports stars, friends of Ali and local dignitaries are paying their respects, welcoming him home. But I've heard rumours he is not going to show. "He may be too tired," the organisers said. Even at 58, and slowed by the onset of Parkinson's syndrome, Ali's schedule still remains busy enough to drain a 20-year-old. He travels approximately 220 days of every year.

That afternoon, Ali and Lonnie were in Frankfort, Kentucky, appearing before the state senate, negotiating funds for the Center. Ali has never liked flying but he rolls with it and flies around more than the Harlem Globetrotters. He makes appearances all over the world. He may have lost his public voice, but his presence can move and inspire a room full of people from Manchester to Marrakesh.

I nearly choke on my beer when I hear a voice behind me say, "Shit, you'll never guess who I've just seen!" A man is talking to a group of people at a bar table.

"Who? Who did you just see?" they ask.

"Muhammad Ali. Can you believe it? Muhammad Ali. He's up in reception right now." Before I have time to digest that statement, my colleague runs into the bar and confirms it. "He's here," he says. "The champ's here." I stand up and get ready to meet Muhammad Ali.

> *"I like walking behind him to watch people walk up to him. The way he makes people feel. He really lifts people up."*
> – Howard Bingham, Ali's close friend.

The Seelbach is one of Louisville's finest hotels. A real grand place. The foyer has ornate marble floors and is lit by extravagant chandeliers. There are also dramatic, swooping staircases leading into the lobby and I imagine Scarlett O'Hara will come slinking down one of them at any moment.

I spot Ali and Lonnie checking in. Ali is wearing a dark suit, white shirt and tie. He's resting his mighty elbows against the reception desk, watching Lonnie fill in the forms. He's wearing that expressionless mask I'd read about and seen on TV. But he still looks good. Whatever the illness has done to his motor skills, he's still a magnificent figure. I feel like a kid standing there looking at the old lion, like a five-year-old if he were in the presence of the real Santa Claus, overjoyed and terrified.

I move to introduce myself and Ali seems to sense my awkwardness. I guess he's used to it. Ever since he charmed the Olympic village in Rome in 1960, Ali has often been surrounded by excited and nervy folk waiting to get an autograph or a quick word. He turns slowly and looks at me and then he stands, stooping slightly, and raises his hands into a mock-fighting stance. His hands tremble, and he looks tired, but he's still got the hint of a gleam in his eye. I smile as he throws a slow combination and I stick out my hand and say, "Hello, champ, how are you doing?" He takes it – his hand is soft – and I clasp the paw that laid out Sonny Liston and sent George Foreman into the land of nod.

Lonnie finishes at the desk and I introduce myself to her. She is a neat and handsome woman, dressed in a dark suit. She smiles and greets me politely and then she touches Ali gently on his elbow and says, "C'mon, honey," and she takes his hand and they both walk towards the staircase.

Lonnie has known Muhammad since she was a little girl. She grew up in Louisville. She was born Yolanda Williams and raised across the street from Ali's mother. Lonnie's mother, Marguerette Williams, would accompany Odessa Clay on her travels around the world to watch Muhammad fight.

Lonnie adored the champ for many years and occasionally, when he returned to Louisville, they would meet and talk. Ali would joke with Lonnie and tease the starry-eyed youngster. Lonnie's been at his side ever since Parkinson's began to take hold in the '80s. She finally became his fourth wife when they married in 1986. Lonnie has become an important figure now Ali's popularity has, once again, gone through the roof. She provides him with an eloquent voice in public.

The reception takes place in a cool, bright room on the second floor of the hotel. It's an informal gathering. Tables draped with clean, white cloths are spread easily around the room. You can sit where you want. I guess everyone is equal in Ali's world, everybody mixes in like one big family. There is an athletic, young, black man serving soft drinks in the far corner – Ali is a Muslim: he doesn't drink alcohol or smoke – and there is a plump, white woman carving a roast on a table next to him – he certainly enjoys his grub. There are TV cameras and the local radio station is broadcasting its evening show from a couple of tables just outside the room. Kentucky sports writer Billy Reed is helping out with the commentary.

Reed, a stocky, solid-looking man in his mid 50s who has worked for *Sports Illustrated* and many other publications, says of Ali, "He put Louisville on the map, but a lot of people didn't like that. You either supported him or you said he's a draft-dodger, a rabble-rouser, a bigmouth. He really galvanised people's emotions."

> *"Muhammad was never like most athletes, never quite like our icons of fame.*
> *In fact there's never been anybody quite like Muhammad Ali."*
> – Diane Sawyer, ABC news presenter.

Most of the guests haven't arrived yet. A man in his mid 60s greets me with a slap on the back and a firm handshake. "How ya doin', son? The name's Bob Thurman, Coach Bob Thurman. And who are you?" I've never met Bob before, but he seems pleased to see me. Southern hospitality, I guess. He is wearing a red Louisville Cardinals baseball cap with matching bomber jacket. He has a good, healthy-looking face, and his blue eyes fix steadily on mine.

I ask him why he is there. "I grew up with the man," he says. "Oh yes, sir. On that street where he's from. He's a good champion."

Earlier that day I had walked around Ali's old neighbourhood. He was born Cassius Marcellus Clay Jr, in Louisville General Hospital, at 6.35pm on 17

January 1942 and he was raised in Louisville's West End, a ghetto adjacent to the tobacco plantation. He began boxing at the age of twelve at Joe Martin's Columbia Gym. Martin once said that Clay "looked no better or worse than the majority when he started". Ali is a great argument against anybody who spouts the old line about any athlete being "a natural". It took Ali years of hard work to master his art.

He took to boxing like most kids take to eating sweets. When he wasn't in the gym he would box with his brother, Rudi, and other neighbourhood kids around the back of Leonard Tucker's grocery store, two blocks from his home. Tucker would gather up gloves that the local YMCA were about to throw out, and he would leave them at the back of his store for the boys to mess around with. "About seven o'clock every night, all the kids in the neighbourhood would put on the gloves and box out there in the back," Tucker is reported as saying. "That's where Cassius and Rudi got their first gloves. Watching them, no one could ever catch Cassius to hit him. I saw a champion back then and I didn't know it."

From the age of 15, Clay would regularly run alone in the early hours, around the West End, down Greenwood Avenue toward the Ohio River. Pounding the streets, eyes bright and alert, fixed on the darkness ahead. Heavy work boots hammering the concrete. He always wore work boots when he ran, even in his championship years. It helped his footwork in the ring. If you can run three or four miles in steel-toed shoes, boxing boots feel like ballet slippers.

His schooling at Central High School would suffer because of his dedication to boxing. Ali neglected his studies. "If he had not been a boxer, he would not have stood out in any way," says Betty Johnson, a friend of Ali's parents. He was described by teachers as one dimensional and boxing was never far from his mind, as this passage from an article by Hunt Helm in the *Louisville Courier-Journal* proves:

"At Central High School in those days, Clay was known as the kid who drank water with garlic in it, who drank milk with raw eggs in it, who wouldn't smoke, who wouldn't drink even carbonated soda pop, who ran and shadow-boxed about as often as he walked, who was very shy, especially around girls (his first kiss, it is said, made him faint)."

Despite his shyness and obsession with the noble art, Clay was popular with his fellow students. He would clown around and make wild boasts and entertain his friends with practical jokes. He was also popular at the Spalding University on South Fourth Street where he worked as a dust-up boy in the library from 1957-8.

Sister James Ellen, who ran the library, remembers him fondly. "He was soft spoken and a nice young boy," she says. "I think he showed at that time the beginnings of what he was later to be – a world interest, who lived life to the fullest."

Once Clay had finished his job he would rush across the road to the Columbia Gym. One day, Sister Ellen came back from lunch to find Clay asleep with his head on a desk in the library. Later she erected a sign above the desk that said, "Cassius slept here."

As his boxing improved, Clay became a local hero after beating the West End, tough guy, Charley Baker. John Powell Jr, who used to work in a local liquor store, described Clay's triumph over Baker in the *Courier-Journal*: "He came through one night and said, 'I'm going to box Charley Baker' on the *Tomorrow's Champions* show. Well, I told him, 'You're crazy if you get in the ring with him.' See, Charley Baker was the bully of the West End. I mean, people wouldn't even talk too loud around Charley Baker. He was huge and muscular. But Cassius said, 'I'm gonna whip him,' and he did whip him. And after that, I said, 'Man, you are the baddest dude I know, now.'"

The West End is still a predominantly black ghetto, a rail road track separating it from downtown Louisville. Freight trains move lazily over the lines. It is mostly made up of small wooden houses with swing chairs on the porch. One shabby house has a hand-painted sign taped to the front gate: "Pit bulls for sale, $150 each." The dogs were lying around in the unkempt garden, dozing in the sun, ribs poking out of their tan-coloured coats.

There were many young, black kids, hanging around, looking bored. I asked a couple of them if they knew where the house once owned by Cassius Clay Sr and Odessa Clay was, and their eyes lit up. I found it on Grand Avenue, a better looking street than most in the area. Ali's parents wanted the best for him and his brother. His father made a modest income as a sign painter and his mother always kept the boys well fed and clothed. The house still looked good. It has been well cared for and had recently received a new lick of pale, pink, paint.

Back at the reception, Coach Bob says, "They bought him a new Cadillac, 'cause he'd won the Olympics and he asked me to put a new stereo in there. He'd turn that stereo right up and you'd hear it from one end of the street to the other. But, jeez, I enjoyed it. I'd never seen one before and, anyways, I'm here to pay tribute to that man." He points at someone over my shoulder and there is the champ again with Lonnie at his side.

He's wearing a black turtleneck and black trousers. He walks slowly towards us and stands a few yards in front of us. Bob greets him enthusiastically and Muhammad pulls a green handkerchief from his trouser pocket and slowly waves it in the air. He holds out his hands, palms down, so we can see that he's isn't concealing anything. He's doing one of his famous magic tricks. Ali still likes to entertain.

We stare at his hands, which shake badly, but Muhammad doesn't seem to mind. He's quite comfortable with it. He wants us to look at his hands. Now he has shown us that there is nothing concealed he takes the handkerchief and pushes it into his left fist with his thumb and then he holds out his hands, palms down once again. The handkerchief has disappeared, and Coach Bob Thurman is laughing hard because I haven't spotted what Muhammad has done with it.

Ali repeats the trick and Coach Bob whoops and squeals in delight like a demented cheerleader and I still can't see what Ali has done with the handkerchief. Ali repeats it one more time and he roles his eyes to the ceiling as though to say, "You is one dumb chump." This time I concentrate and I see that Ali has a latex thumb on his right hand, at least an inch longer than the thumb on his left. Coach Bob continues to laugh and I feel kind of dumb but amused at being conned by Ali. Ali stands with a tight half-smile on his face as he pulls off the false thumb and waves the handkerchief in my face.

The room fills up with some of Ali's old friends and a host of sports people and local dignitaries and Ali performs his trick again for a larger audience. When the handkerchief is revealed, everyone claps and laughs. The trick is a simple one, and I found out later he did the same trick for Fidel Castro in 1996.

It's a poor substitute for the fast tongue and the poetry, but the clapping and the smiles are credible. Ali transcends his illness, as he did his sport, and the people in the room respond to that. They genuinely love him and, anyway, he is enjoying the attention. Ali's friend, the photographer Howard Bingham, reckons this sort of thing keeps him going. "It keeps him alive," he says. "Ali and people. He feeds off the joy he sees in their eyes. Ali is, and always has been, a man of the people."

The room illuminates with flashbulbs as Ali invites people in for photos. I talk briefly to Shirley Lewis, a woman who graduated with Ali from Central High School and the twin of Minnesota Vikings coach, Sherman Lewis. She has a yellowed picture of herself and Ali – then known as Cassius Clay – on graduation day in 1958. They are smiling as they stand wearing mortar boards and proudly holding their graduation scrolls.

"He was just the same even then," says Shirley. "He was always laughing and joking around. I teach first-grade children now, and whenever I get a new class I always look around for another Muhammad. He was special, but you've got to believe that there are others like him out there."

After Ali has satisfied everyone with a photograph, he sits down at the table next to mine. Someone brings him a small plate of fried chicken and he nibbles at it in between signing photos and books. It is past 9pm and Ali usually rises at 5am for the first of his five daily prayer sessions, but he contentedly signs the pictures and has gestures and quietly spoken words for everyone he meets.

Former champion jockey Steve Cauthen, who is a native of Louisville and who now breeds horses locally, watches with me as Ali finishes signing and begins to doodle a landscape of a waterfall, a deep canyon and a rocket shooting off into the sky. "The first time I met Ali was at Governor of Kentucky John Y Brown's inauguration, back in the early '80s," Cauthen says. "I was over in Europe but it was the off season and he'd not long retired. The thing about

Muhammad Ali is he came across as a brash, very outgoing person that thought he was the greatest, which he was, but you'd never hear all the good stories about what he's done for people in a quiet way, helping kids and various people that were underprivileged. Even with his illness, he's carried on doing that. Obviously, everyone admires him as a fighter, the best showman the world has ever seen, but I think everyone admires him for his human side."

When the room has emptied, the champ stays doodling at his table. I don't want to disturb him but I reckon he won't mind. I want to say thanks and tell him I'll see him tomorrow. I place my hand lightly on his shoulder and bow down to speak in his ear. He turns his head and whispers, "You're from England?"

"Yes."

"Eammon Andrews," he says. "Eammon Andrews." Andrews used to commentate on boxing in Britain during Ali's heyday.

"Yes," I say. "He isn't around any more."

Ali looks away for a second and then he turns his head again. "Lennox Lewis," he whispers.

"Lennox Lewis? What do you think of him?"

"I'll knock him out!" he answers sharply. There's nothing wrong with Ali's mind.

"Before I go, I've just got to ask you a question: did you ever find the kid who stole your bike?"

Ali gives me that tight smile. "You know, I never found him, but I forgot about the bike and took up boxing and turned the bike into a Rolls-Royce."

His head is still good and clear and it makes me feel happy to know that. I thank him for a great evening and leave him to finish off his landscape.

"See you, champ."

"Muhammad Ali has travelled the world drawing attention to the needs of children and the cause of tolerance and peace. With his spirit and beliefs guiding it, the Center should inspire thousands of people, especially young people of all races, cultures and ideologies toward the building of a better and safer world."

– Koffi Annan, Secretary General of the United Nations.

26 FEBRUARY 2000

My next stop is the Louisville Gardens, home of the Louisville Cardinals basketball team, for "A Salute To The Greatest". Thousands of local school kids, as well as sports stars and friends, are paying their respects to Ali. The event will take place in an hour and I visit the press room.

I recognise a few faces. Coach Bob Thurman is there, still wearing the baseball cap and jacket, regaling someone with his tale of Ali's car radio, no doubt. Steve Cauthen is there and one or two local basketball and football stars. A local TV station is interviewing the university basketball team coach, a guy called Denny Crumb. "He had a personality that attracted people," he says. "That smile on his face and that glint in his eye."

The first woman to row across the Atlantic single-handedly is there, Tori Murden McClure. A tall and elegant-looking woman, she is a Louisville local and is helping to raise funds for the Muhammad Ali Center. "When I see Muhammad Ali, I see a man of conviction," she says. "The greatest test in life is to make the most of our gifts. For, even in the worst of times, when the test of his religious convictions led Muhammad to ridicule and scorn, he prevailed, using his gifts for the greater good. When I see Muhammad Ali, I see a hero, a role model and a man."

Lonnie says, "Nothing lifts Muhammad's spirits more than lots and lots of children." I guess it is going to be a good day for Ali, then, because hundreds of kids, shouting in excitement, are spilling out of yellow school buses. They've got the morning off and they're going to see Ali. It doesn't get much better than that. Many of the kids are carrying hand-made placards with messages for the greatest, written in felt-tip and crayon.

The kids line up behind their teachers, who look flustered. Suddenly, there is clapping from the press room and a rush for the door. Ali has entered the room. I turn around and I can see his head above a group of photographers. His eyes close as the flashbulbs pop, and he shuffles in and starts to perform his magic trick once again.

As usual, the first time around, they don't see what has happened to the handkerchief. "You're supposed to be intelligent people here," Ali smiles. He performs the trick again until the rubber thumb is spotted and there is applause and laughter. Cameras click again and Ali feigns injury, but he's just clowning – he still does this a lot. After a few seconds, he opens his eyes and throws a few slow punches, and then he stands and waits at the door for Lonnie.

The arena is packed and noisy. Around 5,000 of the 7,000 crowd are local school kids. "A-li! A-li! A-li!" they chant at the top of their voices. A ring, with a blue canvas and red velvet ropes, has been erected at the back of the arena. There are two chairs in the middle for Ali and Lonnie and a podium with a mic for the many tributes to come. Themes from cartoon shows are belting out of the PA system to keep the kids amused while they wait for Ali.

After a short wait, Ali and Lonnie enter the ring to deafening shouts and applause. When the noise has died down a little, the MC, Wayne Perky, takes the microphone. Perky is a DJ with an appealing, oily charm, Louisville's answer to Tony Blackburn. "Today, we've come together, 26 February 2000, exactly 36 years to the day after Muhammad Ali turned the world upside-down and won the heavyweight championship of the world. Today, we recognise this great man." Perky smiles a big, white smile and he begins to introduce the tributes.

Why is Ali so popular once again? Obviously, the Atlanta flame ignited it and it was further fuelled by the Oscar-winning documentary *When We Were Kings*. But it's more than that. Of course, his achievements in the ring and his principled stand against the Vietnam War are still an inspiration to many. In his prime Ali was truly heroic – giving up what could have been the best three years of his athletic career for his principles – and these days, heroes – sporting or otherwise – are as rare as Bengal tigers.

But it's not just the past triumphs of the ring and the courtrooms that have boosted Ali's popularity; his illness also plays a big part. His much-documented battle with Parkinson's syndrome has turned Ali into a symbol of quiet suffering. When he was young and strong, the establishment recoiled when he opened his mouth. When Ali refused to be inducted, Congressman Frank Clark of Pennsylvania said, "The heavyweight champion of the world turns my stomach. I am not a super-patriot, but I feel that each man, if he is a man, owes to his country a willingness to protect and serve it in time of need." But times change and now everyone wants to be associated with Ali. The Butterfly has metamorphosed from the champion of black self-determination, into the torch-carrier for peace and tolerance. Lieutenant Governor Steve Henry takes the stand and says, "Muhammad has often said he is not a hero. That's just not true. He is our hero. He has taught us all how to dream. He has taught us all how to reach our dream."

Many of the tributes are touching and all of them receive ecstatic applause from the Louisville kids. Throughout the hour-long event, Ali sits quietly next to Lonnie. At times, the kids begin to chant, "A-li! A-li! A-li!", but he just sits with his left hand clasped tightly against his belly to ease the shaking, and now and then he shuts his eyes. He used to do that when he was in his prime, but I'm not sure whether he's closing his eyes because he's tired or trying to shut out the praise. Ali is no longer the insecure young fighter who was fuelled by compliments and bravado. He seems to enjoy being a public figure, but he is also a man at peace with himself. I'm sure if he never saw a grinning face in front of him again, he'd be quite content to sit at home signing autographs and reading the Koran.

The final words of the event come from Tia Brown, the senior class principal of Central High School, the only school to have taught three heavyweight champions of the world: Jimmy Ellis, Greg Page and, of course, Ali. One tough school. Tia walks nervously to the mic but gathers herself and says simply, "In my opinion, he is still the greatest, not only because of his championship achievements but his confidence, determination and his willingness to stand up for his own beliefs."

When it's all done, Ali rises from his seat and tries to move among the children. He climbs down from the ring but it quickly becomes apparent that he won't be able to move very far into the mass. He walks slowly and touches as many as he can before being ushered away by his brother, Rahaman, and a host of others. One girl, a fifth grader called Dominique Hatchell, is so overcome, having met Ali, that she bursts into tears. "He made me think of all the stuff in the world and how we can change it," she says.

Soon the kids can no longer touch him, but they don't seem to mind. They are in good spirits and are still chanting, "A-li! A-li! A-li!" As the chant echoes through the arena, Ali finally makes it to the door with his brother and Lonnie at his side. He bows his head and disappears.

> *"Look into his eyes. They have not changed. For me, they speak one thing: Love. Not for some of us; for all. Over nearly five decades, this man has, in one arena or another, commanded our attention, and we're still mesmerised. Parkinson's is no match for Ali. Even at 57. He is a come-to-life definition of his Muslim namesake: 'worthy of praise' and 'most high'."*
> – John Saracino, USA Today, 1999.

Hana Ali

Muhammad Ali's Daughter

People come up to me in the streets quite often and tell me how wonderful my dad is. They all have such amazing stories. That was the reason I wrote my book *More Than A Hero*. I thought, "So many authors are only writing about his history in boxing. A lot of people don't know about him as a human being and how wonderful he is." To be honest, it was going to be a Fathers' Day gift, but my mother thought that it would be a good idea to get it published. It's been out for almost a year now, and I get a lot of fan mail – of course, the fans are my father's! – telling me how wonderful and poetic they thought the book was and how it shows another side of him they didn't know existed or they hadn't seen. I take it for granted. I keep forgetting that people who think they know my father don't really know how wonderful he is. He has a big heart and is such a humanitarian.

My interest in poetry came from the fact that, when I was really young, my father would speak in rhyme a lot, so I would imitate him and write little love notes. Then, one day, I was watching a documentary on my dad and was inspired to write a poem, my first poem, entitled 'Ali' – it was just a short poem about my father and how I viewed him.

See, my dad is like a big kid. He was always real fun around the house, always joking, doing magic tricks, making little rhymes and whatnot. And we always had people in the house, 'cause he liked company – he was very open and he had a very open environment. People would come up to him and want to meet him, and he'd say, "Come on home with me," and he'd just sit them out and do magic. I was about nine when my parents divorced, so we were around a lot, running around, and he was just real open. It didn't matter what he was doing; he just let us run around and have fun.

The world knows my father as Muhammad Ali, but I know him as Daddy, and he's always been a great dad, surprisingly, 'cause he was always very busy, travelling, but he made it very evident that he loved us and he gave us a lot of attention. Nothing was too important. There was never a time the door was closed or even in an important business conference call. He focused on his kids and he made time for his family life as well as the business world.

When I was about five years old, a family friend was telling my father that he had to go train for one of his last fights – I think it was Trevor Berbick – and I was upset I ran upstairs crying and he had come up to tell me to come down. My dad wanted to give me a kiss goodbye. And he said he's not my father; he's Muhammad Ali. He explained that he's my dad, but he's also the daddy to the rest of the world.

I always remember him being there, driving us around town, taking us on walks. I have seven sisters and two brothers. Laila is my only whole sister, so my dad always made sure we were friends. Every summer, our sisters would come down and stay with us in Los Angeles, where Laila and I grew up.

I think I was probably about five years old when I first recognised how famous my father was. We'd go outside and I'd witness all the adulation and all the attention he would get, people shouting, "Ali, you're the greatest," and I was just kind of, like, "Wow, he must be important." I noticed from a very young age the difference in the treatment and I'd use that to my advantage: "My daddy is Muhammad Ali. I can do what I want to do." The effects were there pretty early on.

My father would actually take tape recorders around with us and record us. I still have a few of them now. I have him singing on my answer machine: "Come on, Hana, let's sing now." He would record us at different times of the day when we were real young. He'd say, "Hana, this is you at three. You didn't like to go to bed, and I'm about to go in there and you're going to give me hell!" He has all this stuff on tape, boxes of it. He documented everything, me and Laila singing our ABCs. He'd take me to school and record him disciplining me when I was out of line. He'd pretend to give me a spanking in front of the class! I don't actually remember the incident, but I do remember him saying, "This is important. You're going to listen to this when you're older." And he would save all the little doodles and drawings that we'd do. So he made us feel important, taking his time to save this stuff.

I was extremely close to my father, so it was always really hard on me when he left. It was hard. We grew up with lots of governesses, 'cause my dad was always travelling and my mother would go with him, a lot of the time. Laila was always close to my mother and I was closer to my father. But he would call a lot and send postcards, and we kind of got used to it. That was our life. So I'm used to him being gone a lot. Ever since before I can remember, he was home a week, gone a week, home a while, gone a couple of days. My other sisters, though, have different relationships with my father. If you asked another sister, she might have different issues. But they're pretty much all the same. He always called and made sure we were together in summer times.

Veronica, my mother, is a young mother, about 45. She was in school when she met my dad. She was going to be a doctor, so she had two years down at UCLA, but then of course she left school, married my father and now has a masters degree in psychology. She's real sweet, shy, quiet, pleasant, a real sweet lady. She has a big heart as well, just like Dad. They both weren't disciplinarians, so you can imagine the household was just wild. I remember we would get in trouble for doing something, and they couldn't hold the punishment. It's amazing that we turned out to be so great, 'cause we were wild.

My mother was 17 when she met my dad. He was in a marriage, and it was coming to the end, but she didn't find that out until a little further into the relationship. Men! But, as far as I know, everything went smoothly after that. I was one year old when they got married, and to my understanding, Belinda wouldn't give my father a divorce, so it was an interesting household for a while.

His marriage was rocky then. So Dad goes over to Africa and he sees my mother and he's in love with her, and he's going around introducing her as his wife, so naturally his real wife is on the next plane to fly out there and see what was going on, while Dad was telling her they were having some problems and whatnot. He handled it gracefully, though. A lot of people say to me, "Your father's been married four times and he's got nine kids," but what I have to say to that is that he's an amazing person. He's always a father to all of his kids. And he liked to be married. All of his divorces were settled out of court. He gave every wife half of anything he had, never made anyone sign a pre-nup. He's got a soft, giving heart, he's loveable and he loves pretty women! And I'm glad about that, 'cause we're all here.

My sister Miya never lived with my father; he didn't marry her mother. She's very fair skinned and she doesn't look anything like him. She called him one day, crying, "People are teasing me, Daddy. They tell me you're not my dad and they never see you." So my dad got on the next plane to New Jersey and he went to school with her and sat in every single class that whole day. Then he took her home and walked up and down the street with her so everyone could see that he was her father.

When I was younger and I found out that my parents were getting divorced, I kind of blocked that out. I was only nine years old at the time. I was extremely close to my dad, and I didn't understand it. My mother and father got along, but I think they got to a point where my mother divorced my father. She wasn't happy. She married him real young. I think she needed to be independent and be on her own. They stayed friends, though. I actually saw him more when they got divorced than when we were all living together. I think he was scared we'd forget him. When Mom got remarried, he kept asking me, "Do you have a new daddy now? Do you give him kisses? Do you hug him, too?" He's like a big kid. He'd come over for dinner all the time. They were friends. I don't know how the media portrayed that back then, 'cause I was too young to read the newspapers, but it was a friendly split. All of my father's divorces were friendly – even Belinda, ironically. They're still friends. He doesn't have any malice in his heart. Even people that have done him a great wrong in the past, he forgives them before they even do it. And that's really why what inspired me to write the book. I just wanted to share that side of him, because it's overwhelming. I just try to follow in his footsteps.

A lot of the life lessons he taught me I learned early on. From a young age, I remember I'd run around and brag about the things that we had and go to show and tell and take my best gifts, but my dad would stop me and explain that not everybody was as fortunate as we were, and that I shouldn't take my best toys to school and wear my prettiest clothes, 'cause the girls and boys that didn't have as much might feel bad. He'd tell me about sharing, and how we're all equal in God's eyes, and that, no matter how great he is and how much people love him in the world, he doesn't see himself any different than a homeless man on the street. He's a human being, and we all deserve to be loved and treated with respect and equality. He taught me that everyone is our brother or sister and to love everyone and not judge people, just to accept them for who they are. I learned all this from him, and not just through his words but by his actions, too. And he's put to the test a lot, like all his political stands, including a lot that were off camera, out of view.

My dad would teach me that, when I want to give charity, you can't do it in the public eye, where you know you're getting something back. If you're really, truly going to give something, you don't tell anyone that you're giving it. You just do it. So a lot of the time, you won't see that. A lot of the stuff he does is not televised, 'cause he actually prefers for them not to.

I remember one time, we were coming home from eating out and a homeless man was being thrown out of a restaurant, so my father pulled over and spoke to him and the man was explaining how he was hungry and he just wanted to eat and they wouldn't let him eat, even though he had money. So we went inside there and my dad went up to the manager and said to him, "This man is hungry, and if he's worthy enough to occupy space on God's grand Earth, he can eat in this restaurant." He just charged to the back and sat down. He told the man to order what he wanted, and we sat there for hours. Then he took him to a hotel, put him there for a month and Dad told him that he was going to take him shopping and get him some clothes and he was going to find him a good job. And there's like a million stories like that. He couldn't single-handedly save the world, but he surely did his share of trying!

It makes him feel good, being generous. It's unfortunate, but a lot of celebrities these days want their privacy, and that's understandable, but there's a price you get with fame. These people love you and you're living a lavish life, but something's got to give. It's not always going to be pleasant, and people want to know what's going on. They feel like they know you. They love you. They watch you. They feel like they're part of your family. Dad understands that – you don't get something for nothing; you have to give something back. When people ask him questions about his career and what made him feel the best over the years, he would say that he doesn't feel right if he doesn't give something back. Why should these people come and see his fights and make him and the promoters rich and then get nothing back in return?

When my dad was real young, his idol was Sugar Ray Robinson. He'd wait outside of a Harlem club the whole day and night to get his autograph. Then, when he came out, he told my father he was too busy and didn't give an autograph. So Dad said he would never, never do that to one single fan. He will try to sign every autograph, because if he does 100 and there's 1,000 people there, there's people going home without his autograph. He has Parkinson's, and he's tired, or he'll be jet-lagged, and he'll still try and sign every last autograph. When he's at home, he does his own fan mail. And at Christmas, he'll get the phone book out and look down, pick a number and he'll say, "Call that number." I'll call the number for him, and he'll say, "Merry Christmas. This is Muhammad Ali!" And then, all of a sudden, his face kind of gets puzzled and he's, like, "They hung up on me." So he does it again – goes down the book, stops, picks another number out. It's so funny.

All of my father's wives share one thing in common – they are very beautiful, with sweet dispositions, very light-hearted. He met them all under different circumstances. His first wife he met jogging in a park. That was a short-lived marriage. I think it lasted a few weeks! His second wife, Belinda, she was 17 when he met her, working in a bakery. Then he sort of bumped into my mother in Zaire. Lonnie, his present wife, he's known all of his life. Their mothers were best friends. They grew up across the street from one another. He sometimes would babysit her and she was a friend to him throughout all of his marriages. And now they're married. She takes good care of him – he's happy, she's happy, we're happy with her.

Some people say that he gave a little to a lot and not perhaps enough to his children, but I think it says enough that all of his children – by four different marriages – are all friends. Laila and myself are from my father's third marriage. Then there's Miya and Khaliah, but my father never married their mothers. Then there is Maryum, Jamillah, Rasheeda and Muhammad by my dad's second marriage. He didn't have any kids with his first wife. Then Asaad is adopted. He's ten years old and is with my father's present wife, Lonnie. So there's nine of us. We get along. We grew up together. He always made time for us. He has so much love to give. I think that sometimes he just doesn't know what to do with himself. I think he just sort of incorporated us, put us all together in a big box and just shook us up. Like I said, his home was open. We'd be roaming around. My dad's being interviewed and he has two people that he's met on the street that just want autographs sitting there with him. He just loves to be around people and surrounded by love. He wants to make people happy and make them smile. I think that's what he gets back, when he sees the smile on someone's face and the tears in their eyes when they meet him and tell him how much he did for them so that he knows it wasn't all for nothing. He sacrificed a lot and he stood for a lot, but when he goes out and he sees that people haven't forgotten what he stood for and what he's done, he's so proud, but he's so humble at the same time. It's amazing. He's always saying, "Isn't it amazing that, anywhere in the world I go, they love me? I wonder how many people would just take me in if I went and knocked on their door, if they'd take me in and feed me. Do you think they'd clothe me?" He's always thinking about that kind of stuff.

The simple things make him happy. He likes to sit back and watch TV and have his family around. He loves people. Sometimes, when we're just sitting around in a hotel room, he'll say, "Let's go outside and just go walking." He wants to see how many people recognise him. He likes to sign all their autographs. He feels then like he'd done his duty for the day.

When I look back on old videotapes of him, my father actually inspires me and I think, "Wow! I came from him! His blood is in my veins." And I can see how easy it was for him to inspire people, especially in those times when black people weren't loving themselves. I think that that was probably one of the greatest things that he could have done for his people, to show them that they could love themselves, that they could be who they wanted to be just, that they could believe in themselves and do anything. There are always going to be someone telling you that you can't do it, but that just made him want to prove himself even more. In fact, I think that, without those cynics, he might not be as great as he is today. He would say in interviews that he was not 100 per cent happy, sitting up on a hill and in his mansion, driving his Rolls-Royce, 'cause he knows people are still catching hell down in the slums.

So he was always trying to do something for his people and show them that they could be exactly what he was. He was very focused and he did everything he could to actually get down there in the ghettos and talk to people, to the winos. It's not just lip service. No bodyguards – "Take me to the ghetto, where people are. "He wanted to talk to them and inspire them and to help them the best he could.

I was too young, growing up, to remember my father's fights. My eldest sister, Maryum, sat through some of those. He didn't like us actually being there, but I do recall watching them. Actually, I never watched one of my father's fights all the way through until recently. I don't like watching him get hit, but he danced around so much. But no, I honestly don't like watching those fights, especially in his later years. The earlier ones, when he was just dancing around and they couldn't catch up with him, they're a little easier to watch.

I can see why people might think Dad was arrogant in his youth; it was all an act, really, to sell tickets. He was his own self-promoter and confidant, on top of that. In those days, it was unheard of for a black male to be that outgoing and confident and outspoken. But now, with my dad, what you see is what you get.

And for people that are worried about him and love him and want to know how he's doing, he is amazingly strong and confident. He doesn't feel sorry for himself. His condition is physical; it has nothing to do with his mental faculties. It hasn't affected his memory. He is extremely sharp. Unfortunately, people see him a lot in transition, when he's jet-lagged and tired, and he's not supposed to eat sweets, because the sugar slows him down some more. But he's happy, at peace. He sits at home, does his fan mail on his time off and devotes his life to just being peaceful and helping people, calling his kids up and reflecting on the old times. Of course, it would be nice if he could be cured of Parkinson's, but I think he has accepted that as fate. He doesn't go back and say, "I wish I didn't do this." I don't think he believes that it was brought on by boxing. No one has proved that. People like Michael J Fox are turning up with Parkinson's, and he never stepped in the ring once. It's just fate. He thinks it's slowed him down some so he can be more peaceful and just relax and just focus on spirituality more, so he looks on the bright side of everything. He always taught us that it's easy to hold onto faith when everything is going smooth in life. The trick is to keep that same faith when things aren't looking good, at the eve of your darkest intent, and still know that there's a greater plan. He's living proof of this. He doesn't just talk the talk; he walks the walk.

I think that my father has definitely lived his life being what he wants to be. His only fault is his big heart, but he's taken the repercussions and punishments because of it, no matter what. He just stays true to himself. He can have no regrets if he does that. He says exactly what he feels about everything, no matter where he is, 'cause he knows that people are watching him and he is representing people in general. He wants to be a role model to help inspire other kids to be that strong. A lot of people are shy deep down and timid, but my dad fears nothing but God. He's extremely spiritual. I think that, if you can get on that level, people will be on the same boat. Life has thrown a few curved balls, but he's taken them quite smoothly.

I would have to say the single most valuable lesson that my father has taught me is really to just be a caring person. I don't think people really care about people these days, but he genuinely does. That, to me, is godlike. It's spiritual. My dad was always saying he wished he could build a big mansion and put all the homeless people in the world in it together, or build some restaurants where everyone can eat for free. He talks about it all the time, and he genuinely means it – his eyes fill up with tears. He just has so much compassion for people and life, it's just overwhelming, sometimes. I don't know he handles it all. How you can care so much when the world is just so chaotic and crazy? You can't save everyone. How do you get through the day?

People might ask where all this comes from. I think – and my dad will agree – that it came from God. He was born with it. He had this story he used to tell me, that he is like a little ant – lots of little ants follow him, look up to him, so God gives him some extra power. He feels that he was truly born to do what he's doing. He feels he's doing God's work. If you're an atheist, you can't look at the sun and the moon and know that there's a god. I look at my dad and I know there's a god, that there are angels that are protecting him and watching him to know that he's gotten this far in life untouched and unharmed, especially in that controversial time when our black leaders were being shot and killed. He was a threat, at that time. But he's still here. I know he has his flaws, but I look at him and I think he's as close to heaven as he can get on Earth.

Veronica Anderson

Muhammad Ali's Third Wife

When I first met Muhammad, I was 17 or 18 years old. He was 31 or 32 at the time. It was at a charity function in Salt Lake City, Utah. I was a volunteer hostess and he flew in to take part in it. I did not like him before I met him because he had a big mouth. But part of our job, me along with several other young ladies, was to pick up the celebrities as they came in and escort them to their hotel rooms and then have them come to the function later. I was so tired by the time Muhammad was ready to be picked up, and I said I wasn't going! But everybody said, "Oh come on, come on," so I went.

My first impression was just that he was totally different than I thought he would be. He was quiet, he was very polite, he was humble. I don't know what I expected, maybe for him to just get off the plane bragging and acting arrogant, but he was totally different. There wasn't electricity; I just remember noticing that he was very different. He liked to joke and play. He was a very nice man.

Later, there was a contest for a poster girl to advertise and publicise the fight in Zaire, the Rumble In The Jungle, but I didn't win that. Two other girls won. I was considered too light-skinned to represent the black race. But they asked me and someone else, who also didn't win, to take part in it by teaching people about the country – going around showing slides at different people's homes where we'd have these gatherings and get people interested in going to the fight. And I ended up going to Zaire. None of us knew we were going to go, but we were given a trip over.

Then the fight was postponed for a month because George Foreman got a cut on his eye, so we had the opportunity to get to know one another. I had visited Ali's training camp with a few other people and he invited me back, and on the bus ride coming back we talked a lot – just on a friendly basis – and got to know each other that way. I didn't really know anything about him, really, but I found out that he was married. I mean, there was nothing between us at the time, but he told me he was getting a divorce. I actually asked a few people if he was or not, but most of them wouldn't say because they knew both Ali and his wife. But then one particular person, who I won't name, said yes, they were having lots of problems.

We spent a lot of time together in Zaire, but not all day. I used to come over sometimes and we'd walk along the Zaire River and talk and then I'd go back. I didn't see him constantly. Then, one day, when he was at his training camp in the presidential compound just outside of Kinshasa, he was reciting one of his lectures and it was on friendship and love and all his ideals, and I fell in love with that and started falling in love with him, too. That's the beginning of it. I didn't realised I was in love with him right then, but I can remember that moment of really being impressed with him.

When Muhammad told me he was getting divorced, I never thought of it in terms of him leaving his children for me or even leaving his wife for me. It wasn't an issue He told me some of the reasons he was getting divorced, and I understood. Plus, I was just this Catholic schoolgirl back then, and part of that was being self-righteous – which I hate to say now! But I felt justified because of the things he told me. I was very young and I was in love. Now, today, I would have told him, "OK, call me when you get divorced," but I didn't know better then. Actually, I wanted to go back home, but he didn't want me to.

In fact, it was a whole year before I got back home, when I was 18. I felt I had to ask my mother if I could stay, so Muhammad came up with this idea – he'd call her up and he'd say that they were making a film of his life there in Zaire and he wanted me to be in it. He called her, and the story went on and on. He would say, "Yes, we're riding an elephant today," and I'd say, "Oh my god!" Mom had a pretty tough time saying no to Muhammad, but only to a degree. She's pretty level-headed. But my older sister told me later that she said to her, "Uh-huh. Something's going on," but my mother said, "Oh, no."

Of course, there have been stories that Belinda, Ali's wife at the time, saw me in Zaire and tried to attack me. Nothing like that whatsoever happened. I never even came into contact with her. She was living in a hotel while he was staying in the training camp. I thought that that was part of the reason why they were getting divorced, because they weren't living together. I didn't know that, in training, you don't necessarily stay with your wife. I mean, people know that there was a fight between them over there, but it had nothing to do with me. As a matter of fact, Belinda didn't even know that he was with me then. She herself told me that, when she found out, it was much later on.

During that time, we talked a lot, but he did not talk about his early childhood, specifically about his father and how he was treated. His mother was very sweet. He called her "Momma Bert", and she was just the sweetest person you could meet. Very motherly. He was very close to her. One day, Ali had done something that was questionable, as far as good manners, and she said to me, "Veronica, can't you do anything with him?" She was just so cute. She told me that, when he was a little boy – a baby actually, a toddler – she couldn't control him, and that she used this old piece of fur so that, when he was misbehaving, she would put it on the floor. He was afraid of it – he would stay in the corner!

She also said that, when he was born, he was so small – six pounds, I think – that she was afraid to hold him at first and she had the feeling that she'd hurt him or break him. I mean, you just don't think of Muhammad Ali as being a six-pound baby!

One of the stories that Muhammad told me about his earlier life is that, when he was a young man – still a teenager, I guess – there was a girl that he liked and he got around to kissing her, just on the lips, but he was standing on a stairway at the time, and he was pretty nervous, and he got so excited that he fell down the stairs! He was pretty shy, which is incredible when you think about the personality that he was. Very sweet but shy. He told me that, when we first met, he was afraid. He didn't know what to say.

I don't know why his parents split up – they were split up before I met him – but people think possibly it's because his dad fooled around. As far as Muhammad inheriting that type of trait, people know that he's fooled around in his lifetime. I mean, he has a couple of children that he had out of wedlock, and we were together before we were married. That's not anything new. As a matter of fact, when the TV pundit Barbara Walters came to our house in Chicago to interview Muhammad, she asked him about infidelity, what did he think about it and would he be unfaithful, and he responded basically by saying, "Do you know any man who wouldn't?" Of course there are great men out there and they don't all fool around, and he said that in a joking way, but he did say it on that show.

The hardest thing for me, being married to Muhammad, was that there were people in the house constantly. There wasn't any privacy downstairs. I literally could not come downstairs in my robe, because there were always people there. When he wasn't travelling or at the training camp, Muhammad would sit in his office and people would come and go all day long. He loved to answer fan mail, too, and he'd answer as much of that as he could. And he read a lot, mostly the Sufi teachings – a sect of the Muslim religion – which are very loving, peaceful teachings. He did a lot of lectures at colleges based on some of those ideas about love and friendship and peace. I think one of the most important things for people to realise about Muhammad is that he was always totally sincere about everything he said or did or stood up for. People have questioned whether or not he really meant it when he stood up to the draft. Believe me, he meant it 100 per cent.

When we did get married, on 15 June 1977 in Newcastle, England, that was a fabulous day. I wore a calf-length white dress, not a wedding gown, and the people were very gracious and wonderful to us. We rode in a horse-drawn carriage to the place where the dinner festivities were held. Hana was with us by then. It was just beautiful. It felt like a fairy tale, riding in that horse-drawn carriage!

He was a good dad, although I don't remember him changing diapers. He probably did, though, because he just loved doing anything that had to do with the kids. I remember one time we were going to a Hallowe'en party that Diane, my sister, had arranged. I was someplace else at the time, so Muhammad was going to take the kids and I'd meet them there. When I got there, Laila had a T-shirt on, her hair all uncombed, no underclothes. It was just typical of a dad who is really not used to doing everything and taking the kids out on his own. Now I think it was cute, but back then I was shocked.

But he was a good father in the sense that he loved the kids to death. And they knew it, too, especially Hana. She was our firstborn. My two kids were fortunate enough to spend their early years with him, back when he wasn't fighting as much, and when he was, we were in the training camp with him, so they got to see a lot more of their father than some of the other kids.

He was always happy to have the kids around. They'd bounce around on his couch no matter what he was doing. He'd always let them in, even when it was their bedtime. Hana would scream, "Daddy!" and he would let her come out. She always knew she could get out of a bath or going to bed by calling her daddy, and he'd let her come down and sit on his lap in his office. He liked to talk to them with him whenever he could. His dream was one day to have all his kids in one place living in the same house. There were just so many of them, though, that the summer was pretty much the closest we got to that. They visit him at the farm in Michigan a lot now, but they're all grown up.

He has a lot of kids, too. With Sonji, he did not have any children, because they were married less than a year, but then, with his next wife – her original name was Belinda Boyd but she then changed it to Khalilah – they had a number of children together: Maryum, the oldest; there was a son, I think, who was stillborn; then the twins, Jamillah and Rasheeda; and the youngest of her children was little Muhammad Ali. He also has a child by the name of Miya, who he had with Pat Harvil, but they weren't married. That was before he knew me. Also, there's another child named Khaliah. Her mother's name was originally Wanda Bolton, but she changed it to Aishea. Again, that was before we met. And then there's my two children, Hana and Laila, and there's an adopted son, Asaad. I'm not sure if that's his nickname or his proper name, but his name is Asaad. There's a lot of kids, a whole gang. They used to come over every summer, when we were living in Los Angeles, and it was really fun to have them in the house. It was a huge house, of course, lots of bedrooms, and my kids were still pretty young.

He was there at the birth of both of my children. With Hana, we were in Berrien Springs, Michigan, where his farm is. He came to the hospital with me and I was dilating but nothing was happening, so he put pressure on the doctor. It was so funny, because he was more nervous than I was. He was saying, "Do something or I'll take her somewhere else!" He was very concerned and very nervous. Then, with Laila, we were in Miami Beach, and he was in training at the time. I was in hospital for a week because it was a Caesarean, and he visited me a lot.

He was very happy when we were married – at least, he never gave any indication that he wasn't. I think that was because he loved being at home with the kids. As a matter of fact, when we got divorced, he really wanted to have the kids with him, but he knew it wasn't practical because he was travelling still so much, and I was very tentative about sending them across the country to him without someone there, because he wasn't remarried then. When he was, I was more relieved, so then, whenever he wanted them to visit, they were there.

I don't really think there's any contradiction between the way he treated women and his religion. As far as I was concerned, he was pretty consistent. For instance, he really preferred that I did not go anywhere. I did respect the religion – I wore long clothes and I covered my head a lot of the time. Eventually I stopped doing that, but I did adhere to a lot of his wishes, and unfortunately that contributed to us breaking up. It was pretty much an old-fashioned way of living, after all, but at the time I was very young and I didn't mind it as much, and when my kids were very young I was at home all the time anyway. But then, when they were in elementary school, I wanted to pursue things of my own. When Muhammad and I met, I was a pre-med student, and I had actually wanted to go back and graduate, but he talked me into waiting a semester and then another semester and then, of course, I started having children.

But from my own experience, what he said publicly was the way that he was, and that did change somewhat when Elijah Muhammad passed away and a lot of the restrictions eased up. But I know that he still preferred it the old way. A friend of ours was a very business-like woman, and Muhammad said, "I could never be with a woman like that." He preferred a more domestic type of person that was happy staying home.

I was never expected to be a Muslim myself, though. One of the first things Muhammad said to me when we met was that I was already a Muslim. He said, "Do you submit to the will of God?" and I said yes, and he said, "Well, you're already a Muslim." That's his definition of a Muslim. When I think back about that, I think part of him might have been afraid to ask me if I'd be a Muslim and I'd say no. To me, all religions are great, and really that's how he thinks, too. But it was never an issue, really. I respected His religion. I went to the mosque. I never formally joined, but I thought of myself as a Muslim back then.

He was a hard man to live with. He could be very stubborn, sometimes, and he was hard to talk to when he had his mind set a certain way about something. I remember once we had a little conflict about where to send the kids to school, and he would literally take them out of the school where they were in the neighbourhood, drive them all the way across town and leave them at another school.

I didn't like him boxing, either. I never loved boxing, but I accepted it as what my husband did. I always wanted him to retire, though, and even though it was an impossibility back then, I thought that maybe we could have had a normal life if he wasn't boxing. I was very naïve back then, and we could never have had a normal life, because he'd still be Muhammad Ali. And now that my daughter Laila's fighting, it's ten times worse, in terms of the stress I feel when I'm sitting there watching a fight. With her father, I used to just sit there. I couldn't wait 'til the fight was over. Even though I knew that he would be OK, I also knew that anything could happen in a fight, and that was the scary part. It's the same with Laila – she's very good, but I know that anything can happen.

But Muhammad had a good heart. Basically, he's always been a sweet and a good-hearted, good-natured person. The hard things were having people around all the time, the travelling, being constantly in the public eye, the death threats – having to walk right next to him out in public knowing that he's received a death threat. There were a lot of stresses. The lack of privacy, like I said – he always had an entourage around him. Also, there were a lot of misconceptions about how we met. I never told my story, and he never defended me, either! Later I said, "You should have defended me. You don't have to disclose everything to say, 'Well, that's not true,' or whatever." I mean, I was a teenager still when all of that was going on.

But Muhammad loved having lots of people around, all the time. I remember once someone had actually stolen something from him, and he said, "Well what am I going to do? They're my family." That was how he felt about the people that were around him. I'm not saying that everyone was negative; there were a lot of people there that I love. But, for instance, there was no way that I could come in and ask him to try to get rid of anybody that had been with him for years before I even knew him. There was this bond that they had. I knew that that was an area for me to stay out of.

As a matter of fact, one of the people who was there a lot happened to be one of the Muslim ministers, and said, "Look how much Veronica's taken. Imagine how much more she'll take." Before that, I didn't even think about it – it was just the way life was. I loved Muhammad. I was very young, of course, and my way of thinking was that, when you're in love you're in love – basically, take anything! Of course, that's not healthy, and I know that, but as a young girl back then, that was the culture. That was in the songs I heard, and I thought that was how love was supposed to be, that when you love somebody that's the most important thing, and anything else you just go through.

I know that Maryum, Muhammad's oldest, has called me a "stage wife". She never liked any women around her father. And I've heard that she said a couple of little things about me and I realised that she doesn't approve. I mean, Maryum wasn't really around that much. She came for the summers, when she was older, when Muhammad and I first met, and I realised that she'd heard the other side of the story from her mother, Khalila, and her family. And she also has to feel some hurt regarding me, seeing me as the reason why she wasn't with her father.

But I'll always have love for him. We've never fought each other. We've never been on bad terms. We even went to China together for two weeks when we were getting divorced. He cried a lot when we split up, but he cries a lot anyway. He cries when he sees anybody in pain. He's very sensitive. When things touch his heart, he cries. He cried at Laila's wedding. When he hears a beautiful poem, he'll have tears. I know he's continuing to cry now.

When I got divorced, Hana and Laila were very angry at me for a long time, but that has eased up now. Kids are usually always angry at the parent that they are with, because it's safer to be angry. When they know you love them, they feel safe in being angry at you. And Hana and her father had such a bond, I know that it was a deep hurt for her. But I did what I felt was best for me and the children. I considered everything when I decided to get a divorce.

He divorced Sonji very quickly, though. I mean, it's no big secret that Sonji did not want to conform to the Islamic way of life, and Muhammad is the type that, even though he loved her, he would bear down and take the pain and divorce a person if they weren't right. From what I know, that's basically what happened with Sonji.

He was always full of passion, full of life. He had so much energy. I remember when I was 18 and he was 32, the schedule we kept just knocked me out, but he was still full of energy, running around on not much sleep, going here and there on jet planes. He had an over-abundance of energy. And I was the young one!

I know that, with Ali, it's difficult to separate the icon from the man. Back then, I felt like I was living with the man. I mean, I knew of his status in the world, but at the time I didn't think about him in that way, whereas now, when I look back, I realise it more. We always dealt on a family level, not as him being the celebrity Muhammad Ali. As a matter of fact, in Zaire, when I used to watch him train, a few times I went down to the gym, and he seemed like a totally different person in the ring. It struck me then that this did not seem like the person that I knew. It was a totally different man up there.

When I first got divorced from him, I immediately went back to school, completed my BA, my masters, and now I'm working on a doctorate in psychology. I lived in New York for some time, too. I'm happy. It's been a long, hard road, and a lot of work, but it's very rewarding. I almost never tell anybody that I'm Muhammad Ali's ex-wife, but people find out anyhow. And then, when they do, I say, "Yes, but actually now I'm more known as Laila's mother than Muhammad's ex-wife." But when I first got divorced, I didn't really want to be known as his ex-wife, because I never knew who my real friends were when I was married to him and I just wanted people to like me for me and not because of who I was married to. But I'm still proud of the fact that I was married to him. He was a wonderful man and he still is.

Maya Angelou

Poet

I used to listen to Joe Louis fight on the radio when I was young. It was so important to hear how some black mother's and father's son was the champion of the world. It was fantastic. And then, years later, to hear Muhammad Ali on the radio and on television, that was just amazing. Sometimes he was called "the mouth", but he was so wonderful to look at and great to listen to. His poetry always made me laugh.

When I first met Muhammad Ali, I met him as Cassius Clay. And when I say, "I met him," I don't mean I physically met him; I mean he swam into our lives as Cassius Clay. Then, when he became Muhammad Ali, as far as I was concerned there never was a Cassius Clay, because I do believe that people have the right to be called anything they want to be called. He certainly has that right.

He was a man who made an immediate impact on my life, because he was at once so big and so gentle. He was very strong, but he also was very gentle and had a wonderful sense of humour. You have to be intelligent to have a sense of humour, so I knew then that Muhammad Ali – as powerful as he was and respected as he was, and even feared by some as he was – also had a sense of humour. I loved that. I never trust people who don't laugh, and I trusted him immediately.

Oh, I know that he was criticised, but there are people who criticise any public figure. There were people who criticised Jesus and Buddha. But Muhammad meant so much to both black people and white people. He was a crossover hero. When I was living in Ghana, he came to visit the country and I met him and his retinue at the local hotel and invited him to my home for some chicken. I had told my small boy, who helped me around the house, "Don't mention to anyone that I'm cooking chicken for Muhammad Ali." But when he came to visit, Muhammad couldn't get into my street. The people had jammed it solid and we could hardly eat or hear ourselves talk because the Ghanaians were shouting, "Ali the greatest! Muhammad Ali, the greatest, the greatest!" And the people who worked for me acted the same. They had told everybody. They were so proud.

When I met him back in Ghana, he was very young – it was 40 years ago! He talked about Islam. Now, I'm a religious person myself and I have great respect for people and their religions. I had studied Islam, and so I was able to talk to him about it, although he knew more about Christianity than I knew about Islam. We had a good talk, and it wasn't competitive, combative conversation. I keep the memory of that meal very precious to me. I've not even written about it.

But after that meeting, Muhammad Ali was not just Muhammad Ali the greatest, the African-American pugilist; he belonged to everyone. That means that his impact recognises no continent, no language, no colour, no ocean. It belongs to us all, just as Muhammad Ali belongs to us all. It wasn't only what he said and it wasn't only how he said it; it was both of those things, and maybe there was a third thing in it, the spirit of Muhammad Ali, saying his poesies – "Float like a butterfly, sting like bee." I mean, as a poet, I like that! If he hadn't put his name on it, I might have chosen to use that!

He can be compared to any great man or woman. He can be compared to anybody in the world and not be found wanting. He can be compared to Mahatma Gandhi and to Marie Curie because he belonged to everybody. It would've been nice, I think, if he belonged only to African-Americans, but it was never so with him. As a practising Muslim, he also belonged to the Baptists, and so Baptist preachers would preach about him. So, of course, he could be compared to Malcolm X, Martin Luther King, or Mr Mandela because he is a person of such confidence in his morality. Other people will say that he had this expertise, that he was agile and wonderful, physically, but I think of the moral man. A moral person can be compared to any moral person in the world.

It wasn't that people were more tolerant of him or maybe patronising of him because he was black. Just the opposite, in fact. He had more to overcome because he was a black American, he was male and he was conceived in a time not too far from the time when people lynched black males. But as a boxer, he stimulated and encouraged people who wanted to go into the boxing game, and I think he also discouraged people who knew they didn't have it. As he became older, he knew himself that boxing was not a game for older men, so he simply stopped. But his impact was such that boxers still want to be one-tenth of what Muhammad Ali was.

Some people argue that he's safe now, because he's been accepted by the white establishment in America and because the Parkinson's syndrome has neutered his voice, but I don't think anybody's safe from scurrilous attack, so I don't think Muhammad Ali is safe from some dumb-bell attacking him. But the dumb-bell would show himself or herself to be a true dumb-bell, because he is revered by people now, more than just appreciated and accepted. A part of that is ageing, and a part of it can be laid at the door of his ailment, his illness. But also, a great part of his acceptance has been stimulated by him remaining a man of honour, a man of redoubtable resolve, a man, and there's a world of difference between being an old male and being a man. If you're born with certain genitalia and you don't get run over by an out-of-control truck, you can become an old male, but to be a man is a different matter. A man can be fat, thin, short, tall, white, black. He can be Muhammad Ali or Stirling Baker or Joe Jones. I think that a great deal of the respect and affection that people of every colour have for Muhammad Ali can be laid at the door of his manliness. That doesn't mean bravado or strength. That means that he is a great man. I don't know if he's the last great American pugilistic champion, though. I will have to wait and hear men who can speak not just to the sporting game but to life. When I hear a boxer speak about life itself the way Muhammad Ali has spoken about life, its value and its values, then I will know, "Ah! We have not seen the last of the boxing masters."

Jazzy B

Musician / DJ

My first memories of Muhammad Ali would be from the very, very early '70s, when my parents still referred to him as Cassius Clay. They had this monumental position in the living room, in an alcove, and his picture stood very proudly right there, in the centre. You'd look around the family things and you'd see this picture and it's not my mum, my dad, my sister or my brother, it's – aargh! It's Muhammad Ali. He made all the difference in the world. He was the role model for that period. A real source of inspiration.

I always refer to him as a boxer, and he was the king of heavyweights. King of the jungle. But of course, during that period of time, he was politically very important for us as black people. During the mid '70s, there was a time where a lot of young black guys in Britain – in London, particularly – were involved in a lot of racial fights with skinheads, and then somebody like Muhammad Ali would come along who stood for blackness, who was very proud of being a black man, and I think that really made a difference to all of us growing up. It encouraged us to have our feet firmly on the ground. Obviously, if someone like Muhammad Ali was doing it, he would encourage us young people to feel the same way.

People found it odd that we had to turn to the States for a role model, but the fact is that most of our parents migrated to England from the colonial islands during the '50s. Muhammad Ali stood out a lot, particularly because of the days of Martin Luther King, Malcolm X and the whole Black Panther movement. In Britain, we didn't have that many people to idolise as young black kids. It wasn't until the '70s that people like Clive Best came along, and then it sort of evolved from there. There were a couple of footballers but nobody like Muhammad Ali. This guy wasn't just a sportsman; he was a very articulate person, very much a showman. He had all the elements that you'd want. He's quite ferocious, as well as being gentle, and he knew what he was doing when he was boxing as well. It was something delightful to see him beating the hell out of his opponent. You'd hear him talking in the ring, and then he'd come out of the ring and he'd be far more surreal than the whole fight itself, talking to the commentators. No one else could ever do that, 'cause most of the other heavyweight fighters during that or any period were too knackered or really not that way inclined. This guy had everything: he was jovial, he was very spiritual and he was a very serious sportsman.

The Rumble In The Jungle is my favourite of his fights. It was certainly the most intense one, especially for how long the whole thing went on and what he was saying during that period. Of course, he had to win. It was intense. There was energy in the house at that time. He had an effect on black people's identity across the world, and I think that to some degree he even made a lot of white people question who they were, what they were. He made you want to be black. He didn't perm his hair. He looked like a strong black man, somebody that your uncle or your brothers would look like. He was quite a handsome chap as well, and he kept himself natural. A real nubian man.

I guess I've been blessed, in terms of being proud of who I am, coming from a large family, particularly with my parents as strong as they are. But he reinforced that and made you feel no other way. I was upset when he turned to being a Muslim, being opposed to the Muslim faith, but I think he helped to encourage that somewhat as well.

Muhammad Ali could be a very serious person. He had a serious message, but his manner was about wooing the crowd. This guy was a boxer, as well as all the other work he did. It's amazing that he could go through that type of punishment and still be that articulate. But then, sometimes even the words weren't that important. It's just looking at him and seeing what this man stood for. Even now, when you see him today and suffering from Parkinson's syndrome, you can see how much he's put himself out there, which I think must be quite a gruelling task. This guy threw away his medal because he thought that was all bullshit. You read the things he said when they wanted him to defend his country – it really did inspire all of us. In school, we'd always draw a line from the great poetry he came out with: "Float like a butterfly, sting like a bee." He's always been important. He doesn't even need to say anything. Everything the guy stands for conjures up various different thoughts, and all of them positive ones.

People have said that Ali's poetry was an early form of rap, and I think that's a great observation. Eclectically, it definitely could be. This was around the same time as James Brown, Curtis Mayfield – great guys, as well – and was the whole Philly and Motown era. It was a fantastic time. Maybe he should have made a record, instead of Mike Tyson, who made a few. A lot of them did, even Joe Frazier. He made quite a lot of reggae recordings in Jamaica.

My own interest in boxing really comes from it being one of those physical things, as well as really sharp. It's not just a game of brawn; there's a lot of skill involved. Having spent a lot of time with some of the world's greatest boxers, and one person in particular – Maurice Hope is a very good friend of mine – you can see how intense it is. It's also a very lonely game, in terms of what you've got to go through. You've got to be a really strong person to be dealing with that type of sport. There's no teams to rely on, so it's very much a man's man's sport.

But Ali has got to be the number one, really. The heavyweight champion of the whole wide world. Greats like Muhammad Ali, Nelson Mandela, etc, never go away. Never. People like that are always there. Curtis Mayfield, James Brown, Jimi Hendrix, all these cats, they've been such life-inspiring people, so they are always going to be around somewhere, in your thoughts or whatever. And the media resurrects people's awareness about these people. But the real true encyclopaedias on all these people are always

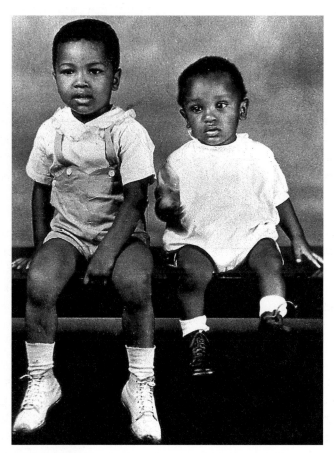

Cassius Clay (left) at the age of four, with younger brother
Rudolph, 1946.

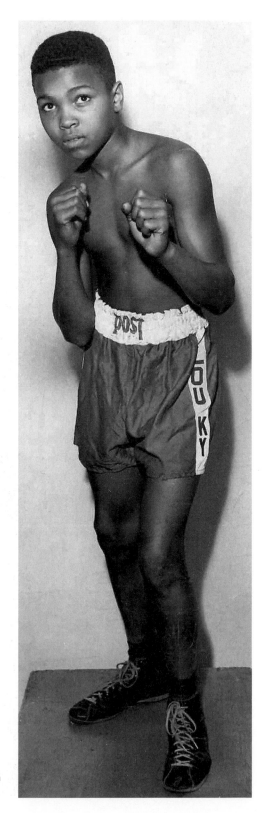

Twelve-year-old Cassius in
an early fighting pose.

Cassius and friend at Joe Martin's gym in Louisville, 1958.

Clay signs his contract with the Louisville Sponsoring Group, 1960.

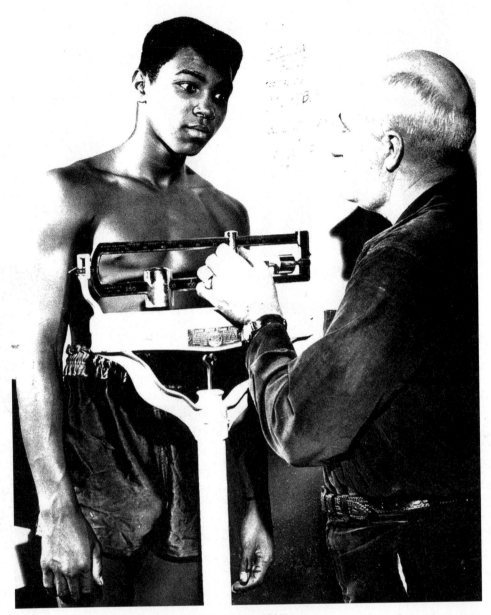
Clay on the scales before his first professional contest, 1960.

Clay stands proudly on the podium with his Olympic gold medal, Rome, 1960.

The Olympic champion is welcomed home by his parents and brother at Louisville Airport, 1960.

Cassius and Rudolph stand outside their parents' home in Louisville, 1962.

there, documented, deep rooted. They're inspirations, because you've got to go through so much in life, and knowing that there's people like that who went through probably even worse and have managed to sustain it is a constant source of inspiration, and those flames never go out.

I don't know if he's still an influence to the younger generation now, because there are people like Mike Tyson and Lennox Lewis and Prince Naseem who have come along and are in the current realm of it all. But I think that, from a sheer educational point of view, if people want to know their stuff, they have to know about all the greats, everyone from Muhammad Ali right the way back to Sugar Ray Robinson, Joe Frazier, George Foreman, etc. It depends on how much involvement you have in the sport. When you come to people who are icons and legends, people like Muhammad Ali, they stand out incredibly like sore thumbs and they are always going to be a source of inspiration for anybody who is willing to dig into the depths of their history.

It's been said that Ali went through a time where he was reviled by a lot of Americans because of Vietnam, the Nation of Islam, and now he's loved by everyone again because he's no longer a threat, and I'd agree. He is no longer a threat to white America because of what he is undergoing at the moment. And it's funny that he's been embraced in such a way. It's odd to see him taking all these accolades from people who wouldn't have wanted anything to do with this gentleman no more than 20 years ago. It's quite ironic, really. To me, it could even be that he's a wolf in sheep's clothing – and I mean that very positively. There's a saying: "You'll be tired of seeing me." And if you can't hear him, you can see him. People are always going to be curious: "Who is that guy? What is he?" Everybody is giving up praises to this chap.

To a certain extent, he's more popular because he doesn't pose any more. He just keeps smiling and nagging everybody, and you'll soon be tired of seeing good old Muhammad there. Everybody's embracing him and thinking, "Oh, what a lovely fellow," and he's looking around now and saying, "What a load of bullshit." It's probably the case that now, through his Parkinson's, he is unable to react in that way, but I am sure that, given half the chance, he'd have so much to say. Sometimes I just look at him and think, "I wonder what's going through his head now," considering all that this man has gone through, all that he has stood for.

There is only one Martin Luther King, there's only one Nelson Mandela and there's definitely only one Muhammad Ali. People can try to mimic and imitate, but you can never duplicate. I can't think of anyone else who would be anywhere near the force of that mighty person, other than somebody trying to act in a play or in a movie, trying to portray exactly what this gentleman has meant to the world. You could never duplicate that.

Victor Bockris

Journalist / Poet

The biggest interview I ever did with Ali was for *Penthouse* in 1974. I was really scared about that, because I thought, "He's not gonna like being in this magazine with all these naked women. Oh my god, what have I done? Am I gonna get shot in the street by the Muslims." But I went down to see him after the magazine came out and he actually shook hands with me and thanked me for it and told me it was the first time he'd ever seen his words printed in a big magazine like that. He wasn't all over the papers at all at that stage. In a way, he was lucky that he escaped a great deal of press coverage that could have upset his image. But then the people he did give stories to were always so appreciative. Somehow, without engineering it, he had the press where he wanted them.

Later, of course, the press couldn't get enough of him. The only boxer in the world today that gets anything like that degree of attention in the press is Mike Tyson. He has charisma, the kind that you can't really understand until you're in the presence of it. Ali had that kind that same kind of charisma. He had a lot of things going for him – he was unusually good looking, with an almost perfect body. He had a combination of things that just perfectly meshed with the moment and the way the moment was changing. He looked great in black-and-white photography, for instance. The hard-edged, high-contrast photo shot was perfect for Ali, perfect for Warhol, perfect for The Beatles, all that essence of youth and exhilaration that those people had.

I went up to Deer Lake one day expecting to do a one-and-a-half-hour interview with him and he gave me eight hours the first day I was with him. We didn't have a tape running the whole time, but we could have. He was very playful – took me on a ride in his touring bus, showed me videos of his fights and took me on a tour of the camp. He was obviously loving being with someone who he could actually have fun with, verbally, and I was surprised by the depth and width of his verbal ability. This wasn't a guy who was just reciting something he'd learned; here was a guy who was actually creative, verbally, spontaneously. As a writer, I was most interested in spontaneous composition – Kerouac, Ginsberg, the beat thing, and also Lenny Bruce, the comedian – this idea of throwing up words and tossing them around, and for the first couple of hours I was with him Ali was laying out extended stories with all sorts of characters, bringing them in and out and going off on tangents and bringing it back and hitting his mark and taking off again, and I was really surprised. He even read me some of his poetry, some of his longer poems, and his timing was really quite remarkable.

Plus when he met me, he was stark naked. It's the only time I've ever seen a celebrity introduce me in his house stark naked. And obviously he didn't just do that without thinking. It was a way of being totally vulnerable, totally open. But there was nothing weird about it. It wasn't like he was subliminally gay or throwing some wicked angle at me. It was just a really lovely thing to do, and I was really impressed. It was a strange combination of vulnerable and all powerful.

But that's exactly what makes him attractive. I think that Ali had a certain kind of genius that I don't think anyone's ever pinned down. But I remember Bob Dylan saying that there was a certain high-mercury sound that he was going for in his records that he only captured in the first three electric records that he made, and that strikes a bell in mind with Ali. There's a kind of high-mercury kind of magic that was just *there* somehow that he was trying to harness, and he did harness it in this particular time, around 1972 to '75.

In that period, what you saw was ten years of preparation, ten years of talking to the press, entertaining people and being very funny now mixed in with a more serious commitment to the Muslim faith and a desire to be a public speaker. He was moving between the worlds of poetry, religion, old-fashioned performance, vaudeville and folk poetry, toying with all this without knowing any of those things, without intellectually thinking about that, but somehow naturally bringing all of those things into play, and then conjuring words in a way that was quite magic and which very few people in his entourage recognised at all.

On one occasion, he asked me to stay to dinner because he couldn't give me the time to do the interview earlier. I said, "Great," and I was quite surprised. I had dinner there with 15 other men, all black, and Ali sat at a separate table on his own with a television set, on which he was watching the news; a copy of the Koran, from which he was jotting down some words; and a big pad of paper. All these other guys were having these wonderful raucous conversations, talking about the day's training, and Ali had no interest in it at all.

I don't think that Ali is Jesus Christ; he's like a folk figure, a folk poet. There's a certain folk wisdom that he has which is very real. He's one of the very few central key figures who came out of the '60s who are still standing – Lennon's gone, Warhol's gone, King's gone and the Kennedys have gone. But the greatest irony of Ali's whole life is that he had two gifts – his athletic gift and his verbal gift – and he worked out this really unique way of dealing with this conundrum. As soon as he was out of athletics, he turned around and used his verbal gift. He understood that he was a character who, because of his ability to tie together the east and the west contingents of Islam, could go into worlds that white people couldn't and do a kind of PR thing just by being very nice and friendly and telling some really very simplistic things but doing it in a very lovely way that bridged gaps. It would have been brilliant if he'd done that in the late '70s. But for him to lose the verbal thing at the last minute, totally unexpectedly, is one of the great ironies of this time. But he's handled it remarkably well. For a long time, he was very, very depressed in the '80s after he lost everything – his money, his wife, a lot of his family and his ability to speak.

But the nature of celebrity is that it's like the emperor's new clothes. Real, top-flight celebrities have charisma, and charisma is an indefinable thing that, at the moment you're around it, creates this wonderful atmosphere in which everything seems to sparkle and you seem to be ten feet tall. It's like a drug. But it's no different from being a politician or anyone who's in the public eye – they always repeat themselves. It's the nature of the game. As Warhol kept pointing out, repetition is the basis of life. But there's nothing wrong with that. That's what people want to hear. It's like when people go to concerts – they want to hear the oldies; they don't want to hear new songs. So Ali always gave them what they wanted. But he did start mixing in a lot of new poems in the '70s, longer, more developed poems than the doggerel things he wrote in the '60s. In fact, when WH Auden died in September '72, around that time the students at Oxford University brought out a petition for Muhammad Ali to be the new Professor of Poetry there.

But the thing is, when I was presented with these poems while writing *Muhammad Ali – In Fighters' Heaven*, it didn't strike me as at all odd that a boxer had written them. When I talked with him about it, he'd been fighting for ten years non-stop and wanted to talk about other things. When I met him, I saw him as a cultural figure. But he was also a blank slate upon which you could write anything. A lot of great celebrities are that way. You can get them to focus on whatever you want them to focus on. I think I was just lucky in that, at that time, Ali was more interested in his poetry than he was at any other time in his life.

To a certain extent, he's become so elevated Ali because he allowed an expanding media to use him in different ways. But then again, even as late as 1972, most people thought that Ali's career was over, and it wasn't that easy to get newspapers to publish stuff on Muhammad Ali. They were like, "Oh, he was in the '60s. That's over. He's not gonna make a comeback. No way he's not gonna beat Foreman." So at the time, people like me had to argue that he was still relevant, still interesting. And Ali talks great, too. I mean, it's surprising how little people really knew about him in 1972. When I first went to his training camp at Deer Lake in that year, there weren't a lot of people visiting. It was very quiet. It was only by the middle of '73 that suddenly more and more people were coming. He was really fighting an uphill battle.

The thing is, because Ali was such a character of the '60s, in the early '70s they were trying to find out what the decade was all about and they kind of wrote off Ali, but by around 1972 the '70s began to find its shape, and that shape was very much defined by a different type of celebrity culture. It was called "the me decade" by Tom Wolfe. *People* magazine was probably the leading exponent of it, and *People* was very much influenced by Andy Warhol's *Interview* magazine. The idea was that you could just take a magazine and run a bunch of interviews with celebrities and that's all you needed.

Ali was perfect fodder for this idea, but back in 1972 people weren't quite aware of that yet. People didn't really know that Ali was a person who was able to maintain hours and hours of conversation, that he wasn't just three-line poem or a funny quip but that he actually could talk at great length. He could develop a point and then leave it and then come back to it. He really knew what he was talking about. And he had this wonderful voice, which could be deep and sonorous or it could be light and funny. It was a very mobile voice. And he had a very expressive face and also used his hands and his face very well. He had beautiful hands. And he really knew how to do all this. I mean, he'd learned it, obviously, but he was very, very good at it. And he enjoyed it. He lit up inside when he was doing that. He loved to perform. I think that one of the difficulties with athletes, particularly boxers, is they only get to perform once a year or something. The rest of the time is spent in secret, training. It's very dull for them. In fact, Ali told me that he needed conversation to keep him focused on his training. He really needed to keep his mind as sharp as his body, and the only way he could do that was through conversation.

But Ali never did live in the celebrity world. He lived in his own world. He had his own castle, his own entourage, his own party. He didn't go to other people; people came to him. That's the way Elvis was, too, and the way it is with a lot of top people. And Ali wasn't really a night-life person. I mean, being a Muslim, all that stuff was completely against his rules anyway. He was such an extreme example of the single celebrity. He didn't even want to be in a room with other celebrities. There was only one star in Ali's world. He was the star. Nobody else came close. And he wasn't really interested in being with other celebrities, because then there was competition. The only celebrity he ever wanted to meet was Elvis.

But then again, he made himself available to everyone. Anyone could go to Deer Lake. You didn't have to be taken up and introduced. It's funny, because he had a lot of baffles between him and the world. When I met Paul McCartney recently, we just shook hands, he looked me in the eye and we had a conversation. Ali wasn't like that. You couldn't reach him on that level. He would put his hand on your arm and be looking somewhere else. He wasn't really into eye contact; he was only interested in people who came to him because they were interested in him and had a particular purpose.

Back in 1975, he went on a tour to support the boxer Rubin "Hurricane" Carter, a middle-heavyweight champion who was in jail, – unjustly, as it turns out. Ali told me about this when I was up at Deer Lake one day. He said, "I'm going to visit this boxer in prison. I don't know if he's guilty or not but I'm going to find out and I might help." It turned out that Dylan jumped on the tour, too. Then, when the tour got to Madison Square Garden for its final and biggest night, Ali came out and did his schtick and actually called Carter on the phone from the stage and talked to him and it was very dramatic. But the interesting thing was that there was a photograph taken backstage of Dylan and Ali sitting on a bench together but some distance from each other and both looking in the opposite directions. Ali had no idea who Bob Dylan was, and that tells you something about where he was at.

Now, regardless of whether or not that was bravado, whether he really didn't know him or wanted to pretend he didn't know him, it's interesting. His attitude was, "I never heard of this guy Bob Dylan before tonight, but he must be a pretty good guy 'cause look what he's doing." And Dylan was Dylan. He wasn't gonna make a big attempt to be friendly with Ali if he didn't want to be. So Ali played a seemingly very big role in the '60s, and yet even at the highest moment of his appearance in the counter-culture he denies any knowledge of it.

The thing is, there's a certain problem in understanding these kinds of people. You can't expect Muhammad Ali, who by 1975 was the most famous person in the world, to be judged on the normal levels that you judge other people. If you make Faustian bargain – I am going to dedicate my life to my fame – there's no way that you can operate on a normal level with other people. The only people with whom you could be judged as having any kind of sympathetic relationship would be your family. Ali didn't have time to be sympathetic to other people. It just wasn't in his make-up.

He had an inner core of hangers-on who would come to him for money. He tried to be very generous, but he got ripped off an enormous amount, and after a while it wasn't so much that he was upset about losing the money as that he realised that these people weren't really his friends. Then he had the normal problems. I always think that rock stars are classic examples. They usually become famous when they're very young and enter a kind of cocoon in which they live for as long as they're rock stars, having no contact with real life. Ali was like that. From the time he was about twelve, he was focused on this boxing as a way to escape normalcy and become a star. And then, by the time he was 20 or so, he was one of the biggest stars in the world, and he wanted to hold onto that. That's all he was really concerned about. He told me, "I eat, sleep, breathe, drink, dream and think about only boxing. That's how I became a champion." But of course later he was saying that there was more to him, that he wanted to be a great religious leader, and he was starting to live and breathe and drink and dream that.

He never considered politics, though. I think that he thought politics was demeaning and beneath him. He had contempt for politicians. The United States tried to use him on a State Department field trip to Africa, but of course he was nuts and they couldn't control him. They didn't know what to do with him.

He has admitted recently that, when he was in boxing, he didn't really conform to the standards of Muslim beliefs and he wasn't really relating to God the way he thinks he is now. Now, there's a certain hypocrisy in that, but if you want celebrities then you have to understand what they are and not judge them by mortal levels. On the other hand, Ali was the greatest publicist of the Muslim faith in the world and he spent a lot of time publicising it in a fairly positive way, so you have to give him credit for doing that. Kennedy was in a very similar position. But these people live, at that level, with a great deal of tension and things like death threats and financial conundrums. They have to make enormous decisions, and you have to give them a little leeway.

Now, of course, he's been absorbed by the white establishment. But of course Ali has always been paid by white people, from the beginning of his career. White people were always in control of his career, and he has no illusions about that. That's where the money is, and he certainly wants money. His audience is largely white. He has no illusions about that, and it doesn't bother him. And with politics, it doesn't matter if you're a Republican or a Democrat, as far as he's concerned. He just doesn't care about that kind of thing. He's way beyond that.

But you can't say that he's sold out black America. Ali was never the voicepiece of black America. Ali was the voicepiece of the Black Muslims, which is a very separate thing. He was never a man of the ghetto. In the '60s, there was a short period when he was friendly with Malcolm X and would walk through the ghetto and sign autographs and let children sit on his knee, but he never really did that kind of thing very much. He didn't go out there and necessarily try to earn the reputation he has. All of these many different hats he wears, in a sense the public put them on him. He's just so mired in history and events that it's almost impossible to pull him out and look at him without all that stuff on him, but you have to if you want to understand him or have any sympathy for him.

I don't think that it would have made any sense to kill Ali, though. It would have been counter-productive. The assassination of Malcolm X, Martin Luther King, President Kennedy – those made sense, but killing Ali wouldn't have achieved anything for anyone. It would have just made a very large number of people angry with whoever had done it. The only person who might have shot Ali would have been some redneck who thought that his friends would like him for doing it, but I think he was too well protected for that. He had a very protective entourage of bodyguards. The Black Muslims are very tough lot. I saw a lot of guns when I was up at Deer Lake.

Through his involvement with the Muslims and by refusing to be drafted, he got pitched into being a sort of cult figure, but his position didn't relate specifically to black people; he was just against the war. His wasn't a black stance; it was a generational stance. That's the moment at which he suddenly became something beyond some brilliant, pretty athlete who grew up at the same time as The Beatles and had the same kind of aura as them. He started talking about the war and taking positions. And of course none of the people – like Ali, in the public eye – who spoke out really knew anything about the war. They couldn't talk about it intelligently. They probably couldn't tell you where Vietnam was , but let's give them their due – they put their names on the line in a way that could have destroyed their careers. To an extent, it did destroy Ali's career.

Of course, it was much harder for him, as a black guy, than it was for a privileged white guy. For example, when The Beatles talked about the war, against the instructions of their manager, they didn't lose their careers. They didn't lose any money. They might have lost a few concerts in America, but that's it. Ali, though, he pulled the carpet out from underneath himself. He found himself banned from boxing, from travelling overseas. All illegal but, you know, he's black so we can do it. And yes, it was illegal. The Boxing Commission had charged him with evasion of draft, but you're still innocent until you're found guilty of any crime. They withdrew his boxing licence before he was found guilty.

In some ways, he's very similar to Lennon. But one of the very basic things to consider about Muhammad Ali is that being a black man in America is a very, very frightening thing to be. A black man in America – anywhere in America, not just in the South – is always vulnerable to being arrested. He cannot walk down the street with a joint in his pocket because he might be arrested and searched. You can apply that across the board to anything. If a black man has a woman, it's much harder for him to protect her or to support her. So Ali was fighting from a very different corner than Lennon or any of the other people we might compare him with.

The only person I ever could compare him to successfully was Andy Warhol, because Warhol came from a family of Eastern immigrants, an even poorer and more downtrodden group than Ali. They were the lowest of the low. And

Warhol had a very similar strength that Ali had and a very similar religious basis to that strength, and a similar charisma. They were the great white man and the great black man at that time.

And of course Warhol produced art on Ali. In the mid '70s, Warhol was trying to expand and develop and he got into a whole new way of working. Rather than having an idea for a painting and painting it, he would get commissions from people. He would get a £1 million down-payment to do a series of paintings on X. Well, he thought about what that X could be, and thought about great athletes. They would be easy to sell because, for instance, the museum of baseball is gonna buy one of a baseball player. It's a good way to start doing corporate art. So he did a series of pieces on ten athletes, and Ali was one. He also did OJ Simpson and Chris Evert, the tennis player. He would do six canvases of each subject and then a hundred prints of each canvas, and then a whole series of posters. When you parcel this out, you can make a lot of money. So he paid the athletes $15,000 each to have their picture taken, so Ali was earning $15,000 for six minutes' work. I was there when the picture was taken and he kept talking about it the whole time: "I'm getting $15,000 to sit here. That's pretty good!" And he wouldn't pose. It was really very funny. That's why Warhol invited me there, to be a buffer between them and get him to pose, which I ultimately did.

But Andy had no personal interest in Ali. It wasn't like he thought, "Ali is a great man. I'll do his painting." In fact, after we left, he kept asking me if I thought Ali was really intelligent, because he'd acted so weirdly. That was because Andy was gay, and Ali was uncomfortable with that.

You hear very little about Ali's family, though. I think that he's always been very careful to protect his family from publicity. First of all, no celebrity wants to have their children photographed a lot, because of the threat of being kidnapped. Then, of course, Ali didn't often make the kind of appearances that often require the trophy bride on the arm. He lived in a very male world, the world of the gang, the entourage, and there wasn't really much room for women or family in that. That was certainly destructive to him, in the long run, and that's why he wasn't able to maintain families and why he kept going through them and having to get new ones. He clearly wanted children and the companionship of a woman, but I don't think that he was that perceptive or knowledgeable about the whole thing. I don't think he ever thought, "Oh my god, this isn't really something that works very well for someone in my position." I think he just kept banging away at it. In fact, the godsend of his life is his current wife, who really is wonderful, like his best friend, whereas his other wives I think thought that it would be fun to be Ali's wife rather than really care for him.

To really understand the essence of Ali is to understand that he is totally unintellectual. Essentially, he is humane. His concern is for the underdogs – the winos and dopeheads and prostitutes and little kids and the brother on the street who can't get a pair of shoes. He had been an underdog as a child and, as he became larger and larger and larger, the underdog then became the whole counter-culture, that whole side of culture that wasn't satisfied with the establishment, that was looking for cultural leaders. But he was very much a figurehead. He would cut the ribbons and go to the boat-launching ceremonies and give the speeches, but you couldn't expect him to have any kind of intellectual understanding of what was going on and write a newspaper account of it.

But I think the public needs people like that. Part of American celebrity culture is trying to find a kind of royal family. That's where you have this lingering desire for Camelot – this horrible, weird desire to keep propping the Kennedys up, for instance. At some time or other, there have been celebrities that fulfilled that function, but they are very few. I don't think there are any now that I can think of. But there was a mythic quality to celebrity that grew up in the '60s.

It all has to do with the aftermath of World War II. When The Beatles first started, it was the first shout of joy from youth that we'd had for many years. After enduring a difficult time after the war, after rationing had finally stopped, suddenly you had this wonderful joy in consuming and enjoying life. The Beatles were given a kind of a royal status, with diplomatic pouches and all that kind of thing. Muhammad Ali became part of that myth. He locked into that mythic culture level. When The Beatles went to see him in '64, when they first came to America, it was very much a recognition between them. He recognised that what they were doing was the same thing that he was doing. Dylan is part of that, too, that mythic level of celebrity. Warhol certainly was. Burroughs certainly was. They weren't just movie stars; they were people who'd invested years and years of training into what they were doing and then did it very, very well.

I admire Ali enormously, and looking at him today, having some sense of what he must know he's lost for ever, his commitment now to spending over 200 days of the year travelling around the world, lending his presence in a positive humane way – certainly in Third World countries – for just causes is remarkable. It's hard for him, with his physical ailments, sitting on these twelve-hour plane flights to Africa and India. It really is a commitment. I mean, he's kind of unattractive now, drooling saliva – he can't really control his mouth – and to be in public like that after being the most beautiful man in the world, admired for your beauty, that takes real courage. He's not doing it for the applause, either. He's had enough of that. I think that there's a real moral commitment to carrying out his legacy.

They tell me that his mind is totally unaffected. If that's really true, then I know that mind, and it's a mind which is racing all over the place. It's full of all sorts of images and thoughts. It's to some extent exuberant and childish and to some extent religious and sonorous. It must be very difficult for him. I'm sure he's focusing on everything around him through religion, and I'm sure he's deeply grounded by his relationship with Lonnie and the new child he's recently adopted, but I think that anyone who would criticise Ali or question his real commitment would have to look at what he's doing now. There's no reason for doing it other than to show that the real moral strength that came out in the '60s is still there.

Ina Bond

Muhammad Ali Center Board Member

When I was in high school, down in Florida, I learned that my father, along with ten other businessmen, was helping support this wonderful young athlete from Louisville, Kentucky, who was apparently a brilliant boxer and a very charismatic, exciting person, so I started following his career. Things just sort of grew and grew and grew, as I learned of his wonderful personality, his sense of humour, his charisma. At that time, everything was a little more chauvinistic, so I wasn't allowed to go to the fights, like my three older brothers, but I heard about them and read about them and followed him in the newspaper. Then, when I was in college, I did go and see the Liston fight on close-circuit television, and of course I bet on him when nobody else did, because nobody thought he'd win. Somehow he convinced me early on that he could do it. He always had this wonderful belief in himself. So many people have a natural athletic talent, but he had this heart and soul that made him never quit.

In Louisville, in the early '60s, there was still segregation. It was the beginning of the civil rights movement, but things were very different then. I didn't pay too much attention, although I probably should have. Of course, now I'm aware of just what a terrible situation it was. I had so many friends that were African-American, and I've always had friends of all religions and all ages. But the fact that these eleven white businessmen were backing this black fighter wasn't a big issue. They liked him. This Cassius Clay was very talented, a superb athlete with great personality and a sense of humour, and they thought he was very clean-cut, a nice young gentlemen, and they wanted to help him. They all really liked him.

I met Ali later, at the Kentucky Derby, and I just remember how friendly he was. I asked for his autograph and somebody who was with me took a picture of us. He is still this way. Whenever anybody meets him, he is not at all arrogant; he never acts like he's the most famous person in the world. He's so kind and wonderful to the person he's with. He makes you feel special.

At the time, a lot of people around here saw him as a hero. They had a huge ticker-tape welcome parade when he came home, but of course everybody's heard the story about him not being served in a restaurant, which is just horrifying. But it wasn't like the whole town was like that one man. Most people were just thrilled. He'd won the Olympics. He always spoke of Louisville, too – "I'm Cassius Clay from Louisville, Kentucky." When he left, we never felt any resentment. Now, I've heard that there are some people that did. But many people grow up and move away. I don't think that means they abandon their home town.

My father was sad that they were not gonna be continuing on as his sponsor, but I don't think he and the others were angry. They realised that he had won the heavyweight championship of the world and he probably didn't need them any more. I'm sure that there are people all the time who've achieved success going on and find new managers.

But we all kept an interest in his career. I certainly did. I had grown up and married, but I followed him and I went to every single fight. I very much had an interest in seeing him do well. I was always happy when he won, always sad when he didn't.

I'm not sure how my father felt about his joining the Nation of Islam and the Vietnam War. He was probably like a lot of older Southern gentlemen. He was more conservative than a lot of people, including me. I didn't understand the Nation of Islam like I do now, so I didn't understand what it must have been like for Muhammad and for so many African-Americans. Now I understand how important that feeling of black pride was and why he was drawn to that movement. At the time, I think people didn't understand it and so they were confused.

At the time, Elijah Muhammad was very separatist. He hated white people so that was somewhat scary. I hoped Muhammad wouldn't start hating me. It was clearly a confusing time, because there was a war and, while a lot of Americans had always had a sense of patriotism, here was a war that was unpopular and the country was divided on whether people ought to fight or not. There were so many movements at that time. It was the beginning of the civil rights movement and times were changing, as they should have. But it was a very volatile time, a very confusing time, and of course Muhammad, at the height of his fame and the best time in his career, was plopped right in the middle of it.

After Muhammad retired and got Parkinson's, I really didn't hear too much about him. Then, maybe four years ago, I was in charge of the, the National Red Cross Convention and someone said to me, "Wouldn't it be wonderful if we could get Muhammad Ali to come help open the convention?" So I thought about trying to find out how to reach him and see if he would be willing to come, and he *did* come. It was just amazing, because usually you ask somebody of that notoriety and someone who's so famous and sought after and they say, "Oh no, that's impossible."

Later, Larry Townsend mentioned that they were beginning an effort to start a Muhammad Ali Center here in Louisville and asked if I'd like to be on the board, so I said I would. That was three or four years ago, and I've just gotten more and more deeply involved as time has gone along.

For the last 30 years, Muhammad has really tried to reach a lot of children and to do good things for them in many different ways. And he's wanted to bring people together and have people love each other. He wants people of all cultures and all races to respect each other and have an understanding of each other and live in a peaceful society. So Muhammad and Lonnie decided to create a place where people could all come together and learn about their differences and hopefully avoid conflict and have a better understanding of each other.

A second dimension of the Center is to inspire all people, but particularly children, to reach their full potential, to be their best. I've heard Muhammad and Lonnie say, as they've travelled around the world, that they've seen so many young people who've given up hope that they could be something, and he wants to inspire them to stay in school, stay off drugs, really study hard or do whatever it is they wanna do in life and stick with it, not give up. That's kind of what he did in his life.

I'm so excited about what they're doing at the Center. There will be a visitor experience with five major galleries. It will not only be entertaining and fun, but it will also have a great impact on each individual that goes through. They'll not only learn about Muhammad's life but, if we've done our job, they'll learn about themselves. It will help the people that go through that to be inspired to be the best people they can and to really work hard to make a difference in our society. It'll also help people to understand those that are different. That's one dimension, the visitor experience.

We'll be also adding distance learning through our website. We'll have seminars and round tables and teacher-training sessions that will help take some of the themes of Muhammad's life and translate them into things that are very meaningful to people around the world. And there will also be a conflict-resolution centre. We've formed a partnership with the University of Louisville to do this. We'll begin training for people all over in how to avoid conflict or, if there is a conflict, how to mediate it so there is not violence. I think diversity is gonna be a big part of the programming of our cross-cultural education. In some ways, I think we're gonna be like the Carter Center, which started as a presidential library and became a centre for humanitarian efforts. We hope that this will be something that will grow bigger and bigger and, in the long run, will be international in scope.

Because of my father's involvement, I feel like I'm a continuing part of the Muhammad Ali story. But sometimes I think this is something that was just meant to be. I have never worked harder on any project in my life. I've given a substantial amount to it as well. I believe in it strongly, because I think it's a really good thing. I have tremendous admiration for both Lonnie and Muhammad. I think it's important for our society to create a place like this. When you see the violence that's happening in America, in the schools, and you hear about violence everywhere around the world, anything that you can do to help stop that is very important. It's also giving young people hope and trying to turn their lives around and helping them lead a more spiritual and productive life, instead of getting in a gang or something.

My father died in 1973, but I think he would be absolutely thrilled that Muhammad has turned into what he has. He always saw the boxing greatness, but I don't think he had any idea of the great humanitarian that he also was. I think he'd be pleased that he's made such an impact on the world. Muhammad has said himself that his boxing career was just the beginning of his work and it's what he's doing now that's the most important thing. It's what he was really meant to do on this Earth. The boxing career made him famous, but I'm amazed at the energy he has, even in spite of his Parkinson's syndrome. He travels over 200 days a year to do good things around the world, and not always just meeting with the upper crust and the kings and the queens; he'll spend a whole day with the homeless in New York or here in Louisville. He's gone to the Home Of The Innocents, which is a home for children who've been abused, have diseases or disabilities, and when he's with those children, he absolutely lights up. I've never seen anybody that has so much love for all people. And through that love, and with his fame, he's been able to do wonderful things. Wherever he goes, he draws a crowd to raise money and then gives it to charities instead of taking it for himself. I think it's quite remarkable.

It's very exciting to work for him. You know you're really blessed when you can do something that's not only work but also brings you joy at the same time. It's not easy, because anything great takes an enormous amount of effort and there are always stumbling blocks. We know that the Center needs to be very big in scope. We couldn't have just a little museum with some boxing gloves and robes or something. It's got to be something that really makes an impact, not only in this city, state or country but around the world. From the beginning, we've been really ambitious with our goals.

It's a labour of love. Something like the Center has been attempted in the past, but they just didn't have the right leadership in the earlier efforts. Ours is an $80 million project.

There's not that much memorabilia or tourist attractions to do with Muhammad in Louisville. The town has been way too slow in doing more for him. The only thing we have, really, is Muhammad Ali Boulevard, and that was done quite some time ago. However, the Chamber of Commerce is about to unveil a huge portrait of Muhammad on the side of a building to honour him. It's not that Louisville doesn't appreciate Muhammad; he's kind of taken for granted because he visits here quite frequently. It's not such an amazing thing to see him walking down the street here like it is in other parts of the world. When the Muhammad Ali Centre was recently working in New York and Muhammad was with our director, Michael Fox, he was on the street for two minutes and 300 people gathered there in that time. I even heard that a bus driver stopped the bus in the middle of Madison Avenue and got off, leaving all of his passengers and blocking traffic because he wanted to meet Muhammad.

Billy Connolly

Comedian / Actor

Muhammad Ali is an absolute natural comedian. I remember when he was Cassius Clay in the Olympic Games, he wouldn't sit down between rounds. He just stood there, terrifying the guy by joking around and then going out and pasting him. I think it was meant as an aggressive move but it looked really funny to me. He said he copied wrestlers in America for his talent for being funny and over-the-top outrage. All that "get up, get up, what's my name?" stuff. I loved every second of it.

He has extraordinary comic timing for a person who isn't a comedian. I remember once he was on the *Parkinson* talk show. Parky said, "Would you like to read a bit of the…?" and Ali got up and everybody thought Parky was going to be punished. But Ali was just kidding and it took the country by storm. That kind of timing's a stunning thing. Not only for comedy but for drama as well.

But I didn't love Ali so much for being funny, I liked him for his outstanding bravery. He embraced American Islam, he wouldn't go to Vietnam and he went to jail. He almost gave his career away for his beliefs, and I thought he was the bravest man in the world. In doing that, he influenced all sorts of people all over the world to stand up and be themselves. I don't think that kind of thing lasts for ever, but at that moment, I'm sure a lot of people got strength. I did and I'm sure all my friends did. We were all deeply impressed when he said, "Vietcong's never done me any harm." It was a very sensible, basic thing to say. People tend to get all complex about a subject like that, so it was lovely to see someone cut straight to the money – "That's why I'm not going" – *biff!* It's a hard thing to do because you tend to mask it in poems, in jokes and stuff like that, but there he was, straight for the door. I just turned a somersault. I loved the guy...and I do.

Throwing the medal away was so courageous. Even if I disagreed with society, if I had a gold medal from the Olympics, I wouldn't throw it away, I wouldn't have the fortitude to believe that much in myself. At the time I remember I didn't like it. I thought, "Nah, that's not good." But then I thought, "Yeah, maybe it is good." Leaders of society are like that, they do things sometimes that scare the life out of you and make you disagree. But then you come back and think, "Yeah, pretty damn good."

The working class all over the world recognise each other, whether it's a black guy from Harlem, or someone from Belfast or Derry. So I identify with all boxers, because you very rarely get posh ones. There was a very famous French boxer once called Carpentier, but he had a big nose as well, which proved he was a smashing boxer. This big, lovely nose was untouched, exactly like he started with. He was wonderful, a gentleman, very well bred and well read. You occasionally get them, but the vast majority of boxers are from the working class society, and you can see social change by looking at them.

Looking at boxers as they're working their way up through society gives an interesting social history. There was a whole slew of Jewish boxers in the '30s and '40s, when they were coming in from Russia, and being poor and going up the ladder. Now all the boxers in America are Mexican or Latino, they've got the bottom rung now. They're kind of wee, so they're lightweight, featherweight, up to about welterweight. In Britain, it used to be all Irish boxers – Rinty Monaghan and Scottish guys. I don't think there are any Pakistani guys – they're too bright, I think!

It's very difficult if you've had a fighting background to go further and use that to teach people, but I think Ali had a smashing education. He said he didn't do well at school but something must have been going on at home. He must have read a lot at home or his parents must have read good stuff to him because something good happened to the guy. He was as sharp as a tack and some of those poems that he would make up on the spur of the moment had me just roaring with laughter. His general bearing, his knowledge, the way he embraced Islam and the reasons for doing it, were absolutely cogent. And when he spoke about war and international politics, he was right on the money. He was as bright as anybody I ever saw without a degree. He was just extraordinary for his time, very courageous.

That's why I like boxing. You get so few chances to see people being brave in your life, and there they are, two guys in a ring staring at each other. I spoke once to John Conteh, the Liverpudlian boxer, and he said, "Everybody's throwing water at you and rubbing you up and waving the towel to get you some extra air and tell you what to do, and then a bell rings and everybody with any sense gets out the ring and then the two guys are like fighting dogs, staring at each other." Now, I couldn't do that.

I was punched once in a class – at a boys' club – by this guy who was supposed to be teaching us to box. I think his hobby was beating up children because he bounced me all over the room. But he did me a real favour, because I never went near it again. I was on the Jay Leno show once, with Joe Frazier, and he put his fist against my face, and it covered all of my face. So if he's then got a glove to go on top of it, and if he hit me with half of his weight – my whole head's flying across the room! The bravery of them just takes my breath away. I admire them so much.

I don't like women boxing, though. But I didn't used to like women playing football and now I love it. When I saw America playing China, they were stunning. But with boxing there's a sort of awkwardness of movement that I don't like, that makes them look vulnerable and makes me feel weird watching it. I feel like a voyeur. I feel as if I'm watching jelly wrestling or mud wrestling and I feel a wee bit dirty. But Muhammad Ali's daughter is extremely good. I saw her fighting Joe Frazier's daughter, which was odd, the two daughters going for it.

I met Ali once. I was nominated for an award in America – I didn't get it so I don't remember what it's called! When the curtain went up, live on stage, there was a semi-circle of heavyweight champions and it was just breathtaking. All the greats – Floyd Patterson, Joe Frazier – were all there, but everybody's eyes went to Ali. They all had dinner suits on and you could see his big hand, shaking in his jacket, and it kind of drew your eye. It also drew your heart as well. Everybody knew what had become of him – this Parkinson's affair – but there he was, this enormous presence. Afterwards, he was signing autographs, with great trouble, for some women and I joined the line. I said, "I just want to shake your hand because I always lose autographs!" and he laughed and shook my hand, and rubbed my hair and chased me away. It was one of the nicest moments of my life. I met Nelson Mandela once and it was as nice as that.

My grandmother introduced me to boxing. She liked all boxers but Joe Louis was her hero. She had all these bizarre theories. Today it would be very politically incorrect, but she said to me, "If it's a black guy and a white guy boxing, put your money on the black guy. I won't tell you why, but put your money on the black guy. And if it's two black guys boxing, put your money on the bald one." That was my granny's theory!

My favourite moment was when Ali was fighting Sonny Liston and shouting at him. I'd never seen a boxer shouting at another boxer before. Liston was on the floor and Ali was shouting and pointing at him. He kept saying, "What's my name?" and made him say his name. "What's my name? What's my name?" That was great. When I saw Ali shouting at Sonny Liston, I thought, "Oh, this is gonna be great for years. This guy is gonna kill everybody – and it's gonna be such fun." The biggest boxer before that was Rocky Marciano, but since then, there hadn't been anybody great. There had been Floyd Patterson, but he was quiet, the peek-a-boo style. But this was the one, this was the messenger we were all waiting for.

My favourite boxing moment, though, was the Rumble In The Jungle with George Foreman. I used to go to the Apollo in Glasgow – the big concert hall – because the fights were beamed in. Me and my pals would get a theatre box, a crate of booze and we'd sit and get sloshed, smoke cigars and watch Ali fight. In that one he just got beaten and beaten against the ropes and we thought it was over. "There's something wrong with the guy...he's just covering himself up. His arms are going to come down and the guy'll paste him...he's a monster."

And then he did it. No one will ever forget it. He just turned round and it only took about four punches. A *boom!* A *boof!* And a *whis!* The whole Apollo was singing and dancing and squishing beer down the stalls. That's the size of the guy. He used to sell out the place, just to watch him fight on the screen.

But I'll tell you a funny thing: if you watch tapes of Muhammad Ali's fights, you'll be amazed at the number of times he's booed by the crowd – in *America*. People have forgotten that. If you look at the fights going back, a lot of the crowds disliked him and everything he stood for. All that fancy dancing and shuffling around and making a fool of people and doing the "Bolo" punch, they would just boo.

It was at the time of "black is beautiful" and some people didn't agree. A lot of guys who go to boxing are a bit strange, a bit on the redneck side of things. They didn't like a flashy black guy throwing his weight around, but that made him even greater for people like me because he took them on as well as the guy in the ring. I really wanted to kick their asses as well, and there he was, doing it. It was just the nicest thing.

Muhammad Ali was the best boxer I have ever seen, without a scrap of a doubt. But he was also a philosopher. A strange kind of philosopher, completely acceptable and funny. "Float like a butterfly, sting like a bee" was magical and it just took the world by storm. He was the best boxer, a great athlete and a kind of prophet, in a strange way, about a new world to come.

Sir Henry Cooper

Former British And European Heavyweight Champion

There was huge media interest in Ali's first fight, but there were previous fights that attracted similar attention. There were world title fights where you had the big hullabaloo. When I used to defend the heavyweight championship, there was always plenty of coverage there. But when Cassius came over in '63, he'd had a few winning fights in America and he had about three or four contenders he had to get in front of, so he was doing all the chat, making poems up and slagging off his opponents, because he knew that it used to affect a lot of the black guys, more than it did the white guys. Half of them were beat before they ever got in the ring with Ali, and he just got in the ring and finished them off. He used to call them everything. With Sonny Liston, he found out where he trained and went round there with a big chain, like a collar: "Where's that big ugly bear? Let me chain him up!" Used to get them right at it, all the time.

Back in those days, champions had to fight their number one or number two contenders. Ali had about four heavyweight fighters, perhaps, in front who were entitled to fight for a world title. So he called them everything under the sun and they all said, "Right, let's make a match with him. I want to fight him." That's how he got into a position to play Liston.

When I fought him in '63, his management identified me as the person to beat before he got to Liston. At one time, I was joint number two contender, so he saw that, if he beat me, that's a good kill. Now I'm getting film crews turning up four decades later asking about this fight. They show it on the BBC every now and again, 'cause the youngsters haven't seen it before. When they make films about his life, anyone under 40 can't remember it. But it's great, 'cause now you've got new people looking at it and admiring the guy, because he was a great boxer. He was the fastest-moving heavyweight of all time. I used to love fighting big guys, six foot four or six foot five. I mean, we had them in them days. They were that little bit slower. But Ali was the exception to the rule. When I boxed him the first time, he was about 14 stone eleven and moved like a middleweight, which is sort of unusual. The big guys are usually a bit slower. Their reflexes are a bit slow. That's why I used to love it, because I could nip in and hit them and nip out before they could react. But Ali was totally different.

We'd seen him in the Olympics and we were reading about him and you knew all about him, but you had to have the right tactics to beat him. The tactics I used – and I still think they were correct, because you couldn't stand off him – were, if you stood off him and tried to box him, he was going to box your ears off, because he had one of the longest reaches in boxing. He was six foot three and a half, so he was in reach when I was out of reach. The only way that you can cut a man's mobility down in the ring is to get him on the ropes, trap him in corners, so when he was in a corner I had to go either left or right to cut off his exits and keep him on the ropes. And that's basically where I caught him, because I showed him one or two left hands and he'd gone back, gone back, because Ali did things very unorthodox in the ring. As kids, when you take up boxing, you're taught that you don't jerk your head away from punches to miss them. Instead, you slip them – you come that way, that way; you bob that way, that way. And he didn't. He did things unusual, because he had such great reflexes. If someone's throwing a punch that you can't avoid, it's better to glance it than come forward. If you come in and come in, you got to go sideways. We were always taught to miss punches and parry, block and parry. Basically, all the great punches come in an arc, and most of the power comes from when the punch is at its height then starts coming down. That's where all the power's generated. And boxers aren't silly – all punches that knock fighters out, they don't see them. If you saw a punch coming, you'd get out the way, but with good punches, you can't. They travel over such a short distance and so fast that you just can't see them. I had the aeronautical people from Farnborough come down to a gym and they had this special camera that took something like 3,000 frames a second. They brought out some fantastic statistics – my left hook over seven inches travelled ten times faster than the Saturn rocket that got the astronauts on the moon, and over seven and half inches it landed with an impact of four and a half tons.

That second Sonny Liston fight, though, from that day onwards, they banned return-clause contracts because Liston had Mafia connections and they found out afterwards that Liston and his manager was cobbing a percentage of his next three defences.

Leading up to my first fight, Ali was on TV and in the papers. Then when he came over, naturally he was on all the newsreels, saying, "If he gives me jive, I'll stop him in five." I was living in Sydenham in them days, south-east London, and they had a big gasworks there. I used to get up early in the morning and run all around that area. And at four o'clock in the morning there used to be middle-aged women who were office cleaners either going or coming away from the offices, and they'd say, "Shut his lip, Henry. Go on, boy! Well done, son."

So that was the first fight. Then after about a year or two, they found out that this basically was just all bravado. It was a way of getting the public's interest. So then the British public took to him. I mean, he's more liked in Britain that he is in America. There are still white people in America that call Ali a draft-dodger because he didn't go into the army. That would have been like me in 1939, when we were having trouble like with Hitler and the Nazis, saying, "I've got no fight with the Nazis. They ain't done me any harm. I'm not going in the army." That was exactly the same feeling in America about Vietnam, because you had people losing sons and husbands. And he refused to go, which I think basically was silly, because if you look at, say, the Louis saga in the Second World War, he did as much for the black people in America, perhaps, as Ali did, but he did it much quieter. He went into the forces. Didn't do any military service, though. He was just doing exhibitions, going around and encouraging and that. I always think perhaps Ali could have done that. But he had to do things his way. He was a very strong character and wanted to make points, because at that time he was just getting involved then with the Black Muslims.

So yeah, after a year or two, they realised over here that that's all it was, just a gimmick, and then the public took to him. When he fought me the second time, I think he got £150,000 for a fight. Now, that was the most he'd ever got up 'til then. I think I got something like about £40,000 when I filled in for the world title, which was good money in them days.

That was a big fight, and there's a lot of preparation you've got to go through. Basically, you've got to control your nerves. Nerves are the most weakening thing. If you let them get on top of you, you can go in the ring like a limp rag. As long as you've trained well, your sparring's gone well, you've done all your road work properly and you've had no injuries, you just have to worry about nerves. I hadn't had any injuries for that fight. The only problem I had was that I was so light, because it was in a hot June. I lost too much weight too quick, and Jim Wicks was always trying to give me something to make me put a bit of weight on. But no, you couldn't do it, because every time I went in the gym, I had no spare meat on me or fat. I just worked it off. Thing is, heavyweights are allowed to get on the scales with their boots on, so on the day of the weigh-in, Jim Wicks cut out some lead soles and stuck 'em in my boots. He also gave me a small weight to hold. It was only a little thing. I could have in my hand and you couldn't see it, but it was very dense metal and it weighed about four or five pound. I got on the scales and I weighed 13 stone four, and I must have had six or seven pounds of lead in my shoes. But Jim said, "We can't let them have too much of a psychological advantage." But I was well light. My real weight was about twelve stone twelve.

The second venue for the fight was Wembley. That was a great venue. I loved it. We had 40,000 people there. It's funny, because boxing comes under theatre rulings. You can't house 100,000 people watching boxing, because everyone has to be seated. You all have to have so many square metres each, so it cuts it down. At Wembley that year, they were only allowing 40,000 in, so we didn't use the round ends of the stadium; we just used the main central stands and then put boards all over the pitch so you had the ring in the centre. It was great, a marvellous atmosphere. I was using the England dressing room.

But I was never a great believer in studying films and videos, because fighters do different things with other different fighters. If you said, "Look, when this guy fights so-and-so, as he comes in, he drops that right hand," and then, if he don't do that, you'd think, "Wait a minute. Where am I? Where's my plan?" I always said boxing was about ad libbing. Whatever comes up in front of you, you have to have something to perform with. I wasn't a great believer in going in there with set plans; what I wanted to know was whether the guy was a good left hand, if he had all his power in his right hand, if he was quick or which way he went around the ring.

Muhammad Ali loved the tall, big guys too. He fought Ken Norton, who was six foot four; he fought Ernie Terrell, six foot six; he fought George Foreman, six foot five. If you look at the smaller guys, they always give him problems. He had three great tussles with Joe Frazier, who was barely six foot. He fought out of a crouch so he was bent over, ducking low. When you're six foot three and a half, the only thing you can see is the top of his head bobbing around. I knew I wasn't short, but I was lighter than him and I was faster than the average heavyweight. All right, maybe not as fast as Ali.

And he had trouble with me, 'cause I was a left-handed boxer. A left hook is a tough punch to have a solid defence against. You can have a right-hand punch so that, when their right-hand punch is coming over, that hand can be moved to block it, but a left hook travels so quick and over so short a distance that you can't see it coming. It isn't faster; it's a punch that, because it's coming from the leading hand, you don't expect, and for some reason it's not as easy to have a defence against. So I used those tactics, and then I had to get him onto the ropes to cut down his mobility because, if I stood off and allowed him to stay in the centre ring, he'd be jabbing me silly. He had a 90-inch-odd reach. I had to keep being a moving target in front of him, and that caused him problems. He looked better against the big guys.

In that first fight, things were pretty even in the first rounds. I found out that he was quite a novice, when we got in the ring. He hadn't learned any inside fighting; he just stood there and held me, waiting for the referee to say, "Break." So I messed him about. I had his nose bleeding in the first round with a lot of short uppercuts, and he kept on looking at the ref, saying, "Well, come on, ref. Say, 'Break'!" But the second fight was totally different. He's a quick learner. When I fought him then, every time I got near him, it was just like being in a vice. He held me rigid. I could hardly breathe, he was holding me so tight. He would just wait until the ref said, "Break," and then he was pushing me back and jumping back as well, because I'd caught him with a left hook.

When it came into the third round, I knew I was winning. I knew I was doing all right. I thought we'd messed him about and we were holding our own. I'd done enough to be in front. When I had him on the deck, I thought, "Great! Now let's see if we can catch him again." But they'd doctored the glove. I was confident that I could catch him in the third with a good punch. My eye had been bleeding for a couple of rounds, because he'd caught me with the heel of the glove. In most fights, the only way you can tell if you're cut is if you can feel the warm blood dripping on your chest. I could feel this, and I thought the ref would stop the fight. When I came back in the third round, Jim Wicks said that we might have to, but I said, "Don't stop it! I can catch him. Just do it up as best you can and let me get out and have one more round."

Then, in the fourth round, I caught him, and I thought, "Thank God for that!" But then the blooming bell went. No one had seen a split glove previously in that round, but suddenly he goes back to his corner, and you could see that the stitching had stretched on the right-hand glove a bit, and he just ripped it and called the referee over. So the referee then had to go to the steward in charge, the steward in charge then had to send someone back to the dressing room, which was 150 yards away, so he had a good two-and-a-half-minute interval. Now, to an athlete who's had a big one on the chin, that's all you need. You could see Angelo Dundee with these little ammonia phials and breaking them under his nose – which is also illegal – and you see him come to. So all that gave him the opportunity to get his wind back. But my eye was so badly cut that he came out and hit me on it about two or three times and it started pumping blood and the referee had to stop it. If I could have gone to him again, perhaps just landed another one, I could have had him. In those days, if I had them on the hook, I didn't let them off it, so perhaps I could have gone on, had the next fight and fought Liston for the world title.

There's a film version of the fight that shows Ali backing away when he sees the eye cut, but that's only in the films. He always says, "I didn't want to punch him." Now, if you actually watch the fight, the only time he comes forward slinging punches is when my eye's badly gashed and I've got blood pouring in my eye. If you look at the archives, it looks like he's deliberately aiming. Of course he was. Don't let's be silly. If ever I was in the ring and I knew a guy had a weakness around the eye, I'd play that, because you play to your strengths and his weaknesses. That's all part and parcel of boxing. I knew that. That's why, when I was cut, I was a bit dangerous, because I knew I had to stop the guy as quick as I could or else perhaps the referee was going to jump in and stop the fight. If I'd have been a negro, though, I would have been the world champion, because I wouldn't have cut so much. The only thing that put me back was my cuts.

That fight, though, people ask me if it was embarrassing to lose out in the fifth round, but it wasn't. In boxing, any fighter who can predict what round he's going to win in and be right is very lucky. Some of the greatest fighters in the world have tried to predict that and failed. You can't, really. Ali did say, "I'll stop him in five," and that he did, but you've got to have a lot of luck on your side. It's just fortunate for him that the thing worked out that way because, if I'd had him a few seconds later, it would have all been over in the fourth round. There's a lot of luck involved in a thing like that.

When Ali went on to beat Liston, I watched it on television. I wasn't surprised Ali won, 'cause I'd boxed him, so I knew. Also, Liston tore a shoulder muscle in training for that first fight. The thing was, he thought that Ali was just a brash kid, a loudmouth. He said, "I can beat him with one hand." Well, he found out he couldn't, because Ali had a lot more than Liston ever thought he'd have. In the first fight, Liston quit in the ninth round, if I remember rightly, because punching air is the worst thing if you've pulled a muscle, and that's what he was doing, because Ali was so quick, and he aggravated the injury.

But boxing's all about training. You train to a peak. Now, the heart of all great trainers is knowing when your fighter is at that peak. If you're thinking he's not, that's worse than being under-fit, because if you're under-fit you can say, "I'll have a go for four or five rounds and see if I can knock this guy out and, if not, I'll blow up," but then you'll be knackered. But when you're past that peak, when you're stale or over the top and you've gone that one day too much, you keep saying, "I'll do it the next round." And that next round never seems to come. It's the worst feeling in the world.

But all great trainers know their fighters – I used to go away for four or five weeks before a big champion fight, and the first week was a novelty – I was getting up at quarter to four in the morning, on the road at four, going to bed at nine o'clock because I was knackered. The second week, I was thinking, "Oh, this is a bit of a bore." In the first or second weeks, Jim Weeks used to say things to me that would go straight over my head. Then, in the third or fourth week, he'd say things and I'd want to have a fight. I'd want to have an argument with him. People say, "Why do fighters go away." It's nothing to do with the sex side of it; sports psychologists have said that good sex before any athletic event doesn't impair your performance. It's the build-up to it all. Fighters disappear before a fight to get mean. You're then looking forward to the fight, saying, "Come on, win that fight!" You want to get to the fight because the fight can be the easy part, sometimes. It's the training which is the hard graft.

So yeah, it's all training. You have a day off every now and then, which slows you up a bit. If you keep on fighting, you're going to go over the top. Jim could see I was the type of fighter that didn't do a lot of sparring. I only used to do six rounds of sparring a day, and that was plenty enough, and I never sparred for more than two weeks before a fight, because I came to my peak too quick if I did. Jim sometimes used to say, "All right, have a day off today," because he could see that I was getting to my peak too quick. I used to knock them out in the ring in a hurry, going through about four or five different sparring partners.

I must say that Ali paid me a great tribute. If you look at all the guys he fought – Ernie Terrell, Ken Norton, George Foreman, all those sort of guys – he always belittled them. He never did that to me. He always said that punch I hit him with was one of the hardest punches he'd ever took in boxing: "Cooper hit me so hard he didn't only shake me; he shook my relations in Africa." He was only ever put down after that by Joe Frazier in the 15th round of the world title fight. He always said afterwards, "I didn't slip. Cooper did hit me." Directly after the fight, he said he slipped, but afterwards he corrected it. He hadn't slipped. The eyes tell you everything in boxing. Eyes register pain, joy, the lot. Whenever I hit a guy on the chin with a left hook, you saw that look on their faces.

It can happen so quick, though – one punch and you're gone. Especially a heavyweight. One punch can turn everything around, if you hit a guy on the point of the chin, two inches up either side. You've only got to look at how Rahman hits Lennox Lewis – right there on the chin, in that perfect spot. But you can have other punches that are more painful. You get one in the liver, just under the rib cage, and the pain can hang on for 20 seconds. You can't breathe and you're trying not to show your opponent that you're hurt, but it's agony. But that's why you do all the special exercises to toughen the muscles up. But a knockout, though – that usually saves the brain from being damaged.

Fat is a factor, too. All modern-day fighters are much heavier than they were in my day. Now they bulk up by doing much more weight work than we used to so they can absorb the punches from these big guys who are throwing big bombs. Unfortunately, when they do that, they lose out on the boxing skills, because fighters don't move as quick as they do when they're lighter. I always think that Lennox Lewis was the best-moving heavyweight in the world when he was just under 17 stone. Now he's 18 stone, he don't move. He slowed right up. It's like, "You hit me, now it's my turn to punch you." And it's the strongest that survives.

But of course certain fighters are drawers and some aren't. Thank God I had a good following in Britain. The halls in London were always full. I never boxed in a half-empty hall. In those days, me and Jim Wicks used to sell up to £9,000 worth of seats on our own, and at Highbury we had 44,000. They allowed more at Highbury than they did at Wembley.

That was a great night. I had a chauffeur car come and pick me up from Wembley and take me to Highbury, where there were literally thousands surrounding the stadium and inside. In the dressing room, I could hear the shouts: "Henry!" And in that second fight, like I said, Ali had learned a lot. He didn't allow me to mess him about inside like I did the first fight. My left hand wasn't reaching the target for the first two or three rounds, and then, in the fourth and fifth rounds, I just started reaching with the left hand, and then *wallop!* The same eye cut came open, like another mouth. The referee wanted to give me an opportunity to carry on, but in the end it was too bad.

Ali wasn't singly a great puncher, but he used to hit with, say, 15 punches in a 20-second burst, and referees had to jump in because they guys were helpless and they could have been injured.

They were the worst cuts I ever had in boxing, the ones I got in the two Ali fights, and that second one was perhaps worse than the first one. I had to have 60-odd stitches in that. It was like plastic surgery. It wasn't because Ali was a better boxer than me, a superior puncher; he won because I had a weakness around the eyes. It was as straight and simple as that.

I would class Ali as one of the greatest boxers but I don't think you can really say one man was the greatest of all time, not in boxing. If you look in the '20s and '30s, there were literally thousands of boxers about, and there were a lot of good fighters. If you look at modern-day boxing, there's only a handful. You only get great fighters when there's a lot of them about. The five great heavyweights were really Jack Johnson, Jack Dempsey, Rocky Marciano, Muhammad Ali and Joe Louis. They'd have surfaced whatever era they boxed in.

But of course he also set a bad trend for subsequent boxers. He did a lot of good for his own race, because he got a lot of black kids interested in boxing, but a lot of them fought like him. Now, he was the original. He was the one who could drop his hands, show his chin and get away with it. People like Errol Graham and Kirkland Lang, they were good fighters, but at some time in a fight they'd start dropping their hands, and they got clobbered with good punches.

And he was a shrewd guy. He knew the ropes. Sometimes, if you look where his left hand was, his left was behind his opponent's neck and he was pulling them forwards so they were slightly off balance. Now, when you're on the balls of your feet, you're not getting leverage like you are if you're on your feet square. So he'd pull them forward and then let them flurry away at his stomach. But he wasn't really taking the punches.

But you had to admire Muhammad. He will go down in history as the greatest-moving heavyweight of all time. His particular style wasn't everyone's favourite – all that jumping about – but yes, he was one of the greatest heavyweights.

Stanley Crouch

Journalist

The Nation of Islam was a sort of cultural/political LSD. It was an emotional hallucinogen that people took and then were actually able to go into this other world in which everything black was great and everything white was bad. It was never a serious political organisation. In fact, it wasn't a political organisation at all. It was a racist cult created by a guy named Elijah Muhammad who taught his followers that white people were invented 6,000 years ago by a mad scientist named Yacub on the isle of Patmos. Even if they didn't believe it, some vulnerable people would say, "Well, I'm with the Nation of Islam, I think the white man is the devil, actually." If you had to travel through the world seeing that paintings of Jesus Christ were paintings of a white guy, white women were supposed to be the most beautiful women and white guys the most handsome, and hearing that white people in general were supposed to be intelligent and black people far less intelligent, then you might embrace that. I remember many people loved to say, with great relish, that the white man was the devil, but I think that is just part of the cult stuff. The fact that Muhammad Ali had embraced it, through the meetings he had with Malcolm X, just showed that he was as vulnerable as a number of people to a cult version of race history that would, more or less, reverse what had been said before.

I don't know that Ali would have been as impressed necessarily by somebody from the regular civil rights movement. He was from the South so he had grown up with it. When he was a boy, people were out there protesting, so he knew about all of that. He knew about the marches, he knew about the sit-ins; he knew about the terrorism being wielded towards the civil rights workers by rednecks willing to either brutalise or murder people to maintain an order in which black Americans were not able to assume that the Constitution applied to them. As a Southerner, he would have heard the horror stories. A guy was walking on a street one night when some bored, drunk, white guys decided to tie him to the back of a truck and drag him to death; another guy came back from the service, wearing his uniform, and some local white guys, who didn't have anything to do, felt insulted that he was walking on the street with this military uniform on and so asked him who he thought he was. He gave his name, rank and serial number, perhaps jokingly, perhaps not. They went berserk and murdered him. There were all sorts of stories like these and, believe me, the overwhelming majority of them were absolutely true. Ali grew up hearing all of that, so to be able to go into an organisation in which people with real fire said, "The white man is the devil, he's a beast," was very appealing to him, I'm sure.

That Muhammad Ali is a creole or a mulatto, a mix of both European and African ancestry, of course, makes it a little bit more complex. But, in America, who asks consistency of anyone? After all, Elijah Muhammad was himself obviously a mixed-blood person, and Malcolm X was a light-skinned guy with freckles and red hair. Three of the biggest voices for black racial purity were themselves mulattos – that's truly American, I'd say.

When the media latched on to Malcolm X, when the Nation of Islam was discovered, it was because they had finally found a black person who paralleled the white races, someone who could come on whenever there was any kind of discussion about whether or not black people should be able to vote in their own cities. There was always some guy who would get up and say something like, "Well, NAACP stands for niggers, apes, alligators, coons and possums" – there were plenty of them, but they didn't have, until Malcolm X, somebody who could get up there and say, "No, no, no, no, no. The white man is the devil, he's always been a devil and he can't be trusted."

When they got him on they'd say, "Okay, we've got this kind of racism with the white people and we've got that kind of racism with the black people." It was a tit-for-tat situation. It had nothing to do with anything other than selling excitement. "This is your version, this is our version."

When Ali said that he was a member of the Nation of Islam and that he was a follower of Elijah Muhammad, that was monumental. Nothing like that had ever happened before in the United States. A major, popular figure, who was black, had essentially embraced a racist cult. It wasn't that he stood up and protested against something. He had embraced a racist cult, a gaggle of lunatics who were espousing a vision that was so insane that it made him seem insane. But it also turned him into another kind of a figure. I remember my sister saying how these white girls at her work were always talking about how handsome a guy he was, so charming and cute. And then, when he switched over to the Nation of Islam, the black women were happy because he was off-limits to white girls. This was one black guy that white women were not going to get.

Part of the reason why Ali went from a pariah in the world of sports to an internationally loved figure was that he took this position on Vietnam. He was out of boxing for a while and, by the time he reappeared, he essentially was not connected to the Nation of Islam. I think that had he remained in the Nation of Islam, his position in the world would be vastly different. By now, people would have concluded that he was out of his mind.

I don't think that anybody becomes a great figure in the world without having some sort of luck. Ali came to manhood because he had certain kinds of interesting fights. He had a war in Vietnam which essentially disrupted the world in that period. He took a stand that guaranteed nothing. Then society itself came to agree with Ali.

Then he had Joe Frazier to fight. In a certain sense, Ali became a different kind of person when he lost the first fight. As people found out more and more about that fight, there were two things that were amazing. One was that Ali was not knocked out because, as Frazier himself said later about the left hook that knocked Ali down, "I reached down to Alabama for that one. And when he got up I was very surprised." When you see that left hook, you actually think it's a knockout punch. But Ali rolled over, got the ropes and stood back up. I'm sure that Frazier, like everybody else, thought, "This is a different kind of person here." So at that point, even though he loses the fight, Ali takes on another size as a fighter. Then Frazier loses to George Foreman and Foreman becomes Ali's second Sonny Liston in a certain sense.

Then he goes to fight him in Africa and that's an even bigger piece of drama, and even more absurd in the way that it's played out. You have Ali, this light-skinned guy with hair more like a caucasian than not, and Foreman, the big negro who, as far as skin tone and facial features go, looks nothing like a white person. But in a bizarre reverse, the real black man is Ali and Foreman's supposed to be the white man's fighter, because he held up two flags at the Olympics when he won. At the fight, it's all black people in the world against George Foreman. So, all this drama is going on in Zaire, too, when something happens to Foreman and they have to postpone the fight. Will there be a fight, will there not be a fight?

Finally, there is a fight, with all these Africans chanting, "Ali – kill him!" and Ali puts on an extraordinary display of his ringmanship. He discovers that he can't knock Foreman out, so he turns it from a boxing match into a bull fight. He essentially does with Foreman what a matador does with a bull, which is he wears him down and then he takes him out. There's that great moment when Foreman begins to fall and, if you look at the footage, Ali could have hit him again. He could have hit him with a hook right then, and it would have been legal, too. But he let Foreman go and immediately took on the dimension of a great sportsman. For all of the really violent, underhanded things that he would say about various fighters in order to whip up public attention, when he got into the ring he didn't exhibit anything except first-class sportsmanship. Everybody got to see that.

After that it was just a regular boxer's life: you stay in the ring too long, then you get hurt and that's the end of that. He tried to become an actor, but he'd already been an actor, playing the best role that he'd ever gotten, which was Muhammad Ali. When asked to play anybody else, he wasn't very good. People said, "Oh, he's a handsome guy, he's so witty, he'd be a good actor." In fact, he's as dead as a piece of wood. He tried to get into politics for a little while. He didn't know anything about that, however, so he couldn't do that either. In fact, everything that people associate him with, he actually couldn't do.

Ali's appeal was based on the fact that he seemed to not take what he did seriously, so he got to make light of a very dangerous profession. But he took it very seriously. He had this little doggerel that he would make up for each fight and he would have this repartee.

He would say things, at certain times, that everybody thought but wouldn't necessarily say. One time, at one of the seemingly innumerable sports dinners at which, I think, Jack Dempsey and these guys were bemoaning the decline of the heavyweight division, Ali just stood up and said, "Wait a minute. What you guys are saying is that you're unhappy that there's not a white champ. Let me tell you all something. If you all were young men, I would beat you, too. Dempsey, I could knock you out." And he just went through the list of people sitting there, saying he would have beaten all of them. "You're all sitting here, trying to pretend that you're not talking about me, but you are talking about me. You wished there was somebody white who could take the crown from me. No such guy exists."

I guess he had a certain sort of unprecedented arrogance for a black guy at that time. He was very handsome, but you could never imagine, say, Billy Eckstine, who had been a singer in the '40s and '50s, and who was more handsome than Frank Sinatra, saying in an interview, "Firstly, I can sing better than Frank and, secondly, I'm a much more handsome guy than him – and if it wasn't for so much racism in America, I would have a TV show and I would also be successful as an actor." Ali's the kind of guy who was saying these things ten years later. He would aggressively take on the society and it endeared him to black people, but not only them. In America, the black person symbolises all outsiders, all people who haven't had a chance to do what they should be able to do; it symbolises the possibility of anybody to come from nowhere and go to somewhere. So, as time progressed, the things that Ali did were seen more as being representative of the voice of the person who wants a fair deal.

Americans have always had an affection for people who thumb their noses at authority. In that respect, he's a cultural figure who travels all the way back in historical/cultural time, to Davy Crockett, John Henry, Brother Jonathan and other figures whose identities were at least partially connected to the fact that they broke the rules.

There aren't black guys who are politically aggressive at this particular time, but when Ali was around it was a different era. Tiger Woods has completely changed the perspective on golf, which is pretty revolutionary in itself – as the comedian Chris Rock said, "I think they need to give classes to these white guys so that they can get accustomed to being beaten by this young black guy every year." Then you've got the Williams sisters. No one in tennis wants to play either one of them if she can get out of it, but if Venus were to jump up and talk about the black women of America, then that's not her job.

Ali came forward when you didn't have black mayors in the South. You didn't have black police chiefs in the south. You hadn't had a black mayor or a black governor of Virginia, which was Robert E Lee's home state. So when he was around, he was talking about very obvious, unarguable examples of racism and restriction. Things are a bit more complex today in terms of what has to happen.

I think Ali played a significant role in making this change, but his significance has been exaggerated. What will make a guy like Ali endure as a cultural figure, though, is that he actually could do what he said he could do. He wasn't like a movie star. Those guys that he got in the ring with were not like the people who shoot at Sylvester Stallone. They weren't like the people that Clint Eastwood gets in fights with in movies, or that Bruce Willis throws out windows. They were Sonny Liston, Joe Frazier, George Foreman, Ken Norton. They were real men, flesh and blood guys who worked a long time at learning how to whip your ass. When they came in, they were not intimidated by what he was saying. Someone like Joe Frazier had one thing on his mind when he got in the ring: that was for him to be vertical and Muhammad Ali to be horizontal. When you come through those real battles, then people look at you in a different way. The other things become charismatic window dressing, but it's the window that really counts. And Ali was all of that. He was the man that he claimed to be, in terms of being a fighter. He was courageous. He showed no cowardice in any fight at any time; fear, of course, because he was in better condition some times than he was at others. But this was a real fighter, a real sacrificial hero.

I don't know that Ali was the greatest fighter, though. Sugar Ray Robinson was probably a greater fighter, but there's no discussion about who managed to emerge from the world of sports and with whom people became more intimately involved in terms of his opinions about politics, his wives, his battles with the government, and his fights. He seemed to move beyond the arena of an athlete.

He also made people realise that there is a greatness – perhaps not always – to fighting, because time is going to knock you out for good eventually. The real fighter is like the great doctor. The great doctor knows all his patients are going to die, but when he goes to work, he fights death as hard as he can fight it every day. Ali is just like a great doctor. He's fighting something and he's showing us all that you should fight whether you're going to win or lose.

The only thing that's important is the quality of engagement. So when you look back at a guy like Ali, you see that in most situations, when it really counted in the ring, he could really do what he was supposed to do. As a person he might manipulate the crowd, he might ruthlessly say terrible things about his opponent, he might seem like a clown one day, a political Swiss cheese another day, he might seem like a puppet of a racist cult. He might say many, many things, but when you hear that bell go *bing* and he comes out, that's when you find something out.

I don't think Ali assumed that he wouldn't make a mistake. I just think he assumed that he could get out of it. If he lost the fight, he could get a rematch and win. Until he got too old to do that. Even when he lost to Joe Frazier, he probably went, "Well, okay, he's not going to catch me with that left hook next time."

One of the things that has to be addressed with Ali, is that he fought in the greatest ever ring fight of all time, the Thrilla In Manila, with Joe Frazier –

the "rubber match" as it's sometimes called. This was essential to Ali's moving from the realm of great fighter into the realm of mythic fighter. These were two very big guys, even for the heavyweight division at that time, in condition, fast, powerful. They fought 14 rounds, with no slow rounds, and it looked like a movie fight. Most people see a fight in a movie and then go to see an actual fight and think that the professional fighters are loafing, because there's not a whole bunch of powerful punches thrown in every round, not a lot of speed and power. Then you see the Thrilla In Manila and you actually do not believe that two men of that size could stand there and fight like they fought for 14 rounds. The sheer output of energy, the endurance and the power is beyond belief.

I saw a film with the former light heavyweight champion, Jose Torres, watching the fight. Around the eighth round, Torres said, "This is beyond boxing. What these two men are doing is beyond boxing. I've been a champion, I know what it means to be in a ring. What they're doing is not boxing. The rest of us boxed. They're doing something that we didn't do." Ali and Frazier were not boxing each other. They were boxing legend. They moved beyond the frame of what we expect of human beings.

If Ali had beaten Larry Holmes and become champion again, just about everybody on the planet would have been ecstatic, or they would have known somebody who was ecstatic about the fact that Ali had the crown again. Now, if Mike Tyson wins or loses the next time he fights, who cares on that scale? There will be people who will be happy, there will be people who won't care. But if Ali had beaten Larry Holmes it would have been dancing in the street. That's the kind of person he represented to other people.

Billy Crystal

Actor

When I first met Ali, I'm a substitute teacher starting out as a comic, and I get a call from Dick Schaap, who had been known then only as a talk-show host of *The Joe Namath Show*. He says would I do this impression of Ali which I was doing in my act at the time at a dinner honouring Ali, this televised local special. Ali is going to be there. I went, "Wow! Do you want to hear the impression?" "No, no, I hear it's great." I was a 25-year-old white kid doing the great black champion – no one was doing that then. But it was funny, and I had the voice down good, so I threw together a tuxedo, this velvet suit, and I bought a bow tie. I get there and everybody else is in suits and ties. It wasn't black tie. I looked like such a dope. I didn't know what I was doing. Pretty much all I had in my act was this little six-minute chunk of Ali and Howard Cosell. So they put me on the dais with all of these other great athletes from all the individuals sports. It was *Sport* magazine's Man Of The Year. There was the great college football player. Neil Simon was there. George Plympton was there. Everybody great.

Then Ali walks in. He looks at everybody, looks at me. "What's Joe Gray doing here?" Dick says, "How do I introduce you?" I said, "Just say, 'Here's one of Ali's closest and dearest friends.'" I was a schoolteacher! So he does and I get up.

No applause. I get to the mic and I just go right into the impression of Cosell, then went right into the Ali. My piece evolved from an imitation of a dramatic piece called 15 *Rounds*. I have a piece of tape of myself when Ali retired at the Forum in LA, where they had a big night in his honour and I closed the show – with four bigger names than I was at the time. I took this imitation and made it his life. There were 15 episodes, punctuated by ring bells, ending with the loss to Leon Spinks in Vegas, when he really was mortal to us.

I started going, "Everyone is talking about Joe Frazier. Joe Frazier is ugly. He can't sing." The place came apart, and he went wild. Ali watched that and he was crying, watching me be him. It's a very funny piece of film.

He started covering his head with a napkin from the dinner and I'd pull it off and back and forth. It was just one of those nights. Afterwards, he comes backstage. There was Richard Pryor and Chevy Chase and all kinds of big, big stars, and he walked up by to me and just grabbed me and held onto me. "Little Brother," he said, "you made my life better than it was." And he just wouldn't let me go!

He calls my mother "Momma". He makes her feel like a million dollars every time he sees her. He gives those who are close to me an extra hug, an extra hello, an extra something, whether it be my wife or my daughters or my brothers. When he hears that it's somebody in my family, he makes them feel like he's in the family too. It's extraordinary to watch. It's just instinct. It's about being a very incredible giving human being.

So that first night started a 27 year relationship. I sat with Muhammad at Howard Cosell's funeral. Howard meant something to me, also. I made my network television debut on *The Howard Cosell Variety Show*. He was always a supporter of me, and he was the one who came to Ali's side when Ali was banned from boxing. He was the one reporter who openly said, "This is wrong" and sided with him and made that horrible time a little easier for him. So we're sitting there at Howard's funeral and he nudges me during this very moving service and says, "Little Brother, do you think he's wearing his hairpiece?"

"I don't think so," I said. "Why?"

"Well," he said, "how will God recognise him?"

"Well, I think once he starts complaining, He's going to know."

Recently, we did a book cover together for Dick Schaap. The three of us are all on the cover of Dick's book, and it was perfect symmetry, 'cause Dick brought us together and the three of us have been friends ever since. We did this shoot in the basement of a hotel in Detroit, where I was shooting a movie. Ali comes and we do the shoot. He's tired and he's not feeling too well that day – he'd been jet-lagged like crazy – but he came because he wanted to do this for Dick. He was there signing all kinds of stuff, but then he took a tablecloth and he started drawing an ocean, submarine, mountains, airplanes and birds with a magic marker. It looked like a child had done it, like stick figures. He was explaining that he was on his way to the Olympics in Australia. He was a boat, but he made it a submarine under the water.

One of the men on the crew was an African-American camera assistant named Baird, and Ali looks over at him. Now, Muhammad is profound, because he doesn't say much, but when he does, it's big. He says, "What is his name?" Baird. "How do you spell?" He told him and he writes it, then writes, "By Muhammad," folds up the tablecloth and gives it to this guy. He was speechless. He could barely talk the next day!

Ali means so much to us. He means so much to people, no matter what your religion or colour or what you believe about certain things. He grabs you. He's Buddha walking. And he's quiet now, but he's almost louder than he was when he was ranting and raving. There's something about him that's so profound and loveable. He's an amazing guy, an amazing force on the Earth.

I love him for different reasons. Yeah, he was a great athlete, an amazing boxer, but he also stood up for what he believed in. He said, "I'm not going to do that. I got no quarrel against no Vietcong. I will not fight." And he didn't. He gave up the prime years of a career. Boxing is different than other sports. You look at these guys now, getting home runs at 37, 38 years old – they're not taking body shots and punches to the head every day in training and sparring. To be as great as he was as long as he was, that's astounding.

But that conviction of his, it wasn't a convenient excuse to get out of the army, like friends of mine did. This was a belief. This is what changed his life. He's still who he is. He'll still pray every day a number of times a day. It's how he leads his life. It's what he believes in, and it gets him through what he's going through now.

He was an extraordinary talent, but he also had a side that wasn't real attractive, back then – the taunting of Joe Frazier, the taunting of Floyd Patterson. But that came out of competition. It came out a side of him that wasn't fully formed yet, and he probably regrets some of that now. But, as far as an inspiration in terms of being yourself and believing in yourself and being an individual, he stands alone. Of all the figures in that time who were taken from us – Bobby Kennedy, Martin Luther King – the one who emerged was Ali, and he was the voice of the time, in many ways. And he's the only one still around.

In the beginning, I have to say that there were times you wanted him to get knocked on his ass. Who could be that verbose, that confident? No one had done that except professional wrestlers. No one had predicted the outcome of a fight. When you predict a round in wrestling, usually you're right, 'cause most of it's fixed, but Ali admired the staging of that, the way they brought people in. Of course, it was all a show, but he could back it up. He was predicting the rounds in an unpredictable sport and being right.

But yeah, there were times you wanted to say, "Oh, get knocked out." Then, when you started to appreciate the genius of his skill, you didn't want him to get hit, and when he did get hit, you'd go, "God, he got hit!" Who else could inflict the punishment or score the points in boxing while moving backwards? Aren't boxers supposed to move forward? He had strategy. He was scientific. He was an artist. Everyone else would plough in, the Sonny Listons, the George Chuvalos, the Ernie Terrells, the Cleveland Williamses. Even Joe Frazier. He was an amazing athlete, but he'd take three shots to hitch one. Ali said, "Why do I have to take three? Why do I even have to take two, or one? I'm just going to be gone." And there was an art to it and a beauty to it, coupled with the charm and the personality. Phew, he was amazing.

The thing about Ali is the fragility of this powerful man, the vulnerability.

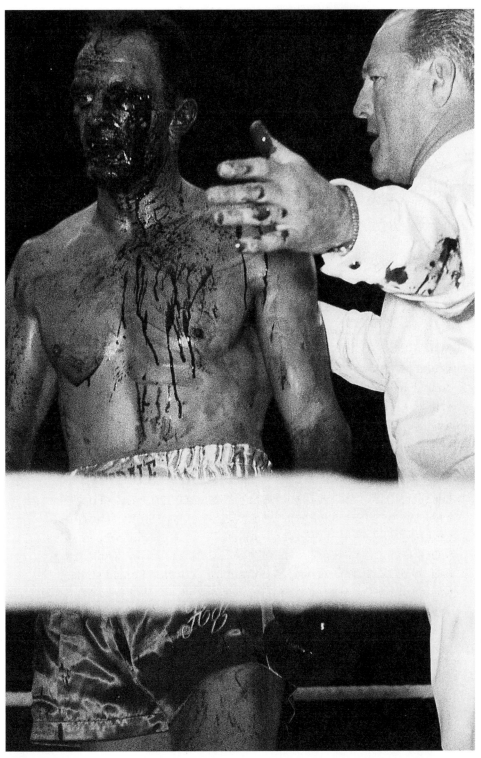

Henry Cooper – eye gushing blood – is stopped by the referee in the fifth round of his first controversial bout with Cassius Clay, Wembley Stadium, 1963.

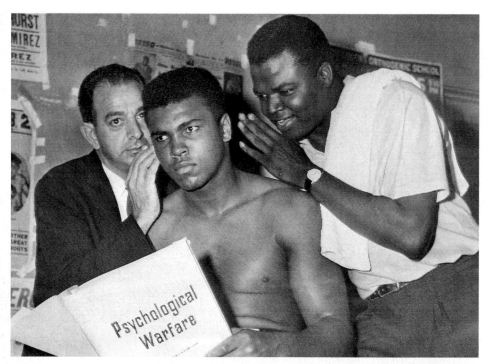

Before the physical warfare came the psychological. Angelo Dundee and Drew "Bundini" Brown ham it up for the cameras with Clay before the fight with Sonny Liston, 1964.

Before their first fight, Liston predicts the round in which he'll knock Clay out, Miami, 1964.

Liston is stung by another Clay jab during their first championship, Miami Beach, 1964.

"Cassius Clay is a slave name" – the heavyweight champion of the world, "Muhammad Ali", discusses his new name with young fans in Harlem, 1964.

When he got knocked down by Henry Cooper in London, I remember screaming, "Get up!" And then he gets up and finishes off Henry. And I remember the genius, the savagery of the Cleveland Williams fight in Houston. That's Ali at his best. Here's someone six foot three, 215 pounds, with a perfect physique, handsome, but the accuracy and the stunning savagery of what he does to this guy is awesome. Anyone who says he wasn't a big puncher should look at this fight. That sequence is amazing. Artistic.

Then, as he became an older fighter, a less mobile fighter, moments stick in my mind. The comeback fight against Jerry Quarry, when it didn't look like he could go further than, say, six or seven rounds, and when it ends quickly we breathe a sigh of relief. There was a realisation that he wasn't the Ali that we loved from three years ago.

When he got up from the punch against Joe Frazier in the 15th round of the first fight, I had tears in my eyes, crying, "Get up! Get up! You won the fight!" I still thought he'd won the fight, even when he was being counted out on the floor. But he got up right away. That's courage. He gets nailed, but he's up at four. I remember getting so emotional about that fight. I didn't sleep for two days after 'cause it was so extraordinary, what they gave and what they took out of each other.

And I remember watching the Thrilla In Manila on television and not knowing how that was going to go, and then admiring Joe and wishing that would be the last fight. Then he went on to what definitely should have been his last fight, against Larry Holmes. I was sitting with a good friend of mine, Julius Erving, who is a fantastic athlete, and we were just so sad that Ali had nothing left. He actually looks away at one point and puts his hand up. It's just sad. And Julius and I walked from the fight site to a hotel to eat, and who ends up sitting across from us but Joe DiMaggio. He doesn't say much during the dinner, but as he leaves he says goodnight, shakes my hand, looks over at Julius and says, "Don't stay so long." And Julius said, "No, we're going to go pretty soon." But Joe says, "No no no no. *Don't stay too long.*" He was telling Julius, don't play one year too long. Get out early. Ali stayed too long.

There were times, too, when I didn't like him. I didn't like him taunting Ernie Terrell in the ring – "What's my name? What's my name?" But that was at an angry time in his conversion. It was an angry time in America. It was important to him that he was treated with respect. But I didn't like that, and I told him that. But he had such courage in the ring. Anyone who says anything about Ali, good or bad, says that he could take a punch.

I'm on the board of the Muhammad Ali Center. That's going to be a fantastic place. This is not a place to look at memorabilia of the champ; this is a learning centre. It's mostly about kids and it's mostly about helping people to learn and understand each other more across the world. It's what he cares about. It's about getting the good word out to everybody about finding yourself and about learning. It's really about kids. At this point, I think his great goal in life is for them to understand who he was, where he came from and that you can do something with your life.

That's what's so extraordinary about him. When Lonnie and Muhammad asked me to be on it, I said, "Absolutely. I've learned from you, and I think everybody can." That's the essence of it, and that's why it's such an important place for him. It's his legacy. What I like about it is that it's valuable, a valuable place. It's not just a mosque to him; it's not just something put together for him to cash in on; this is a legitimate, heartfelt, well-thought-out organisation. He just wants to make the world a better place.

Now, 23 years after he stopped boxing, he's better known now than he was when he was still boxing, in some ways, and more loved. People love him for different reasons. There are people that just love him and they don't know why they do. Now kids don't know about him: "Oh, he was a boxer, wasn't he? Poor Muhammad." He never thinks, "Poor Muhammad," and for one reason: this is a test for him, in his mind. This is who he has been sent to be. It's odd that a man who has spent his life being violent is so peaceful. And that, I think, is the essence of the Muhammad Ali Center. It's a place where people can come and understand that. His essence is the foundation of this place, and the things that he believes in and cares about are hopefully what people will come away with.

I remember giving Ali the Athlete Of The Century Award for *Sports Illustrated* in Madison Square Garden. That was a pretty great night, but what was interesting was it was in Madison Square Garden, where he lost to Joe

Frazier. So he walked up on stage and he almost tripped, coming up, and I was onstage with him. He comes towards me, looks at me, puts his hands up and starts throwing jabs. Then he went to the podium and he spoke. He doesn't say much, but I've been in the Garden a million times and I've never heard it quiet like that. He got to the mic and he thanked everybody, and it was just so simple, so soft-spoken. It was probably an effort for him to do that. It was amazing. That was a great night.

Of course, what was more important was that it was my 50th birthday. We had a party that night and it was like, "Ah, Jeez, when did *this* happen?" Anyway, my wife gets up in the hotel and says, "Somebody wanted to send you special greetings," and she read a telegram from somebody and then she launched into this imitation of Ali. She said, "I do imitations of the wives of famous people." It got a laugh. It was a room of very funny comedians. She went, "Mrs Jack Benny," and it was so funny. Then she goes, "Mrs Muhammad Ali," and she starts with, "I want to talk about Mrs Joe Frazier. I want to talk about… Oh, why am I doing do this? Why don't you say hello to Muhammad Ali yourself?" And he walked out on stage in this tuxedo, and he just held me and said, "Happy birthday, Little Brother. I'm the biggest present you ever got." I just lost it. He stayed the whole night and got back on a plane and went back that night. That was more important than me giving him an award. I can give him a million awards, and I will continue to do that, but he wanted to be there, because he knew that it's more than an impression I've done. When I did the 15 *Rounds* thing, that forever bonded us, and he knows that I do it because I love him. Some athletes, you say to them, "Could you come to my party?" and it's, "Yeah. $100,000 appearance fee." Not Muhammad. "When can I be there? What time do you need me." He just came to be with the family. That was better than that night at the Garden.

I know him in a way that's different. I watch him with his kids, and they care about him and they worry about him. That's the other side, the side that people don't get to see. Maybe they shouldn't. That's private, and that's how he'd like it you know. He's a daddy to them, too.

The day after my party, Lonnie calls me in the morning and says, "Can you come over? Muhammad and I would like to talk to you about being on the board of the Muhammad Ali Center in Louisville."

"Well, whatever you want," I say. "If you want me, you've got me."

"No, no," they said. "Come over. We want to show you the tape of the Center and what it will be like."

So I go over to the hotel and we watch this videotape of the Center, what it will be like. There's film of Ali fighting, but there's also film of Ali with popes, with presidents, with Russian presidents, embracing kids around the world – in Africa, in India, in Israel. Then the film goes on about what the Center will be. As I'm watching this, Ali's next to me and I hear this very loud snoring. I look over and he's out cold. I look at Lonnie and go, "Shall I wake him?"

She's starts whispering, and the more she's whispering, the closer I get. She says, "He had a very bad night last night. He has nightmares. He dreams of his fights, dreams of throwing punches in his fights and he sees fighters. Sometimes I have to restrain him because he gets so agitated, and sometimes I have to get out of the room because he starts throwing punches."

"Really? That's terrible!" At this point, I get hit in the back of the head and he says, "Look out, Joe Frazier! Look out, Joe Bugner! Look out, Floyd Patterson!" Then he laughs like crazy and his great friend Howard Bingham came in and took a picture of me looking embarrassed. He hugs me and says, "Got you, Little Brother. I got you!" It's all a joke, and it's hilarious. It's absolutely hilarious.

And he does these magic tricks. They're store-bought things, but he does them pretty well. So, on the night of his birthday party, there's 20 or so of us in this restaurant, and he's showing the staff this trick. He's stuffing this thing into hand and then it disappears and he brings it back out of a little piece of cloth. Everybody applauds. He then starts to show them again, and you say to yourself, "Oh God, he doesn't remember that he just did it. What's wrong with him?" And someone says, "Champ, you've showed us this."

"No," he says, "I'm going to show you how I did it, 'cause I am a Muslim and I cannot deceive you." By the laws of his faith he's not allowed to deceive people, so he showed the staff of the restaurant how he did it, with this fake thumb.

Later, I was next to Arnold Schwarzenegger and Muhammad at a fundraising party and Ali's showing this same trick to Schwarzenegger. Arnold doesn't get it, and Ali's looking at me – like, "How could he not get it?" He's got a fake plastic thumb that fits over his thumb. It's even a different colour! But Arnold is looking at it and going, "I cannot believe this. I cannot believe this!" Ali's looking at me, and he's even got the thumb out, but Arnold still doesn't see it. So then Schwarzenegger turns to me and says, "I cannot believe this. It's so good. How does he do it?" And Ali's behind him, pulling this face. It's just too funny.

Howard Davis

Boxing Trainer / Former Olympic Boxing Gold Medallist

Muhammad Ali was a superb athlete, but there was also a political side to him. He stood up for something. When he said, "I'm not going to fight in Vietnam; they never called me a nigger," that was a statement to the world and a brave thing to say, and I think just saying that eventually made him an icon and made him revered. But in the end, he couldn't have been right about what he said.

There are people today that say athletes don't stand up enough for their political beliefs, that they're too concerned for their sponsors or their corporate identities, but Ali did, and he had a great impact, not just from the political aspect of it, but he also had an impact on sports in general. Here was a man that was nice looking, articulate, spoke his mind and predicted the rounds, which nobody'd ever done in boxing before. A superb athlete who had intelligence, articulation, that brought something different, not just to boxing but to the world. You had to respect him for that. Without Ali, boxing would have been a mundane sport. It was up until he came around. There was nobody on the horizon, except Sonny Liston, and there was a guy who was a known criminal. He took boxing down a notch or two. Then Ali came along and changed the face of boxing for ever.

The first time I met him was in about '68 or '69. I was twelve years old and playing in a band at the Apollo Theater in Harlem, New York City, doing amateur hour. He's backstage doing a play called *Buck White*. I didn't know who he was at the time, but I remember my father – who was our manager in the band at the time – going, "Oh my god! There's Muhammad Ali!" I was backstage after we'd finished playing, and Ali walked up to me and touched me on my chin with his fist and said, "Get out of the way, champ," and I said, "Oh my god." I was only five foot nothing, so he was an imposing figure to me, but even at twelve years old, I knew this was somebody very special.

That was around the time that he'd had his licence taken from him. He lost the best years of his life because of that. But he still had an impact when he came back in 1970. And I think everybody can remember the fabulous Ali versus Frazier fight in 1971, the biggest event in sports history at that time. I remember going to a close-circuit viewing of the fight and watching the people dressed up in fur coats, and you had celebrities from all around the world there. Not only was it a sporting event, but it was just an event for the world to see, and I think he changed the face of boxing forever.

He was the first Muslim superstar, and I think what he's done for black people is give them a sense of pride. In the '60s, which was a really terrible time for blacks, he gave us a sense of pride when our self-esteem was down. Here was an epitome of a man that stood up against the forces of America and said no. I looked up to him. So when I started fighting I patterned my style right after him. I didn't have the confidence or the articulation to talk like he did, but I patterned my style after him. Whenever he fought, I felt like I was fighting, also. I think most of black America felt the same way – we didn't want our hero to lose. Whether he was fighting somebody black or white, it didn't matter. He was our hero.

I don't know if he was the greatest. I mean, how do you explain the greatest? Do you mean, was he the greatest boxer that ever lived? I don't know. Some people say Joe Louis, you know, some people mention Jack Johnson or Jack Dempsey and so on. But I think that, when he said, "I'm the greatest," he spoke for the people. He spoke for himself, politically. I think *that* made him the greatest, to do what he did. Took a lot of guts. So in that terms of speaking, yes, I think he was the greatest.

They say these days his is the most recognisable face on the planet – next to Mickey Mouse! That don't surprise me at all. What he did politically, that's what really made him famous, not so much his boxing prowess but his politics. He stood up for so many downtrodden people, and people recognise that. Now, he can go anywhere in the world and everybody knows him – dignitaries, everybody.

Now, I've been meeting with him off and on for the last 37 years. I met him again after I won my Golden Glove championships in New York, I met him at a friend's house and then I would see him at certain events. He would do magic tricks. As a man, he's quiet. Not as loud as he is in public. He doesn't really do that much talking, especially now, in the circumstances. He's a reserved person. I remember I went up to his training camp in 1980, and every day, before he started to do his workout, he would sit down and right in the middle of the ring and talk to the crowd. Some days he would do lectures on academic history, and some days he would do lectures on the political realm in America. I was amazed at the guy. He is a deep thinker. I respect the man.

Mickey Duff

Retired Fight Promoter

I first got involved with Muhammad Ali in 1966, when I managed to secure the return match with Henry Cooper. They had fought once before and Cooper was stopped then, controversially, with a cut eye. I also took him on an exhibition tour throughout Europe, when he made appearances and boxed. We had a wonderful time for about ten weeks. He was fantastic to travel with. I never met a more co-operative and down-to-earth man in my entire life. Unfortunately, he's nowhere near the man he was, but I'm happy to say that he still remembers me and gives me a hug when he sees me.

He was a draw back at the time of the second Cooper fight. Muhammad Ali was born a draw, a natural draw from day one. He wasn't just a draw to the British public; he was a draw to the world public, everywhere he went. Britain was just one of the fortunate countries to have him on several occasions.

To give you a perfect example, I made a match with Richard Dunn, in Germany, which really was a disgraceful match, because everyone knew it was a mismatch, and Ali loves giving value for money. Before the fight, I said to Ali, "I need your gloves," because I was doing a benefit night for Chris Finnegan in London. "Those gloves you're fighting in will bring a lot of money at the auction."

"You've got them."

Unbeknownst to me, Angelo Dundee had already promised them to somebody else, but also unbeknownst to me, when Angelo Dundee asked Ali for them, Ali said, "No. I've already promised them to Mickey."

So when the fight was over, there was a race for the gloves. As Angelo took the gloves off his fists, I ran over and said, "They're my gloves, Angelo!"

"You've got them," he said. "But I can't give you his arms. I've got to take them off him first." He was really annoyed.

"OK, OK, I'm sorry," I said. I gave Ali a pen to sign them, then I grabbed the gloves and turn to leave.

Just then, he puts his hand on my shoulder and he says, "Look inside the right glove." He'd written in before the fight, "Ali wins KO, round five." And he did!

That's the kind of the guy he was. He'd considered that he owed the public a show. He didn't care that it would take him five rounds to knock out a guy he should have knocked out in one. He figured that the public had paid and they were entitled to see something of Muhammad Ali.

Like I say, he was born a showman. He was also the most considerate person I ever met. I saw him do such wonderful things. First and foremost, he was an even greater human being than he was a fighter. That was his biggest asset. And yes, he had an ego, and his ego made him what he was, but his character was totally tinted with good thoughts and good intentions. For instance, he was at a boxing an exhibition one year, and the referee there was Teddy Waltham. He was on the plane with Ali, and suddenly Teddy said, "My money's gone!" £500 for doing this exhibition. He put it in his pocket and somebody's taken it. He was shattered.

I said to Ali, "It's a terrible thing. Waltham lost his money."

"What money?" said Ali.

"The money he got for refereeing."

"Oh, that's a shame. He worked so hard."

Later on, I see Waltham and he's laughing and joking. I said to him, "You look very bright. Don't tell me you've found the money."

"No," he said. "Not exactly. Somebody told Ali and he gave me the money." Ali gave him £500 out of his own pocket.

On another occasion, some kid did something for him and he gave him a £2 tip. He said, "That's a lot of money. What are you going to do with it?"

The kid said, "I'm going to put it on my suits."

"What do you mean?"

I just interrupted and said, "You got a suit on HP?"

"Yes."

"Muhammad," I said, "he's paying off his suit. He's going to put it towards the payment."

Muhammad said, "How much do you owe on the suit?"

"£12."

And then Muhammad gave him the other £10. "Now go and pay for your suit." Then the kid walked away, and Muhammad said to me, "There's one kid that won't hate niggers."

Then, one day in London, he said to me, "There's never been anybody as famous as me." He said, "I can walk out there and I'll be out there for less than ten minutes and I'll stop the traffic."

"I don't know about that," I said.

"OK. Come on."

So he went outside and just stood there, and soon somebody came up and asked for his autograph. So he signed, he stood and he waved it, and within ten minutes he was mobbed. In London! He's an American bear in mind. And he stopped the traffic in London. I don't think anyone else could've done that. I'm not saying he's the greatest man that ever lived, but there has never been a human being like him with his particular qualities.

Nobody will ever totally eliminate the problems between blacks and whites, ever, because there are always people that will be that way inclined, but he went a long, long way towards eliminating a lot of racial differences. I think he did more as an individual than any other individual that had ever lived.

I remember one time we were sitting together, talking about all the different fighters, and the name of Floyd Patterson came up. Ali says, "Now, he wasn't really a heavyweight. He only weighed about 13 stone."

"No," I said. "He was bigger."

And Ali leaned over and he said, "Did you just call me a nigger?"

There have been other people that have achieved far greater things, you know. I'm not saying that, because the man was heavyweight champion of the world – and, in my opinion, the best heavyweight that ever lived – that makes him the greatest. It was his character and his general regard for other people that made him different.

He never recognised it, but if one wants to be totally dispassionate, he was almost totally illiterate, both in writing and in understanding what is the thing to do and what not to do. And he wasn't the tidiest of eaters, because he wasn't brought up that way. And he never, ever figured that he had to change. He used to say, "I is what I is," and that's it exactly. He never tried to change.

When I saw the Foreman fight, I watched very closely and I discussed it with him afterwards. He knew that he didn't have the youth and qualities to beat George Foreman. He told me that he knew he could only beat Foreman by letting Foreman hit him until he got tired and then taking over. He sensed that the only flaw in Foreman's character was his stamina. And he kept saying in the fight, "Come on, motherfucker. Is that the hardest you can punch?" And he's letting Foreman hit him. He was half blocking, but a lot of punches were getting through. "Come on, then. You can punch harder than that." He made Foreman punch and punch and punch until he tired himself out. The round that he knocked Foreman out was the first round that he won. He let Foreman punch himself out completely, and then he took over. He said to me afterwards, "One or two got through, but they didn't really hurt." He had a cauliflower body when he finished. But it worked.

If you ask me how the human body takes that punishment, I would say, "You're quite right. It's impossible." But if you ask me how Ali took that kind of punishment, it's very simple: he was a one-off at many, many things, but one of his biggest assets was that he could take punishment. It's all mind over matter, and he just blocked it out of his mind. He had all the physical advantages – six feet six, long arms, long legs, an incredible sense of anticipation and, above all an almost unbreakable chin. And on top of all that, he had unbelievable recuperative powers and a temperament that was good.

When I first signed Ali, me and my associates came to the conclusion that he would draw people by taking a pee. Through signing him for that four-fight deal, I also did an exhibition tour with him all over England, and we did unbelievably well. He boxed three rounds at each exhibition, and he'd invite people in the audience to come in. He was a ham. He liked the attention as much as he enjoyed the money. And if he wasn't working, he was uncomfortable. The amazing thing is, though, that, with all the money he gave away and threw away, he's still not short of it. He now gets up to $40,000 to make an appearance. He can't open his mouth; he's there to be in pictures and shake hands with people. His current wife manages him now, and she does a very good job. She won't look at less than $25,000. I mean, how much money does a guy need? He only needs to live. But he gave away untold millions. He probably earned $200 million, if not more, and that was in a period when that was about $1 billion today.

Ali was essentially a good man, but some of the people around him took him for a ride. Elijah Muhammad and Akbah Muhammad were thieves with a licence to steal. Angelo Dundee gave good value. He got a fixed commission as a trainer, and Ali was always extremely fair to him. Ali was the biggest thing that ever happened and was ever likely to happen to Angelo Dundee. His older brother, Chris Dundee, who was far more money conscious than Angelo, was also very loyal to Ali.

But when Ali turned up to these fights and went around Europe with us, he brought all the hangers-on with him – Bundini Brown, Herbert Muhammad, Akbah Muhammad. It's unusual, because normally the biggest spongers on fighters are their own family, mothers, fathers, brothers, sisters-in-law, cousins. They all want to get in on the action. And the reason most fighters end up broke, even though they made big money, is because the biggest parasites are their own families. They all come from poor families and they have a guilt complex. I've heard fighters say, "How can I sit there with all this money? I've got a lovely house and my mum and dad are living in two rooms." So he buys her a house. The next thing is, the sister's pregnant. He buys her a house. Then, before you look around the brother-in-laws become the managers.

Muhammad Ali was the exception. It was the Muslim thing that cost him millions. He did more for the Muslim movement than any person that ever lived, by endorsing it, and they still robbed him blind.

Ultimately, though, I think he was a great inspiration to black people. Black people that want to boast about what black people have achieved will never boast about it without mentioning Muhammad Ali. For them, he became an idol to worship. He became an image. They no longer felt separate, because Muhammad Ali was a part of them. In that sense, that was probably his greatest contribution to life, being black. It would almost have been unfair for him to have been born white. He would've had too much power. Him being black helped to even things out.

Angelo Dundee

Muhammad Ali's Trainer

I first ran into Ali in Louisville, Kentucky. I used to go there with my fighters – Willie Pastrano, Ralph Dupas, Luis Fernandez. In fact, Willie Pastrano fought Johnny Holman there. That was the first fight they had, in the arena there. I would come to town and these two guys would try and meet me, Muhammad and Jimmy Ellis. They were always around. They were great amateurs. I knew nothing about amateurs then. In fact, the amateur field was such where you didn't see it on TV like they do today. The Olympics right now is big, but it wasn't that big in those days. In fact, a lot of the Olympic champions that came around, people didn't know them.

One day, Willie was fighting Alonzo Johnson in Louisville. So I got a call from the lobby, and the rhetoric went, "My name is Cassius Marcellus Clay. I won the Golden Gloves of Kentucky. I won the Gloves in Chicago. I won the Gloves in Seattle, Washington. I'm going to be a national Olympic champion." This was 1958, so this kid has predicted it two years before it happened. So I listened to him and I said to Willie, "You know, there's a kid down here and…I don't know. It sounds a little nuts to me, but the kid wants to talk to us." So Willie said, "Well, the TV stinks. Let him come up." So the kid came up and we started talking, and we've been talking ever since.

I've known Muhammad since he was 16 years old, and I'm happy to still know him today. We see each other a dozen times a year, running into each other at certain affairs, which is a kick for me. He's a lovable human being – "How is this trainer or that trainer?" And he would never admit that he was very close to boxing, but I was with him at the Olympics in '96. I tell you, it was funny, because I heard that Muhammad was coming and I thought they were going to make him get his medal. He travels all over – goes to India, goes all over the world. He travels more now than he ever did. So I called his secretary, Kim, and I says, "Does Muhammad want me to pick it up for him? He don't have to come. I'm here. I'm doing the ABC radio at the Olympics." I was going to be there for all the fights, and I thought I was doing a good turn. I didn't realise what he was doing. The Olympic torch! It was sort of hush-hush.

The day afterward, we went to the Olympic village and it was like old times, because I made Muhammad meet all the amateur fighters, and all these kids from around the country were happy to meet him. He actually invaded the Olympic village. Actually, we raided a lot of places. And that's when the era started off. But when he come up to the room with his brother, Rudi, the conversation was boxing – "How do you train your fighters? How many miles do they run? How do they abstain from chasing girls?" You know, stuff like that. So he was a very interesting kid.

A lot of people don't know he's a student of boxing. He enjoys it. He'd always try and con me to work with my fighters. He wanted to spar with them, and he'd be waiting in the gym. Two hours before I got there, he'd be hitting a heavy bag. He knew I was coming there with my fighter. So, finally, one day I relented. I didn't like amateur kids working with pros – I think it's wrong – but that was my own gut feeling. But he worked out with Willie Pastrano and I got conned into it. I shouldn't have done it, 'cos Willie was ready. It was, like, five days before the fight. He didn't need the sparring. So we boxed two rounds. Willie will tell you himself that he did everything but turn up loose, so I tried to counteract the reaction. I said, "Willie, you're stale! No more sparring for you. Stale!"

"I got the hell kicked out of me," said Pastrano. "What are you talking about?" He couldn't do nothing with Muhammad! In those days, Muhammad was jump, jump, skip, skip. You know. Willie couldn't do nothing with the kid! We did that twice, you know. We did a number like that years and years later with Ingemar Johansson but, you know, for fun. The thing about Muhammad that a lot of people don't realise is the fun element. You always have fun with him. Never a dull moment. Never a beef, never an argument. First guy in the gym, last guy to leave. These are his qualities. He had a lot going for him.

A lot of people would just see the flash side but he was obviously very serious about his boxing. He never got nervous about it. He just thought it was fun. The biggest problem I had with Muhammad, early on in his career, was getting him too early to the arena, because as soon as he got to the arena, he started jumping around, "painting pictures" on the wall, loosening up. He'd put his boxing clothes on right away – he just couldn't wait. So I used to impose upon the boxing commissions and say, "Please, do me a favour. Don't let us get there too early." Because he was, you know, Speedy Gonzales. Put his shoes on, everything – he was ready to go. Five minutes and he'd be – *boom!* – ready to go on into the ring.

Ali first came to me after the Louisville sponsoring group had sent him to see Archie Moore. One of the group knew Archie Moore, and they heard about the place where Archie used to train fighters, and it had a name about being a tough place to train, so they sent him there. But Archie was light-heavyweight champion then. See, what was happening then was a clash of personalities. I've learned in the profession that there's only room for one star. You're not of star quality; the fighter is the star quality.

Muhammad would ask him, "Archie, when am I going to fight?" Archie says, "You're not ready, kid." "I want to fight! When am I going to fight?" "You're not ready yet." And Muhammad finally said, "I've had so many amateur fights. I've boxed all over the world and you're telling me I'm not ready? I want to fight!" So that was it. What broke the camel's back, though, was Archie asking him to sweep the kitchen. Muhammad said, "I never swept the kitchen for my mother. How you going to make me to sweep the kitchen?" So that didn't work out.

So he went back to Louisville. Lester Mallets, who was Mike Mallets' father, was involved with Horton Bingham distilleries. He was doing their public relations. So they asked him about a trainer. He said, "Well, gee, why don't you get hold of Angelo? You know that guy living in Miami Beach? They say he's training and he's got Johnny Holman and Luis Fernandez." Well, I was training a bunch of guys, a bunch of fighters, so they sent two people down here to interview me, Worth Bingham and some other gentleman. They asked me what I would do, how I would handle him. They were happy with everything, the way I was talking to them.

Later, they called me, said, "When do you want him to come down?" I said, "After the holidays." So I got a call back ten minutes later. They said, "The kid wants to come down tomorrow. He wants to fight. He doesn't want to think about Christmas holidays and stuff like that!" And as sure as God made apples, a couple of days later, him and his brother came down by train.

He came down and got off the train, carrying a little suitcase. I found him a place to stay, and that was it, that was the beginning. Like I told you, he was the first guy in the gym, last out. Went up the steps – "Angelo, line up all your bums. I'm gonna clean up the gym!" Stuff like that, you know. Always fun. Luis Fernandez adopted him. That's where he got his big mouth. And there was Kits, the gym in Miami Beach, where everything happened. So, you know, this is all the beginning of his career. I had so much fun with him.

It would have been very easy to have been upset by him, but he was so good natured. When we first came to England to fight Cooper, I knew the public wouldn't like him, because I'd been there with Pastrano before. Pastrano was a gentleman, soft-spoken. The fans loved him. I was there during the war, when I got to know the English public. They like a gentleman – you know, like Henry Cooper, who got knighted by the Queen. So, lo and behold, "Yap yap yap yap. Run like hell, London!" The public sort of backed off on the kid. But he didn't mean no harm. He was just trying to build something. It was all in fun. He never meant to insult anybody or hurt anybody. But he was doing good old Henry and people didn't like that. Then, when he got into the ring, he wore a crown and a cloak. My god! They really, really blew their stacks. But the point was that, when he came back, he was a serious kid. They loved him over there, 'cause he was the way they wanted him to be, a gentleman. He's always been a gentleman.

He got interviewed once before fighting Duke Sabedong in Las Vegas. Gorgeous George was wrestling the night before, in the same arena, so they doubled up on the two. They figured that those guys were going to be two of the next attractions in Las Vegas at the Sports Arena. So Gorgeous George is on one side and Muhammad's on the other side, and the silent one was Muhammad. Gorgeous George started spouting about how he was going to wrestle this local and he was going beat the heck out of him, pull his arm out of its socket and beat him over the head with it. "If I lose, I'll cut these beautiful blond locks of mine and shave them right in the ring." He went on and on and on, and the kid's listening and watching, 'cause I'm in the wings watching the interview, and Muhammad said, "We've got to go see this guy". So we went to the wrestling show. Sold out. About 12,000 people. He said, "Look at this. I gotta start doing this kind of stuff and getting the people all juiced up, you know?"

And that's what started it. Gorgeous George was the definite innovator of that. We watched him. The bit about pulling people across the ring – "Kiss my foot!" – that came later for Muhammad. He used that technique later on.

The thing was, it was always a different scene – a different theatre, a different arena. We met different people. It was the big thing. It never sounded stale, 'cause once you heard a poem of Muhammad, you heard a bad poem, but we did it to a different audience. But he always had fun. That was the important thing.

See, Muhammad likes people. He's never disliked a human being in his whole life. In fact, early on, when we used to kid around with the opponent, he'd go, "You're old. You're an old man, Charlie Powell!" So Charlie's brother, Ike Powell, who is a former football player, is watching this shenanigans. He wanted to hit Muhammad, but I held him back. "He's only kidding! We're trying to sell tickets!" Well, the place sold out. It was at Pittsburgh, in the middle of the winter, with ice on the streets, and it was sold out! Muhammad did that. Muhammad attracted people.

His big thing was, when he go into the ring, they'd be booing him. Now, there's a lot of people that wouldn't think anything of a boo or applause, and that was Muhammad.

He got better and better as we went along because, you know, continuity is what makes a fighter. Early on, the experts in the profession didn't think he would make it. I'm talking about guys like Al Brooke from *The New York Post*, Red Smith from *The Times*, Shirley Povitch, who were good boxing minds. They didn't think this kid would make it, 'cause he was jumping around too much, pulling and everything else. He does everything wrong but he's getting away with it, so as long as he has the speed and the agility, he's winning.

Meanwhile, they didn't realise that the kid was growing. When he first came, he was 189 pounds, and then he grew. His stature got bigger and bigger because he was a young kid growing up. He got taller, his body widened out – and he'd never lifted a weight in his whole life, never did a push-up, never did a pull-up. To this day, that's my rhetoric about training a fighter: do everything natural. If you do it natural, it turns out right. What you see in the gym is the heavy bag, the light bag, the shadow-boxing. That's all important.

Muhammad ruined a lot of fighters because he brought the mirror into play in the gym. A lot of guys stand up there and they look pretty standing up straight, when they got their chin up in the air, so Muhammad ruined a lot of good fighters, 'cause they tried to imitate him. You can't be another individual. Muhammad was one of a kind. Each fighter is one of a kind. There's no two alike.

The first real big name he fought was Archie Moore. I had Willie Pastrano playing Archie, and I knew Archie Moore was too slow for Willie, so if he was too slow for Willie, what was he going to be with Muhammad? Muhammad was taller, quicker and punched bigger. Naturally, he was a heavyweight, and I knew he could handle Archie Moore. No aspersions to Archie, but Muhammad was just too quick for the guy – he just couldn't handle the speed – and I knew he would beat Archie Moore. I just felt I had to pick the perfect opponent for learning the sequences. And he learned. He learned from all those people.

Also, everybody asks how come I jumped into the Liston fight after the Cooper fight. Well, if you saw the list of fighters in the Top Ten then, they were all tough. So I figured, if you're going to go in with a toughie, why not go for the title? Because in my own heart I felt we could beat Sonny Liston, who was the dreadnought of the heavyweight division. Sonny Liston around today would destroy every heavyweight. I wish I had a Sonny Liston to work right now, 'cause I think I'd do a number on the heavyweight division.

Something that a lot of people forget that's overshadowed by all the flashiness and the hand speed is the amount of guts that Ali had. Take the Doug Jones fight. I remember it very well, that day. Muhammad died. It gave him problems. But, you know, he won. There were no three ways about it. You know, they were rooting for Doug Jones. He was a local guy, had sold out Madison Square Garden. It got to be a hype thing, so Muhammad, in his infinite wisdom…most of the time you saw the picture of the tape over his mouth. I used that as a gimmick in his dressing room. Got the wires. I was always looking for a little extra ink, the best I could get, because Muhammad would get all the ink he wanted. I suggested he injected a little slow stuff. I was going to the weigh-in and I said, "Muhammad, put a tape over your mouth." He thought about it and says, "Yeah, OK, we'll do it." But then, as the weigh-in progressed, he says, "All the newspaper men are here. I can't do it no more." And he took the tape off!

But he loved visiting places abroad. You know, the odd thing was, the first time in London, people avoided us like the plague. We could go out anywhere, go to any movie. We used to walk from the Cumberland Hotel to Iso's, have dinner, walk back. Nobody bothered us. But the second time around – you know, the second Cooper fight – forget about it. We couldn't walk the streets. There were mob scenes. They loved him! We couldn't go to a movie. In fact, we went to Iso's, but everybody knew we were there and the people put holes in the car's tyre so we couldn't leave! So we ran out the back. We knew the short-cuts to get back to the Cumberland. We had to run. But they were fun trips. We always had fun.

In the first Cooper fight, Ali's glove split in the very first round. A lot of people said that I cut the glove on purpose, but I actually didn't. It was split in the seam. I'd tell him, "Keep the glove closed. You don't want to keep it open, 'cause he'll see the split." I thought they would see it in the corner, or the referee would. Then Ali got hit with the left hook.

I ran to the corner, pushed him down, put my finger into the leather and lifted it, then walked over to the referee. I says, "This glove is split. You'll have to get a new glove." The referee says, "Call the commissioner." The commissioner went back to the dressing room looking for gloves, came back and called the referee. They don't have no gloves. He comes back to me. I says, "That's OK. We'll use these." I never took the gloves off. So I didn't do nothing but try to help the situation. See, that's what you're there for. You try to do the best you can to help your fighter without tripping the other guy or grabbing him by the back or something. So, during the interim, Chicky Ferarra was in the corner, putting ice on Ali, reviving him, 'cause he was hurt. That was a great left hook he caught. If the ropes hadn't been there, the fight would have been over, because he just slid down the ropes. Got hit, nailed, eyes closed. I'd seen this kid react like that before, but he wasn't on the ropes. He got nailed by Sonny Banks. He was out going down. When his body hit the canvas, he revived. Remarkable.

The Liston fight was something that I looked forward to. It was a great situation. It was months and months of preparation. There was a situation at the hotel in Vegas where Liston made believe he got a pop pistol and shot it at Muhammad, and everybody went down to the floor. Then Muhammad went to Liston's house, when he was living in Denver, and got on a bus, put the lights on and yelled out from the bus, in the middle of the night, "You ugly bear! C'mon out. I'm gonna lick ya!" He just went on and on. When the fight came close, Muhammad chased Liston at the airport with a cane, as if he was gonna beat on him!

We were big on the name-calling – "ugly bear", you know. Liston was a big, strong guy. Mean. So we gave people monikers, just fun. Later on, Patterson was "the rabbit", 'cause he was of that kind of style. Terrell was "the giraffe", because of his long neck. Chuvalo was "the washerwoman". We used the scheme up these gimmicks. It was nothing. It was just something to sell the fight. The oddity was that Liston was the meanie, while the young, brash kid was Cassius Clay. Two weeks before the fight, my brother Chris and Big Don, the other promoter that worked with him, wanted to commit hari kari 'cause he announces he's a Muslim.

In those days, it was, "What's a Muslim?" People didn't know. I didn't know, because Muhammad never spoke religion with me, and I never spoke religion with him. None of my business. I never even knew he was a Muslim. The funny thing was, all of a sudden, there's the unknown fighter, a bad guy, top sell. I was selling this brash, young kid to fight the toughest fighter in the world. All of a sudden, there were two unknown quantities, and the fans were sort of confused. To me, this was the perfect scenario. Perfect timing. The funniest bit, though, was the way it seemed that everybody made a big thing about it.

At the weigh-in, everybody was there, the commissioner, the doctor and so on. He scared the heck out of the doctor, so much so that the doc wanted to cancel the fight. He reckoned Ali was half nuts.

I spot Ferdie Pacheco in the crowd and say, "Ferdie, c'mon, let's go. I want you to come to see Muhammad with me." We went to the house where Muhammad was living. When I get there, Muhammad's playing on the step with a bunch of kids, so I got on the phone and said I had a Doctor Pacheco who had just examined Ali and he says he's OK. But the thing was, it was strictly a sham, strictly a show, like somebody at the Academy Awards. He was fantastic!

It was beautiful to see! There's never been a better salesman in the profession? We don't have them today. See, Muhammad left boxing empty. Because he was great outside, he was great inside. So the combination of the two always brought people to fights. He was beautiful. He was fantastic. Muhammad had so much going for him, intelligence-wise. He could feel, get the pulse of people. He was sensational. He was just good at that. And, you know, he strictly had fun with it. After the scene would be over, he'd say, "We really got it, man! We really got it!"

Muhammad was always the coolest of everybody after a fight. He was so sharp. He had a pace. He knew what was going on. He was a happy man. He said he was going to beat the guy.

He was sincere. I mean, knowing the kid as well as I did, the way that I worked with him, I knew he didn't have a phoney bone in his body. Honest john. Sincere. I never had an argument with Muhammad. Like I said, it was a fun trip. We got along famously. Never had a cross word, for God's sake. And it's like that today.

At the Liston fight, it was a party in the dressing room. He was getting ready, no sign that he was nervous. Nothing! In fact, people don't know this, but we went outside and watched his brother get licked. He lost a six-round fight. Didn't upset him, though. Nothing bothered this kid.

I knew Liston before the fight. I used to see him in a lot of fights, like at Miami Beach. In fact, I seen him fight a guy named Erne Cab. I had a barometer on him. I felt strongly that Muhammad would beat him because of the superior speed. I saw Liston fight a guy in Detroit one time, a tall, skinny guy, a bit of an awkward size and height. See, Liston wasn't tall. Liston *looked* tall. Big. Muhammad was taller. So I gave Muhammad that thing about, when you get in the middle of the ring, stand tall. Look down, because the guy's shorter than you are. He looked down at the guy and said, "Gotcha, sucker!" And that was it. He really meant it. And he felt strongly about beating Liston.

Even so, we weren't really sure which way the fight was going to go. But Ali was so much quicker than Liston. Liston couldn't get near him. And Muhammad was hitting him with that strong jab that he had, and he kept circling, kept moving and Liston couldn't get to him. I think Liston got completely frustrated, and if you get frustrated, that takes all the snap out of your shots. But meanwhile, Liston was trying to get to him, and then you know what happened – Muhammad busted him up with a right hand. It's my own thinking that they used Monsel solution in the cheekbone cut.

Also, I think that they maybe used carbolic vaseline for Liston's shoulder, or maybe that green linament, 'cause both Muhammad's eyes went. He must have got his head on the guy's shoulder, or he may have put his forehead into the solution – he sweats profusely, Muhammad – and then it went into both eyes. So when he got that, it was scary, because the guy comes back to the corner and he's shaking his head. The referee's looking at the action in the corner, so right away I started putting water in his eyes. Just prior to that, I put my little finger in the corner of his eye and then put it in my eye, and it burned. He definitely had caustic stuff in his eyes. So I got the sponge and washed it out. Actually, I threw the sponge away, then leaned him up with a towel and threw the towel away, 'cause whatever's in there, I didn't wanna keep messing with it. Then he gets up and says, "Cut the gloves off. I'm going to prove to the world what dirty work's afoot."

"In a pig's eye," I say. "I ain't going to cut nothin' off. Take it easy".

Then he started going over to tell the referee, and I pulled him back because I didn't want the referee to come over to my corner. The kid would have said, "Stop the fight," and the referee would have stopped it. So right away, he tried to get that hysteria and contain it. The last instruction I gave him was, "Run!" And that's what he did. He ran, and halfway through the rounds, his eyes cleared – thank God for tear ducts – and then he started doing a number on Liston again.

But that was scary, 'cause he wanted me to cut his gloves off. A couple of guys would have pulled the scissors out. I would've cut their throats, you know, because you've got to contain it. You can't be too hysterical. But he was blind. Everybody says he wanted to quit. He didn't want to quit. He couldn't see that big sucker. If you look at that round, he took a hell of a shellack. Liston was digging in body shots. A lesser human being would have got out of there, but he didn't. He withstood whatever happened to him and made it a plus.

Then Liston had had enough. I honestly feel that Liston didn't want to get knocked out, 'cause he knew that Muhammad would have. I don't know how old Liston was, but then, all of a sudden, all of the aches and pains came in. We were trying to make a thing about his age, but he was neither a bobby sox nor an old guy, but he had been around a long time. Maybe age caught up with him. I think he thought, "What am I doing here?" He'd tell to your face, one on one. "What am I doing here?"

The scenes in the ring were just unbelievable. I got up into the ring and said, "We can't win. We can't win!" Everybody was telling us we couldn't win. But when the scene started getting hectic, you couldn't see me. I went around the edges. I didn't want to be around there. I'm not a big guy. I let them jump and bob and everything else, but I stayed away from those scenes, because there was big bodies involved. I was thinking, "If they fall on me, I might be a little hurt." I always watched those hectic scenes. I never got involved in them.

During the preparations for the Liston fight, I knew something was going on outside the ring. A lot of gentlemen were coming around to talk to me, FBI people, asking me, "Do you know this guy? Do you know that guy?" I didn't know none of those guys. One thing I never did was get involved with my fighters outside of life, personal life, religion. I always stayed away from that like a plague. I never wanted to mess with that stuff. So I told these guys, "Hey, I don't know if he's a Muslim. In fact, what's a Muslim?" I didn't know about that religion, but I got to know Elijah Muhammad. Later on, I got to meet Herbert Muhammad, his son.

The funniest thing was that Elijah gave Ali's brother a name, Rahaman Ali. He comes up to me in the gym and says, "Hey, Angelo, I've got some great news for you"

"What's that?" I said.

"I've got a new name."

"Oh yeah?"

"Rahaman Ali." He spells it out.

I said, "Well, I'll call you Rocky."

"No you won't!"

What's the difference? But I never had a problem. My thing was always being involved with the boxing end of it. And that paid off.

Once Muhammad changed his name, though, the public perception of him changed. In the gymnasium, he was still the same guy. For a while, he got a little quiet because he wanted to get that stately look, but he always reverted to being Muhammad Ali. He was definitely a joy. He was for real, though. He used to read the Koran, and I would know it was going to be a two-hour session, so I would quietly walk out. Naturally, in the press interviews, they would start talking boxing and then they'd go into the Muslim thing. So I told the guys in the front, "Look, guys, let's talk boxing. I know you guys are here to do a job, but we're here to talk about a fight." You know, there'll always be one guy to change the gist to talk about his religion.

But what I didn't realise was that it was part of a much larger political thing. I learned a little about that when I went to Scotland. I had Willie Pastrano fighting, and I made the mistake of going to a Catholic church. Vasilio and Willie, they're both Catholics, and I was brought up a Catholic. Anyway, then we went to church and took a picture with the priest. The worst thing I could've done. Willie was fighting Chick Corduiz, and they didn't buy that, and this played against us. That's when I started learning a little bit about religion. I never knew anything about Muslims because you don't hear about these Far East things.

At the Patterson fight, there was quite a lot of name-calling before the fight and again some more overtones about Ali, calling him "the great white hope", and Patterson said he was going to get the heavyweight title back to America. I didn't like that. I thought that it was overdone. I thought Patterson calling him Clay was overdone. The guy has the right to have himself called whatever he wants to be called. But I felt sorry for Patterson, 'cause all he did was prolong his agony. Muhammad did a number on him. I would've liked to have seen the fight stopped, period, because his back went out and everything else. To me, it was a methodical job Muhammad did on the guy. I didn't like it. Naturally, though, I didn't like the name-calling stuff, either. It was ugly. But a lot of people forget that, when that bell rings, Ali is a fighter, a tough guy. You can always see the way he reacts to getting prepared for something. He was a complete fighter. I mean, to me, he did everything you can ask a fighter to do.

As for the Liston rematch, I've got a copy of *Seed* magazine in my office, a Swedish magazine. They have a sequence of pictures where the guy did get hit. The guy's left foot picked up off the canvas. He got hit with a punch like I teach my fighters today. Pop, slide, *bang!* Liston didn't see the punch. Liston threw a jab. He was facing the cameras. Got nailed side of the head. Down. And he rolled over. There was no doubt about it – he got knocked down. I walked across the ring and say, "Tough luck, son." He looked right through me. He walked right by me. He didn't see me. He was still out of it.

At around that time, with the problem Muhammad had with Vietnam, it was a relief to get away to Canada and England and Germany. We were in Germany for the Mildenberger fight and Muhammad entertained the troops. He had them come back to his hotel! He would tell them stories. He was very popular with the military. Never had a problem. In fact, for the fight in Cleveland with Chuck Wepner, we went around and distributed tickets to the army bases. When we went to England, we would go to the American air bases to see their latest equipment. He would get up in the jets, you know. He never would take a ride in a jet, though. He had a hard time with that flying, early on, but now he knows he's gotta fly, because I said, "If you want to be a superstar, how you gonna see everybody? You gotta fly." So I talked him into it.

He never talked to me about the Vietnam thing, though. All I talked about with Muhammad Ali was fighting. Nothing else. I never put my nose in. I've been in service. From '43 to '46, I was over in England, France, Germany, Belgium, waving the flag. What's the baloney? A man's got a right to his convictions. The man felt what he felt. Later on, it came out, "Hey, he was right." But the point was, he was the only guy that did that.

You know, this is the guy that some restaurant Woofie's took his title away from him. That was a disgrace. How do you take a title away from a guy? The guy deserved it...he won it. But, you know, that was asinine, what they did then. "He can't do that. He's got to go to war." Everybody does what they want to do in life, and Muhammad believed in what he said, what he'd done.

When they stripped him of the title, that was when he was in his prime years. He had looked the best he ever looked to me in the Folley fight. But, you know, *que sera sera*. Naturally, he was not the same guy. In fact, I used that rhetoric with the Tyson fight, that Tyson will never be the same again, because of his incarceration. Muhammad wasn't incarcerated, though. Imagine the guy being in one spot all the time, not being able to be a free soul and do his thing.

When he got his licence back, immediately everybody was saying, "Ali-Frazier", the undisputed champions. All the papers said that they respected each other but really didn't like each other, but that's a one-sided thing. Muhammad likes him. Muhammad always liked everybody! It's Joe. I think he could not understand that this kid was popular. Joe was never that popular. He was a great fighter, but he didn't have the popularity. That's why you got to be yourself. Don't try to be another individual. He just couldn't understand why the guy was so popular. The other thing, of course, is that, if Muhammad wasn't around, where would Joe Frazier have been? You wouldn't have had those three fights.

In New York, we couldn't even leave the arena. We were stuck in Madison Square Garden all day. I couldn't go back to the hotel. There was a ring of humanity around Madison Square Garden. I had to send everybody out of there while I stayed with Muhammad. We ate in Madison Square Garden. We walked around Madison Square Garden to walk off the food we'd eaten. He slept on a rub-down table! But it was such a bizarre situation. We couldn't go noplace.

The build-up to the fight was absolutely incredible. It was big, and I mean *big*. On the screen, you don't see the people who were there. Some guy yelled my name when I was on the apron: "Hey, Angelo!" "Yeah?" It was

Frank Sinatra. Isn't that nice? Nice feeling. It was a happening. That fight with Joe Frazier... Naturally, I'm biased. I don't think Muhammad lost that fight, but then we wouldn't have had the other two fights.

Muhammad had two bad rounds, the eleventh round and the 15th round. I don't know how Muhammad survived the eleventh round. It was lucky he was a ballet dancer. He was reaching out and trying to grab onto Joe. I don't know how he survived. The 15th round, though...getting knocked down and getting up was not surprising, and Muhammad was throwing punches at the end. The voting was very close, in the end. One guy gave it split naturally – eight-seven, something like that. It was very close voting. But that's passed, and you should never look back. But the point was that Joe should feel that, without Muhammad, he wouldn't have been that popular.

Very often, when you get a big build-up like at that fight, the fight itself is a disappointment, but Muhammad built up the guys he was fighting, he stood up to the fight. In fact, there was a kind of down feeling in certain fights, like Patterson and Terrell. I could give you the names of fights where it was built up to a level and then flattened out. These things happen. So, in boxing, we've got to be realistic.

The fight with Ken Norton, though, people ask me if I asked him to quit, but no. I asked him in the first round. I told him his jaw was busted. I told Muhammad, "I have to stop this fight." He said, "No, you ain't. I can beat this guy." Muhammad – no excuses for him – we got to the town and he wasn't in the greatest of shape. I figured we had another ten days. I could get him in shape. But he got in even worse shape, because the promoter took too long parading him around all the places. I think he was running for a political office or something. He took him to every bar. He tried to hustle tickets by running Muhammad around, because Muhammad was the guy that would build the fight up. Nobody gave Kenny a shot, yet Kenny Norton was a good fighter. So Muhammad had a broken jaw. Well, you learn something every day of your life. I found out that it was because of a compacted wisdom tooth. In the physical examinations of fighters, they should X-ray the fighter's teeth and see if he had compacted wisdom teeth.

The Norton and Frazier rematches, they got him back on the path, although both fights took an incredible amount out of him. I mean, Manila – phew! What a murderous fight. I was exhausted, working the fight. It was *hot*. It was about 100 degrees outside, but inside it was hotter because the arena had this tin roof. It was literally just a tin roof. I don't know how Joe and Muhammad survived. It just shows you the strength of a fighter, the condition of a fighter. That's what I mean when I say that fighters are the best conditioned athletes in the world – the way they train, the way they prepare themselves.

Anyway, at one point during the fight – I forget what round it was – Muhammad came back to the corner and he really flopped, you know? I just went about my thing, with the ice and everything, cooling him off, and he made a crack that that was the closest he'd fought to death. But I didn't pay no attention to him, 'cause I wanted to get him juiced. But, you see, what happened with Joe Frazier, he just ran out of steam. And that's not a knock on him. He was in a murderous fight. He got hit some voracious punches later on. But after the fight, he was exhausted. Completely exhausted. In fact, we were all exhausted. But he was a completely physically exhausted individual.

Muhammad always used to seek out weaknesses. He always had that knack of digging them out. I don't know where he got it from, but he had it. He would always come up with something. Later on, when he fought Larry Holmes, I stopped the fight because I was afraid he was going to get hurt. He was really laying in the clinches… I was afraid for his eyes. He hurt one of them. So, when he came back, I said, "No more. Forget it. You're not throwing punches back." You get to know your fighters. You get to know to what extent they can go.

Manila was an incredible event, but the Rumble In The Jungle was great, one of the greatest of all Muhammad's events. He really lucked out in that fight. We were there, facing the Congo River. Or the Zaire River, they called it. We were staying in a place away from all the activity. We ate, talked and slept boxing. The arena was right there at the gym, where we trained. Foreman couldn't take that kind of living. He went into Kinshasa, which became Bourgainville when they changed all the names. That's in the

Belgian Congo. I remember going to South Africa, and Bourgainville was one of the stops. Anyway, that's why the fight took place, because Zaire wanted to let everybody know where Zaire was.

Bobby Goodman and I used to go to press conferences in Kinshasa, which was 45 minutes away. We had a guy driving us who I used to "AJ Forte". The government themselves told me that, if you're driving in Zaire and you hit somebody, don't stop, 'cause the people didn't like mechanised things. They would hit you back. If you hit somebody, run to a police station and don't stop. Those were the instructions we had.

Anyway, there was a guy there who used to hold press conferences every day. One day, he wanted to take us to lunch. I said, "I don't want to eat lunch. I gotta be back in 45 minutes and be with Muhammad in the camp." I would go back every day. But every day, it would be, "Get there at eight o'clock in the morning. We're going to have a press conference." That bum would draw up and say, "Let's go eat lunch." I'd say, "Forget about it. We're going back to camp." When we were at the camp, though, there was nothing to do but train, prepare, and Muhammad got himself in the best shape of his life. It was remarkable, the way he trained. You can tell that by the end result.

That night, when we came out to the ring, it was a great scene, with all these people in the stands. Everybody was there. It was an awesome sight.

During the fight, he was laying on the ropes a lot, and I didn't like it at all, because the ropes were loose. Those hemp ropes they used got loose because of the intense heat. This was at four o'clock in the morning. It was so hot. The ropes had stretched and the turn buckles weren't big enough to tighten them. In fact, during the fight, I yelled at Pat Patterson, "Go tighten the ropes!" He only loosened them more. When Muhammad was laying on them, I was afraid Foreman would throw a punch and he'd be out of the ring, like those fights where kids go through the rope. It was a short apron, too. If Muhammad went through the ropes, he would've broken his back, 'cause they had the ring up high so everybody could see, and that would've been a floor drop. It would've been disastrous. That's why I was sweating out.

In fact, one time during the fight, when Muhammad was in my corner, I actually smacked him on the butt and said, "Get the heck off the ropes!" You know, *bang!* But, thank God, everything turned out all right. He was making Foreman miss punches by a hair and Foreman got tired. I work with Foreman now, and when he tells the story – and he'll tell you whenever you want to hear it – he says he heard all these voices in the corner yelling, but he heard my voice above the other guys. After a couple a couple of rounds, I get shrill. So I yelled, "Get the heck off the ropes! Don't play with that big sucker!" Then Foreman heard it. Muhammad says, "He was looking to hit me with a real good right-hand shot." When he saw that, Muhammad moved off.

Generally, though, I don't pay no attention to what Ali says in a fight. Actually I'm so intent on the fight itself, a lot of that stuff passes me by. But I hear him giving the same rhetoric: "C'mon, sucker. S'matter? Can't hit me, sucker?" You know, all that kind of rubbish. And it took a lot of self-confidence on Ali's part to adopt those tactics. He's supremely confident. He's a professional. And he knows what he can do. He knows what his limitations are. The accolades of Muhammad will go on for a long, long time, thank God, and they'll say, "Gee, who's that little guy in the corner with him?" *I'm* the short guy. To this day, when I send pictures out, I'll put down, "I'm the guy on the left," so that people won't get us mixed up!

He made his own decisions, though. Muhammad had no time to take advice from anyone. People say he should have resigned after Manila, but I'd be the last guy to tell him. I never tried to play god. I think a man does with his life what he wants to do, and Muhammad did – and still does, to this day – what he wanted to do. Everybody is trying to make something out of this Parkinson's situation. I don't think it's attributed to boxing, specifically, but you gotta be honest: the shots he took didn't help the disease, whatever the disease is. But they have no cure for the disease. They don't know what creates it. And people from all walks of life get Parkinson's disease.

I remember the Holmes fight, though. That was something that should not have happened. The doctor gave Muhammad thyroid pills, which sapped his strength, although they made him look beautiful, physically. He looked like a picture of health. He never looked better. But the tank was empty. The thyroid pills ruined him. I thought he was taking vitamin pills. What harm could *they* do? I didn't know they were thyroid pills. I would've objected, if I'd known. But, you know, you don't tell a doctor what to do, and I didn't want to impose myself upon the situation. Had I known they were thyroid pills, I definitely would've blown my stack, because I would've checked it out. I would've called my doctor friends, and they would've straightened me out and said, "Yeah, you shouldn't let him take them, 'cause they have bad effects on people." In the end, it was me who decided to stop the fight. He couldn't do nothing. He wasn't punching back. He wasn't pulling out that special Ali formula – socking it up, you know. Ali was empty that night.

Then, the fight with Berbick, that was a disaster. I tried so hard, but he had promised some guy in Nassau that he would come there. Like I say, the last guy he shakes hands with, that's his buddy. He didn't have an enemy in the world. Anyway, this guy was having an ego trip, and Muhammad went there in no kind of shape. None. He looked like Chubby Checker.

Even though I didn't interfere with his life outside the ring, we were very close. We've been close from the git-go. Him and I respect each other very much, and when we see each other, we hug and I tell him, "Hey, we've got to stop doing this kind of stuff," 'cause he pats me on the butt and I pat him on the butt. "Guys are going to start talking." But yeah, we're very close, naturally for two human beings that have worked this long together. Ali's a friend. I've known him since he was 16.

I think he came around at the right time, when heavyweights had this image of being slow, sloppy, clumsy. The Carnera era. Then along comes this guy who's got the bounce to the ounce, the quickness, and he uses this agility to beat bigger guys. He had that balance of reflexes. Also, he liked boxing. He'd never admit it, but he liked the people involved in boxing. He'd like that guy, he'd like that camera guy, he'd like the guy with the sound because he knew he was in action. He was that kind of guy. He loved the media.

There was a guy called Cope in Pittsburgh, a well-known radio guy, and he called him Mickey Rooney, and there was a newspaper guy from *The Post* called Harbutt, and he used to call him "the gangster", because he always had the cap and the raincoat on. They loved having him around, because it was always fun and they always got new ideas. They were like that because we were in action. There's only one disease in this profession, and that is silence. When the press isn't looking to talk about boxing, we're dead.

When you talk about Muhammad Ali, you're matching an era, a time where boxing needed someone to bring out the quality, and he *was* quality, at all times. Quality, intrigue – everything went on with him. It was a great time, and everybody had a lot of fun. All the TV guys, the newspaper guys and radio guys had a ball because he was there. As a kid, he used to attack press conferences. We used to go into the press rooms and get to big fights. I'd say, "What do you want? You want some poetry?" Ali, he was more, "Well, whatever you want to do."

He was an original. There'll never be another Muhammad Ali, just like there'll never be another Henry Cooper. He's one of a kind. To me, fighters are very rare individuals. They gotta have that certain quality to make a fighter. And not everybody can be a fighter. I'm not just talking rated champions; not everybody can be a *fighter*. It's a tough profession, and I'm the advocate. I tell these kids, "If you think you're gonna make it quick, forget about it. It takes time." He was the greatest at what he did. He changed the whole scenario, made it fun. To me, he was a great individual. Muhammad Ali brings a smile to me whenever I talk of him, because he was a great guy.

Jimmy Ellis

Former Heavyweight Champion

To become a world champion, you have to fight. They don't give it to you. And when you fight to get it, then you know you really did something. Ali was the Olympic champion, and after he won that he came on back to America and he said he was gonna be the world's heavyweight champion. And he did what he said he was gonna do. Someone might have wanted him to fail, but he wasn't gonna fail because he had made his mind up what he was gonna do and weren't nobody gonna change it. He was gonna win that heavyweight title and he fought and he fought and he fought and he beat a lot of guys and he won the title.

He was a crazy man. When he came up to a fight, he would come in behind me and choke my neck and I'd say, "Turn me loose!" and we'd mess around, boxing and punching at each other. And when he accidentally smacked me, I said, "Oh, I'm gonna kill you now," 'cause I didn't like to be smacked. I'd rather for you to hit me than to smack me. But he's a good guy, a wonderful guy.

We both grew up in Louisville, but I was a country boy and he was a city slicker. It was a nice town in the '50s. I was born and raised there and I'm still there. I don't wanna go nowhere else. Not without Mary. My wife was here, my family was coming from Louisville, so it was the place I would always be. I wanted to stay and I did.

I thought of maybe going into boxing back around '57 and '58. Started training and everything. I went to the different gyms that I wanted to go to. I went places I wanted to go you know. Got a chance to go to Chicago. It was a new career. But I was considered as a hoodlum because we used to fight in the streets. I would go over to Mary's, on Lexington Road, and sometime would get in trouble. I would get in a fight. I never would start a fight, but I would end a fight. At this one restaurant, most of the time the people was nice, but some nights I got in fights because I maybe said something wrong or he might have looked round or something like that and I would knock whoever out. I had to fight my way out. I wasn't trying to hurt nobody. The white guys were always wanting to jump on me, and if they did, they'd be sorry. I'd go into bars and it'd be white guys in one area and blacks in another. I would knock 'em out. But I never would start anything. If I get in a fight, I get in a fight. If somebody wants to try to whoop me, they can try. If they beat me, good luck to them, but if they don't beat me there… That was it, the way it was.

Muhammad got into boxing 'cause someone stole his bicycle and he wanted to train to get them back. Ali had beat a friend of mine named Donny Hall, so when I learned to fight, learned to box, learned my skill, I wanted Ali, because Ali had beaten my friend. Then I said to Donny, "Hey, Ali, he beat you. I'm gonna beat him. I'm not sure I can do it but…" The first time I met him, I didn't beat him but next time, I did. We didn't fight no more after that.

At that time, Cassius stood right out in the crowd wherever he was, 'cause he had a thing about him – he would walk tall no matter what, no matter what you'd say: "I can beat you." He'll tell you that in a minute. When I fought him, I didn't know whether I was gonna beat him or not, but I thought, "Well, I'm gonna try. I'm gonna do my best." I had calmness in myself. And when we grew up, we were staying in the same room together and Ali said, "I'm gonna be a heavyweight champion," and I said, "Well, I'm gonna be a champion, too." At that time, I was a middleweight.

Ali went from light-heavy to heavy. And both of us did become champions of the world.

Ali was gonna beat anybody in boxing. He was, "I don't care whether you're white or whether you're black." Hey, if you was black and he was good, he was gonna beat you. Same as if you're white, he was gonna beat you. There was something about him. He believed that he could beat anybody at that time, that he was coming through. He was gonna be a winner every time.

We were sparring partners. Mary, my wife, says that's one of the reasons why he was so good. She says that, when I fight, she see some Muhammad Ali in me, and when he fights, she sees some of me in him. I mean, sparring's an important business. When you box and spar with different guys, you really wanna be the great guy. Being the great guy means that you're the best guy out there. And Ali was great. I was in Louisville, training as a middleweight, and he was down in Florida. I went with him to train when he went to England to fight Henry Cooper. He had a lot of fights at that time. He was doing pretty good, beating everybody. Regardless of what they say, he was still beating everybody that he fought at that time.

The gym in Miami that Ali trained at with Angelo Dundee, it was a good gym. There'd been a lot of other partners that Angelo had and they used to train there too. Then, I got to go down with Muhammad and box with a lot of the other guys. A lot of good partners came through that gym when Muhammad and I was there, and even before that. That's what got me warmed up and got me going, with Muhammad Ali down there. I said, "I gotta hang out with him." We were helping each other.

A daily schedule was get up in the morning, do your road work. The first thing was to go to the park and run two or three or four miles, something like that. Me, when I come back from my road work, I'd get me something to eat and go to my job. Ali, though, he'd get up in the morning, he'd run and then he'd get hisself some food and eat and get to the gym at twelve or one o'clock to work out and do everything he's supposed to do. Sometimes he might work out two hours, maybe two and a half.

Sometimes just an hour. Then, when the evening comes, he'd get something to eat and take a rest. And then, the next morning, he's up doing exactly the same thing. That's what you gotta go through when you're in training.

Angelo Dundee trained Muhammad, worked his corner. He's a great guy. I won the world champion title with him, and when Muhammad Ali was with Dundee, he won the heavyweight championship. So we were back to back. I was glad to see him win the world heavyweight champion, because he came up as a young kid and he said he was gonna be the world heavyweight champion. Everything he said he could do, he did.

I remember when Ali fought Sonny Liston, watching that fight and thinking Ali was gonna win it. I knew Sonny was good and had beaten a lot of guys, but when Ali went in the ring with him, he didn't know that Ali was as fast as he was and he could punch. He thought that he was gonna come in and beat Muhammad Ali the way he was beating the other guys, but Ali was a different guy when he was fighting. Liston thought Muhammad Ali was just a talker but he didn't know that Muhammad Ali was a talker *and* a fighter. He could do both.

I didn't know nothing about Islam when he changed his name. But he was his own man. He had a decision to make for himself, and if that's the way that he went, then I guess he knew what he was talking about. I guess that's what he wanted to be. He wanted to do it and he did it. That's all there was to it. It didn't upset me or nothing. My father was a minister and I was a Baptist and I believed in what I believed in and nothing was gonna change my mind. I think they tried, but they weren't successful. Muhammad Ali, he was the same way. He went into what he thought he wanted to be in and he stayed in that, so I gotta give him honour. Whatever he believed in, that's what he did. I wasn't worried when all these tough characters started hanging around him. I wasn't worried about nobody messing with him too much, because I knew he could handle himself.

I remember liking London when I went over there to train with him. I was there for both the Henry Cooper fights. Cooper was a good fighter, but he couldn't beat Ali, no matter what. I was gonna try to fight Cooper on my own, 'cept that my career ended before I had the chance. But that Cooper, he could take a punch. He could take you out of there. But with Muhammad Ali it was like, "You might hit me, and you might drop me down, but I'm gonna come back and I'm gonna get you. I'm gonna make you pay for it." And he wound up winning.

In '67, you heard stuff in the papers where he'd said, "I'm not gonna go and fight in Vietnam." Then he gets his title taken away from him. They held a tournament for the title and for me to get in I had to beat a guy by the name of Johnny Pearsall in New York. I knocked him out in the first round. Eventually, I won three fights and the tournament. After I beat Jerry Quarry, that made me the heavyweight champion of the United States of America. And I kept the title for two years, until I got beat in New York by Joe Frazier.

When he didn't go into the service, it was weird. My brothers, they went to the service. I was lucky that I didn't have to go. I was married and had kids and if you had kids, they didn't like to draft you. I've got a younger brother that didn't have to, either. That was just one of the things that happened at the time. But if I'd have had to go into the service, I would have gone.

Ali, though, he did something good with boxing. He won the title, he fought hard and he respected people. He changed the face of boxing, when he started fighting the way he did, and that was a good change. They changed some of the prizes, moved the money up. Now you was talking about having a fight for a million dollars. Ali would always look out for his friends. They were the greatest asset to him, and he made us big money. I fought a lot of fights and didn't get paid for them until Ali came along and I got a chance to do a lot of travelling with him. Then, after he lost the title, he was still in my corner when I won it. He figured that, if he lost it, I could win it, and he was right about that. I *did* win the title and I held it for two years.

Without Ali, though, I don't know. Life would have been good, but it was a lot better because of him. I'm not a talker. I'm pretty quiet, most of the time, but Ali is a talker. He talks all the time. He could talk and he could sing a little bit – especially 'Stand By Me', he sang it all the time – and he could speak to people and get their attention.

I fought against him in 1971 for the heavyweight championship. I remember that was a good fight. I thought that I could get him, but hey, in that last round, with only 58 seconds left, he comes in with some good shots. When you got hit by him, it's like, you wake up and say, "What hit me?" That's the only way you had to deal with it. Was it the right hand? Left hand? I don't know what it was, but I got hit. And no matter how good a fighter you are, if you get caught with some good shots, you're in trouble, and he caught me with some good shots. He could hit you so hard with a right punch.

After you've been in a fight with Ali, the next morning, you're all swelled up. He was either gonna knock you out or shake you up real bad. He was the kind of guy that, if he hit you with just three or four shots, they were good shots. "Float like a butterfly, sting like a bee. Rumble, young man, rumble." And if you couldn't rumble with him, hey, then you were in trouble. Ali would open up on you. And if you couldn't take it, you'd be outta there. But even Ali would be pissing blood two or three days after a fight. He wouldn't be able to eat properly. His body would hurt. And this was the world champion. This was the greatest fighter of the time. It's a tough business.

The late '60s/early '70s was a unique time in American sporting history. A lot of fighting went on and there was some good fighters back then – Muhammad, Joe Frazier, Oscar Bonavena, a lot of good fighters. You don't have the same kind of fighters now. When Muhammad Ali came along, he made a lot of guys come in the ring that probably didn't wanna fight. They just wanted to fight him. After his comeback, everybody was trying to get him: "Yeah, I wanna fight him. I wanna fight him." But no matter what they might say, they weren't gonna beat him.

They gave me a gold ring just after I won the world championship and it's something that I'm gonna keep on my finger as long as I'm living, something that I was really honoured to get. There's a lot of other fighters that got the same ring, only their name isn't on it. I'm proud of it because I *know* I was the world heavyweight champion and my friend Muhammad Ali was the world's heavyweight champion, too.

Chris Eubank

Former WBO Middleweight / Super-Middleweight Champion

For the BBC's Sportsman Of The Millennium awards in 2000, I was told I had around two minutes to make a speech on Muhammad Ali. When I got to the venue, I found I had 30 seconds. Thirty seconds to explain what this man stood for. It made me angry because all the other people who were there only really spoke about him as a sportsman, but the real crux of Muhammad Ali is nothing to do with how well he did in the ring. After actually saying what he achieved, Muhammad Ali's hand came over and gripped mine. I got emotional and started to stutter and then the presenter came in with some silly little joke.

The reason I was angry is because people are missing the point. It is not about the man's boxing ability, or how he brought boxing to be the number one sport in the world. It is about taking a stand and using your position to actually highlight what is right.

A couple of years ago, at a birthday party at the Hilton, I found a piece of paper and wrote: "Moses, Jesus Christ, Muhammad, Nelson Mandela, Muhammad Ali – thank you very much, Chris Eubank." As I explained to his wife, I'm not an idiot. This is what the man means to me. Muhammad Ali was a role model as was Moses and Jesus Christ and Muhammad and Nelson Mandela. And Bob Marley for his words, although he never got the opportunity to fight for his cause, as Ali did. But it was never about what the individual did – it's what they stood for.

I know that I have integrity. But would I have the strength of character to actually stand up against what is wrong in this world today? I don't think so. I would be too afraid of character assassination because of my children, my wife, my family name. Would I have the courage? Probably not. You can't speak about me and Muhammad Ali in the same way. I'm well behaved, I have good manners, I contribute towards the system, I go around schools and talk to the kids about conduct, about how they should never take the easy route in anything and they should always take the right route. It's easy to use drugs and be rude and cut school, it's hard to keep a schedule – it's hard to say no, it's hard to do the right thing. But that's about as much as I can do. Try to compare that to what Muhammad Ali stood for and you can't. We shouldn't be spoken about in the same decade. It's not for my boxing ability or his boxing ability, it's for what he stood for.

We had similar media images, though, controversial and marketable. I was only being real. I didn't think it was right that I should walk towards the ring smiling and saying, "Hi, hi, hi." I thought I should exude the way I was feeling, which was fear. I was terrified, I was about to have a fight. I didn't cultivate any of the image, it happened instinctively or naturally. It's quite a compliment to think that I was clever enough to actually premeditate this!

I don't believe Muhammad Ali premeditated it either. He had that psychological advantage, because it was natural. With an opponent, if you can do what they don't expect then you have them thinking. If they're thinking about you then they're not thinking about what they should be doing. And if you can distract their attention from what they should be doing then you'll probably beat them.

As time went by, I achieved things in boxing, but it's not about how good you are, it's what you use your position for. The difference with Muhammad Ali is that he stood up for something, he stood up to be counted. He wasn't "Okay be a good boy, stay down, don't talk too much, don't be too clever". The fact that he stood up against the government and in so doing stood up against the media, this is what strength of character means. I've had people crossing the road on seeing me – until about four, five years ago – because they didn't want to be next to me. That's the perception that the media can give you. Fighting a George Foreman or a Joe Frazier is not even to be compared to standing up against a media. Because if you stand up against a government that's what you are doing, you are standing up against a media and they will character-assassinate you – which nobody wants. Ali stood up against the media.

For me it was tough, in the particular sense that it was lonely. People don't understand me, I'm actually a nice person. And I'm thinking inside out – not outside in. Why should people treat me this way? This is the way I earn my living, it's actually quite noble. You shouldn't treat me this way but the fact that you do is only because you're being told how to think by the people who control the minds of the people – the media. It's only a matter of time before I am able to convince you because I will continue to speak my truth.

Ali would have coped with this very easily. You see, the truth lies within the individual. The fact that nobody else understands that is tough. It's only a matter of time. When you practise that quality of integrity, what happens is this: at the time you're doing it, people will dislike you immensely. But, in years to come, they'll grab you and say, "Wow, what a guy."

Sport didn't really interest me as a child. I never looked up to people like sporting individuals as role models. What attracted me was anyone who was living their lives by, or using the quality of, integrity. My common sense told me that if a man can do something, then I too can do it because he's just a man just like me. But strength of character, now that's a different matter. That a man would get up and speak when he should really be quiet, this is what inspires me. Muhammad Ali was willing to stand up and say, "No Vietnamese ever called me nigger." Now that, for me, is strength.

When I was a kid, I remember watching a fight in black and white in 1974. I don't know who the opponent he was fighting was, but everyone was just talking about Muhammad Ali. Gradually over the years, the understanding becomes more clear. All everyone talks about is his boxing ability and when you're aspiring to be a fighter of genuine worth you realise you can't compare yourself to anyone, because you end up being bitter. There'll always be greater fighters than yourself.

For great fighters it's a matter of integrity, that's the measure of a man. If you're in the ring and it's really tough, you're exhausted, you fall back on a principle which is taught to you when you first begin. When you're feeling exhausted, it's not going your way, the chips are down and you want to quit, stay there and take your beating. There is no escape because if you take a way out – which means you go down from a punch that you can really get up from, or you pretend to be concussed – you have to live with yourself. Forget about living with the public, after the fight you have to live with yourself. I can't pretend. I'll take my beating. Ali took his beating as any person who practises a quality of integrity does. In so doing, even in defeat people will say, "What a guy. You inspired me." Whereas if you quit...

There's a nobility to boxing. There are rules to abide by and in abiding by those rules you are being noble because it's a desperate, frightening, terrifying experience. When you step up to the plate, you know the rules, you can't cheat, there is no gouging, there is no kicking, there is no biting, no rabbit-punching or hitting the man low. We have constraints in which you have to work.

You're not taking advantage of anyone. You don't humiliate an opponent, you've both had three months in which to prepare, and there's no malice involved. When I hit you, it's just the point I'm scoring. And if I can acquire more points than you in the contest, then I will win and improve my reputation and make better my standard of living, maybe defend successfully my world championship – but nothing personal.

I've had one or two fights where it has been extremely personal but this was not through the combatants themselves, this was through the hype. And sometimes the hype becomes real. Ali, on two or three occasions, was accused of belittling his opponents, either in pre-fight or even during the fight, Floyd Patterson specifically. But what happens is, to give the fight publicity the promoters say that these two characters hate each other. Oh, they can't stand each other. And sometimes it becomes real, because you feel threatened, the fellow's talking you down and he's disrespecting you and then you start taking it personally.

There was one particular fighter who always referred to Ali as "Cassius Clay". He persisted with this because it annoyed Muhammad Ali immensely and he made him pay physically for it. But it's not supposed to be personal, this is brought on by, first, the promoters to sell the fight, and then the media because it helps sell newspapers.

Muhammad Ali is famously Muslim and having faith is a help to a fighter, no doubt. When you're in the ring, the only thing you can really rely on in the world of reality is patience. Now sometimes you need help and so to have faith in something that cannot be seen is good, because it's almost as though you can peg yourself onto it to help you through that time. With regards to my beliefs, I'm a buddhist, a christian, a Muslim, an atheist. I believe in everything and everyone. I don't put on it any particular denomination.

With regard to Muhammad Ali's Nation of Islam links, each to his own. A man goes through particular phases and each man is an individual and each man does his thing a little way different. His good work supersedes everything else. There was a surgeon who invented the heart bypass. He was a womaniser, but that doesn't take away from his achievement. We all have our flaws. I am not Muhammad Ali and so I don't have his mind. I've developed now to the point where religion is all encompassing. When you ask the question do I believe in Jesus Christ, really the question is also do I believe in Buddha, because the objective is the same. Be good to your fellow man – in fact no, be good to yourself and in so doing you will be good to your fellow man.

Cathy Freeman

Olympic 400m Gold Medallist

I first became aware of Muhammad Ali as a child, when I heard his song, "flies like a butterfly, stings like a bee". I think that entered into my consciousness at a really early age. Everybody was talking about this Muhammad Ali in the magazines and on TV shows, so I couldn't help becoming a little bit more interested in him as time went by. And certainly I became intrigued with him and interested in the things he stood for. He was strong and a leader, somebody who stood up for what was in his heart. Just recently I saw the movie, *When We Were Kings*. There's some kind of magnetism about him and the legend of Muhammad Ali – even though he's obviously still with us, he is an icon. Take away his sporting prowess and all of the titles and all of the achievements and you still find yourself being pretty much attracted to him, just because of his flair and that sparkling way he has. And the way he can mix with people is really powerful I think. I'm not one who takes a lot of interest in people who are surrounded by a lot of hype and attention, but especially myself being black, and being someone who was looked up to as a leader in my own country for the Aboriginal people of Australia, I find inspiration from him a lot, through books or on the internet. Everybody loves him, it seems.

Ali had a tremendous impact on Australia. I'm a little bush kid from the red country of Australia, and I didn't have to travel far to hear all about Muhammad Ali. Even if I wasn't leading the life I lead now or if I hadn't achieved the things I've achieved in my running career, I think I would have been interested in the man and interested in his story – interested in his people and where he comes from and why he has chosen the way he has chosen. He has this magnificent personality that just sort of grabs you. I've never met him but maybe one day I will! I don't think we'll ever see anybody like him again, not in my lifetime. He's such a magnificent character.

Muhammad Ali was one of the few sportsman to transcend the boundaries of his chosen sport. That stems from the fact that he was always going to be true to who he is. I don't think it was a question of courage, I think it was just a question of him saying what he felt. Very pure, very honest, very instinctual and very comfortable in his own skin. He didn't need to be led around by what other people wanted or expected, he marched to the beat of his own drum. As it turns out, everybody else was soon marching to the beat of his drum, and still to this day. He's smart, articulate, charismatic, good looking and I've heard wonderful stories about his kindness and generosity – especially toward children and those who are less privileged than himself – but I think the overriding thing is just his absolute honesty and integrity. And his messages were so clear. He was telling kids to stay off pot and brush your teeth. The way he carried himself was so dignified.

The strong can withstand criticism. Withstand or ignore, it's the same thing. But you have to be so totally sincere about it otherwise people are going to see through it. It's not about being an opportunist type of person. You understand that people actually do listen to you and take note, but it's not about abusing anybody, abusing the time you have on TV or that piece of space in the newspaper. It's just about following your heart and sharing with people things that are important to you.

Muhammad Ali had an amazing following all over the world with people in boxing, with people in sport, with people of his religion, with people of his colour, with people from a working class background. I'm sure the indigenous people of Australia idolised him, and still do. He is like a god but he is incredibly human at the same time. There's always something to

Armed with bear collar and honey, Ali goes on a hunt for Sonny Liston – whom he dubbed "the big ugly bear" – before their November 1964 rematch.

With actor Steppin' Fetchit at his side, Ali discusses his first workout since a hernia operation forced the postponement of the Liston clash, February 1965.

Fearing attempts on his life in the wake of Malcolm X's assassination, Ali is flanked by bodyguards as he arrives at a Black Muslim convention, February 1965.

Attorneys from the DA's office who sought to prevent the Ali v Liston rematch on the grounds that it was a "common nuisance".

Ill feeling continues as Liston glares at Ali checking his weight, Lewiston, Maine, May 1965.

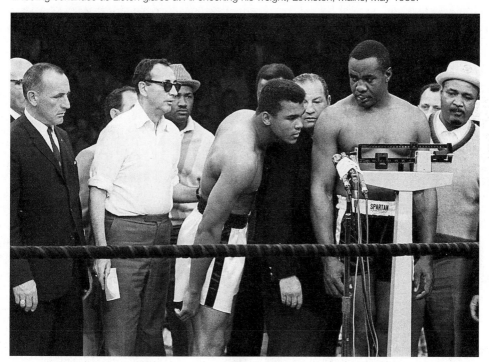

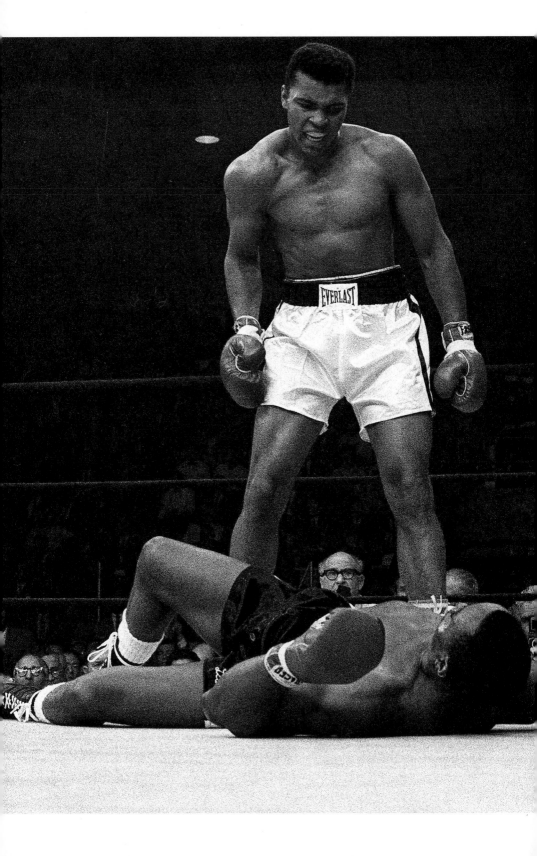

"Get up sucker!": Ali can't hide his frustration as Liston goes down in the first minute of their controversial rematch, May 1965.

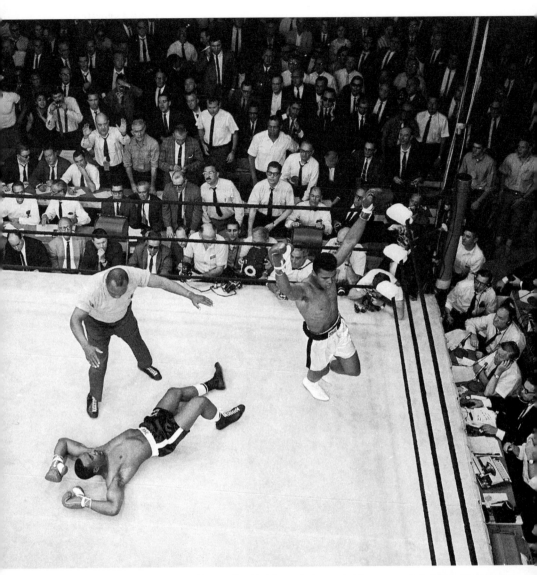

A stunned crowd watches Ali celebrate. But his bizarre first round victory prompted nationwide calls for a probe of the fight and a demand for federal control of boxing, May 1965.

learn from him and God only knows that the indigenous people of Australia – and especially the men – need somebody to feel inspired by and look up to. Muhammad sets a wonderful example of how our indigenous men can be.

I think, like Ali, through everything I've achieved I've tried to remain ultimately the person I was when I was a little girl. I don't have a problem remembering the things that are important to me, such as the relationships around me, my loved ones' health, my space. The things that I enjoy doing are being with my husband, being with my cats. But I work hard and I find true strength in tragedies that I've overcome personally which makes the victories even sweeter. I'm very close to my family and I'm very proud of my heritage and it all stems from having that strong and very clear sense of self. In terms of what other people see, it really doesn't matter as much as what I see. But certainly my achievements are acknowledged, and it's really special. When people have allowed you into their minds and into their hearts, it's not something you get blasé about. I take it very seriously. When a little child remembers you, when they're all of three or four years old, and they live halfway around the other side of the world, it's really not me they're embracing, it's where I'm from, so that's pretty cool.

I'm too young to remember the reaction in Australia when Ali lost his licence over the Vietnam issue, but I guess one of the most amazing things about it was that it would have made people stop and really think about the issues and about the meaning of what the Vietnam War meant and what really could be achieved by it.

I wasn't privileged enough to see Ali fight at the time. I've only seen recordings of the fights, years after they actually happened. TV was nowhere near as evolved as it is now and often in small towns in Australia we only had one TV station!

When Muhammad Ali lit the Olympic flame at Atlanta in 1996, my immediate reaction was "Why is he shaking so much?" And then, of course, you realised it was Parkinson's syndrome and that the man is human. I was so happy for him that night because he has represented and symbolised so much to so many people all over the world for so long. I think everybody felt part of him when he lit the cauldron. I was proud for him, for his family, for everything he stands for. It put him in the spotlight again and made us all remember how much respect we have for the man.

When I lit the flame in Sydney in 2000, I was more concerned at the time about falling down the stairs or falling in the pool of water, to be brutally honest! I have to admit my main priority was racing and trying to win the gold medal. But certainly I understand that what actually went on was a powerful symbol of hopefully what is yet to come for Australia in terms of the black and white relations and our sense of identity. I am a powerful symbol of what Aboriginal is in Australia, and being young, being a woman, I know a lot of indigenous people, and a lot of Australians, were very proud. I don't know if I warrant being compared to Muhammad Ali, but it's nice that we share that common ground. We've both got Olympic gold medals and world titles and we both lit the cauldron. But I've yet to work on the larger-than-life sort of poetry that he spoke and the showmanship he displayed, though – I'm a bit too shy for all of that! I'll have to practise!

Berry Gordy

Motown Founder

The first time I saw Muhammad Ali or heard about Muhammad Ali was before his fight with Liston. Here was this brash, young, cocky kid screaming and talking about what he was going to do. And here Liston was, this big, monstrous character who was a destroyer! Usually when a person brags that much you don't expect very much. We just thought, "Here's a kid promoting himself, trying to make a fast few thousand dollars." So when he proceeded to knock out Liston that was a shock and we started paying a little more attention! Being a fighter myself – I was boxing as a featherweight probably when he was a little boy – I knew he could have had a lucky punch. But I soon realised it wasn't luck.

I went to see his first fight with Frazier at Madison Square Garden. I had taken Diana Ross, my son and Barry Diller, a friend of mine. There had been so much publicity before the fight that everybody was there – we saw Sinatra in the ring corner shooting pictures and he was all excited. It was a major, flamboyant event, with people dressed like you've never seen before, men with fur coats and suede and women you wouldn't believe.

It was a great fight and it could have gone either way, but Muhammad lost that decision. Diana was extremely upset and I remember her jumping up and running back to his dressing room. I thought she would never get in, but he later said that when he looked up and saw her there and she was crying, he was moved. People were very upset that he had lost. But, of course, he came back and beat Frazier because he was a smart boxer. I've always admired him for his dexterity. He and Sugar Ray Robinson were my favourite fighters. Muhammad Ali was probably influenced by Sugar Ray, as most of the great boxing fighters were, but Ali took it to another level. He put all the pieces together – the promotion, the showmanship, the wit, the humour, the class and he was cute! He had convictions and character and integrity and all the things that you wouldn't expect a fighter to necessarily encompass.

He was a major showman. I remember when Ali fought George Foreman for the championship. That was a strange fight. Up until the eighth round I think he had been very tired, and I was worried that he might lose, but he fell against the ropes, covered himself up and recovered and won the fight. He later called that move the "rope-a-dope" – he created a name for it! He was very clever and smart and since perhaps he was not in as good a shape as he should have been, he just did something that probably no one else has ever gotten away with. And then he came back and talked about it like it was planned!

When Ali said he was not going to serve his country in Vietnam, I didn't know what to think. It was a confusing time. For one, I had to go to Korea to fight for my country and now here's this talented kid who has changed his name and who now won't join the army. But also, there was a lot of turmoil going on everywhere. We were having the worst race riots Detroit had ever known and the Black Power forces were developing.

As a record company, Motown was looking at the events. There were tanks and armoured cars in Detroit and there were curfews, but our people refused to stay at home. We had an inter-racial situation in that our whole sales department was white. There was a Jew, there was an Arab and the guy who was running the department was Italian, and they all came to work in this neighbourhood with the armoured tanks and the race riots.

We put out records to try to deal with it. Our writers were very into what was happening with the war and we came up with records like 'Ball Of Confusion', 'What's Going On' with Marvin Gaye, 'War' by Edwin Starr and two or three others that were about the feelings of the times.

We were very busy with all of the problems that that entails, and also with the civil rights. I was a follower of Martin Luther King – he was actually under contract to Motown! – and he was losing power, so it was a tumultuous time. And Muhammad Ali was just right in the midst of all of it.

When Muhammad Ali refused to go to the army, there was a tremendous reaction against him from the American people. I had served and other people had served and so it made it sound so bad that he was singled out for his beliefs. We didn't know about conscientious objectors and stuff like that, so the world as a whole compared him to all kinds of people, like the black Benedict Arnold, saying this guy is horrible. He had defied American tradition. He had defied the whole power structure of America just because of his beliefs.

Through all this confusion I wasn't emotional about Ali one way or the other, but I was watching him and when he made the statement that "those Vietcong have never done nothing to me. They never called me a nigger, none of the Vietcong has ever called me a nigger", it made me think. I thought, "Wait a minute, the Koreans didn't either, they never bothered me." I hadn't thought about it like that. I did not want to go to the Korean war myself, but for a totally different reason. I was just scared not to. I didn't want to go and get killed, but I had to fight for my country, because it was the law! When I heard Ali talk about his convictions and that he was going to go jail for his beliefs, I really became convinced that this man was serious and I loved him for what he was doing. Not only was he talented, not only was he clever, not only was he all these things, but he was a serious man who had great convictions. He made me think about things I've always felt but never focused on, so I always thank him for that.

As far as black people were concerned, Muhammad was definitely a hero in that he was willing to fight for what he believed in. They took his licence, they stripped him of everything – and he was going to jail for five years. All that and he still stood up. He did not bow one moment. I think that lingers with him throughout his life, because he felt that the black man was not treated properly. Not only here, but certainly those people in Vietnam hadn't done anything to him. He wanted to get this straightened out over here before he'd go over and fight people he didn't know. He had some cute saying – "brown people with brown things" – in which he poetically described not fighting those people.

He was smart enough to make the thing live for people here. By saying "they never called me a nigger", all black people had to think how many times we had been called niggers over here and how many times have our ancestors and what has happened to the whole racial situation in America. It brought up a lot of things you think about. It made you think about the equality in the world and how to do something to help that situation.

My feeling about people is that they're all basically good, but we come up in such a way that we accept things and we have to protect ourselves from other people. Ali inspired people to think and believe in themselves and by example he was willing to give up everything that he had worked his whole life for – for a principle that he really believed in. I realised that principle is always big. There are no small principles. My feeling has always been that less than one per cent of the people in all the world ever reach their full potential. And it's because they get off the track with their principles or with their ideals, and they let obstacles affect them in their path.

Ali didn't do that. He was not a theory person. He was an active person and he did it. He knew the principle was very clear and he knew nothing else in his life was more important than what he believed in. So I think he instilled that into a lot of people. I just would like to see it now go further and I'd like for people to really understand this man's legacy and make it even more meaningful.

Ali was the same kind of person as Marvin Gaye, in my estimation. With Marvin, who worked with me, it was something he had to do. It wasn't whether it was right or wrong. He wrote things like *What's Going On*, one of the greatest albums of all time, because he wanted to know what was going on at the time, and he put it into great art. He was one of the great masters of his thing.

Motown was heavily into music of all kinds, but it all dealt with the emotions of people, making them feel good, with creativity and talent and art, when all the turmoil was going on. It was a sign of the times. When Ali came along, he was just an additional sign of the times. Whether he influenced the writers and the producers, I don't know, but he was big at the time and he was doing what he was saying and they would listen to all the stuff that was going on in the world. But he certainly had a personal influence on me.

Ali and I became very good friends and I found him to have an incredibly bright mind. He would come by my house and we would talk about everything under the sun. He used to ask me a lot of things because I was a conservative thinker as far as he was concerned. We would talk about life and emotions and feelings and why people do what they do and all that stuff. He was really into that. He would also read or recite his poetry to me. It was different from what he would say on the air, but it was similar in the style because he was very brash and he had such convictions. Some of the deep poetry he read to me was just brilliant. In fact, he had different phases of it where he would rap – before they called it rap – and he would say things and they made so much sense. I would try to define what it meant to me. Really, the guy was brilliant and I hope he saved these things that he recited.

He had some transformations in his own emotional system from different times because reality would be one thing and he was constantly searching for just the right thing. That's why the world continued the groundswell of liking this guy, not just because he was a great fighter and a smart, witty brash prophet. He was a star even before he was champion. Before, he was just a personality that people loved. They fell in love with Muhammad Ali. Whatever his religious beliefs were, they fell in love with the person, the personality, the human being. Because they could see his character. And that's all it takes. It's not a complicated world when it's just about truth and simplicity.

So when you want to sum up Muhammad Ali for all the things he's achieved, you have to take a phrase from him – and that is simply "the greatest".

William Greaves

Filmmaker

When I first became aware of Muhammad Ali, at the beginning of the '60s, he was this brash young man who shouted a lot. Then, of course, when I saw him fight, I knew instantly that he was hot stuff and that he had every right to boast. As a kid growing up in Harlem, I boxed myself, so I knew a good fighter when I saw one, and he certainly had all the skills that were necessary to become a major figure in the ring. And of course people all over delighted in his in-your-face persona. It's not that he confronted the establishment or that he challenged racism in America; he was very immodest, and in that particular period in American history the silent negro was the most acceptable type, so he gained the ire and displeasure of many people in mainstream America, particularly when he resisted going into the Vietnam War.

And given the degree of racism I imagine was present in his home town of Louisville, Kentucky, I'm sure that boxing was a way of expressing himself and gaining respect for himself. All boxers have that need. Of course, when he cracked through to championship status, he realised that he could use his celebrity for a direct encounter with the forces of racism and injustice that were taking hold in America at that time.

Some believe that, at that time, there were people out there who thought, "Here's a man who's articulate. We can use him for our cause." But really, he didn't need anyone to do his thinking for him. He only got perceived in that way by the way in which his persona unfolded in public, in contradiction to how he behaved in his one-on-one private encounters with people. He was really two completely different personalities – on the one hand he was a very quiet, reserved, low-key person off camera and on camera he was brash. But I think that he saw it as a strategic way to proceed, both from the standpoint of him attracting attention and also because it gave him the opportunity to express himself in a very candid way, hiding behind this bravado, using it as a means to assist his need to protest and challenge whatever he felt he should protest and challenge.

Of course, I'm sure he was referred to by Southern and Northern racists as an uppity nigger for daring to confront white America with it's violations of human rights, for shattering a lot of the preconceptions of black males. But American history is replete with those kinds of individuals, who protested and challenged and fought and died to gain their civil and human rights in the country, so he was very much appreciated because he showed another side of the black American experience.

And white America tried to either absorb him or crush his spirit. Because he was knocking out both white and black people in the ring, it was very difficult to suppress him, because he'd made good media copy. He was very much sought after by journalists, so nothing really could stop him, except when he made a political decision that flew in the face of the law of the land. When he refused to go into the army to fight in Vietnam, then he handed his opponents an easy opportunity to condemn him, to suppress him in other ways. That was the only major way that could be constrained or restrained from being as vocal as he had been – but he nonetheless continued. He felt that he was in a sound position to object, and that his objection would translate into a political statement, which of course it did.

People at the time were surprised that a boxer could be that articulate. He was not your run-of-the-mill boxer, certainly. I've spent time with him, and at times, when we've been alone, he's taken me to his room and opened his various folders where he would keep notes on the various issues in

American life that he would speak about in public. I was struck by the fact that he felt that I was someone he could share his intellectual reality with, that he felt that I would appreciate his intelligence. Really, I felt flattered that he would open up in that way to me.

A lot of his talking points revealed him to be philosophically and poetically a person who thought in a very profound way about the cosmos, life, society and the values of some of the world's major thinkers. He was an intellectually gifted person, and if you studied the way he conducted himself in the ring, you would have to conclude – if you knew boxing and if you knew the art of war – that you were in the presence of a very intelligent, thinking individual. So it's not surprising that he would articulate and express himself more than any other boxer that had come down the path of that profession.

Of course, having worked on making the movie of the Ali-Frazier fight, I got to know him quite well, and it was terribly interesting that he had these other sides to his personality – the quiet, subdued, unpretentious individual; the intellectual; and then the other, public persona, this very expansive, in-your-face truculence which was not him but which he knew would gain him a great deal of ink and time on television. And he was absolutely correct. He synchronised with the mood at the time. Young America, both white and black, was in a very confrontational state of mind, because of the nature of the various problems that were developing in the country – the assassination of Kennedy, the Vietnam War, the excesses of the forces of reaction which led to the civil rights movement and so on.

As I became closer to Ali, it was the intellectual side that surprised me the most, the simplicity of his behaviour, the unpretentiousness, the seriousness. He *was* a very serious person, not like the flighty image that he managed to generate before the cameras. But that kind of behaviour had its own strategic objectives, and at the time, as an intellectual, a person who had decoded the American pop-art culture, he knew that it would be a perfect fit.

If he'd grown up at any other time, there's a strong chance that he wouldn't have been the Muhammad Ali that he is famous for today. The thing is,

America is a fascinating country in the sense that it continues to change. If there's one word that would typify America, for me it would be "change". It has gone through a number of changes – industrial changes, cultural changes, social changes and political changes – and in the '60s we saw the change in status of African-Americans in the body politic, the change in the social arrangements that were made. The social contracts in relation to black Americans were all torn up in the '60s and redrawn. It was a very volatile period.

Then, of course, there was the Vietnam War, and again the young people in America who had been accustomed to a certain amount of luxury and pleasure suddenly found themselves being called to fight in a far-off place. They didn't quite understand why they had to do that, other than the fact that there were people over there who had a different political system, and so the youth of America was very confrontational about that. Then the women's liberation movement developing in the wake of the civil rights movement. As a matter of fact, the civil rights movement spawned a number of rights movements focusing on other minority groups within the American body politic – the aged and the disabled, for example.

So that whole period was a very active period, and it altered American society considerably. When you study American history, you can see that it keeps changing, more than any other society on Earth, I think. It has this capacity to shift and evolve. On the one hand, that's part of the country's strength, but on the other hand, it makes it appear at first glance to be weak. But it always seems to bounce back in a relatively positive way, and I think that probably the American creed – the Declaration of Independence, the Bill of Rights and all those things – are residual concepts that somehow or other help to nurture the need to move in the direction of something resembling more justice of one kind or another.

So it's entirely possible that, if he were born ten years earlier or ten years later, Muhammad Ali wouldn't have been Muhammad Ali. He came along at a time when the youth of the country were looking for a certain kind of leadership. The black Americans were looking for a certain kind of spokesperson, and he came along at a time when he was synchronous with what was needed. If he'd been operating, say, 20 years before, he would not have been as popular. But then, of course, America was under the scrutiny of the world much more during the '60s than ever before.

Muhammad understood that he had some influence, but I don't think he was on an ego trip. I don't think he saw himself as a messiah. My feeling about him was that he was very humble. He was a great fighter, but he understood that to be a great fighter is not about being an egomaniac; to be a great fighter is to adapt to the psychological make-up of one's opponent and not to oneself into thinking that one is greater than one is. I mean, when he said, "I'm the greatest," he didn't believe that. He *was* terrific, but he knew how hard he worked to be terrific, just like Tiger Woods or Michael Jordan today work very, very hard. There are disciplines that one must follow in order to achieve that, and he understood that. There was something inside him that said, "Listen, if you want to be great, this is what you have to do and you have to work very hard at it. You're not great yet." It was all right for him to say that he was, because it would scare people or maybe get him some press, but he knew, in his heart of hearts, that he had to keep working, and he had a very demanding regimen of exercises that he pursued prior to a fight.

Then, of course, straight after he fought Sonny Liston, he changed his name twice, first to Cassius X and then to Muhammad Ali. There were many people who were fairly outraged by this, about him hooking up with the Nation of Islam. The Muslims were perceived as not a renegade group but a group that was outside of the American mainstream. A lot of the people who were part and parcel of the Muslims were people who had come out of the criminal justice system, out of the penitentiaries, and despite the fact that they were very well rehabilitated, because of the Muslim religion, they were perceived as being people to shun.

But within the black community, they were not as negatively perceived as they were by white America. As a matter of fact, there was a fair amount of acceptance of the Muslims, because they were very positive in many ways. I think that, when he joined them, Cassius Clay was attracted to their interest in economic self-reliance. He felt that the black community needed to be more self-reliant economically, politically and spiritually. That was what he was most interested in. I mean, at one point he talked about wanting ten states to be separated off for the American blacks, in accordance with the Nation of Islam's separatist philosophy. Now, while he was a member, he probably subscribed to this idea, although I don't think it's a good idea at all, because it's fraught with all kinds of problems, and I don't really think that he thought that strongly about it. America at that time would not have been that friendly to a ten-state black nation.

Nevertheless, Muhammad Ali was an icon, certainly for black America, for people of colour, who were continuously being bludgeoned by the psychological warfare of the Western media, the white media in America. He was an inspiration, because he showed that there was no justification for the second-class citizenship that black Americans were forced to accept. He also gave a certain amount of hope to people in the colonial world, who were also in a state of oppression. In that sense, he was politically very useful in raising the consciousness and the public's awareness of these people. I think you could write him down as being one of the most significant figures of the 20th century, and indeed even the 21st century, because of his work in areas other than in the ring, his contribution to the human race.

Bonnie Greer

Playwright / Critic

My earliest memories of Muhammad Ali are from 1964, right before he decided not to go to Vietnam. When he won the Olympics in 1960, back when he was Cassius Clay, that didn't make that much of an impression on me, but I do remember '64, because that's when television sport really started to come into the mainstream in a serious way, and there he was. He was beautiful, he was young, he was opinionated and it was very exciting for us growing up, because we saw a black male athlete who actually spoke up to people and then was able to do what he said. I mean, he would make predictions. He'd say, "I'll knock him to the ground in the fourth round," and he did. I think that his articulate nature was the first thing I remember about him, and of course the fact that he was beautiful.

My father just adored him, because I think, for every black man, whether of Muhammad Ali's own time or whenever, he's the incarnation of everything that you think about yourself as a black man. This guy actually embodied it, and it was the very first time that a black male was so public and was able to demonstrate not only his physical prowess but also his verbal ability. This incandescent young black would say that the word "black" was used as a bad word, that people used it as pejorative term. We were negroes. We were coloured people. We weren't black. But Ali made it a very empowering word for us. In fact, he used to say, "I'm not a negro. I don't know where Negroland is." But we were all coming onstream as well, using the word "black" and coming to understand what it meant, and here was a man who said it in public. Here was a man who wore his hair in a way that, when I was a kid, only people who grew up in the country wore it. He looked like a hick, but he wore it high. Didn't do anything to it. Then, in the '60s that was an amazing physical statement. He was the embodiment of what blackness was. We learned from him to actually understand how to be proud of your skin colour, to be proud of your nose and your lips and your natural hair and the way you spoke, what you thought about your *raison d'être*. In that way, he was a rebel, because our parents grew up in the generation where to be black was to risk your life, so they brought us up to be afraid of talking too loud, making ourselves visible, making people we knew see us too much, wearing our colours. We were taught to keep down and keep quiet.

Then Muhammad Ali would come onto the media with his mouth this big and say what he wanted to say. For us, it was like, "Yeah! This is today's generation! This is what we want to do." And, of course, when he stood up and said that no black man belonged in Vietnam fighting other people of colour, my generation we were saying that as well. This was not our war. This was no reason to die. He said that loud and then he didn't go, and it destroyed his career when it was at its peak. He put himself on the line like that for us, who were just beginning to understand what it meant to be young and black. Here was a guy who put his career on the line, and it was a huge career, a massive career. No one's ever done that since.

We saw him get stripped of his opportunities and we said, "If this guy can do this, then we can march in the streets and stand up to our teachers and stand up at university and say, 'No! This war's wrong!' Not only for young black people but for young people, period. We're going to be the first generation that says to the older generation, 'We ain't gonna fight your war. This is your problem. You deal with it.'" That's what he did, and he was very important to us, in that sense.

My personal involvement with boxing began when I did a show in New York. This show was about a male boxer, and one of his fantasies was about how his sister inspired him to train, even though she couldn't box herself, so I had to actually learn to box and fight with him on the stage. I had to take lessons. I mean, I'm only five feet tall, and this guy was something like five foot ten! And what I learned was that boxing requires not so much physical strength but the ability to think two or three punches ahead. You have to be able to stand up on your feet and be able to anticipate a punch and also think in the body of the person opposite you.

At the same time, boxing demands the ability to balance yourself, to use the hand that you're good at, defend the hand that you're weak at, and also to understand that the person's gonna come for you on your weak side. And you have to know how to take a punch. But the thing is, it's also entertainment, so the people out there are watching to see how beautiful you can make this. Since Mike Tyson, of course, it's become about brute strength. In a way, he lowered the atmosphere, because he brought in boxing as taking a punch, but I believe that boxing is more about *not* taking a punch, about delivering a punch as soon as you can, getting your opponent off his feet and being able to end the match standing up and being beautiful.

Boxing is a great, a noble sport. On the level of Prince Naseem and the way Chris Eubank fought in his day, on that level you get to see the beauty, you get to see the nobility of it. What's so wonderful about Muhammad Ali was he was a heavyweight. He was a huge man. I was in a lift with him one day and his fist was as big as my head. But to see this guy actually be able to stand up on his feet, deliver the grace of a person two or three degrees of grades below him and demonstrate that kind of balance while weighing in at 180 pounds plus was massively beautiful.

There was no boxer who's been like Muhammad Ali. He was one in a generation. It was a real privilege to be able to see him. There's been no one like him. There probably won't be anyone like him for a while, either, because the game has changed. We might see someone like him coming from the developing world, but from the West I think that's pretty much finished. I think Ali represented a kind of feline, almost feminine beauty in the ring, that ability to use intuition to fight. He fought with his mind first. His body came after. You always knew all the time what he was thinking, what he was feeling. He also realised that it wasn't really very serious with him, and that's quite a feminine thing as well.

His attitude about it in the ring was that it was always a game. Outside of the ring, he understood that he was a role model, which meant that he knew that we, the younger generation, were watching him. We were learning from him how to be people. We were learning from him how to be black, about America's place in the world, about being privileged enough to being born black in America, about our obligation to ourselves and to other black people outside America. Muhammad taught us what that meant. We knew that here was the true ambassador of the sport. He was saying to us, "Be the best in the ring. It's just a game. It's not the end of the world. It's not the beginning of the world. Outside of the ring is where it matters." He continues with that message to this day. With him, it was playfulness. Now, sport is like a life-or-death lifestyle thing which I think is actually kind of wacky and goofy, but Muhammad Ali showed us the playfulness of it. That's why I love him. That's why he's still important to me.

But when I see him now, I wish that he'd stopped fighting 20 years ago, because I think he took too many blows. You see him now and I guess his inner kindness and his inner sense of fun is the thing that's to the fore, but I can't help remembering this beautiful creature who seemed to be the incarnation of the age of my youth, my kind. When I see him now, I think of all the music that was around then and the clothes. I think of the clamour of the streets. It makes me sound very chauvinistic, but I think ours was the last generation where our parents really wanted to be us, but they couldn't pull it off. It's not like now, of course, where you can walk around and you can be 50 and you can actually sort of semi pull it off. To actually watch these adults scramble to raise their skirts, to do their hair, to actually wanna be their kids, that was something. That was really empowering. And Muhammad Ali he was one of the symbols of that time, 'cause everybody wanted to be Muhammad Ali. Just for a moment, you'd wake up and think, "I'd give almost anything just to look like that, be like that, act like that, talk like that, fight like that." And the whole world – black and white Americans, non-American, female, male – were saying, "I really wish I could be that guy." I don't think anybody was ever like that, before or since.

I think that Muhammad Ali represents nobility. I think he represents the way that sportsmen can be. We don't have anyone like him any more. We don't have anyone who understands that sport is a thing in itself and that it's also a metaphor, a metaphor about being in the world, how to be in the world, how to relate to yourself, to your body, to other people. He reminds people of a time when people could look at a sportsperson as being a champion outside the ring as well as inside, someone who walks the walk. He exemplifies a kind of genius on an everyday level. He inspired people to think, "If I can never be a boxer, I can still exemplify some of the qualities of this person in my life. I don't have to aspire to be world champion in the ring; I can be champion of the world in my life or with my kids." It wasn't about a guy who could buy five Porsches or who lived in a big house; he stood for something that mattered.

And it's good to be old enough to have that past, to be able to say, "Yeah, he's great, but boy! You'd have known him 30 years ago. You should have seen what it was like to have been a kid and run to the television set because Muhammad Ali was boxing on television and you knew he was gonna win." He'd stand in front with Howard Cosell, the sportscaster, who was a half a foot shorter than Ali, and Ali would say "Mmm... Let's say I'll do it in three." And he did! Not a scratch on him, no blood, didn't break a sweat. Nobody's done that since.

Of course, he had a reputation as a womaniser, but Martin Luther King was a womaniser. Robert F Kennedy was a womaniser. Malcolm X was a womaniser. Nelson Mandela's been married three times. This may sound really crude, but I really fancied Martin Luther King and Muhammad Ali. I could understand why people fell for them. But I don't think a person's private life has anything to do with their public stance, and I think we're too concerned with people's private lives. What's important is what they say and how they affect themselves in public. What they do after 6pm is their business.

But I don't think Muhammad Ali stopped any woman from doing anything she wanted, and obviously he didn't stop his own daughters, because one of them's a boxer.

We were the children of men who had been in World War II or the Korean

War. My dad was here for D-Day, so if you see the film *Saving Private Ryan*, you don't see the blacks 'cause they all got segregated. Black men didn't carry arms, except in emergency situations. Now, when the guys came out of that, they fought in the United States to make the rest of the country understand that black people were not cowards, so we grew super-patriotic, in that sense. We went off to fight for our country because we had to constantly prove ourselves. We had to constantly, constantly, *constantly* prove that we were not cowards.

But then my generation re-examined that and said, "Hang on a minute. We're not gonna go into the service. We're gonna break that bond." However, at the time, there was still conscription. You were drafted into the army. You didn't have any choice, so all of my friends from secondary school, the minute they graduated, if they didn't get accepted at university, they were classed as "1A", which meant that they went into the army. If you were black, you probably didn't get accepted in university, so you were cannon fodder automatically.

Now, if you didn't go into the service, you were automatically sent to Fort Leavenworth, where you were given hard labour. If you were black, you would probably be up against a whole lot of Southern redneck crackers, who made up the military class, so you would get triple hard labour. On top of that, your record would show that you refused to fight for your country, so you probably wouldn't be employed for the rest of your bloody life. You could have been attacked, as well, because people knew that Fort Leavenworth was where the deserters went, where the people who wouldn't go were sent, so to refuse to fight like Ali did could ruin your entire life. Now, we're talking about people who were 18 years old, who had the rest of their life to look at. So it was a huge risk that you took as a young person to say, "I'm defining the rest of my life by saying no." And for Muhammad Ali, a man who had a huge career in front of him – he was set to make millions of dollars – it could have been the end of the road.

But Ali was photogenic. He was funny. He knew how to use television. And he was black. He was the perfect person to stand up and say no. He had everything. He was a combination of people today – Tiger Woods, in terms of his ability; Naomi Campbell, in terms of his beauty; Richard Blackwood, in terms of his ability to work the medium. And he had something extra, that extra thing that you can't define. He could have been a movie star. He was everything.

Janet Guerin

Muhammad Ali Center Board Member

We lived near the Clays. Mrs Clay was a lovely lady. She would bring the birds out and they would sing and I would say to my grandfather, "Listen to her birds." Cassius was good looking, quick with words, the quips. I never paid attention to boxing. He used to be on TV, of course, fighting and on some little local programme, but when he became famous it was like he would want you to spend money to go to a boxing match! I never would have done that. But he made boxing more sophisticated. I heard from my father all about Joe Louis and how dumb he was and how he lost all of his money, and of course the people here that backed Cassius knew that. They were young entrepreneurs, and wealthy in their own rights, and made a vow that Cassius would not wind up that way. It's obvious that they put him on the right path. They were decent guys, decent business people. They had reputations.

At that time, Louisville was segregated, but there was no signs. You knew, but I don't know how you knew. I don't remember my parents or my friend's parents sitting down and saying, "Now, you do this. You don't do this." You just knew. But I had a very good childhood. The black community was very close-knit. Everybody either knew you real well or by extension. It was really like a little village set apart from the big village. Until I became involved in the whole immigration thing, the law, the marching, the sit-ins and became aware, I didn't know that you didn't have to like this. There used to be a cafeteria here that wouldn't let blacks in, and I remember marching past one day. We knew that there was some blacks in there, and so the whole thing was that we would stop in front of this cafeteria and then would be approached. "You're not allowed in." There were black people in there eating, but they were fair-skinned blacks. They went in and ate and nothing happened, and of course they thought that they were white. The black community wasn't as large, but it was very Southern in it's flavour. I think of it still as a Southern place.

When they changed the street from Walnut Street to Muhammad Ali Boulevard, there was uproar. There was a segregated private club on the street that did not want it to be changed. It was owned by these very wealthy people, movers and shakers, and they really put up a fuss. The club was only integrated ten or twelve years ago. It's only been recently that they let Jews and women and blacks even become members. Of course, it's totally illegal not to allow coloured members, but it was like the last bastion. They said, "Well we'd have to change our stationery." It's like a bank saying, "We have no money." You know that's what banks are for.

I remember my parents were not very pleased at hearing that Martin Luther King was abdicating. I felt just the opposite. I remember them telling me, "Well, if you get locked up with all this marching, don't call, because we are not coming to get you out for something that you knew not to do." But I was still young, I found out that, if you were under 18, you didn't go to jail; you went to some sort of holding place and you wouldn't have a record, so I just marched and marched and marched. My thinking when the war was going on was… I had a brother, five years younger than me, who graduated and went into the military and went to Vietnam. Every night, we'd watch the newscast to see how many people were dying.

When the Black Muslims had made the connection with Muhammad, it was like he had turned against us. He was no longer Protestant. He was no longer one of us. Then he steps out and says that he's not going to go to war, which puts him against the rest of the world. It didn't really bother me, but when he said that the Vietnamese hadn't done anything to him, I grieved. Why did my brother had to be over there fighting. For what?

A lot of people privately and publicly were against him. I don't think that people understood it. Some people were getting out of a draft through politics, money, going to Canada, but then and, in some ways, now, blacks were held to different standards, and I think that he was caught up in that.

An awful lot of blacks and Hispanics were killed in that war. And maybe privately people will say that defending your country is all about patriotism, but I don't care how patriotic you think you are. What sense did it make? When Ali said, "Those Vietnamese ain't done nothing to me," that was enough of a reason not to fight for me. Now, it's easy for me to say that because I am a female, and I wasn't going to get called up, but I think that it was very brave on his part. He was following his heart.

My grandfather and his brother lived two doors down from us. When you got sick and needed emergency help, you would call the police and they would take you to the hospital, if they could. My grandfather was a heavy, stocky man, and he had a stroke. My mother and me went round there and tried to call the police, and they wouldn't come round. They said they couldn't lift him. He was too heavy. Well, how could we take him ourselves, two women? But then the neighbours – including Ali – pulled in and took care of him, saying, "We will carry Mr Fall." When I think about that now, why would I be surprised that he is a man who is compassionate, who's a premier humanitarian?

When he was first famous, he built a house for his mother. Oh, it was big. Huge. Maybe you can say, "Well, that's what famous people do. Football players do this." But we didn't have this before. We had nobody like that. My grandfather used to keep my ten-year-old younger sister after elementary school, and when she didn't show up one day, of course, he was just horrified. He's huffing and puffing, out looking. Everybody's out looking. Then Muhammad comes up and my grandfather tells him, "My little granddaughter's missing!" He was sweating he was so worried. And Muhammad went out looking for her – and found her! She had gone home with another friend.

He was a teenager then. I knew him from my grandfather's neighbourhood, so it was like it is when you don't pay attention to your best friend's brother. He was just somebody in the neighbourhood. But when we graduated from high school, his Central prom was the same night as my high-school prom, and I remember that, until he had won the Olympics, he didn't have a date. I can remember seeing him that night, out at the glass-house, and he was gorgeous. I kept thinking, "Damn, is this the same guy who used to run along the side of the bus?" You know, you would just want to die. I saw him all the time when I was at my grandfathers, and I was at my grandfathers about two or three times a week. He was just another kid to me. But when he became famous, it wasn't exactly, "Oh, gee, I can't wait to turn on the TV and watch boxing." It wasn't exactly a girl's kind of thing. I don't think that any of us dreamed that he would be famous.

When he was at school, we thought of him as a nerd. He wasn't a football player or a basketball player, for God's sake; he was a boxer, and boxing to me was foreign. Girls went to the basketball games and the football games as cheerleaders and cheerers, but boxing was different. And then he was running along the side of the buses. Do you actually want to go out with somebody that chased along the side of a bus? When that happened, I remember slinking down in my seat – you know, here he comes. He'd wave and call out your name. How embarrassing! My friends at Central never talked about him as if he was somebody they wanted to go out with, and I wonder about all those women now – what do they think? I know what I think: a lot we know!

It was interesting when he started all that "Louisville lip" thing and the poems and, "I'm a pretty this, pretty that." We'd never thought this before. He mesmerised us, and finally the scales fell off our eyes, and, "Yeah, he is good looking." I watched him in the Olympics and I thought that he was really something. All of a sudden, he'd got bigger. When he was a neighbourhood kid, he was strong enough to help carry my grandfather, but not like he was when he was in the ring on TV.

I don't remember seeing a whole lot of Mr Clay. My father used to go to the barber shop on what is now Muhammad Ali Boulevard. I remember him saying how talented Mr Clay was, who painted a lot of signs on the blacks businesses. But I saw Mrs Clay. She was a homemaker, like I say, she had these birds in cages, and she'd put them out on her front porch and they would sing and she would talk to them. I thought that was really something. I don't remember saying a word to her, just watching her. She was a light-skinned woman, very attractive. My father and my mother say that Mr Clay was a dashing, good-looking, dark-skinned male that probably got Ali his swabby kind of style and profiling. But I think the inner core of him is his mother. She impressed me as being gentle. When I remember watching her with the birds, I think that that's the essence of him.

When I talk to white people I grew up with in Louisville that are my age, they don't even remember how racist and truly segregated the town was. It seemed like we were invisible. When Ali got outside this country and saw a whole different thing, where it didn't matter what colour you were, he had done something the rest of us at his age didn't do. He obviously forgot, when he came back here. But there was people there that will not let you forget. I have white friends who were my age and went to school with me, and one woman in my high school – a good, wonderful person – asks us, "How come we don't ever see you at Sutton Ferry Park?" And I knew that she was not trying to be vicious. She just didn't have a clue. My friend and I looked at each other and I said, "Patsy we can't. We are not allowed to go there. We are black." So, if the world is your oyster, you're not going to be aware if you have everything. How could I expect those people to notice? To them, I couldn't come because I didn't have the money to get there or just didn't want to go, not because it wasn't allowed.

Then I remember we moved to 1423 South 32nd Street when I was four years old, and the woman who lived nearby said she had to get away from the niggers and she moved just one block away to get away from us. I don't know if I could go back to that. I don't ever want to go back to that. For Ali, the shock was he went to another country as a young person and saw that, when you go someplace and you don't feel anything like that, it's like the scales come off. It's like they say, once you take them to Paris, you can't bring them back to the front. I can remember the first time I went overseas and found that things were totally different.

All that "I'm really pretty, I'm the prettiest man", though, the black people had quite low self esteem. The good looking guys knew they were good looking. They're the ones that stood around in the little groups at the parties and held their heads to the side – we call it styling and profiling. Ali would have been in that genre, and when his time came, he used it all. I think that he was a very astute observer of the human condition, and when it came time to use it, he used. He used his brain that nobody thought he had, and he used his quick wit. You couldn't make up those kind of poems. Ali has never deserted us. He is planning to move back here when the Center is completed, and here in the United States we'll get a chance to know what people in other countries feel about him and know what's happen because of that association.

But Louisville today is different from the city 40 years ago. A lot of that has to do with the city fathers and what they want for this city and also the people that have come in from other places that have relocated to Louisville and brought their progressive ideas. Is it fully grown? No. Are we ever finished? No. But it's a much more sophisticated city that Ali would find now than the one he left behind. I'm not sure we'd know him. We've maybe not cared as much as we should have or been proud as much as we should have. But there are some good and decent people here who wanted to make sure that he is honoured in his home land. So, much like the prodigal son, when he comes home, he gets what's due, he gets his fatted calf. It does us good, that we get to know what this man – who has been an ambassador around the world – has done for so many other people.

It's extraordinary that this nerdy guy is going to have an $80 million building built in his name, but I think it's wonderful, too. I can't wait until its up and running. My grandsons don't know him as a boxer. He autographed a photograph and I brought it to them and they said, "Oh, Muhammad Ali. We've learned about him in our conflict resolution class," and I never even got around to explaining to them about the boxing. That's what they're learning in school, and that's what the Center is about. Yes, the boxing will have a place in it, and the memorabilia and all that he has done, but this is his legacy. This is what people respond to when you go to this little town in the Gambia and this little town in the hills of Italy. When you mention you're from Louisville, Kentucky, in these places and they say, "Muhammad Ali," it does the heart good. He is a proud citizen and an example of our sleepy Southern town.

Richard Harris

Actor

I've broken an old law of mine to do this. I never take part in these biography features. I've been asked to do things on Marlon Brando, Kirk Douglas, Charlton Heston, Richard Burton, Peter O'Toole, Roger Moore and I refused to do them because I just don't think that actors have any legitimate place in history. I think we're a crowd of buffoons who get paid far too much money and run around pretending to represent the ordinary man. But we never meet the ordinary man; we're full of bodyguards and private jets and stretch limousines. We never see anything.

I feel the same about athletes. They haven't advanced humanity any more than actors, but Ali is a different case altogether. He is special, very special.

Actors and athletes are all diminished by time, forgotten. But Ali seems to have grown with time, he seems to have got bigger and bigger and bigger and more respected. Although his boxing career ended years ago, he seems to have become more illuminated in the world. Every single boxer in the world would sell their soul to become the heavyweight champion of the world. What did Ali do? He regained his soul by giving it up. He said, "I can be heavyweight champion, but if I can't walk into Harlem in 20 years' time and hold my head up high, what's it all been worth?" Very mature. To me, he stands shoulder to shoulder with Mandela, who is one of the world's great heroes.

I remember the first time I met him. I was in New York and he was training for the Foreman fight. His two favourite movies were *Man In The Wilderness* and *A Man Called Horse* and through a mutual friend he requested I come up to Deer Lake, his camp, and bring the two films so he could show his sparring partners and his crew up there. So I did. I think you must ask yourself why these are his favourite films, because this gives you a real insight into the man: *A Man Called Horse* was the first American movie to dignify the American Indian, the first to dignify a minority group in America and show them in this beautiful light; and *Man In The Wilderness* was about survival and dignity, a man who was up against the elements, up against his time.

When we went up there to see him, he was totally different to his image. He was the most gentle, the most hospitable, the kindest man. We were there for a whole day while he was training, and he knew what he was doing, he knew he was going to win, but he was a quiet, lovely, gentle man. He would talk to me about Irish poets like Yeats and so forth.

I think Ali was the most sincere person you could meet in your life. You can name any actor you like and I'll say, "Insincere. Don't turn your back on them." I've no time for actors, I don't mix with them. I don't go to the award shows, I don't go to their clubs. All my mates are guys from the streets. Genuine, decent, sincere people. Ali is that – he's got nothing to do with the people that are in my business.

He was always so sure of himself, though. He never felt that he suffered by comparison in anybody's company at all. It was wonderful to see him surrounded by kids, and he had the greatest respect for old boxers, but he always held himself with fantastic dignity. He didn't feel he was a token guest in anybody's house. He knew he was Muhammad Ali and he had this wonderful, gracious, almost sort of regal presence that you were in awe of. I don't care from what mountain you stood on to look down at him, you were in awe of this man and his presence.

I met Mandela in South Africa and in New York and he had that same thing. Frank Sinatra had an incredible aura about him, too. I remember because I knew Frank very well. But the difference was, when Sinatra made an appearance on stage, he walked into an aura created by the audience already. They left the space in the centre of the stage waiting for him to walk in and fill it. Whereas Mandela and Muhammad Ali brought the aura with them. They came on and you went, "Ooh, look at that."

I remember talking to Mandela about this. I said, "You know that you have this wonderful aura of saintliness about you. Were you like that before you were incarcerated or did that all happen to you in jail, through suffering and depravation?" He said probably yes, in jail. Similarly, Ali wasn't well treated. You know what happened when he won the Olympics. He was a black man in America, and he had to challenge that prejudice, he had to establish himself as heavyweight champion of the world. Then the Americans took his world titles away from him because he wouldn't comply with the American laws. Ludicrous. He grew from the experience, though, and I don't think he was ever angry at all, which is a wonderful quality. He had a lot to deal with, and now he's got Parkinson's and somehow or other he deals with that with dignity. I don't mean to be sentimental, but I'm actually proud to live in Ali's time.

I was in New York for the second Frazier fight in Madison Square Garden. It was absolutely extraordinary. I remember sitting there with a couple of friends and the place was a jamboree of excitement. When Smokin' Joe came out it seemed to be to a flashbulb, like from a Baby Brownie. But when Ali made his entrance it was like thunder and lightning, as if God had put a thousand watts of light onto this guy. It was absolutely astonishing and you were just in awe. He came into that ring and danced around, did his little shuffle and it was extraordinary. He was a great showman.

That was the only fight I saw, because with acting you are always all over the world. You go from location to location and then, when you've finished the movie, you're off selling it in Sydney, Australia one week, Christchurch, New Zealand the next week, and Bangladesh the week after.

Ali had that amazing capacity to change himself, I think. He literally created "Muhammad Ali", because he certainly was not that. It's like all of us. I was born Dickie Harris but I became Richard Harris – I invented a personality. Peter O'Toole invented a personality, Bono has invented a personality and Madonna never stops. Every year she invents something new. We all do it. But Ali was very smart. He invented a personality which drew the attention of the world to him while he could project his skills, which were quite enormous.

There's a great story about his shoes. We were up there in the camp to meet this man who danced about in the ring, was as agile as Nureyev, but I noticed he seemed to be sort of heavy-footed. Whether Ali was sparring or just walking around the bed, he seemed to be very cumbersome. I mentioned it to Angelo Dundee and he said, "So would you if you were wearing lead boots!" The day Ali signed for a fight, he put on these lead boots. He ran nine miles in the morning in them, he did all his sparring in them and he only actually took them off in the dressing room just before the fight so he could feel light on his feet.

He knew where he was going in that fight, though. He said to me, "I'm gonna take Foreman in the eighth round."

"How did you get the eighth?"

"Well, he can't count beyond two, so when he gets to eight he'll be totally confused, I'll have him by then."

Unbelievable.

I love boxing. I remember sitting up all night in Limerick, listening to Joe Louis fighting Billy Conn on the radio. There was no television in those days, but I have most of the great fights, even the black and white fights, on tape, like the Joe Louis, Arturo Godoy fight, the Tommy Farr fight, Tony Zale, Bruce Woodcock and Rocky Marciano. I love it.

It was the Sonny Liston fight where I noticed Ali. I couldn't believe my eyes. I had studied, in an amateur way, all the black and white films of all the great fights and all those great middleweight champions, but when I saw Ali fight Liston I couldn't believe what I was watching. For the size of the man, the speed and the grace he had was amazing. He turned the whole world's eye onto boxing.

I think boxing is a joke today without him. You can tell by the awe he's held in, in particular by other boxers. A couple of years ago, Ali was in London for the Sportsman Of The Millennium awards. He was staying under a false name at the Savoy, but I called his suite and said I'd like to come and pay my respects. I said, "I don't know if he'll remember me, but I came down with my wife, my brother and my best friend as his guest when he was training for Foreman."

"I don't know if Muhammad will remember you," this voice on the phone says, "but I certainly do – come on down."

I spent around two hours with him, but I wasn't the only one. Prince Naseem, Henry Cooper – you couldn't believe the stream of celebrities calling up to ask if they could come and see him and maybe spend half an hour in his company. It was like royalty. This sort of thing wouldn't even happen to the President of the United States, or the Prime Minister of England. But it happens to Ali.

Gil Scott Heron

Musician

There's a poem I wrote about Ali called 'Over The Hill'. It's a description of the bout between Muhammad Ali and George Foreman. I went downtown to see it with my brother and sat next to the coach of the Redskins at the time, George Allen, and he had a bunch of players that he called "the over-the-hill gang". But him and all of these people, they were rooting for George Foreman, saying that Ali was too old and he wasn't going to make it, so I was real pleased to have an opportunity to tell him that he shouldn't give up on over-the-hill people at the end of the fight.

I thought that was just a masterful thing, that Ali was not only physically the equal of the people that he fought but that he was smarter than a bunch of them, and that oftentimes the strategy that he employed was as important as the practice.

He has always been an inspiration to me, because he stood up for what he believed in. Every once in a while you're so overwhelmed by the size and the breadth of the government and the different people who are the authority figures that you forget yourself. You forget to stand up for what you've always wanted to say you're about. And when push came to shove, a better man stood up. I'll always love him and respect him for that. I believe that was a tremendous thing to do.

There were a lot of people like me in the '60s, angry about the situation in America, the race problem, but Ali was actually speaking out, and he was important because of his earlier international visibility. You can wait for your senators and your governors and your representatives to stand up and speak up when something is wrong – they didn't get where they are by being stupid; they know when things are wrong – but somehow they get mind-locked. And you forgive people who are even part of the same movement that you're involved in when they get mind-locked in and can't open their mouth at the right time.

We found a tremendous amount of courage within the things that Muhammad Ali did. He was sacrificing millions of dollars. Every time he said what they didn't want to hear, he gave it up – the prime of his life, the prime of his career – to stand up for what he believed in. There's not much of that going on no more. We've changed from a humanity of concepts to a humanity of substance – if you can see it and you can't buy nothing with it, then it's not important.

It's important to look back at people like Muhammad Ali. I put him in the same category with Nelson Mandela, who stood up for a whole lot of folks by just staying where he was and saying what he believed in. I would like to at some point be able to say that what we were doing has some kind of influence in the same direction.

Some people point out that I always spoke for a community or a nation, whereas the things that Ali was saying – "I am the greatest" – were personal, but that was all hype.

He refused induction into the armed services. He took up the Muslim faith and stood with the Nation of Islam at a time when they were under great pressure and great denigration. I'm saying, you're not going to be a silhouette of everybody you admire – you're not going to necessarily admire the clothes that one person wears or the hairstyle that one person has or their attitudes – but you have to admire their gut-level instinct to believe in something, say something and stand, sometimes against great opposition from the masses. This was a man whose opportunity was slipping away from him, because he was saying the things that he believed in. He said them anyway. Eventually, of course, the fact that he didn't want to go to war and didn't want to hurt nobody became America's feeling, and it said a lot to the young folks. Then, they got a chance to really listen to what he was saying.

I believe that there ain't but two races, men and women. I believe that, as soon as you need a blood transfusion, you find out that all the others count. If you're going Type A, you don't care if it's a purple midget. All people are beautiful who stand for what they believe in, like Lou Haymer. She was a short black lady who dared to go out there and lead folks. And we have songs about Dr King and David Walker. We have songs about Malcolm X. We have songs about people who actually stood up and said what they believed in. When I played Johannesburg in 1975, a lot of folks were saying I should wait because this is not the issue. But when Mandela was finally released, they said, "Well, you should play now, 'cause it was too soon earlier." I said, "Hell, he's been in jail for twelve years. *He* don't think it's too soon."

I'm not an African-American. I'm not a Caribbean-American. I'm a black American. That's a whole brand-new people, 'cause we've got European and Indian and Chinese and some others. We take special pride in the folks who come from us and say thanks that everyone in the world can agree with them. Muhammad Ali was just such a person, and we admire him for that.

I've been credited with giving birth to rap, but the first rap was done in 1789. You can go back as far as Pearl Sweetly and Jupiter Jones, who had rhymes and poems but didn't write them down. I believe that Ali's attempts at rap were a part of the spirit of the brotherhood, that he brought youth and excitement and enthusiasm for what he was doing to publicise and promote his activities. I don't see nothing wrong with that, but I don't necessarily believe a whole lot of folk are going to sit down and study Muhammad Ali's poetry!

We have to remember to separate the different parts of him. He was an athlete, he was a figure of some spiritual conviction and he was a showman. And he brought people to the fight. First, people wanted to go and see him win, then they wanted to go and see him get his ass kicked. He didn't care if they just came to fold up the chair, of course; he just wanted them to come right on in there, so he made himself known that way by saying what he was and doing what he said.

He was friendly with Malcolm X and then turned his back on him, while I wanted to contribute to everybody that wanted to do something positive for black people. I am not anti-white; I am pro-black. I play for the Black Panthers. I play for the Nation of Islam, Lou Haymer, anybody who stood up and said we need to do better and try to raise some money to help somebody. I did not want to join a particular group, because I didn't want any other group not to allow me to help. But I believe in anybody who stood up and said something.

I believe that it was Ali's right to stay with the Nation of Islam, if he wanted to. I believe that Malcolm X had the right to change his mind, if he wanted to. I think that, like with a lot of Baptists, Methodists, Presbyterians and Catholics now, I don't believe it's necessary to have anything to do with that. I believe it was another direction that Malcolm X wanted to go in, something that had more of a feeling for the community that he was living in than what the Nation of Islam were saying. I believe that both of them were doing what their religious convictions told them. I wished both of them well, and I was very sad to see both of them penalised the way they were.

Now, in the modern day, we're seeing the fruit of this labour. We have more opportunities than we ever had before. We have more students going to college and more people getting jobs than we ever had before. There's a widening gap in America between who can do something and who can't, between those who have and who do not have. And not just in terms of black people but in terms of white people, too. People often forget that there's some poor white folks out there, because they're concentrating on the ones that are considered the ethnic minority. I'm saying freedom ain't the easiest thing in the world. A hell of a lot of people would rather not have it, 'cause before we had freedom we could say we succeeded because of our initiative and our determination, and if we fail, it's 'cause we're black. They pull a rug from under us, once you get to make any choice you want to! Ali is now embraced by the whole world, but he was very unpopular when he made his stand. As long as you want to find out how this society got to be the way it is, you've got to see where it came from, and he was a very important figure in that.

My favourite fight of Ali's was the Rumble In The Jungle. I've got all them at home, and I look at them every once in a while, just to remind me of when I was doing this thing myself. But one of my favourite memories of him was when everybody else stepped forward at the Louisville induction ceremony and he stood his ground. I'll always remember that. What you believe in is more important to you than what anybody say.

I'm not sure that, if Ali hadn't been a boxer, he would have found another way. But there ain't no sense in putting him in no other suit. He wore that one and done it well. He was an athlete. He was a person who took extremely good care of himself and made sure he did damage where he showed up. I believe that, if he hadn't have been a boxer, he wouldn't have been Muhammad Ali.

Dustin Hoffman

Actor

I was a young actor, acting in Boston in the '60s with Bob Duval in a stock company, when I first saw Muhammad fighting Liston. I remember the derision he got from the sportswriters. He was not a popular man. He was considered a loudmouth. How dare a black man not know his place.

When he changed his name from Cassius Clay to Muhammad Ali, they refused to call him Muhammad Ali for ages. In the papers they continued to refer to him as "Cassius".

The next big thing I remember is when he refused to go into the service. He said at the time – a pretty conservative time – he knew he would not have to fight. He knew he would be boxing in the army, like Joe Louis did, so it certainly wasn't a matter of cowardice. And he said, "No Vietcong ever called me nigger." An extraordinary thing to say at the time. A brave and courageous thing to say. It reverberated with people, and one of the things it said to me was he spoke of the thousands of blacks who had fought and died for segregated America.

All entertainers and athletes understand what it is to give up three or four of your prime years. We understand just how precious they are; just think of it as being one third or one half of our careers, because that's what it calculates to. Ali gave up his best years for what he believed in. I witnessed all this while growing up during my years of unemployed actorism.

In 1970, my friend said, "Do you want to go see Muhammad Ali?" He had just fought Jerry Quarry and now he was going to fight a guy named Oscar Bonavena, an Argentinian, who had never been knocked down, never been knocked out.

"You wanna go to the weigh-in at Madison Square Garden?"

"Sure."

That was the first time I met Muhammad Ali – and he recognised me. I was shocked. I'd never been recognised by a great athlete before. He never said my name, though. He kept calling me "Midnight Cowboy, Midnight Cowboy". I thought, "Does he think I played that part?" Angelo Dundee was there and he said, "He loves westerns. That's why he went to see the movie – he thought it was going to be a western."

He did the weigh-in and he was going to fight that night. There was a college basketball team practising at the Garden and Muhammad asked them to throw him the ball. From mid-court, I swear, he hooked it and *swish*, it went in. Being an actor, I looked at him to see if he was surprised, and he was, but he covered it quickly and I thought, "There is something going on with this guy."

I asked Angelo Dundee if Ali was nervous. He said, "Well, he's been up since 5.30, taking the subway from the South Ferry to Harlem, shaking hands with everyone on the train – back and forth, back and forth – before the weigh-in."

Ali asked me, "What are you going to do for the rest of the day?"

"I don't know. I was going to go home."

Then we started talking about a film I did, called *Little Big Man*. I told him there was a documentary made of it, and I had it at the house. He said, "Let's go up and see it." This was in the afternoon and he was fighting that night! I kept saying, "Are you sure?" He said, "Yeah."

He brought about six cars full of friends over and we watched the documentary, because he loves anything about westerns. It was about 40 minutes, and then we went upstairs and were talking for about two hours before I realised that Muhammad was no longer there. I went downstairs where we had watched the movie, and there was my three-year-old daughter being coached on how to do pull-ups on the jungle gym. All the time the rest of us were upstairs talking, he was downstairs playing with my kid, and with a fight awaiting him in a few hours.

When I got to the fight, they said, "Do you want to go backstage to see Muhammad?"

"No, I don't want to bother him."

"But he wants to see you," they said.

I went back and there he was, in a very cold, very dark, little room, sitting on a stool. It was like he was meditating. I sat next to him but I didn't say anything and we sat in silence for a while. Suddenly, he looked at me and said, "You know, I'm getting a little old for this." I said I'd leave him alone, and I shook his hand and kissed him.

When he came out, the whole place – 19,000 people – chanted, "Ali! Ali! Ali!" I swear they had mixed emotions about him, but they chanted. Then Ringo Bonavena came out and there was nothing for him.

The fight was judged on a round system. The first round Ali lost. And the second, and the third. Between each round they were still chanting, "Ali! Ali!" In the fourth round they stopped the "Ali!" a little bit and by the fifth round there were none. By the sixth, he hadn't won a round which meant that he couldn't win on rounds. To win he had to knock Bonavena out, and he had never even been knocked down.

Then, in the seventh round, like some strange thing that could only happen in the movies, these 19,000 people switched from "Ali!" to "Ringo! Ringo! Ringo!". They wanted to be on the side of the winner. But in the middle of the tenth round, Ali not only knocked him down, but he knocked him out. I wish I could write so I could have described it better.

Ali is what all people are. He is like you, he is like me. He went up and down on the subway because he feeds off the people and he gives to the people. That is what he is all about. He is a child and remains a child. They are right when they say that fighting was his profession, peace was his passion and grace is his essence. How lucky we are to be a part of life where he has shone on us.

John Jay Hooker

Lawyer And Friend

I was the democratic nominee for Governor of Tennessee in 1970. We didn't win the general election – that was a very unusual election – but I thought there was a good chance that I'd get shot because Martin Luther King had gotten shot and Bobby Kennedy had gotten shot and I was a part and parcel of that circumstance. I also was strong against the war. It's not that I don't love my country, I just haven't got anything against those fellas over there, and I think it's the fair and right thing to do. So, I would walk around Tennessee campaigning and you could feel the hatred. People would walk across the street in order not to have to speak to me. That's part of what drew me to Ali. He is not thought of generally as being a civil righter, but to me he was the ultimate civil righter. He risked going to jail when he told the nation and the world that his country was wrong.

There are those that feel he didn't really understand the war and the draft and just wasn't interested, and then there are those that felt it was something that the Nation of Islam said, "We've got this heavyweight boxer on our side. Let's make a stand." And there are those that feel he knew exactly what he was doing and he felt it was wrong. But the most important thing that ever happens to a person is which womb they came from. Ali inherited his mother's basic good sense, kindness and love. But he also had a business side. People believed that Ali was not a person of intelligence, but truth is that I've never known a more intelligent person than Muhammad Ali. Einstein said that the ultimate intelligence is imagination, and Ali is the most gifted man, in terms of imagination. As a consequence, he had that facility to see around the corner. He didn't just look at something down the street. He perceived that the war was wrong and decided – on his own – to stand against. He wanted to use his position to resist it. He did it for that purpose and for no other.

There was hatred when he did that, just like there was when I ran for government. Fathers and mothers had their children over there, killing and dying, and anybody who cast aspersions on the war was thought to be unpatriotic, disloyal, callous, selfish, all the things you don't want to be and all the things that Ali is not today.

When Ali went to Harvard to speak to the students, they gave him a resounding ovation. But throughout middle America, they thought he was an awful traitor, a loudmouth, that we'd have been better off if there'd never been any Muhammad Ali. But he carried on. In addition to losing his source of income, and in addition to losing the opportunity to do the thing he loved the most, he had to contend with the proposition that he had been made into a villain. And this was no superficial image, either; it was for real. People were furious when the Supreme Court reversed the Trial Court and didn't send him to the penitentiary. It's hard to overstate the animosity.

And to boot, there was all the racism. The fact that he was a black man and saying this made him twice as vulnerable. It was the double whammy, and looking back on it, it's remarkable that he didn't get shot. Martin Luther King and Bobby Kennedy got shot because they were considered to be disloyal to the country. Muhammad Ali was considered more disloyal than either one of them.

At that time, Bobby's brother, Jack, was very much entertained by Muhammad, but I don't think he ever thought it was possible to deal with him on a political basis and embrace him for fear of what he might say or what position he might adopt. Between '63, when Jack died, and '68 when

Bobby got assassinated himself, Bobby came to feel that he couldn't afford to do that, either, that it wasn't politically feasible to be involved with Ali. Ali wasn't trying to be involved, but there's no question that he had tremendous respect for the Kennedys. He thought they were good for the country and appreciated their stance on civil rights.

Of course, after the Sonny Liston fight in '64, Ali publicly associated himself with the Nation of Islam. If you were a cynic, you could say that that was the smartest marketing decision anybody ever made. All of a sudden, he reached out and took a constituency on a worldwide basis. Who could have thought of a more intelligent thing to do if you wanted to sell tickets? There was a wrestler from Kentucky named Gorgeous George, who had the same sort of personality as Ali, and he used to say that, if you're going to be a wrestler or a boxer, you have to sell tickets and you have to sell to two types of people: those who come to see you win and those who come to see you lose. As a consequence, Ali learned that, "If I rabble-rouse and make them mad, they'll come to see me lose, and when they come to see me lose, they gotta buy that ticket." So he created a world-wide franchise by being a Muslim that he couldn't otherwise create by being the great grandson of a slave.

It soon became apparent that there was a method to his madness. It was comparatively small to start with, but it was there. He knew how to look like he was crazy, and he knew how to exploit that. If your opponent thinks that you use good judgement and you protect yourself, that's one thing, but if he thinks you're crazy, that there's nothing you won't do, it scares him. Ali had learned how to put this act on and make people think he was crazy. First, he directed this at his opponents, but then he directed it at the people who defamed him. This was a way of one-upping them. It became obvious this fella had a game plan, that it wasn't just an accident, that that guy who was standing there in Miami shaking his fists, laying down there on the ground, joyous with jubilation, was a man of substance. As he took on these substantive positions, his constituency began to grow – slowly at first, because people didn't want to understand. Racism was rampant in America as was disgust for anyone who didn't support the law the war everywhere. Ali not only won; he won on his terms.

But all that apart, for Muhammad Ali, God Almighty comes first. You can count on that. I've never known a person with whom I more emphatically believe that. Changing religion wasn't just an ingenious marketing gimmick; that was just the unsolicited consequence. He changed his religion because he believed in it and still does today.

The Nation of Islam are often perceived as being a much bigger organisation than in fact they were, and yet the American people thought they were extremely dangerous, that they were unpatriotic, that you couldn't be a part of the Nation of Islam and be a fully-fledged member of this nation, that there was a conflict of interest. He had a tremendous uphill fight.

The way I see it, he was enormously gifted by God Almighty. He not only had a balance athletically, in the boxing ring; he had a balance between his ears. He was a man of a tremendous common sense. At the same time, he marched to his own drum about his religion, his relationship with the Muslims, about the way he wanted to live his life. He had the facility to be involved, but he didn't have the need to run out and seek headlines in this world of civil rights. He didn't think that was his role. He thought that his role was to carry on doing what he was doing. No other black artists or sports people seem notable in the sense that they stand up in the same way that Ali did. They didn't have the courage, the form or the vision that he had. Today, sportsmen and -women are effectively politically neutered. They are reluctant to make political statements because the money is too important to them. Of course, men and women are undeniably the children of circumstance. Ali came along at *that* moment and was on the stage at *that* moment. But the zest doesn't exist now. There is no cohesive civil rights effort in America today. Many of the civil rights leaders are part and parcel of the establishment. The consequence of that is that there is nobody who's going to do what Ali did. Perhaps not even Ali could do it at this time. He had to do it in the context of his circumstance, which was so pregnant with opportunity for leadership.

He picked the right fight when he picked the war to vent his disgust with the indecency of man's treatment of his fellow human beings of whatever colour, wherever in the world. He reached across racial lines, he reached across intellectual lines and he reached across religious lines, and he was situated to do that in a way that nobody else could. The so-called celebrities, whose positions emanated simply from being celebrities couldn't do it. *His position emanated from the fact that he had a different passport to everybody else. His passport was that he was the spitting image of courage, of a man who'd take them all on.* The consequence of that was that he had an enormous glamour, which permitted him a licence that other people didn't have.

Of course, it was also a consequence of an extremely fortunate series of events. He's a heavyweight, which is the most popular in boxing. You couldn't get a more Shakespearean environment – a square, twenty by twenty, and no place to hide. One man wins, one loses, but both get hurt and both on occasion almost die, so the winning is less well defined. Ali could well have won the fight in Manila and died in that ring before he got out. There was another side to winning, the cost of winning could be death itself.

Some of his success was due to a series of remarkably fortuitous events coming together. Some say he didn't wanna come out in the fifth round of the Liston fight, that Dundee pushed him out. That was a defining moment. Had he not won that fight, we'd never have heard of him again.

Winston Churchill is one of my heroes. There were so many moments in his life in which the ball bounced the wrong way or could have put him out of business, but somehow he kept coming back. There was something, some will inside of him, some urge never to give up his goals. I think Ali, too, had goals that were very well defined to him, not only intellectually but emotionally. He had a desire to be regarded as the greatest fighter in the world, and he pursued that task. And as a consequence of pursuing that task, certain things happened to him, some dreadful such as that thing with the war. But that turned out to be, in many ways, the greatest experience of his life. It gave him the opportunity to become the world's greatest fighter outside the ring, to show that he had principles and that he was willing to pay the price.

And more than anybody else, Ali was willing to pay the price. That's not to take away from Martin Luther, who paid the ultimate price, and many others – like Congressman John Lewis from Atlanta, and those people who were involved in the marches. But to me, Ali was a man who had the facility to sublimate his ambition, to share it with everybody else and lead those who needed a leader, to help those who needed help and to create a fountain of energy and faith. With him, it's real. He does believe in God Almighty and he does believe that he was sent down here for a mission and he does believe that he was working on it on a day-by-day basis.

He's a man with a number of messages, and they are seen by many in different ways. I watched him fight Holmes in Las Vegas in 1980. About two weeks prior to that, he had come to Nashville, Tennessee, to a roast for my 50th birthday, and at the roast he made fun of me for getting him to come to Nashville and break training. "Why should I come? You're a white fella. Why should I come to Nashville and break training? I'm fighting the other greatest fighter in the world. What the hell, what am I doing here?" He was tremendously humorous, making fun of me, making fun of himself.

A couple of weeks later, I went to Las Vegas to see the fight, absolutely convinced that he's going to win because, when he was in Nashville, he had told me that he thought he was in tremendous physical condition and he thoroughly anticipated winning. But Holmes hits him and hits him. The lights are so bright, you could see the perspiration fly two feet off his face as Holmes kept hitting him. It was soon obvious to me that something's wrong. My man's not himself. I sat there and watched my friend get beat up to the point that I thought he would definitely get hurt.

After the fight was over, I go back to the suite and there were all the people that you have back there, so I just sat in the corner perhaps for a couple of hours. Finally, his great friend and photographer Howard Bingham comes out and says, "Champ says come in. He wants to see ya." So I go in and he's sitting on the edge of this bed. His feet are hung over the end and he can't lift his head. So I get down on my knees on the floor and look up at him, and he's looking down at me, and I'm just absorbing the pain of what's just happened to my friend. I'm so distraught that tears start rolling out of my eyes. And then he takes his hand, puts it on my face and wipes my tears away, and he says, "JJ Hooker. JJ Hooker, don't cry. Don't cry. I'm still Ali." That's who he is. He's together. He's comfortable in his own skin, even though he'd just been humiliated, beaten up, hurt, he still hadn't lost sight of that inner belief in himself, in God and in what he was doing.

There have been moments in my life in which I have faced some things that hurt me greatly, but I've been able to put my head on the pillow with the thought that I'm still John Jay Hooker, and that's an inspiration that I got entirely from this man. If you have that inner strength, that inner reliance, defeat is not the end; it could well be the beginning. And so I think his message begins with this inner understanding of who he is and then this profound longing to serve God and to please God and to do so by acting out any kindness that he can that elevates the spirit of somebody else.

I first met Ali through a man named John White Brown, who was Governor of Kentucky and chairman of the board of Kentucky Fried Chicken. At the time, I was chairman of the board of an oil company called STP. John White called me and asked me to start the Muhammad Ali Boxing School using some of STP's money and some of his money. So I got the opportunity to meet Ali on a one-on-one basis and became enthralled with him.

On my first encounter with him, I picked him up on the STP jet to bring him to Kentucky. On the flight, I told him that he was my hero, and he looked at me askance – he couldn't believe it. He said, "You're a white fella. I'm not your hero."

"Yes, you are," I said.

"Why? Why am I your hero?"

"Because you stood up against the war and you were willing to take the punishment," I said. "Then you get in the ring with these fellas, and they're obviously trying to hurt you, and I have great admiration for that."

By this time, he thought, "Well, maybe he's *not* kidding me. Maybe I *am* his hero. So he opens up and says, "JJ Hooker—" he always called me by my full name, even that first meeting "—do you know about the half-dream?"

"Pardon me?"

"Do you know about the half dream?"

"No," I said.

"When I fight," he says, "I get in a half dream. Somebody hits you so hard that you don't know where you are. You see all these lights and your head is swimming and you can't think, and so you drop your hands. Sometimes, they hit me so hard that the alligators start playing the saxophone and the snakes start playing the drums and I don't know what happened. I'm in a half dream."

"When I get in the half dream, I put my hands up and so they can't hit me. All these other boxers, they put their hands down. He said I don't know why I put my hands up – nobody knows why I put my hands up – but I do, and it makes me the greatest."

I said to him, "There's a poem called 'If' by an Englishman named Rudyard Kipling and there's a line in it that says, 'If you can hold on when there's nothing within you except the will that says, hold on—'"

He says to Bingham, "Bingham, write that down."

So when we get there, he has this ceremony with his high-school mates, the greatest show of affection both ways I ever saw, and we spend the day together, go to the races. A couple of weeks later, he calls me and asks me to come to Chicago.

When I get to Chicago, he's in this reception line, so I come through the line and he says, "You. If you can hold on when there's nothing within you except the will that says, hold on," and then he starts trying to talk me into going to Manila. Of course, I don't end up going, but I think about him every day.

Finally, the fight comes. In the 13th round, *whap-whap!* Frazier puts him in a half dream. If you look at the tape, you can see he rocks back, he's gone. It looks just like he said – up go his hands. Frazier can't knock him out. During the 13th and 14th rounds, Dundee wants to stop the fight. Ali says no, gets up, goes back in the ring. Finally, his eyes snap into focus and he goes to work. Then, in the fourteenth round, *whap-whap-whap!* He's got Frazier in the half dream. The round lasts 30 seconds after that. Frazier's gone. He can't answer the bell for the 15th round.

After the thing's over, someone puts this microphone into Ali's face and says to him, "Well, Ali, what do you think about Frazier now?"

Ali says, "The first thing I wanna do is talk to Elijah Muhammad," and he talks a bit about his religion to the camera. Then he lifts his head up and says, "I wanna say hello to my friend John Jay Hooker." And you can imagine, I'm in this movie theatre in Fort Lauderdale, Florida, watching this fight.

The next day, I call him up and he's asleep, but he comes to the phone with this wonderfully cheerful, clear voice: "John Jay Hooker! 700 million people, John Jay Hooker! Did you see it?"

"Of course I saw it," I said. "The greatest thrill in my life! And there were 5,000 people in the theatre. I was so thrilled that I started to jump up and say, 'Folks, I am John Jay Hooker!'" He just laughed. Then I said, "How did you happen to do that?"

"John Jay Hooker, if you can hold on when there's nothing within you except the will that says, hold on…"

My life has been greatly enriched by knowing Ali, and there are a lot of others who feel the same way. I had the opportunity to play only a small role, compared to others. I remember that, at one point, he wouldn't take his medicine, Lonnie kept calling me up and saying, "Look, John Jay, come up here and talk him into taking his medicine. Please."

"Lonnie," I said, "if you can't talk him into taking his medicine, how can I talk him into it? You're facing him at breakfast. You sleep in the same bed with him. If you can't talk him into taking medicine, I can't talk him into taking it." But I went up there anyway. "Ali, why don't you take this medicine? It'll make you better." At the end of the third day, Ali said, "JJ Hooker, I wanna ask you a question. Do you think that if God didn't want me to be shaking, I'd be shaking?"

He's a man of peace. He's turned his attention to God. Now, the hand that knocked people out pets them. The man who acted crazy is now very humble. The man who was totally invulnerable in the eyes of many is now very vulnerable, and yet he wraps it all together in indomitable courage. He's not deterred by his shakes. He's not intimidated by acceptance. He's figured out that it's OK to be happy, that he doesn't have to fight any more, that he's no longer a fighter. He wants to lead by example.

James Earl Jones

Actor

I have a recurring nightmare that I, just a farm kid, am going up to a professional boxer. My only aim is to get into the ring and approach him. Then I wake up in a cold sweat. The fighter is not Ali, but I'm sure the nightmare comes from the experience I had of getting into the ring and approaching the great fighter Muhammad Ali. It was just a stunt. In '84, Junior had heard that Ali was in the neighbourhood, when we were doing the film of *The Great White Hope*, a film about Jack Johnson, and he invited Ali to come by the set and we stripped down to our waists. We were both were then proud to strip down to our waists. We were in great shape. Well, I was proud to be in great shape – he's always in great shape. We put on a pair of gloves and got into a real ring and started dancing around. Then Ali said, "Come on, James. Throw me a good hook." I said to myself, "Now, he won't hurt me. He's saying throw me a hook." I said, "OK, here we go," and I threw him a hook. He raised his hand. I broke my thumb. I broke my thumb against his defensive gesture. So my nightmare came true!

But I adored Ali from the beginning. When I first met him, we were doing the play of *The Great White Hope* on Broadway. He had been on Broadway previously in a play called *Big-Time Buck White*. He got up on the stage and started reciting some of my lines. I've loved him ever since then. I feel I've been friends with him ever since. I never hang out with him – I wouldn't know how to hang out with him – but occasionally, when we're in the same city, we'll find a way to get together.

The last time was in his own city of Louisville. I did a cameo role in a movie about his life called *The Greatest*. I played Malcolm X. I looked nothing like Malcolm X, of course, but I had the great pleasure of saying a few lines in his movie. But the strongest memory I'll always have is getting into a ring with gloves on and approaching this great fighter like I know what I'm doing, thinking he won't hurt me.

Ali felt a great affinity with Jack Johnson. He was a man of great hubris. I'm afraid our movie *The Great White Hope* dealt only with the social issue, which is small potatoes – the guy has a white girlfriend and the boxing establishment doesn't like him. But he went up against the establishment – that was really backed by the US government – in the name of sport, in the name of the heavyweight champion title, and he did things that Joe Louis chose not to do and Patterson and all the great fighters since then have chosen not to do. Not even being that hostile, but just "I am who I am. I will do what I do in my reality. When I enter that ring, that's my reality." That was Ali. He came backstage when he saw the play and he said, "James, you remove the issue of the white woman and you replace it with the Vietnam War, and that's my story. Come on up and get in the audience. I'm gonna go on the stage and do that role." And Ali did it with much more charm, but they were similar in that they were heavyweights, they had *chutzpah*, they had hubris and they dared to be themselves. So when Ali said, "That's my story," in a way he was right.

My father was a prizefighter before he was an actor. There's a photograph of him in the *New York News* when he was fighting as an amateur in New Jersey. He'd won the fight, but you couldn't tell who the hell he was, he was so beaten up. But he raises his own hand in victory. I don't know how much that hurt him. He never encouraged me to be a fighter, but then he never encouraged me to be an actor, either. But when I was doing *The Great White Hope*, my father was very helpful to me, in terms of explaining the

Ali sits before the Illinois State Athletic Commission, February 1966, following his remarks against the Vietnam War. He said he was sorry for protesting after being reclassified as 1A in the draft. However, he refused to make an apology for "unpatriotic" remarks.

Questioned by the press outside the Louisville draft board, March 1966.

Ali listens to the words of Elijah Muhammad at a Muslim rally, August 1966.

Ali and Cleveland Williams feel each other out before their fight at the Houston Astrodome, September 1966.

Mobbed by the press after an all-white jury found him guilty on charges of refusing to be inducted into the US armed forces, 20 June 1967.

A crowd protests for Ali outside the US Army induction centre in Houston, Texas, April 1967.

asceticism that such athletes have to go through in their training to purify themselves in mind, heart and body. But we always had boxing gloves around the place, and my uncles all said, "Your nose is too pointed and your knuckles are too sharp to ever be a boxer. You'll just be flattened." I took their advice.

I don't think that, even if I had been a fan, I would have watched all of Ali's fights. The last fight I thought I'd ever see, I saw a Manchurian fighter get killed in Spain. He got into the ring with a very large Spaniard. I knew something was wrong from the beginning, because his second in his corner would never let him sit down or drink water. Eventually, he got decked. He never got up. I was filming *The Great White Hope* at the time, so that was a breath of reality for me. I sort of swore I'd never go to a fight again, but I have since. I saw the Tyson fight with Holyfield. I even have a little gymnasium in my home which I use in a feeble attempt to stay or to get in shape. And I have a big photo of Ali standing over Sonny Liston. I'm not comparing that with the fight where Tyson misbehaves on Holyfield's ear, but you can see in that picture with Ali the proper way to express that kind of dominance and fury. He's knocked the man down and he's standing over him, daring him to stand up. It's a beautiful photograph. His body is beautiful. I had that in my gymnasium as an inspiration.

It's a brutal sport, but it has this basic appeal, for the same reason that the whole society were into who held the heavyweight crown in Jack Johnson's time, and certainly in Ali's time. I think Ali revived the importance of that symbol of dominance. Otherwise, except for a few fighters like Sugar Ray Robinson and others who had finesse, who had craft, it's a slaughter. But human beings have to have some places, some arena, where we can exercise our the need for championship. It's that simple. We have a lot of sports that go for the championships every season, but boxing is a symbolic sport about who's the best, one on one, *mano e mano*, And that's why it's always been important. I wouldn't do it and I wouldn't want my son to do it, but I respect those who can do it well.

My only comment about the racism in boxing is that, like cycling in Europe, it's a way in America for a young man to get out of the ghetto. There's nothing about African-Americans that make them better fighters. I think we're paying too much attention to what colour the guy is before he gets in the ring. Once he gets in the ring, it's not important. I don't like to give race too much credit. It's not that I want to ignore it, because it is a part of reality, but it's not an important reality. So I think it's just a passing factor, the fact that, when you turn on the TV, you see a lot of coloured people in the ring. In many cases, they have no better way to elevate themselves, in terms of better pay and better status.

My biggest problem was when Ali became a member of the Nation of Islam. I always think the phrase "Cassius Clay" whenever I say "Muhammad Ali". For me, he is the American Cassius Clay. Of course, the Nation of Islam had their own particular reasons for dropping names that didn't have a genetic, cultural and ethnic root, but I like being American and I like having an American name, but that's just my chauvinism. When he made that, choice I thought how brave he was. And he was a conscientious objector, too. That's an act of extreme bravery. As an ex-soldier myself, I know that my fellow veterans have a hard time with my saying that. But it takes a lot of bravery to give up your status and say, "I am not gonna be a combatant for this nation. I'll find some other way to serve." People have comments to say about men who want to become President, but that was an act of courage that we are yet to understand, objecting to the war and to being a warrior. Of course, it would not have been my choice, and not out of any great patriotism on my part. I just thought, "This is my home and this is my army." It was very simple for me. I didn't get all wound up as a patriot about it.

I stayed out of the civil rights movement. I didn't think I was very good at carrying a placard, and I was hoping to find some other way to serve. I did that for myself, but I am not sure I did it to the satisfaction of activists. I'm out of step with a lot of that. I think that activism has lost its way. I don't think Ali was that much involved, either, but he had the label. He took on the mantle, largely because of Malcolm X and the Muslim faith. But he's not a big mouthpiece about it. He has other things he loves to talk about and poeticise about, but it's not that he's disinterested.

His new faith didn't define him, except to give him another name. I didn't see a great change in him. We all like to have better diets and better habits, whether they come from a religious route or just knowledge of good medicine. I entered the army just as the Korean War was winding down, and so I expected to go to war and die just after I got out of college. You don't put on that uniform without thinking, "I could die with this uniform on." That's a certain kind of fate. It was good for me to confront the issue of death that young and realise that it wasn't all about fear. Like, "What is this commitment worth to me, to my family?" I encourage young black people to study the Civil War beyond just to find a reason to be disenchanted about Lincoln, disenchanted about the fact that the war was more about the union than our freedom.

So when I came out of the army, I brought home enough weapons I was trained to use that I could have held the block in the city I lived in, New York City, if there was a revolution – and I fully expected there to be one, frankly, when I heard Malcolm X saying to the American black people, "Get your shotguns." I prayed that I'd find a way to serve the cause of civil rights without ever having to use those instruments. Then, when I became an actor, I thought, "Well, maybe this is that chance." I'm not gonna try to justify it. For me, it's an alternative way of serving. Whether it pleases others or not is not important to me.

Ali had found his own way to serve. The fact that he was banned from boxing was part of a national tragedy, the same way that Paul Robeson was banned from acting and singing. We were not big enough to handle it. I think we *are* big enough, but we didn't *feel* big enough. Americans often don't feel big; we feel puny and inferior, unlike the British – they've always felt big and superior!

I think everybody of my generation who is male and was at least six foot tall and robustly built had hoped that there would be a film about Malcolm X and we could be in it. I remember one in particular, Billy Dee Williams, contending for the part with me. We were both hoping to get a shot, but it didn't happen in our time. But it did happen, eventually, with Denzel Washington, and that's important. Anyway, I researched it some, although I never met him.

When Alex Haley wrote the autobiography of Malcolm X, I went to see him.

It was a winter and under four feet of snow where he lived in Rome, New York, but I trekked from the airport to house and knocked on his door. He opened it and said, "What do you want?"

"Mr Haley," I said, "I just read your book, and I think it would make a wonderful movie." I didn't say I wanted to be in it. "Can I come in and talk?" And I became a friend of Alex's from that time on. Without becoming a compatriot of his, I stood in admiration of Malcolm. And I stood in some confusion, too. I didn't understand the need for separatism. I think they chose the same states that these white separatists choose, Utah and Montana. Everybody who wants to be a separatist wants to go out there, where there's not much communication. The blacks of the Muslim movement wanted to do that. I didn't understand that. Why would you separate yourself? And I knew that there were some principles that probably didn't originate from Malcolm's mind but he was obliged to propagate. There was some foolishness that I didn't understand.

But otherwise, he was a brave man. We still celebrate Martin Luther King in most corners of the world, but it took a long time for the pacifist civil rights leaders to venture into the South. Being from Mississippi, I said, "Why isn't Malcolm raising hell down there?"

Of course, Muhammad Ali was friends with him for a while, but even as a student reading about it from such great writers as Alex Haley, I don't understand the inner workings of that relationship. I can only speculate, and it's not proper for me to speculate about something that important. I don't know what went wrong between Malcolm X and Elijah Muhammad, either, and it doesn't interest me. That's like the man and his wife, the man and his best friend. That's their business. But once Ali took on the mantle of the faith, if the faith said that Malcolm X was an outcast, then he had to say that. It looks like Ali had to make a decision between the faith and a very deep personal friendship. He was torn. But I'm afraid the only person who can address that is Ali himself, and I would not want to second-guess what was going on there, except to say that I think a faith like the Black Muslim faith was born on a political need, and it still has a strong political agenda, a strong political framework. You never know what's politics and what's belief in the almighty. I'm confused about a lot of what goes on in the

Middle East because of that. I'm not quite as confused about what goes on in Northern Ireland, 'cause that's clearly very political. They don't argue about whose concept of God is correct. They're arguing about power and who has it and who don't, who deserves it and who don't, and those are important things to sort out. We haven't found better ways yet.

When I was acting with Ali in *The Greatest*, I certainly didn't hang out with him. I don't hang out with anybody. I met him on the set. We enjoyed working together. We didn't have time to talk, 'cause I had a very short role and they'd fly me in, fly me out, and Ali had a lot of lines to learn. We were staying at a hotel in Miami called the Fontainebleau and, wow, this is a great hotel. I went down to get a shoeshine one day, and there's Beau Jack, the great lightweight champion fighter, shining shoes. My dad and my granddad used to talk about this guy. I gotta get my shoes shined and I get them shined by Beau Jack! I said, "How much?" and he said "$500." I said, "OK, I'll go upstairs and get it." I don't think I ever told Ali this. He probably would have said, "You fool, nobody should pay $500 to get his shoes shined."

I love Ali, personally. This whole country loves him. We got a little confused about the Vietnam War, but we were also confused when other people of sense said, "That's a wrong war." I was lucky that I had retired from the military by then, but believe me, I was ready to send my brother to Canada over that war. We all had a lot of confusion about it. I was in North Africa, and the kids on the streets there recognised my accent and said, "Hey, Yank. Do you know Cassius Clay?" That's all they wanted to know – did I ever shake hands with Muhammad Ali, did I know who he was, did I ever meet him. He was an idol and always has been. The other stuff, the religion, standing about the war, his colour – it's all irrelevant. And the proof is how we adore him now. That adoration has always been there, partly because of his mouth. This is a kid who just said it, "I'm the greatest," and he said it with poetry. I don't mean just the poems that he wrote but with the poetic energy, the poetic spirit. He doesn't say a lot now, but I sense he's at peace with that, because who wants to shoot off their mouth all the time? He was trapped in his own mouth, and now he can be quiet, and there's a twinkle in his eye that says he's probably enjoying a lot of that peace. I had lunch with him and his family when we were in Louisville. He would nod off. You'd think you were having a conversation with him and he nods off, and his wife or Howard Bingham will say, "Don't wake him, 'cause he sometimes wakes up and he goes crazy, you know. He'll start fighting." So you're tempted to go and wake him to see how crazy he will get and see if he will jump up. He wasn't nodding off at all! But he loves to do that. It sounds like a kid-like thing to do, but he loves to play with you. But that identifies the way we have always loved him and always will. It's that simple.

People ask me, if he hadn't had this great boxing talent, if he would have found another route. I really don't know. I became an actor. I don't think he ever fulfilled himself as an actor, but he might have. We all learn, and he would have learned. Arnold Schwarzenegger learned beautifully how to render that craft, after all. I'm not saying that acting would have been his best thing to do, but he could have done it. He would have projected something to us. That's the nature of the person he is. And he would also have been capable of being very quiet. You can see it now, he's capable of being very quiet. But he's in strong communication with mankind. Like, he has said that boxing is just a preparation for his current role, the Ali Center. That's exactly what I mean. If he hadn't been a great fighter and a great entertainer, he would have found some other communication with humanity, with fellow mankind.

Tom Jones

Singer

I never saw Ali in his prime. I met him in around '69, during the time when he was forced out because of his beliefs. But I mean I was very much aware of him, because he brought back heavyweight boxing. Since he's retired, it's not the same. But I was fortunate enough to know him and become friendly with him, and that was very important because I think he was the greatest heavyweight that ever lived, and he had strong beliefs and lived by them. Yes, he was an entertainer, too, but he could back it up, and he knew that he had to.

Boxing before Ali got into it was at a bit of a lull. There wasn't much happening. He realised that he had to get something going, not only just to get into the ring but to get people interested enough, and so he made that happen. When he fought Sonny Liston, he wasn't just saying, "Oh well, I've gotta get something going here so that people will come and see it"; he wanted people to come and see him beat Liston. And he wanted to get Liston riled up enough to fight him, which is exactly what he did. Even if you liked Sonny Liston or the other men he fought and thought, "They are going to destroy Ali," they never could, because he was so good. He said he was and he proved it.

At first, I didn't like that. You think, "Can he back up what he's saying?" Until he fought Liston, he hadn't really fought anybody, so it was, like, "Who is this young guy to say he can do all this?" But then, when you saw him do it, that's when the respect built for Ali, because there was nothing else you could do. You couldn't fault the man, because he was as great as he said he was.

As far as I was concerned he was a great boxer and he lived by his beliefs, which I think is very important. If you feel strongly about something, you don't compromise. When he refused to fight in Vietnam, his career was on the line. They say if he *had* gone, maybe they would've just had him there, you know? Not made him fight. But it wasn't enough for him. It wasn't that he was scared to go to the front; he didn't agree with that war. So he put his career on the line, lost the most important part of his boxing career, when he was at his peak. A lot of people wouldn't have done that. They would have found a way around it, in order to keep boxing, but he said, "No. I don't believe in it. This is what I want to believe." And he didn't care if people were gonna dislike him for it. As it happened, it was a split thing anyway at that time – so people were gung-ho about Vietnam, but there was another movement that was on his side, that didn't believe in it, so he became a part of that group. Some of the old soldiers, the old diehards, they were more for Joe Frazier than they were for Ali, when that fight came up, so that became something more than just a fight. Frazier was representing one group of people and Ali was representing another, so it was like a war itself.

When I first met him, I was playing in Cherry Hill, New Jersey, where he was living at the time. He came to the show, and… Well, once you're in a room with him, his charisma is even bigger than what you see on television. You feel his presence. Every time he came to see me, he would repeat my name all the time – "Tom Jones! Tom Jones!" That night, I said to him, "Why are you saying that?" Apparently, it was the first thing his daughter said when she used to see me on television. He remembered that. And we became friends from that day forward.

When he was going to fight Larry Holmes, he was training outside Atlantic City, where I was performing, so he invited me to his camp, and we thought it would be a good idea to have a knockabout, because he knew that I had been in a ring as a kid and that, if I could get in there with him, it would make an interesting photograph. So I got in there with him and said, "Look, now take it easy." I mean, a big man like that, if he makes a mistake, you know? And he said, "Well just try and hit me."

"OK."

So we start moving around, and I was just doing it for the pictures, but he wanted me to try and hit him, so I threw a left jab and a right cross – not hard, 'cause I didn't want to piss him off! But they both connected and by reflex he shot this left jab at me. I was backing off at that point, 'cause I realised what had happened, and he caught me in the teeth, moved them a bit, 'cause we weren't using gumshields. I thought, "Uh-oh! I'm not going to do *that* again!" But he was telegraphing everything that he was throwing at me, playing with me. But it was enough for me just to stop the weight of his arms when he was hooking, and he was letting me know they were coming! So I thought, "Jesus Christ, can you imagine being hit by this man if you don't know when it's coming?"

Then he said 'OK, give me a tap and I'll fall down." So I did, and there was this picture of me standing over him, like he had done so many times with his opponents. The funny thing was, I'm friendly with Gene Kilroy, who used to work with Ali, and he told me that, when the picture went out worldwide, Ali's fans were writing in saying they thought it was about time Ali packed it in, 'cause Tom Jones could knock him down!

When we became friendly, I would go to see fights with Ali in Vegas. On one occasion, Larry Holmes was there. "That's Larry Holmes," Muhammad said and told me what he was gonna do to him – you know, always the showman. "C'mon, Larry. We could do it now. Let's do it now!" And Larry Holmes said, "No. I don't want to." And I was in between the two of them. I mean, they were only playing around but, you know, to stand in between two big men like that!

So Larry Holmes said, "Tom, you're an educated man. You've got to tell this man not to fight me."

"I'm not going to tell him anything," I said, and as I did, Ali was coming around, trying to get him.

I was there when Ali actually fought Holmes. That was a sad fight; one fight too many. There was a spark there for a moment, when Ali started to move around the ring again, but I think he'd just lost too much of the weight he'd put on, trying to get back to his fighting weight, even though he still had the ability. Ali definitely tried, but Larry Holmes was younger and stronger.

I can understand why he kept on fighting as long as he did, though. The lure of the spotlight, the adoration of the crowd, is like a drug. You get used to it. It's hard to give it up, because it's your life, it becomes part of you, and to live without it would be very difficult. Also, you want to take your talent as far as it can possibly. Sometimes, of course, you don't know when that time is, but it'll tell you. Like, with a singer, when you can't sing as well, you think, "I can't do it" and you stop. And with an athlete, he's got to be pushed to that level, where he then knows that he can't do it, and that's what Ali did – he took it as far as he possibly could. But you have to go that far in order to realise that you have to stop.

He always was a funny guy, though. He sees the funny side of life. He could have been a comedian. I remember in New York, I was waiting for this vocal group to come over for a rehearsal and Muhammad came into the hotel. My son saw him and said, "My father's upstairs." Muhammad said, "I gotta go see him. Tom Jones! Tom Jones! I gotta go!"

I was in there lying down, taking a nap, 'cause I was a little jet-lagged. The next thing I knew, my son was telling me the group was there, ready to rehearse. "OK," I said, and I woke up, and Ali comes into the bedroom, where I was lying down, with a newspaper up against his face. He's about the same height as this tall bass singer in the group, and I was looking over at him and he went, "Boo!"

He was friendly with Elvis, too. That was interesting, Elvis and Ali, because they seemed to admire each other so much and yet they couldn't quite connect because they were so far apart – race and whatever. But they both respected one another, because Ali was as big as Elvis in his field, and was respected as much, and Elvis knew that. At one time, Elvis presented Ali with a white robe that had "People's Choice" on it. That moment was a massive moment, really, because it welcomed Ali into something that transcended sport, really.

He came to see me in Vegas about twelve to 18 months ago. The only thing I noticed about him that was different was that he couldn't speak very well, but you could tell that his mind was working. But his daughter knew what he wanted to say, so she's become his mouthpiece. But he came to see me at the show there. And he didn't fall asleep! He was right there with it, so I was glad that I could do that for him, that he enjoyed coming to see me. He came backstage and we talked again. He's still says funny things, even though his daughter has to say them for him.

But I think that, when you've been around a long time and you've proven your worth, which Ali definitely has done, there is even more respect for you, because then people can't deny it. You look at old footage and you realise what the man really did achieve. And that's why he's had the acclaim that he has. And this Parkinson's syndrome – he's not a punch-drunk fighter; it's a disease that he has, and he would have had it if he wasn't a fighter, according to the doctors. But he still goes out and he still wants to be a part of life. He hasn't just said, "Well, you know, I can't do it." He still goes out and does it, and I think he's gained respect even now because he will not give up.

George Kalinsky

Photographer

I first met Muhammad Ali back in 1966. I just happened to be out walking when I saw him crossing the street on his way to the Fifth Street gym in Miami. Now, at that point in time, I was just a photographer for my family. I just took pictures of whatever everyone else takes pictures of relating to their own family. But I followed Muhammad into the gym and Angelo Dundee stopped me and said to me, "You can't come in here unless you pay your buck."

"But I'm the photographer from Madison Square Garden." I did have a camera, but it was just the family camera. That just came out of my head. "OK, comedian," said Angelo. "Come on in."

So I walked into the gym and Muhammad was there with Howard Cosell, who was doing an interview with him. I thought, "Wow, this is great!" So I took some photos of Muhammad working, or Cassius Clay, as he was known at that point. I took two rolls of film that day.

Later on, I was riding in the car and I saw that Cassius Clay is top of the news, so I took my film to *The Miami Herald* and they wanted to use the pictures, so it goes over the wire service and the next day it's all over the world, from this roll of film I took of the first athlete that I'd ever run into.

A week later, I went back Madison Square Garden in New York and I saw John Condon, who was in charge of boxing there, and I showed him my roll of film and he said, "If you have the *chutzpah* to come here with one roll of film looking for a job, then I have the *chutzpah* to hire you." And that's how I started being the photographer for Madison Square Garden, which I owe to just following Cassius Clay into the gym. Now, I've been here for 35 years.

The first official assignment I ever had to photograph Ali was when he fought Zora Folley at the Garden in 1967. I met Ali in his hotel room across the street from the Garden. He was lying in bed and we started talking, and I took some pictures of him lying in bed reading, shaving, washing, taking a walk around Central Park. Also, he was colouring in these military colouring books. This was around the time of the controversy over Vietnam, and I thought they would make a great prop, so I took a picture of him colouring in these pictures in bed. Whatever he did, I just followed him. I wanted to take candid shots of him. What I didn't know is that I was the first photographer to take those kinds of pictures. Before that, everybody just took pictures where fighters posed.

The Ali that I knew was always humble. He was a wonderful showman, but when the camera wasn't on him, or he wasn't in public, he always spoke very softly, courteously and respectfully, and I found him to be eventually a very good friend. I really got to like him very much.

He was the first athlete to realise that self-promotion would bring in the money, and he had the natural ability to speak in front of people and this charismatic ability to entice people and make them want to listen to him. But he worked very hard at that. It was definitely planned. He said himself that he looked at some of the wrestlers like Gorgeous George and saw how he promoted himself. He took some of the charismatic qualities from other people and tried to use them himself. Now, not all of us have the ability to do that. Joe Louis was a great fighter, but he didn't have the charisma of Muhammad Ali. Sinatra has that charisma. Pavarotti has that charisma. Joe Frazier does not have the charisma. The people fell in love with Ali.

Ali is just one of those people – whether it's an athlete, an entertainer or a politician – that just comes about at the right time, like Michael Jordan, Frank Sinatra, The Beatles, Babe Ruth. He came about at a time when no athlete had ever promoted himself. You'd see at an athlete and you'd just see what this person was like on the field. Occasionally you'd see an interview, but never one that would captivate the audience like Ali did. He was perfect for the time, and he certainly made very opportunity to create a tremendous market for himself, which eventually was the bottom line in creating the most famous person in the world.

When I spoke to Ali when his career was waning, I said to him, "Ali, why are you still fighting?" And he said, "I have to fight. It's my only stage. If I'm not on the stage, people are gonna forget me, so the only venue that I have is the boxing ring." When I asked him if he was afraid of getting hurt, he said, "I am, but until I go into something else where I can start to do other things, I want to stick to my stage, which is the ring. I consider myself the most famous man in the world." And he says this humbly, not in a bragging way. "That's what I'm selling, and I can't do it in any other place but the ring." He thought of every conceivable way to create and market himself. He had the natural instincts and the pure talent of being charismatic – the face, the expressions, the body. He was quick and he had all the lines.

Of course, he practised a lot of the lines. He still did them, because those were his words, but he just wanted to make sure that when he was speaking in front of the public that he had it down right. Drew Bundini Brown used to give him a lot of his lines, but he practised them and he became a great showman. You have to give him a lot of credit for that. He captivated the world. Most athletes have to work hard to captivate just their city or their town or their state. Everybody fell in love with him. We all bought it.

It made me feel sorry for Joe Frazier. When I first knew Joe, back in the middle to late '60s, he was actually in awe of Ali. He couldn't wait to fight him. I remember sitting with him in front of the TV watching Ali fight Henry Cooper and Joe telling me that he could beat Ali, if he only had the opportunity. He said he would attack the body, because he knew that, if he attacked the body enough, the legs would go. But there was no animosity at that time. That started with their first fight, the fight of the century, where Ali really took the time to mock Joe. Joe took that very seriously.

I also thought that, to some degree Joe was envious that Ali had this ability to be able to speak, to take aspects of Joe's life and harm it a little bit. There was a time when he helped Ali. He helped him with money and he helped him with a licence once, and he felt that Ali should be kinder. But knowing Ali, I also knew that Ali was just trying to hype the fight.

Arguably, that fight was the greatest sporting event of all time. Everyone who was anybody had to be there. The audience was as important as the fight itself. It was an incredibly star-studded fight. When I first heard about the fight, my one wish was to get Muhammad Ali and Joe Frazier alone in one place, which turned out to be in Joe Frazier's gym. What an opportunity! Joe had never really touched Ali before, in the ring, but I had to get a shot of them both. I wanted to show the emotions of both fighters, that feeling of power.

But Ali was great. He had tremendous precision. He was missing my camera by a quarter of an inch. I could not believe that a man could miss a camera by that much, and I felt very confident about his precision. Then, at the end of the round, Ali says to Joe, "I beat you. I am the champion. I beat Joe Frazier." That was a great moment for me.

Then I told Joe I want to do the same thing with him and he stepped in the ring and started swinging, and he didn't have any of the precision that Ali had. That took about ten seconds, because I felt the camera was gonna go down my throat! "That's enough, Joe."

"No no no. Let's do this."

"Joe," I said, "I'd love to, but I don't want my head to get hurt." So we stopped, and then I got the two fighters together for the first nose-to-nose, head-to-head shot, which was shown on posters and covers all over the world.

That photo shoot was really interesting. Ali was wonderful, a showman. He started to look like he was in the middle of the fight. Joe was more straight, but Joe had one thing on his mind. This was his first opportunity to be face to face with Muhammad Ali, so he started to hit Ali lightly, then a little more heavy and a little stronger, and the next thing I know, he hits Ali with a left and Ali goes almost down! He was saved by the ropes. Ali was stunned. He looked at Joe and said, "You can really hit."

"Wait 'til the night of the fight," said Joe. "You'll know what it is to be hit."

At that moment, I really felt Joe was going to win that fight, partially because Ali had not fought much in the last couple of years and Joe was in his prime, and also because Joe had the confidence. Ali realised that Joe could really hit and actually had a little bit of fear at that moment and probably going into the fight, too. That's probably what swung it.

Later on, about a month or less before Ali's fight in Zaire with George Foreman, we got a call from him asking us to come over and see him and John Condon, from the Garden. Condon was like a father to him, and to me, too. People loved John, and Muhammad was no different. So we met in the Garden one day about six o'clock and went up to the press room and we talked. He had mentioned on the phone that he was really concerned about the fight against Foreman. He didn't really think that he could win, and he just had to talk to somebody else about it. So there's just the three of us alone in an empty Garden in the press room, and Ali's talking, letting his hair down, saying how difficult it was going to be to win against George Foreman. And while he was talking, I looked at him and I thought of the very first time I ever saw him, at the gym in Miami, and I thought of many other times when he was working out with sparring partners, when he would lean back against the ropes and let them hit him. He just got pounded in the belly, and no one hit him in the head. I never saw anybody else train that way, only Ali. And I said to him, "You know, Ali, any time I ever saw you train, you always train with your back against the ropes, leaning against the ropes, and you let your sparring partner hit you. You have a lifetime of being hit in the stomach. Maybe if you tried this with Foreman, lean back against the rope, act sort of like a dope and just let him hit you, maybe he'll use all his strength up."

"Yeah," said John. "That's a great idea, Ali! That's how you train. Maybe it'll work."

I said to him, "You know, act like a dope on the ropes."

We were all saying variations of that until "rope-a-dope" came out. Ali thought that it might be a good idea, that he'd talk to Angelo and see what happened.

Of course, on the night of the fight, that's exactly what happened. He acted like he was hurt, like he was out of it. George Foreman kept charging and charging and giving him everything he got, and Ali was concentrating to make sure that Foreman would hit him as much in the stomach as possible. Eventually, Foreman wore himself out, and then Ali started looking George in the face and started to get his confidence that he could win the fight. It must have hurt to be hit in the stomach by George Foreman. Foreman was a big guy. He was the one guy that stood in the way of Joe Frazier. He was absolutely powerful, but if anybody could do that it was Muhammad Ali, because he'd trained like that all his life.

But there's another side to that story. About a year ago, I was sitting with George Foreman and I had to tell him the story about the rope-a-dope. I looked at him and said, "Don't hit me, but I got a story to tell you that I've been dying to tell you for years, the story behind the rope-a-dope." So I told George about how the rope-a-dope came about, the conversation between John Condon and myself with Ali and the strategy that started that night.

George looked at me and he said, "You know, Ali went into that fight the right way. The right way to go into that fight against me was to be afraid. My mistake was that I was over-confident. He went into the fight looking at me with fear. Eventually, his confidence came about, because I went about it the wrong way. My strategy was all wrong. I should have gone into it with the confidence but also with fear."

One of the qualities about Muhammad Ali which hit me the very first time I saw him was this charming, child-like innocence. It just added tremendously to this charismatic wonder, this great showman. As outspoken as he was, he was as wonderful person who could captivate an audience like no one else could. I remember riding in the back seat of this white Cadillac with him in Florida, just before the second fight with Joe

Frazier. He was having a lot of fun, practising some lines. Bundini was in the front seat and we were just kidding around. The top was down, and every time we stopped at a corner he would try to entertain the people. He would get up and says, "One of you out there is Joe Frazier. Come on here, Joe Frazier. Stop hiding. I'm gonna whip you!" You just can't believe the looks on the faces of people. He just wanted to give of himself to everybody. As much as he practised being the most famous man in the world, part of that was his truthfulness, his honesty, the fact that he was a real person.

Then we came to one red light and there were three construction workers working on the road. One had an pickaxe pick, one had a shovel and the other had some other tool. They were big, strong guys, and Ali gets up and says, "One of you guys is Joe Frazier. One of you guys is Joe. Come on over here." Well the guy holding the pickaxe evidently was not in love with Ali, and he started coming closer to Ali. Ali was still going, "Are you Joe Frazier? Are you Joe Frazier? I'm gonna whup you!" And Muhammad starts signalling to me, like, *Get the car moving!* And he's still going, "Joe Frazier – you Joe Frazier? Get the car moving! I'm gonna whup you!" We didn't know what was gonna happen. Most people, when they see Muhammad Ali on the street, they're in love with him. They just want to touch him. He's bigger than life. I don't think any athlete or entertainer has captivated the world as he has.

Hank Kaplan

Boxing Historian

I worked with Angelo and Chris Dundee at the beginning of the '60s. Chris was one of the top three promoters in the United States. Boxing was kind of dull at that time, because television had come in and all the small clubs had died off. There was once a time in America where there was a boxing club in every town and hamlet in the country. Then, by the 1960s, all those clubs died off. So there weren't too many promoters, and boxing was really in need of somebody. In a way, it was fortuitous that you got great fighters like Frazier and Foreman, but boxing really needed someone like Muhammad Ali, and when he came along, it increased the newspaper coverage. But that was limited to Ali only. He stole all the thunder and it made the other boxers jealous. For years, everybody in the ring was saying, "Hell, nobody knows me." You look back at the fights now, Jimmy Ellis fighting Frazier, and they were great fights, but they almost seem slightly incidental to the key Ali fights that were going on then. Every writer was following this very charismatic kid who came out of the Olympics and was known as "the man with the lip". He was picking up believers every single day.

I first met him in late October 1960, after the Tommy Hunsaker fight. Angelo Dundee brought him into the gym and he sparred with a young heavyweight named Tommy Alangi. This is something that I've never forgotten: he came in with a very unorthodox style, with his hands dangling at his knees, and he flit around the ring, dodging punches with his feet. And he had this very unique athletic move, rolling back so that his opponents missed with the right hand by a hair. I recall how some of the old-time trainers felt at what they saw. One of them told me, "Listen, this kid's gonna get killed." They didn't believe that his style would hold up, that his methods, his unorthodoxy, would make it. There were a lot of doubters all over the place, but they did recognise that his style was different, that it was unique, and that he depended a lot on his feet.

At that time, I was doing public relations for Chris Dundee and working with some of Angelo's fighters, writing up the little promotional pieces for them and whatever their needs called for. You might think that, when Ali – or Cassius Clay, as he was then – turned up, because he was so good at self-promotion, that I might have been in some way kind of redundant, but it wasn't like that. For me, it was something new. It was stimulating. I mean, the guy used to crack me up with some of the things he said, but everybody listened to him very intently. I thought that there was a lot of charm in the way he promoted himself. He wasn't arrogant; he was just telling it like he thought it was.

One evening in early 1960, I had been managing some fighters of my own and looking after him at night in another gym. This particular gym was called New Black's Gym, right behind the same building that the Sir John Hotel was in, a hotel which used to bring in a lot of the old burly Afro-American singers – soul singers, guys like BB King. It was a very popular night spot for some of the local people. So one night, I'm walking out of this gym with Sel Bonetta, a friend of mine who actually trained my fighters. We walked out to get a little air and a little smoke, turned the corner and there was the entrance to the Sir John Hotel. As I approached the door, I could see young Cassius Clay looking through the window, listening to all that music coming from BB King. And I said, "Cassius, you oughtta be in bed. What you doing up so late?" It was after nine o'clock. So we just struck up a conversation. Of course, he knew me from the gym, and he was a very friendly kid. We chatted, and then I took a pack of cigarettes out of my shirt pocket, pulled one out, put it in my mouth, and as soon as I did that he pulled it out of my mouth and said, "You shouldn't be smoking. It's bad for ya." So we just continued talking, and then he reached into my pocket again and took my pen out of my pocket and he signed this cigarette. I was amazed you could do it on a cigarette. So we just kept talking, shooting the bull, and he hands the cigarette back to me and he says, "Here, you keep this. It's gonna be worth a lot of money some day." So I put it back in my pocket. I didn't think about it. Eventually, I got another cigarette out of my pocket and I lit it up and smoked it. Recently, a guy by the name of Ron Palliger – the world's biggest Ali collector, a guy who travelled all over the world collecting Ali stuff – visited with me, 'cause he loved to talk Ali, and he fell in love with that cigarette, so I let him have it. Eventually, his entire collection went to auction at Christie's, I believe, and that cigarette sold for $1,900 and made the newspapers all over the country. The whole collection went for two point something million.

Then I was at the famous first Sonny Liston fight in 1964. That day was electric. The town was jumping. That fight didn't get any artificial hype; it was just a natural hype. It was one of the great naturals of all time. Young Cassius Clay, who at that point in time was the most charismatic heavyweight fighter in history, fighting the most formidable guy that we've had around in years. Without even thinking about it, I doubt that anybody ever gave Ali a chance in that fight. Sonny Liston was considered the favourite.

One of the things I recall is the famous weigh-in scene. I was there. I went with Joe Louis' wife, Marva, and we stood together. The weigh-in was held on a stage-like structure, and we looked up and of course we watched Cassius Clay and his histrionics. I laughed at the time. I thought it was funny as hell, because everybody else took that thing very seriously, including Marva. She says, This boy is a lunatic! This boy needs to go to a psychiatrist." She was all excited about it, but I laughed.

Then, of course, on the night of the fight, there were all kinds of celebrities there. I sat with several of 'em, people like Sinatra and Jimmy Brown, the football player. Liston has his towels under his robe to make himself look bigger. Then the fight began. Some people argue that Ali won the fight even before the first round, because he so intimidated Liston in the first round, when he came out and refused to be intimidated by Liston.

To be honest, I never thought Cassius was gonna win that fight. I was nervous as hell. The fight was touch and 'go til the very end. When Liston didn't get up from the stall, I was puzzled, very puzzled, and so was everybody else.

For that fight, there was some problems. Like, a few days before the fight when the statement broke about Ali being a Muslim, and I think that hurt the promotion a bit. There was also a story that Malcolm X was asked to leave town because it was hurting the promotion so badly, but I don't think that had anything to do with the match, unless it's information I wasn't privy to. I don't think Muhammad Ali ever changed after he joined the Nation of Islam, though. He was just as nice a guy before as he was after.

I wasn't there for the second Liston fight, but I've watched the bit with the "phantom punch", the fall, over and over and over again. You can see the punch being thrown. I don't see it looming, but the timing was so exact and so perfect that I can easily conceive that that fist landed onto Sonny Liston's chin. It looks like you can see his feet going off the floor at that point. Ali had a pretty fair, straight right hand. It kind of toppled Sonny Liston, so that it looked like he was a little off balance. The impact of both punches coming together reinforced the power of the punch.

I didn't go to any of his later fights, because I was working full time for the federal government, but I did go on an exhibition tour with him in 1965 to the Bahamas. It wasn't unusual for a boxer to be boxing and performing outside the boundaries of the United States, particularly in the Caribbean, which is pretty close. It served two purposes. One was it was always good for picking up some extra money, and secondly it kept the fighter in shape. It kept Cassius Clay in condition when he was between fights. It also helped to prepare him for fights which were coming up. That tour did a lot for his timing, for his stamina, for his general condition.

When I watched him fight later on television, I could see a progression in his technique. His style didn't change, but his skills did. He was very fortunate in having Angelo Dundee as a trainer, one of the greatest boxing minds of the past century. Angelo was very, very astute about the way he handled Ali. Now, Ali wasn't the kind of a guy that would do a whole lot of listening, but Angelo Dundee, if he had something to change, something to improve, he would make it seem like it was the fighter's idea. Angelo was the kind of a guy that wore 17 different hats. He was a great psychiatrist, a great corner man, a great teacher and a great conditioner. To some extent, Ali must have recognised, because he stayed with him, where a lot of boxers seem to chop and change and they leave their managers, try new ones. Ali was loyal, though. He was just a human being.

When he refused to join the armed forces, I thought it was very damaging to his career. It was big news both in the boxing community and outside of it. There haven't been too many incidents where athletes as great as Cassius Clay were refusing to fight with the military at a time of war, so it made a lot of headlines. The whole country was interested in his case at that time; he showed that he believed in what he was doing. That took an awful lot of courage, and of course in some circles he was very much admired for that. But generally speaking, I didn't believe it was a popular move on his part. It really split the nation. He was hated by a lot of people.

When he came back in 1970, after three and a half years away from boxing, a lot of people didn't think he had any chance of regaining his title, but I really believed that he had the ability to become champ again. He was a great athlete, he still had all of his assets and he hadn't been a couch potato during those three and a half years. He worked out and he exercised and he stayed in pretty good physical condition, and he did a lot of thinking. I really believe that he became a better fighter because of that lay-off, because boxing is a game of the mind, not only the muscle. When a fighter depends on muscle only to become a great fighter, he doesn't make it.

I remember watching the first Frazier-Ali fight, the so-called battle of the century. I thought at the time that Ali would win, but Frazier gave him a very, very rugged fight. I wouldn't say there was cruelty with Muhammad. Some people say that he took things a bit far in his promotion, but that's just him being a great actor, a great showman. A clown, if you will. He loved people listening to him and laughing at him, he thrived on it, and he didn't realise that he was hurting these people in any way. These were professionals that he was calling various names, so they should have realised that he was just clowning and working up the promotion. I think they should have realised that, and a guy like Frazier should not be angry at Ali. But I believe that Frazier's long-lasting feelings about Ali go deeper than just the fact that Ali called him various names; I think that Joe Frazier – who was a great fighter himself – feels personally that he was a greater fighter than Ali but that, as luck would have it, he didn't get the same recognition.

The Rumble In The Jungle I watched on one of Chris Dundee's close-circuit presentations, and that was a very exciting fight for me, because I realised that George Foreman was a very formidable guy. But of course he cut his eye just before the fight and he wasn't able to train as well as he usually does. Still, Ali had a big job on his hands, and I was worried about him. I was shaking like a leaf in that fight.

I remember when Ali knocked Foreman down. It was incredible. Ali was very, very astute. He was one of the great strategists that ever lived and treated every fight differently, and him and Angelo Dundee decided that he was going to tire Foreman out and that, after Foreman got good and tired in that heat, and with the psychology of the crowd against him, then he would put his power into use, which is exactly what he did. Foreman looked horrible even back in the third round, when he was throwing punches to Ali's body. He could hardly lift his arms. Of course, he could have been mentally tired as well as physically tired, because Ali's tirades during the promotion in the weeks preceding the fight was enough to get to Foreman. When Ali put that right hand over and hit him on the chin and Foreman went down, that was just an unbelievable sight to witness, 'cause first of all, you know, Foreman wasn't supposed to get hit on the chin and hit the deck. He's too strong, too big, too powerful. It just couldn't happen. But it happened.

Ali's fought as a professional for 20 years, but it wasn't unusual for a boxer to go on that long, and neither is it unusual today. Look at the case of Roberto Duran, look at Larry Holmes, look at Saul Mamby. There are many instances where fighters have fought for seventeen years and up. Of course, he had to change his strategy when he got older. When he first started, people were talking about his footwork. Then, as his legs slowed down as he got older, he adapted to new methods, like for example the rope-a-dope in the Rumble In The Jungle. He allowed Foreman to get tired hitting his gloves and hitting his arms. He was good at those kind of things.

At the Thrilla In Manila, he claimed that that was as near death as you can ever get, and it felt like it at the time, too. You wondered how these guys could go on fighting the way they have been, using all that energy and depleting themselves, getting hit as often as they were getting hit. You wondered who was gonna go first. Well, Ali had an unbelievable kind of courage, an incredible determination, and he had a great chin. So what he's trying to say is that his heart carried him to those last few moments. He suffered, he struggled, but he wasn't gonna give in.

I didn't think he should have fought Larry Holmes, though. That was killing me. I went to Vegas to see that fight, and I was at one of his last workouts, two days before the fight. I was standing there with two writers, one of which was Jerry Eizenberg, and we watched Ali warming up in the ring. Then we watched him put his hand wraps on and saw him shadow-boxing in the ring. He was practically tripping over his own feet. I knew then that his legs were gone. I knew that he didn't have a chance with Holmes. I watched that fight live, and I was trembling like a leaf. I was hoping that Larry Holmes would hold back on him, but thank God for Angelo Dundee. He stopped it just at the right time.

I'm not sure whether he was the greatest boxer of all time. The term "boxer" is a loose one, you see. It could mean a lot of things. I think you need a subdivision of that word. Was he the greatest puncher? Was he the most scientific boxer? Was he the fiercest boxer? What was he, actually? In my opinion, he probably will not go down in history as being one of the greatest punchers of all time. There's something to be said about his straight scientific boxing ability, but had certain variables which are more important, perhaps, than the other two. One, and the most important, is that he had determination, courage, a desire to become great. He had that in copious quantities. He was one of the greatest defensive heavyweights that ever lived, and that's great because, when you don't get hit, your career can go on and on, 'cause you're not damaged. You've got more chance of going a 15-round fight to beat your opponent. Plus he had such terrific hand speed, able to punch his opponents with good combinations going backward, which he did many times. And he had great accuracy, a great eye, and he never wasted anything. He had a beautiful jab and a great chin, and these qualities – plus his very, very educated feet – are what made him so great.

From the very beginning, when we first saw him, we thought that, stylistically, he had the ability to do some great things in boxing, but we never thought he would achieve what he actually did. I remember a few years ago we watched Ali surrounded by a bunch of people as we were sitting having our dinner and I said to Chris Dundee, "Do you believe what happened to this kid?" And he looked up at me and he grinned and he shook his head. No way.

BB King

Musician

Muhammad Ali's a good friend of mine. I knew him before he won the Golden Gloves, so we've been friends for a long, long time. In fact, we've been friends all of his career. There have been a lot of things we've both had to fight hard for, although I suppose he fought a little harder than I did. He hadn't always had it easy at all. I watched him as he grew, finally winning the Golden Gloves, then challenge, challenge, and then finally the champ.

As a musician, to start with I was playing to predominantly black audiences. That then started to spread to white audiences. By Ali standing up as he did, that gave many of us much more courage. That gave us much more hope than we'd ever had before. Some people were afraid for him – me, for one. Very afraid for him. But we couldn't do more than we were doing, like Ali entering the political stage. I never really felt like following him, though. I'm not a politician. Some people drive trucks, others fly airplanes. They can't make the truck driver fly an airplane and an airplane pilot fly a truck. There are some people that are politically inclined, and they do it very well, but I'm not a politician. I never have been, and I don't think I could be very good at it, for several reasons. They call me placid, in some ways, because I always feel that it's not just black and white; I always feel that there is a little bit in between where we can mediate, where we can come to some kind of agreement. I've always believed that way, and I still do, so I wouldn't be a very good politician.

As much as Muhammad did, as much as he tried to bring people together, standing up for what he believed was right, they could have put him in jail for the rest of his life. They could have called it treason. They could have called it many things. They could have done more, and had he not been such a proper man, they would have done more. But to see someone doing something like that now, a lot of people don't know what happened, and a lot of people didn't understand it. We need to let people know what a great guy the man really is.

At one time, 50 per cent of the American population didn't like the man and they really felt that he deserted them during Vietnam. But that wasn't all of us. It wasn't that I thought he should or shouldn't go; I was afraid for his life. And I think a lot of people felt as I did. But any man that can stand up to the US government and say, "No, I'm not going to do it." Well, I was very afraid for him. And from that time to now you can see that he truly believed in what he was saying, what he was doing. Not too long ago, while I was driving through some of the countries that we'd been at war with, I thought to myself, "How could I kill one of these people? How could I hurt you? I couldn't hurt you." So I can imagine how he must have felt, going over to fight people he don't even know. Like I said, I'm passive, I guess. I couldn't hurt anybody. This is what bothers me about people today in the US. They hurt people for no reason. I couldn't do it. I'd rather hurt myself first.

Mark Kram

Author Of *Ghosts Of Manila*

I recently wrote a book criticising the myth of Muhammad Ali. That came out on 22 May 2001, and since then there's been a tremendous amount of heat. I've been called a fascist, a racist and I've had threats at home. It's inexplicable, for the most part, but it seems to keep in tone with the atmosphere in America, where hero worship is extremely intense, almost over the emotional top. People are comfortable with their myths, and they don't like to have their myths disturbed. It's like, when it comes to legend and history, if there's a decision that needs to be made, they prefer to go with the legend. And if anybody reads the book, they won't come away with that myth.

I never intended to write a book about Ali. I didn't want to reinhabit that world. But I saw that the books that were coming down the pike were mainly hagiographic, saint-making books. They really weren't looking. They didn't present the Ali that I had seen for almost a dozen years, through travelling with him extensively across the world, getting to know him as well as anybody could. In those days, you could hang around a lot. It wasn't the period of the mass press conference, with kind questions and kind answers, so there was a lot of down time to sit around and talk to Ali, at least as much as you could possibly talk to Ali. You never interviewed Ali. One smart journalist referred to him as the world's worst interview. You never really had a conversation with him. There was no give and take, especially if you pulled out a pencil and a notebook. He was always interested in putting forth the Muslim tract and he would improvise a whole lot into it. So I thought that it was time to write a book that would elevate him above a human cliché and put some flesh and blood on him.

I don't know why people are so emotionally invested in Ali. This hero worship for him is rather baffling. I can only put it down to a theory that's gaining ground in the United States that talks about something called the "god" part of the brain. Neuroscientists have come up with the idea that there's a part of the brain that provides us with a god because we're so afraid of death. It dominates our every day, buffering the very fact of death. Now, I sometimes suspect that there's a part of the brain that insists on heroes. If not, perhaps we become so bored, without these focal points of intense interest, that it would be difficult to cope with everyday, mundane life, day in and day out.

But Ali has supposedly accepted that he was a man with flaws, but is that enough to exonerate him of the many things that he did wrongly over the years? I mean, every human being is obviously flawed, but history is history. I dare say that, if you examine the lives of Douglas MacArthur, General Patton, Field-Marshal Montgomery, one might come to the conclusion that they did admirable work in the field, but at the same time one might also see that they were narcissist and borderline psychotics who left a lot of people buried in the service of their own ambitions. So Ali's life has to be examined, not through the lens of hero worship but through the lens of history.

I was with him mostly every step of the way, and so I got to know not the man that many people see but a different kind of man. For instance, his public persona was a lot different. He was often a brooding fella, given to long periods of silence, except when he saw that he could be on stage and move his beliefs a step forward. I don't say I'm totally right and that everybody has to agree with me, but I do believe that my analysis of him over the years is accurate and honest.

There's no animosity at all. In fact, I like many parts of him – his generosity, his kindnesses. The parts that came from his mother. She had a very good nature, and you would often see that on display with Ali. He was in many ways a politician who pressed a lot of flesh over his career, and that has served him in good stead. I spoke to Khaliah Ali, his daughter, a few days ago, and she said that she was talking to this man and he said, "Well, Ali changed my life."

"Oh, really? What happened?"

"He shook my hand and my life was changed," he said.

"Oh? What did he do?"

"He showed me some magic tricks and then he levitated."

"And then what? What did he say to you that changed your life?"

"Well…he just changed my life."

What else? Well, there never was a what else. There was just this vacancy in his eyes. You encounter that with a lot of people. They have no explanation why he compels them to think in such a manner about him.

He used to have a large crew of people always around him in the '70s. For instance, on the trip to Manila, he had about 38 people on the roster. I'd say six or seven actually did work in one capacity or another. The rest were people that Ali needed around him. He loved a huge entourage. He loved the idea of taking people he knew from his boyhood or friends that he just met on trips. It cost him a tremendous amount of money over the years. I mean, these people would eat five or six meals a day and make an extraordinary amount of transatlantic calls. But he enjoyed having them there, and I think the reason for that was because he became bored very quickly and these people somehow infused into him the will to go on. He liked to be entertained, he liked to be amused, and these people provided that.

Sometimes he would become infuriated, though. For instance, when we were in Japan for that stupid event with the wrestler Inoki, we were on the bus going to Korea and he got on and said, "I take you niggers all over the world and you don't appreciate it!" He was miffed about the fact that some of them had gone into the Japanese bars and started taking pictures, which they were properly arrested for. So he was like the sheriff of a small town, and he enjoyed it immensely.

It's argued that Ali is up there with Martin Luther King as an agent of political and social change. Some people have even said to me that he's like Gandhi. I'm not so sure. I've looked into his life with a sharp eye to see exactly what he did or didn't do, and I have yet to find it pure. People come at you with these words – symbolism, legacy, hero – but these are very mushy words. You can look throughout the history of the world and see how they've used symbolism, and behind it is always a heavy lobby and the hand of propaganda. You could see it with President Marcos in the Philippines, the Third Reich with their elaborate ceremonies, all in the service of symbolism. The fact is that Muhammad Ali didn't change a thing. He wasn't for civil rights, the counter-culture or women's rights, and he wasn't against the war in Vietnam. He was not savvy enough, politically or geopolitically, for that kind of reasoning. He would go into colleges, put on one of his shows, make sure the room was cleared of LBJ signs and marijuana, and then he'd be on the stage holding up his draft card and saying, "See? I didn't burn mine."

And you have to understand, too, that the Muslims were anti-black. The whole Muslim hierarchy was filled with very light-complexioned people. In fact, Elijah never characterised the Black Muslims – which was really the equivalent of a storefront cult – as sub-Saharan blacks; they were always Asianic blacks. So that was part of Ali's thinking, too. He made some pretty bad remarks on Africa over the years.

But was he a hero? Well, a hero in my mind breaks the normal ranks, goes out on his own and acts spontaneously. Ali never acted spontaneously in this particular world of revolution. He was always dictated to by the Muslims, from beginning to end. There was a bright line of manipulation by the Muslims. Even now, after he's retired, he's manipulated by a lawyer on Capitol Hill. He appears almost robotic, doing what people tell him to do, saying what people tell him to say.

I first saw him fight in Miami, against Sonny Liston, in February '64. Obviously, I wasn't that close to him at that point. I was part of a pack of journalists, acting as a stringer. That was an eventful fight, to say the least. Everybody felt Sonny Liston would destroy Ali, and Malcolm X had just brought Ali into the Black Muslims, much to the chagrin of Elijah Muhammad, the leader, who hated boxing and fighters. The Muslims were so uninterested in Ali that they didn't even send a reporter down from their paper, *Muhammad Speaks*, that's how sure they were that he was going to lose.

Now, there was a lot of hysteria surrounding that fight. Some say that Ali was putting on an act, but I didn't see it as an act; I saw it as a man who was terribly afraid of Sonny Liston. This is a remarkable thing about Ali – he was a fearful fighter, he worried about his face, he worried about his brain circuitry, yet he was able to go into the ring and perform at such a remarkable level in spite of those fears. That impressed me tremendously. He was not a natural-born fighter mentally, but he certainly was physically. He had a pair of Rolls-Royce legs, a great reach, an explosive left jab, a head that was on a swivel, and he instinctively understood the geometry of the ring and the open spaces and he could send his punches zinging.

And yet he was capable of great kindnesses and humility at times. He didn't have the ego that people think he has. He had extreme vanity, but often he seemed to want to unload that burden of ego that he carried around, day in and day out. In fact, he often felt insecure.

I've had some amusing moments around him. And I don't dislike him.. I'm just baffled by the hero worship that's sprung up around him. I keep trying to figure it out and I come up empty. I don't understand how people can have such barren lives that they can invest such emotion into one human being. Ali's supposed to be for peace and reconciliation. Well, you can find anybody on the streets with half a brain that's for peace and reconciliation. What does he do? He travels here, he travels there. He's a great presser of flesh you see, like I said. You only have to be in an airport with him and see how the people drop down in front of him like sparrows. Then, suddenly, there's a long line and he may show them a magic trick or he may sign autographs and give them a Muslim pamphlet, and that's it – they think they've seen God. I think any enlightened person would not want to become so brainless as to think that Ali was somehow beyond their ken. They're trying to make him a theologian. It baffles me.

Ali came into boxing when the mob had a lot of control. Sonny Liston was pretty much owned by the mob, but Ali he really didn't really know anything about the them, except what he heard here and there and maybe what he saw in the movies occasionally. But he feared that element, and that may have been one reason why he hooked up with the Black Muslims.

But another thing about Ali was that he was hypocritical about the women, because he was a Muslim and therefore had very strict rules about adultery. In fact, if you were an average Muslim and you committed adultery, you were taken back to the temple and worked over. Now, Ali would say constantly that he didn't fool with white women. He almost wanted you to believe that he was celibate to his craft and would accuse Joe Frazier of having a white girlfriend. But there was a whole train of women that followed him around, among them many white women, and yet he made such a moral exhibition of his refusal to even touch white women or be around them that it became an outright...well, not a lie, but an outright subterfuge.

But sure, Ali loved women. He loved sex. I mean, some people might call him an unchained sexual melody, in many ways. I remember when he was fighting Joe Bugner in Las Vegas. It was about three in the morning, and on the night before his very close friend and a man who worked as a publicist and arranger of fights at times, came down shaking his head. "Man, the champ is a come freak. There's a hooker in every room on his floor and he goes from room to room."

But really, Ali didn't have very much to say about anything. I mean, take his politics. He stayed very close to the tract of the Muslims. His verse amused many people, but it was like he had the voice but he didn't write the lyrics. Bundini Brown wrote the lyrics. He was the true genius behind Ali, the colour of Ali, the magnetism behind Ali, but Ali had the presence to present it.

And of course, that fostered the rivalry between him and Frazier. There's a blood feud between those two that stretched out over 30 years or more, and that's because of much more than jealousy. You can't carry a feud on for 30 years on jealousy alone. Frazier was stripped down to his heart and battered to his soul by the fact that Ali had robbed him of his identity, turned him from a black man into a white man and isolated him from the black people in such a way that he could never get over it. I mean, when you call someone a black man in white skin, that should cut to one's very centre, and it did with Joe. Most people think, "Well, this is Ali hype," but those fights with Frazier never had to be hyped. They were absolutely natural fights. Tickets were sold out in advance for six weeks. He simply came to dislike Frazier and wanted to isolate him to a section of life where he no longer appeared to be any kind of black man. Well, Joe was a live-and-let-live sort of guy. If you liked him, he liked you. He went to see Nixon because Nixon invited him, and Frank Rizzo, the police chief of Philadelphia, had done a lot of good things for Joe, giving him around-the-clock police protection when the death threats came in. He didn't pretend to be a revolutionary.

When you look at the lives of the two men closely, Ali grew up in a lower-middle-class family in segregated Louisville, and once he turned into his teens and people saw that he might have some talent, a lot of things were done for Ali. People were very, very nice to him. At the same time, Frazier grew up in the low country of South Carolina, one of the oldest slave settlements in America, and he grew up desperately poor – the outhouse was a hundred yards away from the house and there were holes in the roof. He was forced out of town because he interceded on behalf of a black boy against the foreman that was whipping him, so he went up to Brooklyn and stole cars, because he couldn't do anything else. So Ali lived a cosseted life compared to Frazier, and I find it very amusing that the world flocked to Ali's side when Joe's beginnings were very much more part of the black experience.

That fight in Manila, though, nobody expected that calibre of fight. That fight turned out to be the most dramatic fight of Ali's life. Not the best, technically. It didn't measure up to his first fight against Frazier in Madison Square Garden in 1971, but it reached a dramatic level. It was a surprise to see what was left in the two fighters, and there was also such a change of fortune throughout the fight. When you saw the vicious body punches rain down on Ali, his cheeks would balloon and you'd hear a low *whoosh* from him. You knew he'd been hurt. Also, Frazier always claimed that he was blinded in one eye, but he somehow managed to change his style to correspond to his deficiency. Ali put a tremendous raking on him in the early rounds, but Frazier came back and turned the fight around. By the tenth round and I was sitting right under Ali's corner and he looked grey as death. He absolutely did not wanna come out. Then Herbert Muhammad shouted up to him, "Get out there! Move, nigger!" So finally Ali dragged himself up.

He's said before that he fell through a trapdoor that morning into a place where he had never been before, and how he was able to come back again is one of the remarkable things of his career. But he did come back, and by the end of it he was hammering Joe with lead right hands. Joe's left eye was so swollen. I mean, if he never could see out of it, he sure as hell couldn't see out of it then, so he wasn't picking up that right hand. And by the end of the 14th, Eddie Futch had a major decision on his hands: "What should I do here? Can he get to Ali like he did in the 15th round in their first fight in Madison Square Garden? Has Ali finally had it? Does he have enough to go on." Futch, one of the great trainers in the world, who had seen four fighters killed in the ring, decided it wasn't worth it and said, "Sit down, son. It's all over."

To Ali, leaving the ring must have been like an out-of-body experience. He sort of floated. He was clinically exhausted. Then, strangely enough, he gets to his dressing room and finds that the security guard on duty there had been fanning himself with a pistol and accidentally blew his brains out, and Ali – who hates the sight of dead bodies – became hysterical. They had to put him in another room. He didn't want to come out for the press conference, but when he found out that Frazier was coming out, he dragged himself there.

Years later, I visited him in Hancock Park and I said to him, "Ali, let's watch the fight in Manila." He looked at me with vacant eyes and said he would show me any fight that I wanted to see but not that fight. "I don't wanna look at hell again."

But, of course, there comes a time in all athletes' lives that they have to decide whether they are an "is" or a "was". Ali went to Manila as an is but left as a was. The game was over and he knew it. He took my hand and rubbed my fingers over his forehead and there was a ridge of bumps on it.

He was very worried about brain damage. He should have called that fight the end, and yet he continued on. Why? Was it ego? No, I don't think so. Finances? Quite possibly. He had a lot of people to take care of, and he might have looked around the heavyweight division and seen some very easy pickings – there was no Joe Frazier out there – and decided, "Well, nobody can reach me. I can go on forever and make all the big money." So he went on and on, like an actor who's stuck in a play and has to go on playing night after night after night. Even after Manila, you can hear that his speech is thickened, his reactions are lazy and slow. He seemed like a different person. You might say that, with the exception of the two Frazier fights, he took all his head shots after Manila. The fighters were getting to him very easily then. And he was disappointing a lot of people, too. I mean, you could make the case that the officials and the fans only watched what Ali did and not what the other guy did, so there was a lot of contested decisions, especially his last fight, with Ken Norton in the Yankee Stadium. So would he have been in good shape had he stopped in Manila? Most definitely.

At a rough estimate he must have fought about 15,000 rounds in his life. That's counting all the gym rounds, which can't be tossed away, because he took a lot of damage in those rounds. He'd hang on the ropes and let his sparring mate pound him to the head and to the stomach. I never was quite sure what he was trying to prove there. That he was Superman? That he was the new black man? That he was just too lazy to go through the gym work and/or he wanted to sharpen up his defence? But he took a lot of pounding. Gym work is very hard on you.

And it had to have an affect on his brain. The brain is a floating organ, and when you're hit in the head, it will swish and slosh around in this cerebro-spinal fluid that's up there, and it gets damaged. Little bits of scar tissue are built up constantly. Sometimes, you only have to get hit once, but quite a few fighters come out of it undamaged in some way or another. With Ali, though, there's no question that brain damage had set in after Manila.

And now a lot of people are writing books and making films about him and cashing in on his fame. Why do we keep writing about him? Well, a lot of those people are hangers-on and sycophants who think they have something to say, but Ali is part of history. The fact is that he's a good subject. There's a certain complexity about him. But most of the books that have been written about him have been extremely long suffering of Ali. They rarely talk about his defects. I mean, you could read some of those books and still not know who he was. My book, rightly or wrongly, cuts to the core of what I saw, what I heard, what I observed.

The $150 million film about his life is based on Ali's autobiography, which is really a joke, a book that has no truth in it at all, totally fabricated by the Muslim propagandist Richard Durham. There's so much stuff in there that didn't happen, it's unbelievable. So are they gonna go with the legend that's perpetrated in that book or the oral history that came out later, when all of us around Ali sort of had our say? Well, the fact is that you can trust very few people around Ali, to tell you the truth.

I've not really been chastened by the reaction to my book. I've always tried to write pretty much what was on my mind. I don't know how it is elsewhere, but the media in America is into building up stars and legends, and keeping legends lofty. It's in their interest, see, because they're into names. They're not into real stories. So you constantly keep hearing the same old things repeated about Ali. I mean, Ali can hardly speak now. I was last with him in 1990, when we went down to the hospital to get his blood changed. The doctors there said that his condition is due to pesticide poisoning. I said, "Have you looked at any of his films?"

"Yeah," said the doctor. "I looked at the films and I didn't see him get hit in the head." What was he watching, *Abbott And Costello*?

There are two points that are hard to get to in any story about Ali. One is the complexity of Ali that lies inside him which made him decide to become a Black Muslim and which is probably unreachable now. The other complexity is the response of the world to him. I don't know if either of those questions are answerable. I *can* offer some thoughts of my own, though.

Ali grew up in a segregated Louisville, a very fearful child. There was a big part of his mother, Odessa, in him. She was a big, round woman who was extremely good natured. Then, there was another part of him that really magnified his father, an actor. Not an *actor* actor but a man who went through every day of his life as an actor. Some days he would pose as an Arab sheikh, other days as a Hindu. Ali was split between believing that the white man was the devil one day and the next wanting to blend in with the white man. And his father told Ali stories from early childhood about the whites hanging blacks in trees. This created a lot of fear in young Cassius Clay, and I think he grew up extremely insecure, wary of the world out there, needing to find some wall to put around him. The Black Muslims became that wall. He wanted to be led and wanted to believe in something other than himself, and the Black Muslims became that for him. But in giving himself to them, he gave up all individuality, because from the beginning he had to follow the Muslims and their politics.

So he was not an individual. He was part of a group mind and he saw that he could invest emotionally in Muslims. Somehow, he deemed himself a preacher. He liked that whole thing. He couldn't hardly read or write, but his memory wasn't bad at all and he could spout off all this stuff and it made him feel like he was more than just a fighter.

He didn't have much liking for the ring. When he was a very young kid, he used to listen to the fights from Madison Square Garden on the radio. He would hear Sugar Ray's name introduced into the ring or see him on black-and-white television, and this stirred him. He probably knew the gifts he had, although he didn't have the natural killer instinct of a fighter. But, at that time, he was enthralled with the glamour of it all, and I think he always seemed to wanna be much blacker than he was. Again, that probably came from the days when his father thought he was a revolutionary.

But even Ali could not have failed to notice that his father vacillated at times and also wanted to be a part of that white world. He fancied himself a painter – an artiste, so to speak. Once, I was standing with him looking at Andy Warhol's tomato can and he just looked at it and he said, "Gee, these white folk'll fall for anything." In other words, he dismissed Warhol as an artist not on his level.

But was Muhammad Ali the greatest? Well, that's an interesting question. When you really examine it, he was the greatest fighter who ever lived, with Sugar Ray Robinson a close second. There was nobody like him in a ring, so in that sense he stands apart. As a social force, though, as a personality, I guess on stage you would call him one of the great entertainers. He certainly made a lot of people laugh. But as a social force, he was zero.

Neil Leifer

Photographer

Muhammad Ali is a very special human being and there's probably never been an athlete or even a politician that had his ability with people. I've watched many people react to Muhammad and I agree with them. He is just an amazing people person, and it took a while but I think that finally people saw that. He always had fans, but then he had more fans and then he had more fans, and something happened in Atlanta when he held that torch at the opening ceremony at the Olympics in '96 when the few people who weren't on the Ali train came aboard. Some people even see him as godlike, and maybe the way he's portrayed in my photographs supports that, but I don't see him that way, and where I am ringside has nothing to do with that. I photographed Sonny Liston and Mike Tyson the same way. I certainly wouldn't look at either of them as godlike. I mean, I'm a boxing fan. I've got to know too many boxers who clearly in no way represent God, or certainly no god we'd want to know! Muhammad is just one of a kind.

As far the newspapers were concerned, it didn't really make any difference that he was a black athlete. The heavyweight champion of the world had been black for a long time, and I don't think it entered into the equation at all. However, that certainly changed when Cassius Clay announced that he had changed his name and was a Muslim, particularly a member of a sect – the Black Muslims – that were not necessarily looked at in a nice way by most of white America. Then he introduced race into the equation, not because he was black but because he challenged people. He insisted on being called Muhammad Ali when people were still calling him Cassius Clay. It wasn't because people were racist about boxing but because of how outspoken he was and how strong he was in his beliefs. By then, boxing – certainly the heavyweight division – was almost all black, and nobody would have paid attention to the fact that Ali was black. A Black Muslim, though, was a different matter.

My best-known picture, without question, is my picture of Muhammad Ali standing over Sonny Liston in Lewiston, Maine, in 1965. The interesting thing is that it wasn't nearly as well received when I took it as it is now. The picture sort of grew in importance as Ali's legend grew. In a lot of ways, I like to think that the picture and Ali – and maybe my career – travelled the same path. That was just a dream moment for a photographer.

There is a misconception about what a photographer has to do. I mean, this fight in Lewiston lasted only two minutes and eight seconds, or something like that, but God, you work hard! People would say to me, "Two minutes? God, it must have been terribly disappointing." Well, no, because at a fight, whether the fight goes 15 rounds like the first Frazier-Ali fight or ten seconds, the only picture an editor is looking for is one moment: the moment of the knockout.

Look at all 14 rounds of the Ali-Frazier fight in Madison Square Garden. The only moment anybody published on the front page of papers all around the world was when Frazier knocked him down in the 15th round. When this happened exactly in the right spot for me, this is what I hoped would happen. People have asked me many, many times over the years what was I thinking. Well, I don't have a clue. I was so concerned about focusing the damn camera and making sure that everything was set up right, but still, I knew it was in the right place. And as far as I was concerned, once it happened in the right place for me, the only thought I had was, "Stay right where you are, sonny. This is just perfect!"

Of course, it's difficult to cover all the ring. The way a magazine like *Sports Illustrated* or UPI or other wire services would cover it would be that you would normally get two ringside seats – because they're precious; there are so few of them – and you'd try to put one photographer on each side of the ring so that one of them would hopefully be lucky. The irony about the picture, with Frazier knocking Ali down, is that there's a guy in the picture, Herbie Shaftman, who was the other *Sports Illustrated* photographer that night, you can see him looking at Ali's rear end. On that night, he was clearly in the wrong seat. I mean I was just very lucky.

But like I said, that picture of Ali standing over Sonny Liston in Lewiston is my best-known photograph. *Sports Illustrated* did an issue last year that had the theme of "the greatest sports photos of the century", and they chose this photograph to be the cover of it. Obviously, I'm very proud of it. I also know just how lucky I was to be in the right place at the right time. That could have been Herbie right here! However, having said that, a good sports photographer is being paid not to miss when you get lucky like that, and this happened. I was in the right seat at the right time.

But, for whatever reason, that seems to have become the picture that most people look at and think of as the way they want to remember Muhammad Ali. I think it really is that simple. I think people want to remember Muhammad Ali just like this, and as the years have gone by it's just become the picture that people seem to talk about when they talk about what a great fighter Ali was.

I've often been asked what Ali was saying when that shot was taken, because clearly you can see he's saying something in this photograph. The thing is, I spent so much time just worrying about getting the damn thing in focus that I have no idea. I mean, these were not auto-focus cameras we were using.

The next day, of course, Red Smith wrote a piece entitled "The Phantom Punch", I believe, suggesting there was no punch. Now, I've seen the film a few times, and I remember seeing a punch way back then. I've seen other heavyweight title fights in which you can't see the punch, either. Who knows? I always say about this fight: the proof that Liston didn't just sit down was that he got up and they continued fighting. People forget that. They fought for 15 to 20 seconds before the referee was told that he had already counted to ten. Liston didn't go down again. He clearly looked as though he were about to finish the round. I mean, they were well into the final minute of the round when the referee stopped the fight, so I don't know. If you're going to take a dive, you should go down again pretty quickly. He didn't.

That expression on Ali's face, though, that's pure Ali showmanship. It's very hard to say whether or not the expression on Ali's face is disgust, victory or what. Ali just had a way of doing something special. I mean, before Muhammad Ali came along, the weigh-in of a fight was boring – one guy got on the scale then the next guy got on the scale. Ali would do things like wink at the other fighter at a weigh-in. He would emote, do something that suddenly made the weigh-in picture a photograph that appeared on page one of the paper the next day, when nobody ever cared about a weigh-in before. He made the weigh-in visually exciting. With Ali, you could never predict what he was going to do.

I've often been asked if the press corp increased because of Ali. The thing is, in the '60s, there weren't 18 belts in four different divisions like today, when nobody knows who the heavyweight champion of the world is. I mean, there are three or four of them at any given time. Muhammad Ali just was the latest in a long line of great champions – Jack Dempsey and Joe Louis and Rocky Marciano. Back then, a heavyweight title fight was big period, so there was always a lot of press corps there, and I don't know that it increased with Ali. I certainly think that there was interest. For example, I think Ali got women interested in boxing, because he was such a great-looking guy. But then, I think women liked Joe Louis, too.

There's also a picture I took at the Ali-Patterson fight at Las Vegas, after his victory over Sonny Liston at Lewiston, Maine. Patterson had been heavyweight champion of the world, and Ali just gave him a boxing lesson. That was a fight that Ali thoroughly dominated. It was also probably the first time that people realised that there was a new heavyweight. Floyd Patterson I happen to think was a wonderful fighter, but Floyd Patterson on a good day weighed 195 pounds while Muhammad Ali was 210 pounds. He was in terrific condition, didn't have an ounce of fat on him. He was just much, much bigger. While you wouldn't expect Sugar Ray Robinson to have fought Rocky Marciano, in a funny way the weight differential was almost the same. I think Ali dominated Patterson at that fight because I think he was a much better fighter and because he was so much bigger.

At the time of that fight, things were getting very politicised. I read that, just before the fight, Frank Sinatra went into Patterson's dressing room and gave him a big pep talk, that he had to win this fight for America. There was no question that there were an awful lot of people rooting for Patterson, because he was *our* black man, and Muhammad Ali was someone else. Ali played that card. He played the race card. I think he would tell you that a whole lot of it was to build a gate and to build interest in the fight, to sell tickets, and I'm not he didn't use this to help.

I also took a picture of the Cleveland Williams fight in the Houston Astrodome in 1966, and Muhammad was just unbelievable against a very good fighter. A lot of people will tell you that Ali's real greatness is measured by his opponents, and of course you don't create your opponents. Cleveland Williams would probably have been a legitimate and a very good heavyweight champion in any other era. Ali just had a relatively easy fight and knocked him out in the third round, I think. But I took my all-time favourite picture right after, an overhead shot of Cleveland stretched out on the canvas. That picture is my favourite because, unlike the one of Ali standing over Liston, that one came from my own head. I planned that. Everything in that picture I put there. Nobody ever put a camera in the centre of the grid above the ring. They used to put it off at an angle so you might see a little bit of the fighter's face. The next fight after the William's fight, I remember getting to the arena and there was six photographers vying to get this centre spot, to try to recreate this picture.

It's a photograph that couldn't be taken today, because so many things have changed in boxing. Just look at the trunks that they wear. I mean, it looks like a wrestling match today. Boxing used to be very much a tradition – the champ wore white, the challenger wore black. The ring was plain canvas – there was nothing on it. Today, the canvas is a series of commercials. You couldn't get the picture that I took in 1966 today. The ring is just is too busy.

When Muhammad Ali fought Joe Frazier in 1971 in Madison Square Garden, that was just one of the greatest 15-round fights of all time. And Ali lost a fair decision – I think he was beaten even without the knockdown in the 15th – but the boxing fans were eager for a rematch. They couldn't wait. Then Joe took what he thought was an easy fight for a lot of money against George Foreman in Kingston, Jamaica, and lost the title. And I watched Ali during that period, and as time went on I don't think Ali thought he'd ever get another chance.

Then, when he took the fight with Ken Norton, I was there at the fight and watched some of his training, and I just don't think Ali cared. I don't think that it was so much that he didn't train hard enough for the fight; I really think that he was just bummed out by the fact that what he had wanted was a rematch with Frazier. He wanted to avenge the only loss on his record and knock him down, and then that wasn't happening. So he didn't care a whole lot about the Norton fight. I don't think the public cared, either. I don't think my editors cared. For example, we normally sent two or sometimes three or four photographers to a heavyweight championship fight. For the first Norton fight, in San Diego, I was the only photographer. We were not doing a major piece on it. Even when Ali got beaten and got his jaw broken, we didn't do a major piece. We did one spread. Not a big piece. I got in the dressing room at the end of the fight and got probably the only picture.

By this point, George Foreman looked like invincible. He was the new champion, and he looked like he'd be around for years, and people were beginning to lose interest in Ali. I remember going to either the weigh-in or the pre-fight press conference. I came in with Ali, and as we were walking from the parking lot into the arena there was a young black man selling T-shirts for the fight, $25 shirts. He hadn't sold a damned shirt. Muhammad walked over to him, as he knew that this was a good picture situation, and he went, "Hey, brother. How come all these shirts are there? They should be sold by now."

"Well, champ," said the guy, "they're not selling."

And Muhammad said, "Well, you're not doing your job right. Move over. Let me show you how to sell." And Ali got behind this box with the T-shirts and he started shouting "Hey! T-shirts $35!" He raised the price. Suddenly, two people came and bought a shirt and took a picture of Ali. Then there were four. Then there were eight. Ali must have been there only half an hour, but he sold every one of those damned T-shirts. People were getting him to autograph their shirts. Then he walked away and said, "See? You do your job, now. You sell them all, too." But the interest in the fight wasn't there. The interest in Ali wasn't really there.

But then, when interest in Ali grew and he became heavyweight champion, the amount boxers got paid went up dramatically. Certainly, when he and Joe Frazier got $2.5 million each to fight in Madison Square Garden, people said, "Wow! Where's the money coming from?" Well, all of a sudden there were new ways of making money. The idea of being able to show the fight pay per view had arrived. You saw the fights in a movie theatre and you paid $25 a pop, only now it went up to $50 a pop, in the big cities of New York and Chicago and Miami. Everybody made a profit, and the fighters were suddenly getting their fair share of the profits. You look at today's figures and you see fighters that you've never heard of or care about making huge amounts of money. I think it's one of the great marketing coups of all time.

People think about making a movie, when a film makes $100 million it's hugely successful, and usually it takes some time to do that. You can make $100 million in 30 minutes with the right fight. Holyfield and Tyson made a lot more than that. It's a matter of supply and demand. If in fact the fight can generate $200 million worth of income, the fighters are gonna get $20 million apiece. Why shouldn't they. They're the people that are in there bringing in the money. But it just was a matter of earning potential that the fighters suddenly began sharing it.

But Muhammad Ali's fight with George Foreman in Zaire, I still remember the press conference for that. You had 200 American journalists looking at each other – "Where's Zaire?" Nobody had ever heard of it. So Ali brought half the world's press to this fight in Africa. That was when he was at his promotional best, in Zaire. He really built that fight. The whole of Africa fell in love with Muhammad Ali. George Foreman was clearly the underdog there, and yet people thought Ali was fighting an invincible champion.

When Muhammad would go out amongst the people of Zaire, after training, he was like the Pied Piper. I've got great photographs at Ali's training camp just after a workout one afternoon. He'd just started walking and suddenly there was two kids following him, then there was six, and it just kept growing. And no one would touch him. No one would come over and ask for an autograph. They just wanted to be in his presence. Before long, there were a few hundred people just trailing along when he took his afternoon walk. And he loved it. He soaked it up and would play to them. And my camera recorded it.

But George Foreman was a powerful fighter. When he first came along, I photographed him winning the Mexico City Olympics, and he was bigger than Ali then. He looked invincible. He looked like he had the punching power to finish off Ali. And we'd already seen Ali go down when Joe Frazier hit him, and when George Foreman hit them, they stayed down, so you had to think that Ali's only chance was to keep away from him.

In fact, the young Ali, when he boasted about how pretty he looked and how there were no marks on his face, what people didn't understand was that he was the best defensive fighter that ever lived. I mean, you can't beat a guy if you can't hit him. So, while Ali never had the punching power of George Foreman or even Joe Frazier, it was impossible to hit him. That was his strength. Going into Zaire, you assumed that if he could keep away from Foreman he'd have a chance. He had great jabs, still. He could cut him up. But the one thing you couldn't do was mix it with Foreman. You had to keep away, and that was Ali's skill.

So, early in the fight, Ali started this rope-a-dope, as he called it, when he'd lean up against the ropes and just invite Foreman to whale away at him. I had no idea what he was doing. I certainly didn't think it was the right tactic. I mean, I'd watched Foreman knock fighters out one after another – Ken Norton, Joe Frazier. Suddenly, here was Ali inviting him to hit him. It looked to me like disaster, and one had to assume something was wrong with Ali – either he was hurt or just unable to defend himself. It was only later that I found out what his rope-a-dope theory was. Then, when it was happening, I just thought that it was the dumbest thing I'd ever seen.

Ali gives a Black Power salute before entering Madison Square Garden to fight Oscar Bonavena, January 1971.

Taunting Joe Frazier before their first bout, 1971.

Angelo Dundee watches over Ali before the Frazier fight, 1971.
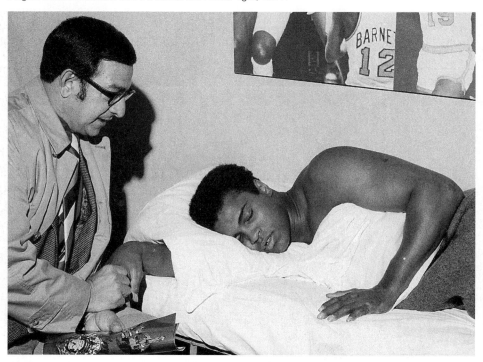

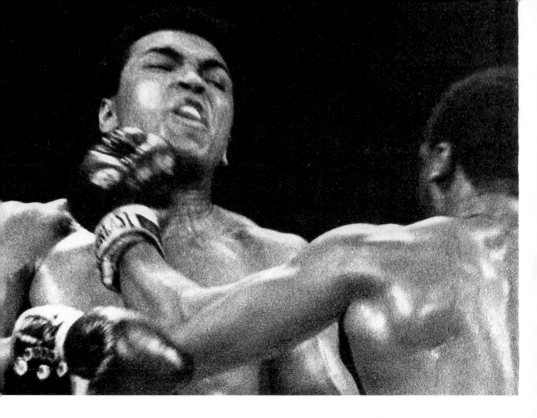

Hammered to the canvas by Frazier in the 15th round of their first fight, Ali eventually loses on a unanimous decision, Madison Square Garden, 1971.

A loser but still a winner: Ali receives an award from Alpha Phi, America's
oldest black fraternity, Milwaukee, Wisconsin, 1971.

Attired in traditional dress, Ali kisses Mecca's Holy Black Stone (said to have been given to Abraham by
Archangel Gabriel, and towards which followers of Muhammad face when praying), January 1972.

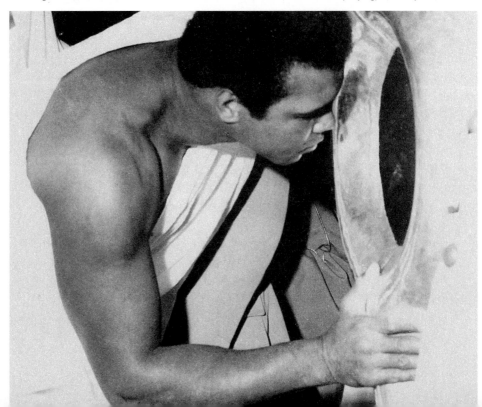

Midway through the fight, though, there's a great moment. I mean, when you think about boxing photographs, mainly it's my picture of Muhammad standing over Sonny Liston, but the pictures that are most remembered are punches landing. Well, I took a picture in Zaire that is among my all-time favourites, because it's subtle. It's at about the end of the sixth round. Ali has spent two or three rounds now doing this rope-a-dope thing. Foreman has hit him with everything he had and nothing happened. The bell has just rung to end the round and you can see by Foreman's face that he knew the fight was over, and so did Ali. That picture says more than any punching picture could have said. That picture told the whole story of the fight. Foreman had thrown everything but the kitchen sink at Ali and nothing happened. Don't forget that, while Foreman was doing all that, Ali was peppering him with jabs occasionally, and those jabs were hurting him – his eye was cut and his spirits were down. He knew he wasn't gonna beat this guy.

And then there was the Thrilla In Manila. I've covered over 30 of Muhammad Ali's fights, but none come close in terms of excitement to that fight, the third of the three Ali-Frazier fights. At this point, Ali was in wonderful shape. He'd been fighting very well and Joe Frazier had already started to slip. He'd just fought Joe Bugner and won, but he didn't look very good. So when we got to Manila, this was kind of a reward for us for doing a good job. We were all gonna have a good time. No one really cared about the third fight – it was going to be an easy Ali win.

It's funny. In photography, you get nervous when you're ringside – you want it to go well – but I remember being, very, very calm at that fight, because nobody was gonna care. I was just hoping my editor wouldn't kill the story. I certainly didn't expect it to become an important story. When the fight began, Ali just dominated in the first and second rounds, and I remember thinking to myself, "You should be watching what's going on. This is gonna end soon. If it doesn't end in the third round, it'll end in the fourth."

Then the third and fourth rounds sort of went – nothing happened. Then, in those middle rounds, Ali started piling in and Frazier started hitting back. And, God, they were the hardest punches I've ever seen in a ring. He was connecting with every one of them, just as Ali was connecting with that great jab of his and everything else in his arsenal. Then through the fifth, sixth, seventh, eighth rounds. By the time you got to the tenth round, this was already a great fight. These guys were throwing punches like lightweights instead of heavyweights, and it was taking its toll. They both looked like they were having a hard time standing by the twelfth round. I remember, when the fight ended, thinking to myself that I'd never seen a fight that good. I didn't think I'd ever see a better one.

I went to the press conference after the fight and photographed both of them. You certainly couldn't tell that Ali was the winner, and Frazier looked like he'd been hit by a truck. It was just an incredible evening. What followed was a party that President Marcos and his wife, Imelda, held at the palace, which I was lucky enough to go to, and Ali was so beaten he could barely lift his fork, but he was too proud not to go. Frazier didn't make it to the dinner.

As a fan, after Manila I was hoping Muhammad Ali would retire. I think he truly was the greatest fighter of all time, and I think that Manila was the perfect swan song for him. But then a friend of mine was asked why Ali continued fighting and he said, "Because fighters fight." There's a lot of truth in that. Muhammad obviously wanted to come back, and the thing about his comeback – and I think you can really see this in photographs of his later fights – it that he didn't lose his ability to fight. He lost his ability to defend, though, and so much of his success was based on the fact that you couldn't hit him. By the time he got to fight Larry Holmes, he was easy to hit. Earnie Shavers hit him all the time in their fight. A lot of people think Shavers won when Ali got the decision. Clearly it was no longer difficult to hit Muhammad Ali. What people had discovered – actually, they'd discovered it in Manila – was that he could take a punch. No one had known that. Everyone thought, "The first time this guy gets hit, we'll find out that he can't take a punch." Well, he took a punch better than anyone else. Unfortunately, he was taking too many of them. I mean, Larry Holmes was a great fighter, but when he won, it was more because Ali was in decline than because of Holmes' great abilities.

Most people think that Muhammad Ali retired from the ring and suddenly became this icon of world sport, but he really didn't. He just sort of began disappearing. I saw him a number of times, in the years after he retired, and he'd still draw a crowd, and certainly people respectfully waited for an autograph or two, but a new generation of fight fans grew up with other heroes. My son grew up thinking Mike Tyson was the greatest fighter and he wasn't a whole lot interested in Ali. Ali was of my generation, just like Joe Louis was my father's generation.

But then things changed when Ali lit the torch at the 1996 Olympic games in Atlanta. Then the world fell in love with him – certainly America fell in love with him – and he grew bigger than ever. Also, because we were nearing the end of a century, everybody was doing retrospectives – books were being written on the greatest this, the greatest that, of the century, and all of a sudden people were realising just how special Muhammad had been. So *Sports Illustrated* took over Madison Square Gardens and he was made Athlete Of The Century, and the more of those things happened, the more his legend grew.

I also think that a lot of people were taken by how courageous he was. He clearly has you know a pretty debilitating disease. His Parkinson's has taken away so much of what was once thought to be the great mouth of Louisville. He used to be a guy who just moved so beautifully; now he has difficulty walking and difficulty speaking. And yet his magnetism is bigger than ever. I marvel at the way people react to him and how unaffected he is, personally, by his difficulty in walking and speaking.

And, of course, now he's married Lonnie, and she has been absolutely wonderful for him. Among other things, she was able to handle the business side of Ali, what became a big business, and took a lot of pressure off him. Muhammad doesn't have the ability to say no to anybody, so he was doing an awful lot of things that just he didn't need to do, and Lonnie has been able to give him a reasonable schedule. It's still outrageous – Muhammad is gonna be 60 years old in January and he keeps a schedule that a healthy young man would have difficulty keeping – but Lonnie has juggled that.

I've photographed him a number of times in the last three or four years, and he's still a devout Muslim. He doesn't run around town preaching these days – he used to never let a press conference go without praising the honourable Elijah Muhammad. Instead, he keeps things very much to himself about his religion today. But he prays regularly.

It's been said that he was just a dupe, a mouthpiece for the Nation of Islam. Now, I certainly am not an expert on Ali and his religious beliefs, but I think that, when you look at him today, 35-36 years after he changed his name and took on his new faith, he is still a devout, practising Muslim. I don't think there's any question. In addition, he's an intelligent guy. He is so much his own thinker that it's awful hard to believe that he was used by other people. I just think that he did what he did out of conviction. I certainly haven't seen any evidence to refute that.

It's interesting, though. First off, when you look at what some could call Ali's racist comments of the '60s, you have to put them in the context of the times. This was the middle of the great civil rights movement in America. There were front-page pictures of police in Birmingham hosing down innocent kids. It was quite a tumultuous time, and maybe Ali's comments just fit in with the time. You take them out of context if you put some racist motive on him.

The only evidence I can give you – personal evidence – is that there was a period of time – certainly in the mid '60s – when Ali was surrounded by some pretty bad characters. They were not very big on the light press that was covering Ali. I had a number of instances where I would go to photograph Muhammad for a cover to preview a fight for *Sports Illustrated* and I'd get there and the Muslims that surrounded him were not very nice and not very receptive. It was, "Hey, champ. You don't have time for this guy." And the minute their backs were turned, Ali would always wink at you and let you know that everything was going to work out fine. It didn't happen once; it happened over and over again. And it always did. So, from my personal experience, I think that one of the reasons the press loved Ali was that it was impossible not to succeed with Muhammad Ali, no matter what you were there to do, even when he was surrounded by people that clearly didn't like you because you were white. I've never seen a prejudiced bone in Ali's body. I've seen his generosity with blacks, whites, Asians – you know, he's a people person.

But that was a pretty scary time in American history, but I never covered a fight with Ali and thought that someone was going to take a shot at him. Given the fact that we lost Martin Luther King and then Robert Kennedy, maybe I should have thought that way, but I didn't. You know, we live in a world today where you go to the Olympic games and... Well, airport security today is nothing next to what the security is to go into a stadium at the Olympics. At every fight in Las Vegas, the security is tight, and I'm sure it's the same around the world. I don't remember that existing when Ali was fighting, even though the threat was possibly more real than it is today. The only danger at a fight was a bum decision. I certainly was at a couple of fights at Madison Square Garden when the referee got a wrong decision and chairs and bottles would come raining down on the ring. But they were never directed specifically at a fighter; they were usually directed at the judges and the referee who called the fight wrong.

A lot of people think he's brain damaged. Now, I am certainly not a doctor, but I know that Ali and Lonnie are positive that he has the best Parkinson's doctors in the world, and they say that he contracted the disease at least 20 years ago, that he's been suffering from it for that long, that the damage that's so evident when you watch him is all related to the Parkinson's and not the fighting. There are plenty of people who dispute that, but I don't see any reason for his doctors or Lonnie to dispute that. There's too many feet of footage of Ali getting pounded in the Holmes fight and the Berbick fight and the Shavers fight. But he is certainly not brain damaged. Muhammad doesn't miss a beat. I just spent an entire day with him, and he hears everything, he reacts to everything, he gets involved in any conversation he wants to get into and he misses nothing. What he does have difficulty doing is speaking, and he certainly is much, much, much slower than he once was. It's just that you're used to looking at footage of Ali when he was so outspoken and so vocal and so loud and his playfulness with the press, and so when you see him now it's very easy to confuse the damage that Parkinson's syndrome has done to his ability to speak clearly with brain damage.

But he was a great man, and had he never contracted the Parkinson's he would still be a great man. I don't think we think that because of pity. I think that the Parkinson's has added to the way people react to him, certainly in Atlanta. He had difficulty holding that torch – he was shaking so badly, but he did it so proudly. In fact, he had difficulty lighting the torch, not because of any difficulty of his but it just didn't catch, so he had to stand there for an extra period of time, but he damned well wasn't gonna give up. I think it just captured America. In some ways, yes, people do feel sorry for him, most people who do have never met him.

If you spend ten minutes with Ali, you realise that he doesn't feel sorry for himself at all. Nobody's helping him walk; he's not driving around in a golf cart. You want to take a walk with him, he takes a walk. Nobody's helping him when of course he could have that, if he wanted to. Parkinson's doesn't appear to stop the Pope, who not only has advanced Parkinson's but is an old man. I think Ali is going to age that way.

Robert Lipsyte

Journalist

Muhammad Ali transformed boxing. Boxing before Muhammad Ali was what it became after him and what it always is – the corrupt Third World of sports, with strong men and hunters and civil wars of all kinds. When he arrived, he was the first non-political figure to transcend boxing itself. When he appeared – particularly in 1964, when he first won the heavyweight title – he was beautiful. He was much more of an entertainment figure than he was any kind of traditional athlete, certainly not a traditional boxer, who did their talking in the ring and who were silent, laconic, sweet-tempered killers who never boasted.

He transformed the sport. He was on the cover of *Time* magazine in the days when that meant something. Before he won the heavyweight championship, he went into Greenwich Village coffee shops and read poetry. He boasted, "I'm the prettiest," which to an America that was not quite attuned to the black athlete was exciting and different. Of course, a lot of African-Americans were not so charmed by this, because they understood right away that this aspect of a black star was really kind of a pimp style. But he was very fresh and exciting, certainly for boxing, which had just come through a series of champions that it never could quite deal with: a Swede who had a girlfriend back in times when, you know, one didn't have girlfriends; Floyd Patterson, a fine fellow but fearful and neurotic; and Sonny Liston, the ultimate thug. Now, suddenly, here's this adorable boy.

It was generally assumed that he would be destroyed very, very quickly, and that's why I became the boxing writer for *The New York Times*. I was a feature writer there, and when Cassius Clay fought Sonny Liston for the first time, in February 1964, *The New York Times*' ambassador to boxing could not be bothered by such a waste of his time and so sent a kid down there to cover the fight.

But I was thrilled to be there. Unlike a lot of older reporters, the younger guys didn't see Cassius Clay as some sort of stain on boxing; we thought it was great. We were the same age as he was, after all, and it was wonderful and it was thrilling.

I remember the very first moment that I saw him in the flesh was in the Fifth Street gym in Miami Beach, which is now South Beach, and The Beatles had shown up there for a photo opportunity with him, very early on in their American tour. They were herded into the gym and they kept looking at their watches. They were really mad because he was late and they decided that they weren't gonna wait: "Fuck it, let's go." When they started to move out, the press agent signalled to these huge security guards and they just pushed The Beatles into a locker room, and I got pushed along with them, because I was talking to them. So the five of us were locked in a dressing room, waiting for Cassius Clay.

So I introduced myself to them: "I'm Robert Lipsyte from *The New York Times*, a very important person." And these four cute little guys introduced themselves. John Lennon said, "Hi, I'm Ringo," and Ringo said, "Hi, I'm George Harrison," and it was all very jolly. But they were very pissed off – *where the fuck is he?*

Then, suddenly the door burst open and this voice said, "Hey, Beatles. Let's make some money!" At first, The Beatles gasped, and so did I because that first glimpse of Cassius Clay was thrilling. He was so beautiful and perfectly proportioned. You could never really tell from photographs and from television just how big he was. He filled the doorway – six foot three and over 200 pounds – and he was carrying a big staff like a prophet. He'd been up the beach, harassing Sonny Liston. And there was a wonderful, hushed moment when the five of us just looked at this gorgeous creature from another planet.

I think that that's the kind of impact he has. Even today, with his face a mask, a shambling shell of what he was, there is still that kind sense of presence. I'm not sure how much of it really is him, his spirit emanating from him, and how much of it is people of my generation and older remembering him how he was when he was this magical youth.

But it was amazing. Cassius Clay and The Beatles climbed into the ring and, as if they hadn't just met each other, they went through what seemed like a total choreographed routine. There are wonderful photographs of this, in which he pretends to hit the first Beatle and they all fall down like dominoes and caper and scamper around the ring. Then they go off to their history and he goes off to his. Then, a few minutes later, he called me over and said, "So who were those little faggots?"

The young Cassius Clay grew up in a segregated city in the South, pre-civil rights, during a time when there was an incredible lid on the opportunities of African-Americans, particularly the males, particularly for somebody like him, who was not going to go to college and law school. He was functionally illiterate, the sweet joke of his school. I've gone back to his high school and people remember him as this really kind, loveable boy who ran alongside the bus to school because he was working out to become a boxing champion. He got what they call in America "social promotions" – he was waved through school, as many athletes have been. He was the kind of boy who would wash the blackboard for the teacher, and of course he had a part-time job at a convent. He was just a lovable human being and everybody remembered him in that way.

The iconography that's grown up around him – the famous story about his bicycle being stolen – it might very well be true, but it certainly is in character with what we came to know that he was. He was in many ways the perfect athlete for '50s America. He satisfied a lot of stereotypes, he was dumb, he was beautiful, he was non-threatening and he was a black man who was willing to work for the white man. After he won the light-heavyweight championship in the 1960 Olympics in Rome, a Russian reporter asked him how he felt about '50s America, about the lack of opportunity, about segregation and lynchings, and he said, "Well, we have good people working on those problems, and at least we're not living in mud huts with alligators," which was very winning to white America and showed his global sensibilities.

Then, when he came back, he became chattel for the so-called Louisville Sponsoring Group, who were the white princes of Louisville, Kentucky, important businessmen who owned racehorses and fighters, and he became their fighter. Now, what that really meant was that not only did he have this wonderful personality but that he was not mobbed up. It was very rare, in those days, for a fighter with real talent not to have any ties with organised crime, and that was very alluring as well. He was clean. Sonny Liston was not clean.

The thing is, when Cassius got a chance at the title, he was really not the next person in line to fight. There are a lot of people, too, who feel that, in the fight that he had earlier with Doug Jones, one of the qualifying fights, he was given the fight. They feel that Doug Jones really won. But then, of course, he won the title, a seven-to-one underdog whom nobody really thought would win.

There was that moment just before the bell rang, when the two fighters came together in the centre of the ring for the instructions from the referee. We all gasped – he was so much bigger than Sonny Liston! I mean, by this time we had begun to believe what we'd written about this kind of Grendel's mother's incredible monster who was gonna destroy this magical youth. Then the fight began, and Ali took charge immediately, and except for that moment where he thought he was blinded, there was no question that he was in control. But Sonny Liston knew that he would have another shot at him, a return bout. He certainly had that kind of jailhouse mentality. Like Mike Tyson, he would not be humiliated. He would rather blow the thing up – bite him, whatever he needed to end the scene.

But really, that was the first sign of the Muhammad Ali that we know from the middle period. Before that, there was the magical youth that was Cassius Clay, and there is now this beautified saint of today with his Museum of Tolerance, this frozen-faced, large, black Mother Teresa cruising through our sensibilities, available for any openings, sanctified out of all proportion. But he is so symbolic, and this is the importance of Muhammad Ali, the hope that he gave to so many people, the resolve and strength he gave to so many at a time when many Americans needed to know that they were not cowards or crazy. After all, if the heavyweight champion of the world was stepping away from the Vietnam War, that meant that *their* stepping away from it was not merely self-indulgent cissiness.

But in the middle was this great fighter. The morning after he'd beat Liston – Liston was grinning, happy that it was all over – Cassius Clay gave this quick interview about the fact that, now that he'd won he could be a gentleman, he didn't have to be this crazed person any longer. The older reporters wrote this down, and they were very happy and left, but the younger reporters we were really unsatisfied. What? It was all a shuck and jive. You mean, you weren't serious?

And there had been rumours that he was a member of the Lost Foundation of Islam, the so-called Black Muslims, and it was known that Malcolm X was keeping a low profile after coming down to Miami Beach to give him support to him in the week leading up to the fight. So somebody said to Clay, "So are you a card-carrying Muslim?" And that phrase "card-carrying" really evoked the '50s, as in "card-carrying communist", with Senator Joseph McCarthy and the dark horrors of the Cold War. I'm sure that Cassius Clay had no sense of what it meant, but it seemed to flip a switch. He said, "In this world, bluebirds stay with bluebirds and redbirds stay with redbirds. I don't want to go where I'm not wanted, and I don't have to be who you want me to be; I'm free to be who I am."

That, in a sense, was the athletic Declaration of Independence in ways that went far beyond Cassius Clay/Muhammad Ali. Athletes and sports really began to seriously change at that moment. That quote really led to the failed boycott of the Moscow Olympics, to the fists on the victory stand of John Collis and Tommy Smith, to the revolt of the black athlete against being put in particular positions and, later, against being persecuted by white coaches. Eventually, of course, once they realised that they weren't going to win that battle, that turned into the self-indulgent, totally selfish Michael Jordan syndrome of today. But Muhammad Ali set that in motion, and that's why he's such an important character. He was one of the people who really both reflected the 20th century and helped define it, certainly in sports and perhaps even further than that.

There were periods in the '60s and '70s when he was the most famous face on the planet. He could go anywhere in the world and draw a crowd, and he would love to do that. He would just go out on the street and see how long it would take to get 5,000 people swirling around him. That really began the morning after that fight. He won the fight, he destroyed that monster and then he made this declaration. After that, the sporting establishment slowly coalesced to stop him and to crush him and to kind of understand. American society didn't really understand the depth of black patriotism in America. In 1967, when he refused to be drafted, there were people in the Justice Department who sincerely believed that they wouldn't get any more black soldiers. These were white people who didn't understand that there was no monolithic African-American sensibility, that African-Americans were loyal Americans and weren't gonna stay away from the army because this loud-mouthed braggart who talked like a pimp told them to.

That was a period of great turbulence and unrest in America. There was a lot of controversy about the Vietnam War. There were hearings going on in the senate. America was divided between hawks and doves, and the doves – who felt that we should not be in Vietnam – were being called communists, in a kind of hangover from the Cold War. It was in this environment that the Louisville draft board – who, up until then had classified him 1Y, which meant that he would not necessarily be drafted – reclassified him as 1A, which meant that you were ready to go. The general feeling was that the 1Y had been a favour to "the lords of Louisville", the Sponsoring Group, who didn't want their treasure to be drafted. But now, of course, he was a Muslim who cared.

Coincidentally, I was hanging out with him to do a feature story. We were sitting on the lawn in front of a rented house while he was preparing for another fight. It was three o'clock in the afternoon. Girls were coming home from high school and he was trying to get them to come into the house. And the telephone rang and he went inside. When he came out, he was very angry. He had just heard about his reclassification from a wire service reporter.

Now, his very first reaction, his very first reaction, was, "Why me? I pay so much money in taxes. I buy so many bombs and guns and helmets and airplanes. Why don't they draft some poor kid." But then, his second reaction was, "How could they reclassify me without finding out whether I'm smarter or dumber? They didn't give me another test." That was because a lot of people who were classified as 1Y were illiterate or stupid, and there were rumours that he was gay. So he was fulminating, and over the course of the afternoon, as he became more and more angry, people started to show up and laugh at him: "They're gonna get your ass out there on the grenade range. Some white cracker sergeant's gonna drop a grenade down your pants. They're gonna get you. They're gonna send you to Vietnam."

Later, television trucks and reporters started to show up and there were more phone calls, and someone asked him, "Well, how do you feel about the Vietnam War?" And he didn't know. He didn't know where Vietnam is. Then the questions became very embarrassing. And finally, somebody said, "So how do you feel about the Vietcong?" And it was in this spirit that he said, "I've got no quarrel with them Vietcong." I was sitting right there and I heard that, and I think my news instincts must be very poor because I didn't get it. I'd been there for so long, and this was just a natural progression of the hectoring that he'd been getting all afternoon. In a sense, he was caught in amber in that line, and that line which became a defining line of the '60s in many ways was less of a defining line of him than people thought it was, but he carried it right through. But he didn't know right away what the principle was that he was standing up for, and that's one of the wonderful things about Ali, this sense of becoming, this sense of change.

After he refused to step forward, every boxing commission – most of which are politically appointed commissions – refused to sanction any fight and his championship was illegally withdrawn, so he had to make a living making speeches on college campuses. Going with him to college campuses was very embarrassing and awkward at first. He would go on a campus and he would look down, horrified because there were these interracial couples, and he would say something really snide about how blacks and whites should stay together and then we'd get up and leave. Then he would sniff the air and say something really stupid about marijuana and the heads would all get up and leave. It took a while for him to understand his new constituency. He would do the Ali shuffle – tell some jokes, talk about the Nation of Islam and why pork is bad for you. In fact, he was pretty boring in the beginning, but then it would go into a question-and-answer sessions, and the kids would talk to him about Vietnam, and it was there that he learned about Vietnam. That's where he understood finally a war in which white people sent black people to kill brown people.

He had this magpie quickness, in the same way that he remembered doggerel and made fun of opponents, and he was sensitive to the needs of whatever reporter he was talking to. He began to understand the politics of the day, and in a sense he grew into the principle that other people thought he was wearing. That was a very loose garment in the beginning, but eventually he did come to fill it, and in that sense he became very, very important. I think that's why he's such an emotional benchmark for the boomer generation, men and women in their 50s who were in college at that time, why he is so meaningful to them.

Of course, in a sense, he hung testicles on all these guys who were being called cissies for avoiding the draft. The heavyweight champion of the world, Mr Man, the toughest man in America was saying, "This war is wrong and I'm not gonna fight it." But it was these kids who eventually taught him what that meant, when he spoke at their campuses. In the beginning, he refused to fight because he was a Black Muslim, because he was scared, because he was backed into a corner by American society, but eventually, in his own revisionism, he refused for all the right reasons.

After the war, though, I think we all knew he would fight again, because he was such a great talent. He was one of the very few boxers who really could draw crowds and make money for the industry. He was a crossover character – so big, so important. It seemed inconceivable that he wouldn't box again, even though you know he thought that he would go on to become senator or president or emperor.

I've always suspected that Cassius Clay was abused as a kid. His father was a violent man, an alcoholic who threatened me on stuff that he didn't like. There are even some police reports of him having beaten his wife. I wouldn't be surprised if emotionally he terrorised Cassius and his brother, Rudi, because there's a kind of pleaser quality to Cassius/Muhammad. He was always looking for older men to take charge of his life, whether it was as a trainer, a manager or the Louisville Sponsoring Group. Of course, the Nation of Islam were a good fit. Their kind of spookiness fit in well with Clay, who wanted to reject white society and black Christianity. I mean, for a boxer in training, not eating pork was fine; not sleeping with white women... Well that was probably a safe thing to do anyway. So the outward restrictions were not all that difficult to adhere to. Of course, in time, he would ignore them anyway.

I knew Malcolm X pretty well at that time, and he was a very powerful figure in Ali's life – warm, funny, shrewd, smart, really a great older brother. The honourable Elijah Muhammad, though, was a creepy shaman. They were well ahead of the curve on black is beautiful – the evil white man, the blue-eyed monster, the white devils, the seven-foot guys coming down in the spaceships saving us, Armageddon. It was really a kind of Voodoo Christianity for Muslims, and the pseudo-intellectuality of it was great for a kid who couldn't read and, I think even more importantly than that, for a kid whose father was this dissatisfied, drunken, out-of-control guy. Here were these members of the Nation of Islam – particularly the Fruit of Islam, their old police arm – they were clean. These guys were reformed drug addicts and ex-convicts who had cleaned themselves up, had jobs and were taking care of their families. So it was a kind of muscular African-Americanism that was very alluring to Cassius Clay, particularly at a time that civil rights was bubbling up. It was strong and empowering, and I think that, in those days, the Nation of Islam did more rehab than all of the city agencies that were going.

But they were a very controversial group, because white America was scared of them and was scared of Malcolm X. Again, it was that Cold War sensibility of the evil empire, being scared of Russia. But it wasn't until Malcolm X left the group and began moving leftward and towards a rapprochement with white society that he became truly dangerous. I've always felt that Malcolm may not have been murdered if Muhammad Ali hadn't moved away from him.

Malcolm was really the best-known spokesman for the Nation of Islam, the frontman and, by everything I've seen, the most vital, intelligent, progressive man they had, the only one who might have made a real difference in American society. And at that time, he was in a state of growth and changing – he'd come out of jail, gotten cleaned up through the organisation – and in a way I suspect that Elijah Muhammad understood that he needed Malcolm to bring in new members and also to have a public voice that made sense. At the same time, though, he was probably jealous of Malcolm's growing fame and power, so when Malcolm made that one slip after John F Kennedy's assassination, saying that it was a culmination of violence in America – "chickens coming home to roost" was the phrase he used – he was suspended. It was this limbo period in which Malcolm was hanging out with Cassius Clay, before the first Liston fight, eating ice cream – vanilla ice cream – in celebration.

But what happened soon after was the eventual pulling away, as it became obvious that, for all the strictures about Muslim men – about them being real, true fathers – Elijah Muhammad was fathering children by his young secretaries. I interviewed him once in his mansion in Chicago and I remember we talked downstairs on couches and chairs covered in plastic. He was a soft-spoken, dogmatic little man, and I remember wondering why all these young, pregnant women in their late teens and early 20s were padding around the mansion. Of course, this was the prophet casting his seed. But it was this that caused the split. Malcolm went to Mecca and created his own organisation.

But I think that, if Ali hadn't stepped away from Malcolm, it would have been very difficult for them to murder him, but he did and soon afterwards Malcolm was dead. I think that, if Muhammad Ali was a more politically sensitive person, it would be a case of "J'accuse", but he's not. It's all tied in with the serenity that we see in him now, this sense that, behind the mask, he's this kind of placid ocean liner moving inexorably through seas which part before him. He's so self-indulgent, so selfish, so absorbed in himself that almost everything he does, even his greatest acts of kindness, are really about embracing the world on his terms.

I talked to Malcolm X about him, and Malcolm was absolutely charmed by him. He thought that he was just delicious, and his kids loved him. But I think he understood that he had not really, totally cracked through. When

Malcolm was murdered, I don't think there ever were *bona fide* attacks, but I think Ali's apartment was burned. But then, the second time he fought Liston, in Lewiston, Maine, in 1965, ticket sales weren't going well and a rumour was begun by a press agent, I believe, that a car filled with black gunmen out to avenge the murder of Malcolm X was driving up from New York to Maine. That excited us all in Maine, and of course the tabloid writers were writing about it. That was about the zenith of the idea that somebody was out to get Ali. The promoters of the fight were thrilled. They felt that a lot of people might tune in to see a live assassination. But, of course, there was nothing like that.

I think that Ali's protected. A friend of mine, a civil rights activist and comedian named Dick Gregory, often talked about Muhammad Ali being the baby of the universe, that everybody really understood that babies in their innocence need to be protected, even if they cry, even if they make noises, no matter what they say, and that, in the same way, everybody would protect Muhammad Ali. Nobody wants anything bad to happen to him because in a sense he epitomised all our hopes for the future, all our senses of something naïve and innocent in the process of becoming. I think that everybody understood that Ali through the '60s was still on a journey. He hadn't hardened. He was still on his way to becoming something else – which he was. He left the Muslims along with three wives, many women and a dozen children and reinvented himself. And now, again in this beautification period, he is once again the baby of the universe.

I really don't know him that well, though. I've known him for 37 years, but I'm a reporter and he's a subject. I think the only real intimate, human conversation that we ever had in that time was when both of us were having daughters born at about the same time. We were both kind of edgy about when it would happen and I remember him complaining about it taking so long. But I'm not really convinced of the depth of his emotional interactions with people. I mean, there are obviously people who say that they're great friends of his, and certainly I would say Howard Bingham has to be, but so many people have moved in and out of his life – some of them go off to get murdered under strange circumstances, others come in and rip him off. There's something about Ali that's like Africa, in the sense that he hasn't been totally developed, and there are all these colonising forces –

corporations, religious groups, lawyers, accountants, entrepreneurs and hustlers – who all have these wonderful ideas of how this incredible natural resource should be developed, whether it's to endorse something as sleazy as a cockroach trap or as lofty as a Museum of Tolerance. But this man, for whom a Museum of Tolerance will ultimately be named, has never seen me in the last five years without saying, "Bob, what's the difference between a Jew and a canoe?" And every time, when I pretend I don't know the answer, he says, "A canoe tips." Museum of tolerance? Yeah, right.

I remember once I was with him for some barnstorming week, writing a magazine article, and we were running through a small airport in central Florida, very late for our plane. All of a sudden, a little old lady jumped up in front of him, held up a camera said, "Wait, champ," and took a picture. I didn't want to miss this plane, so I grabbed him and said, "Well, come on. Let's go!" And he said, "Wait, wait, wait." Very carefully, he reached over to the lady and said, "Your lens cap was on." He plucked the cap off and he said, "Now you can take my picture." We made the plane, of course. The plane was probably waiting for him.

But in the same way, I remember him talking about why it was possible for him to have sex with five or ten or 15 women in a single day, and the reason was – although he never said this – that he never came to orgasm. I thought of this in the same way of him plucking off that lens cap or stopping for an autograph or being kindly to a fan. He understood that this was such an opportunity for them to be with the champ. So this was like a sexual autograph. He was leaving all these little sexual autographs. I found it kind of charming, in some ways. He wants to please people. He doesn't want anybody to be disappointed.

Mike Marqusee

Author Of *Redemption Song: Ali And The Spirit Of The '60s*

Up until the late '60s, there was a system in Kentucky and, indeed, across the South that was very much like the Apartheid of South Africa. It was legislative – it was actually illegal, for instance, for black and white people to get married or to have sex in most of these states – and was also executed in practice, with black people being excluded from direct participation in social institutions. For instance, it barred them from direct use of virtually all public facilities – famously, there were public drinking fountains marked "whites only" and "for coloureds" – and in most of these states they were also denied the basic right to vote. Without understanding, that you can't begin to understand the forces that shaped Muhammad Ali.

However, the young Cassius Clay's principal motivation to go into boxing was more that it was a fantastic stage to show off from. He was clearly an insecure and slightly immature kid, but he loved an audience, and the boxing ring was a place where he could display his love of jokes, role playing and teasing people and at the same time have a certain protection, because, of course, he could win there. It wasn't just the segregation. You have to look at it in a larger context than that.

However, that segregation was nevertheless an experience that he shared with hundreds of thousands of other young black Americans across America. It determined the entire context of their lives. It was an inescapable, ever-present reality. They were reminded of it every time they walked down the main street and saw which shops they couldn't go into, which public facilities they couldn't use. That experience drove all kinds of people in all kinds of directions. It drove large numbers of people who were exactly Ali's age and from very similar backgrounds into the civil rights movements in unprecedented numbers. For Cassius Clay, though, it ultimately drove him into the arms of the Nation of Islam, which at that time stood very much apart from the civil rights movement.

It's also true that, while Cassius and Rudi enjoyed a relatively stable home situation, there were very serious and sometimes quite explosive tensions that existed between his parents. But let's put this in context. There is something of a myth that Muhammad Ali came from a middle-class background. This was a working-class background. His father was a sign painter. That's exactly the kind of myth that could only grow up in a country like the United States, which manages to completely deceive itself about the reality of class distinctions. Muhammad Ali's background was just like that of the hundreds of thousands of other people who got into the civil rights movement: black, working-class southerner.

In his official autobiography, *The Greatest* – which, incidentally, Ali later claimed that he'd never read until after it was in print – there is a great deal made of the impact of the murder of Emmett Till on the young Cassius Clay. Emmett Till was a young black man from the North who was visiting his family in the South. It was alleged that he looked the wrong way at a white woman and was beaten to death. Till was the same age as Cassius, and this could have happened to him, his brother or any of his other contemporaries. And that was an impact felt widely across the black community, both North and South, and a turning point in the development of a more militant race consciousness among black people of his age.

So boxing became a very important sport for the black community. There is an incredibly rich tradition of black boxing and of black boxing lore that has great currency in the black communities in the United States. In the first half of the 20th century, the most famous black Americans were boxers. First there was Jack Johnson, the first black heavyweight champion, who was persecuted, effectively forced into exile and ultimately imprisoned for the crime of having sex with and marrying a white woman! And then there was Joe Louis, who managed to overcome a great deal of that racism but was still profoundly affected by it. His fights were some of the most symbolically charged sporting events of the first half of the 20th century, particularly his fight against Max Schmelling, who was a German champion and was seen as the embodiment of the theory of Aryan supremacy. All kinds of ideas about racial equality, about democracy, about the state of black people in the modern world were contested in these fights. And they were listened to with incredible emotional intensity in the black community. People in Harlem, for example, organised Joe Louis radio parties. When he was fighting and it was broadcast live on the radio, people wouldn't just sit at home listening to it alone; they would gather together in bars and in churches and in community halls and listen to it collectively.

This was a political activity. The Communist party – which was really the main political party concerned with racism at the time – organised some of these Joe Louis radio parties. They saw the black folks' emotional involvement in Joe Louis' fights as something that needed to be built on, as something that could be used as a platform for the lobbying of black people's collective interests. And people from several generations of black activists – Maya Angelou, Richard Wright, Langston Hughes or, later, John Lewis, Julian Bond or Andrew Young – will talk about the huge impact that Joe Louis had as world heavyweight champion.

Jack Johnson was the first heavyweight champion, and he was subject to the most vile racism, not least because he was outspoken, highly independent, impatient and insubordinate. He refused to define himself according to what the white media wanted and, as a result, he was persecuted and hounded, and the black fighters who came after him weren't even given a shot at the title for many years, until Joe Louis came along. And Joe Louis and the black middle-class people who handled him, advised him and trained him decided that they were going to avoid what had happened to Jack Johnson by ensuring that Joe was polite, patient and did not challenge white authority in public. Joe never smiled when he beat up on a white guy in the ring, and above all was never ever seen alone with a white woman. That was the kiss of death, as far as the white press were concerned.

And this strategy worked, because the context of the times. This was Roosevelt's "New Deal" America, and the Democratic party were pursuing a populist agenda, trying to unite large numbers of Americans around an agenda of democracy and anti-fascism. And so, for once, the demands and aspirations of black people – symbolised by Joe Louis' success in the ring – were actually not in contradiction to what a lot of mainstream America wanted. So, on the one hand, you Roosevelt's New Deal and what the left called "the popular front" at the time – their need to project a multi-racial image – and on the other you had Louis' willingness to tailor his image to the requirements of white people.

And then Cassius Clay – later Muhammad Ali – arrives on the scene. There are two major moments when Ali defines himself in new terms and which initiated new eras in popular culture. The first was the day after he won the heavyweight championship of the world, defeating Sonny Liston and upsetting all the pundits and experts. He's 22 years old and, as he says, he "shook up the world". Now, usually, what you do when you're 22 years old and you've just won the world heavyweight championship is that you go to a luxury hotel and you join the cocktail party with the rich and famous, but the young Ali refused to do that. Instead, he went back to his blacks-only motel, in the blacks-only section of downtown Miami, and spent a quiet evening – without alcohol – with a number of his friends, including Malcolm X, Sam Cooke – the great gospel singer – and Jim Brown, who was a great American football hero and one of the early spokespersons for black rights in sports.

And after those discussions that night, the next morning he met the press. In those days, of course, the press was exclusively white and male, and this 22-year-old African-American looks at them all and says, "I don't have to be what you want me to be. I'm free to be what I want to be." Now, that in itself was pretty shocking to sports reporters, who thought that all young professional sportsmen – and especially all young black professional sportsmen – should be what they were told to be. But what made it absolutely earth shaking was the fact that the young Cassius Clay wanted to be a member of the Nation of Islam, the most reviled political organisation of the time.

He was repudiating Christianity in a predominantly Christian country and at a time when most Americans knew even less about Islam than they do now. He was repudiating the integrationist agenda of the liberal civil rights movement only six months after its high point, with the great march in Washington, when Martin Luther King made his marvellous "I have a dream" speech, a vision of an America in which colour no longer mattered. And most importantly, he was repudiating his national identity as an American in favour of an identity that went beyond the borders on a map. He was saying, "I'm not an American. I'm a member of the Nation of Islam" – or, to give it it's full title, "the Lost-Found Nation of Islam in the Wilderness of North America".

All of that was an awful lot for a mere boxer to do. These were themes that within a few years would be commonplace in the black ghettos among the black intelligentsia and would appear in American popular culture without people being too shocked, but in February 1964, when Cassius Clay first articulated them, they truly did shake up the world to a much greater extent than just beating Sonny Liston.

The second moment at which Muhammad Ali advanced on the world's stage and redefined himself and his era came two years after he'd won the world heavyweight championship. It happened in February 1966. He'd already made himself unpopular by being a very public member of the Nation of Islam, but now that the war in Vietnam wasn't going according to plan, and so the Pentagon announced that it was expanding the draft call-up. They needed more American soldiers because they weren't winning the war. As a consequence of this, Muhammad Ali became eligible for the draft.

In fact, the reporters discovered this long before Muhammad Ali did. He was in training for a fight at the time – again in Miami, Florida – and the press called him and said, "Champ, you know, they may draft you. What are you doing to do?" At first, he was pretty confused about that and he avoided the question. But then, of course, he finally refused to fight.

In the spring of 1967, he met with Martin Luther King in his home town of Louisville. They met there because there had been a series of demonstrations by the local black community there, who were demanding access to whites-only residential areas, and in return for their pains they had been badly beaten and assaulted by white racists and the local police. Ali was outraged by this and went into the streets and made a statement about why he was not going to Vietnam, because of what he had seen in Louisville, and I think that that's not only the greatest political statement that Ali ever made but also one of the most beautiful expressions of the true spirit of the '60s. "Why should they ask me to put on a uniform," he said, "and go 10,000 miles from home and drop bombs and bullets on brown people in Vietnam while so-called 'negro' people in Louisville are treated like dogs and denied simple human rights? No, I am not going 10,000 miles from home to help murder and burn another poor nation simply to continue the domination of white slavemasters over the darker people of the world. This is the day when such evils must come to an end. I have been warned that to take such a stand would put my prestige in jeopardy and could cause me to lose millions of dollars, but I have said it once and I will say it again: the real enemy of my people is right here. I will not disgrace my religion, my people or myself by becoming a tool to enslave those who are fighting for their own justice – freedom and equality. I either have to obey the laws of the land or the laws of Allah. I have nothing to lose by standing up for my beliefs. So I'll go to jail. We've been in jail for 400 years."

That refusal reflected an underground development within the black community – and also, increasingly, among white students – of people redefining what their real loyalty to America should be, when America was the aggressor in a terribly unjust war. It also reflected the internationalist consciousness that the young Ali had imbibed from Malcolm X and the Nation of Islam. But at this time, although there was growing anti-war sentiment, not a single major Democrat or Republican political figure had spoken out against the war. Not a single major newspaper had editorialised it. Not a single network had broadcast a serious programme criticising it. Indeed, those who were against the war were routinely derided as dropouts, people who needed to take a bath, communist dupes. And now here was Muhammad Ali, a man who really had a lot to lose, making a stand with people who were completely derided.

At the very moment that he made his statement, the Number One hit song in the United States was 'The Ballad Of The Green Berets', which is an extremely jingoistic song that celebrates American violence in south-east Asia, so he was really standing against the grain in the most remarkably brave way. But to understand exactly how he did that and why he did that, you have to look at something else he said rather quietly on the same day and which only appears at the very bottom of the *New York Times* article about this day: "Boxing is nothing, just satisfying to some bloodthirsty people. I am no longer Cassius Clay, a negro from Kentucky; I belong to the world, the black world. I'll always have a home – in Pakistan, in Algeria, in Ethiopia. This is more than money."

Now, I'd suggest that those people who retrospectively have decided that Ali only blundered into his opposition to the war in Vietnam, that he was really a bit thick, that he didn't even know where Vietnam was and that he mispronounced the name and systematically called it "Vietman" have missed the point completely. This guy had already thought and felt more deeply about the real issues in Vietnam than all the academics and intellectuals who were advising the Pentagon at the time. He knew where he was going and, through the Nation of Islam, he had come into contact with the world community. He had redefined himself. He had said that, as the world heavyweight champion, he was not accountable just to the American establishment; he was accountable to black people, oppressed people, all over the world; and, strangely enough, he felt accountable to boxing fans all over the world. And all over the world, boxing fans *did* support him, because they thought that his position on the Vietnam War shouldn't determine whether or not he was the world heavyweight champion, although it came to do so.

What's significant about his great statement to the press, "I don't have to be what you want me to be; I'm free to be what I want," is first that it's a ringing declaration of personal autonomy, personal independence, and that's one of the great themes of the '60s. That cuts across all sorts of different theatres of '60s politics and culture, the drive for self-expression and independence from cultural norms. Speaking as a child of the '60s myself, that had huge influence on myself and everyone of my age. But it's also more than that, because what's incredibly important about this moment for Ali is that the drive for his personal self-definition is political and is shaped entirely in the context of a collective struggle for human dignity and human rights – first and foremost the civil rights movement, which was happening all around, and secondly in the form of a global movement against the remnants of colonialism, against America's Cold War policy.

During the Cold War, the US establishment very much wanted to project itself as liberal and tolerant and multi-racial society because they were in a competition with the Soviet Union for influence over the emergent nations in Africa and Asia. The problem was that the US wasn't actually like that. The world that emerged after World War II was polarised into the two great power blocs, both dominated by white people. The advent of the American civil rights movement and, more broadly, the African-American freedom struggle was the key moment at which that whole thing exploded, because it proved the lies and hypocrisy on both sides of the power game and it exploded certainly Cold War America's self-image and the image it wanted to project to the world. So the black liberation struggle in America was one of the starting engines for all of those struggles that we call "the struggles of the '60s". The other principal ones were the struggles in south-east Asia, Latin America and Africa. These were coming from the two sides – one within the very heart of America and the others on the very margins and fringes of what you might call the American empire.

It's these two things, starting at once, which immediately become interactive with each other. In fact, Muhammad Ali's whole life demonstrates that interaction but without those sparks of all the other things we talk about in the '60s, including all the stuff about fashion and music and sexual permissiveness. Those come from that initial challenge to the consensus. And once the consensus was challenged, at it's most grotesquely dishonest point – the Hollywood movies of the '50s, for instance, are lies about what the US was really like then – people stood up and suddenly were exposing that, not only before the nation but before the world, and that shook the house. Then, all kinds of other things started to become unearthed and other grievances and other forms of protest were unleashed.

So what starts as one young man's commonplace desire – a very legitimately, central human desire – to be what he wants to be, not to be defined by the older generation, is in this context – the context of the '60s – also a very political comment. And that's what I find so fascinating about Muhammad Ali, because in his career and in his persona these various dynamics of his era – the personal and the political – come together and strengthen each other. Each strand becomes more powerful because it's part of the other.

The scale of civil-rights protest was quite extraordinary in the '60s, and not just in America. One of the significant things about 1968 was that it was a global chain reaction, where events in Paris or Prague or Mexico City interacted with events in Harlem or the southern United States or Chicago, and they in turn had an impact on them. And it wasn't only between Europe and the United States but really between the First World – the developed world – and the emergent Third World. And so this was a kind of emergence of a global consciousness from below that took hold among youth from many different cultural backgrounds across the world.

Now, this seriously worried the establishment, and the level of repression and violence meted out to protestors on a global scale cannot be overstated. I mean, never mind the degree of violence meted out by the American war machine against the civilian population in Vietnam and Cambodia and Laos. In the United States, the FBI launched the persecution of "black militants", as they called them, paying ghetto informants to provide them with the names of activists. In 1969, at least 25 Black Panthers were murdered by the police and thousands more were jailed. Between 1964 and 1969, virtually every American city witnessed major rebellions in the black ghettos, so-called "riots". In the end, something like 500 people lost their lives in these riots, and nearly every single one of them was black and was the victim of a police bullet. 50,000 to 60,000 were arrested.

This was a pretty intense level of civil strife, and that policing operation cost the American government many millions of dollars. And that's just the black movement. If you move on to all the other fronts of protest social movements, you also can see similar rising levels of violence. So the attempt to turn the '60s into some sort of soft-focus nostalgic era, when we all had a lot of fun going on protests – the *Austin Powers* view of the '60s – is a complete rewrite of the reality, and that is really quite shameful. These were serious issues. Real human beings lost their lives. Real human beings had their lives damaged.

The reality is that the 1960s were about a complex series of overlapping social movements, but these were movements that started from below, on the margins of society, and advanced against huge obstacles and resistance into the mainstream of society. Above all, the 1960s were about the emergence of a global consciousness from below – the ideal of solidarity, first among black people, ultimately across all national borders, across all borders of colour and, later, across borders of gender and sexuality. This is one powerful idea working itself out from the bottom of society with frankly very little assistance from the powers that be.

I was lucky enough not to go to Vietnam. I was the last year the draft applied, and in my year Nixon imposed the birthday lottery, and my birthday was pulled out 350 or something, so I was not called. But I never would have gone, anyway, and like most people of my age I had determined that, from the age of 14, I would not do this. But for the American troops involved in it, the war was a remorselessly brutalising experience. They found themselves as heavily armed foreigners in a land that did not want them, where they were asked to perpetrate the most horrific atrocities against the civilian population.

At the time that Muhammad Ali first spoke out against the war in Vietnam, the United States was using napalm, which is a chemical that burns the skin off its victims and cannot be extinguished with water. The US was practising crop destruction as a routine and deliberate policy, water-source destruction as a routine and deliberate policy. Torture. The rounding up of civilians who *might* be associated with the enemy. And of course the destruction of whole villages and village populations, most famously in My Lai.

All of this was well documented by the anti-war movement and by the independent and foreign media, but not by the mainstream media, so most Americans could claim that they didn't know about it. However, I think that, as the war unfolded, that claim fell apart, and the American GIs themselves went into a massive revolt against it. One of the reasons that the war came to an end was that American working-class soldiers – many of them black, but also white solders – simply refused to follow orders. By 1970, opinion polls show that, when asked who their great heroes were, the American GIs at the front line mentioned Malcolm X and Muhammad Ali. And when a draft dodger is the number-one hero of your front-line troops, something has gone seriously wrong in the war effort. The more the American establishment tried to win hearts and minds to its war effort, the more it alienated people, because the realities of the war were unrelentingly horrific for all concerned.

Of course, they were worse for the people of Vietnam. We're talking about two million dead over an eight-year war. We're talking about environmental destruction from which Vietnamese people being born now still suffer. We're talking about the destruction of a whole way of life and a whole society. It's one of the great atrocities of the 20th century, and it says something about things that one of the first persons to speak out most boldly about it was a completely uneducated boxer from Kentucky.

When Muhammad Ali first came out against the war in February 1966, the reaction was ferocious. In fact, over the next year, he became easily the most reviled and hated sports figure in American history. It's hard to believe that now, because very few people will now admit to the fact that they ever criticised or disliked Muhammad Ali, but his stand on the Vietnam War and, particularly, his refusal to comply with the draft led to him being condemned in virtually every newspaper in the country, as a traitor and even as a coward – which is something to say to a world heavyweight champion – and as a thoroughly rotten example for young Americans.

And it wasn't only the white establishment that roasted him, either. Very significantly, most of the leadership of the civil rights movement – most of what you might call the black middle-class leadership – were absolutely appalled. They felt that he'd let the side down terribly, because their idea was that black people should prove themselves to be patriotic, loyal Americans, and by doing that they would then stake a claim to an equal place in American society. Muhammad Ali and an entire younger generation of black and more militant black people that he spoke for and that he was a part of had given up on that because, as far as they could see, they had repeatedly proved their loyalty to America, and in return for it they were still second-class citizens.

Of course, he was pursued by the Justice Department and ultimately indicted, tried, convicted and sentenced to a five-year jail term for draft evasion. He appealed against that and he remained out on appeal until, ultimately, the Supreme Court quashed the conviction on a rather complex technical ground three and a half years later. But, in the meantime, his passport was confiscated from him, so he wasn't allowed to leave the United States, and the United States was the one country in the world where he was not allowed to practise his trade as a boxer.

No sane person would have bet that he would ever fight again. No sane person would have bet that he would ever reclaim the world heavyweight championship, and definitely no person, sane or insane, would have bet that he would finish the 20th century as the most beloved, revered sports figure in America and in the world, and that's because, in 1967, no one predicted the rising tide of protest against the American war in Vietnam, both inside and outside of America. No one predicted that, by 1970, the anti-war movement would be able routinely to put one million people – most of them young – on the streets, month after month, in major demonstrations and basically destabilise the American system.

It was in that context that Muhammad Ali's appeal against his conviction for draft evasion finally reached the Supreme Court. Nixon most definitely wanted Muhammad Ali sent down for some serious prison time, but the Supreme Court judges took a slightly more realistic view. After all, this was only months after Nixon's invasion of Cambodia had sparked off the biggest student demonstrations in the history of the United States, resulting in the killings of students at both Kent State and Jackson State Universities. They realised that locking up one of the biggest heroes of the anti-war movement – and, indeed, someone who had a global following, particularly among people of colour, measuring into the many hundreds of millions – was not a very smart idea at a time when the establishment was for once looking pretty isolated.

And so, after a good deal of internal negotiation, they came up with a technical formula by which they could quash Muhammad Ali's conviction without setting a precedent that would allow other people also to claim exemption from the draft on the same grounds. They restored his passport, and suddenly he was allowed to fight again. But it wasn't the Supreme Court that did that; it was the millions of young people – and, it should be said, not just the young. People all over America, black and white, had been protesting against the Vietnam War, and on the back of that tide of public sentiment the Supreme Court and the American establishment yielded and Muhammad Ali was able to re-enter the ring and begin the second phase of his career, which is just about as amazing as the first phase of his career, although in a different way.

His first fight after his exile from the ring was in Atlanta, and Atlanta in the very early 1970s had become something of a capital for the new aspirant black culture, which had matured through the struggles of the 1960s. Virtually every black celebrity in America turned up at ringside on that occasion. By this time, Ali's support among all black people – whatever their politics and whatever their income bracket – and among very huge numbers of white people was very well established. But the hatred against him by racists, and also by all of those who took the love-it-or-leave-it approach to American foreign policy, was still very intense. There were death threats, and he was even sent the dismembered body of a dog while he was his training for that fight. Contrary to some myths, that racism in America did not die away after 1966, '67 or '68. The passage of the civil rights movement was a momentous and wonderful thing, but it was by no means the end of racism. Muhammad Ali continued to be hated throughout all his boxing career by many of those people.

One of the strange things that happened was that, because they hated Ali so much, they came to identify with anyone who fought against him, including black fighters. And poor Joe Frazier! You have to feel sorry for Joe Frazier. He's one of the greatest boxers of all time, and he is one person who really does have a legitimate grievance against Muhammad Ali. Through no fault of his own, he became a symbol of white America, and Muhammad Ali used that against him – brilliantly, in some ways, theatrically – to sell the fight on television. That was demeaning to Frazier. But in the end, the fact was that most of his supporters were people like Nixon and the Ku Klux Klan and the Hawks in Vietnam and everyone who had a grudge against Muhammad Ali. And of course Frazier himself came from a desperately poor Southern black background and was the most ludicrous figure to embody either the American dream or, in particular, the white power establishment!

One of the many paradoxes about Muhammad Ali is that he demeaned his black opponents with language that compared them to animals. He talked about them as being ugly, as being gorillas. If a white fighter had used this kind of language, the fight would have been boycotted by black people. But this is, of course, the complexity of black identity – it can be turned inside out, used for all kinds of nefarious purposes, although it can also be used to promote the liberation of black people from oppressive structures. But it's sad that Ali sold the Thrilla In Manila and some other fights on that basis, turning his black opponent into a subhuman figure, because after all that was just playing to not only the worst racial stereotypes but also to the worst stereotypes about boxers in general. And here it came from the mouth of someone who did more than any other individual to dignify boxers and to say, "We are human beings. We have a right to political, social, cultural and religious opinions and a right to express them."

One of the things that most offended the establishment was Ali's insistence that he should decide what his name was. Over a ten-year period, between 1964 and 1974, he fought quite an amazing battle to have what he called his "own name", which is what they call it in the Nation of Islam. *The New York Times* – the so-called "paper of record" – refused to refer to him as anything other than Mr Cassius Clay until the mid '70s, and I think they're pretty ashamed of that now. The irony is that it was always very commonplace for performers of various kinds – including sports performers – to change their names in America, but in the past it had usually been white performers with ethnic names – Jewish, Polish or Italian – who changed their names. John Garfield and Edward G Robinson, they both had Eastern European Jewish names and changed them to these mainstream whitebread names because they wanted acceptance.

So it was a total hypocrisy on the part of the American establishment. Changing your name for commercial reasons was perfectly OK, but changing your name for political reasons – and, in particular, changing it to a name that was explicitly and self-consciously not American – completely flummoxed them. Nowadays, of course, Islamic, Swahili and other African- or Asian-type names are common and, frankly, not only in the African-American community, and that's been a wonderful loosening-up of cultural boundaries and a redefinition of what it is to be an American. And, of course, don't forget that the only native Americans are a very tiny minority of the population, most of whom were extinguished by the ancestors of the rest. So it was that Muhammad Ali's bravery – ironically enough – freed other ethnic groups to reassert themselves. Now, of course, Italian-Americans do not change their names when they go to Hollywood, as anyone who follows Robert De Niro, Al Pacino and Sylvester Stallone knows.

In 1964, the Nation of Islam was the longest-established, best-organised, most widely known and most definitely wealthiest black nationalist organisation in the United States. From the 1930s, after the demise of Marcus Garvey, it had been the principal vehicle for the whole tradition of black nationalism. To oversimplify things, black nationalism is a tradition that states that black people form a nation within America, an oppressed nation, and not just a nation within America but a nation across the whole African Diaspora, and which therefore defines them as having interests separate from and frequently opposed to the interests of their oppressors.

This had been a hotly debated idea within the black community ever since the liberation from slavery, really. "Where do we belong? Are we Americans or are we something else?" Elijah Muhammad was the founder of the Nation of Islam, and he was largely illiterate and totally poverty stricken when he came to the revelation and he put together the most curious and, ironically, typically American amalgam. There are bits of Islam there, but anyone who has actually read the Koran will know that the Nation of Islam as it was led by Elijah Muhammad was nothing like anything that can remotely be called orthodox Koranic Islam. There were bits of the Judeo-Christian tradition, there were bits of Marcus Garvey and there were bits of popular science fiction. Part of their teachings was that a superior race of beings would come in a sort of mothership to liberate black people from white people. Part of their teaching was that white people were the result of a eugenics experiment done by gigantic scientists which had gone badly wrong.

All of that seems pretty wild, but on the other hand you have to ask why it was that so many very intelligent people – not least Malcolm X and Muhammad Ali – were willing to accept a great deal of this. That's because, in the light of the direct experience of black Americans within the United States, some of these theories actually did not seem so preposterous. Something had to be explained here. How else could you explain the outrageous and disgusting position that black people endured? The white commentators' explanation for it was that that was what black people deserved. Even white liberals really thought and said that. But here was a group of people saying, "No, white people are evil. America is evil. We are good. We are beautiful." And that was why Muhammad Ali was attracted to them.

But the Nation of Islam had other elements in its make-up. Its members really rejected the whole modern world. They were anti-gambling. They were, ironically, anti-sport, and it was a big problem for them that their most famous adherent was principally famous as a competitive, commercial sportsman. Elijah Muhammad regarded competitive commercial sport – along with gambling, alcohol, drugs and prostitution – as a white vice that had been inculcated into the ghetto in order to destroy black people. Elijah Muhammad was an autocrat, and this was an organisation run with an iron grip from the top down, and dissenters could be dealt with very severely. Of course, the most famous dissenter was Malcolm X, who was ultimately not only ostracised but in fact murdered by members of the Nation of Islam – although, of course, there continues to be considerable debate about who was actually responsible for organising his killing. Nonetheless, there can be no denying that he was denounced in rather lurid terms by both Elijah Muhammad, Minister Farrakhan and other leading members of the Nation of Islam.

They were also completely homophobic and deeply misogynistic. They believed that women were second-class citizens and that the best protection for black sisters in a white, racist society was for them to submit and subordinate themselves in the role of the home maker to black Muslim males. Both Muhammad Ali and, to some extent, Malcolm X went along with this, although both of them also questioned it later on.

Finally, the most important aspect of the Nation of Islam is that it was actually a very apolitical or anti-political organisation. At the very time when black people in unprecedented numbers were taking to the streets and joining picket lines, demonstrations, sit ins, rallies and voter-registration drives, the message of the Nation of Islam was that this was all a waste of time because America was irredeemable. It could not be changed. They were saying that what was needed was a separate black nation, either in America or elsewhere. Throughout most of the 1960s, the teaching of the Nation of Islam was against engagement and politics, and this was the main reason why Malcolm X split from them. Malcolm felt profoundly guilty after the Birmingham bombing that took the lives of four young black girls, the white racist response to Martin Luther King's appeals for interracial harmony. After the Birmingham bombing, Malcolm X was commanded by Elijah Muhammad to do nothing, but that wasn't good enough for him and so he turned away from the Nation of Islam in the last year of his life.

Muhammad Ali, though, was actually attracted to the fact that the Nation of Islam disapproved of political activity. This is one of the ironies of his career. When he first announced his allegiance to the Nation of Islam, one of the reasons why he was doing it, he said, was that he didn't want to go on demonstrations. He didn't want to move into an all-white neighbourhood; he just wanted to be left alone to be a proud black man. But guess what? In 1960s America, that was not going to happen. The irony is that, by persecuting him for his allegiance to the Nation of Islam, the American establishment actually turned him into a much more sophisticated and politically engaged and politically significant figure.

For Muhammad Ali, like many other very talented young black men in the '60s, particularly, the Nation of Islam offered a refuge from racism. It was a safe, all-black haven, and it was a place that said, "You can go out into the world and be successful as a black individual but also, at the same time, wall yourself off from the realities of this horrifically racist society." So it was very appealing to ambitious young black people – Muhammad Ali, Sam Cooke, Joe Tex, another great soul singer who was a supporter of the Nation of Islam. Black businessmen flocked to Elijah Muhammad's banner. He offered them an apolitical response to the struggle against racism, the struggle of the civil rights movement. But they kept running into a basic problem, which is that the white establishment would not let them be.

In Los Angeles, in the early '60s, the police staged an appalling raid on the organisation's headquarters. There are no two ways about it – they openly gunned down several of the activist members. People who were unarmed, standing in their own office, were shot and murdered. After that, Malcolm X went to Los Angeles and said, "We've got to organise. We've got to fight back. We can't just let this happen." Elijah Muhammad told him to say and do nothing, because Elijah Muhammad wanted to keep the organisation strong and, it must be said, rich, but in a world of its own. He just wanted the white power structure to go away. But they wouldn't.

To some extent, this explains why Elijah Muhammad was prepared to collude with even the Ku Klux Klan, with whom he tried to negotiate a non-aggression plan at the very time that the Klan was lynching activists in the South. It was a pretty disgraceful moment in history of the Nation of Islam and something that turned Malcolm X's stomach and turned him away from it.

Muhammad Ali had a much more ambivalent attitude. He really liked being a boxer and he really did just want to go on being famous, being popular, having fun and exercising the craft at which he was so brilliant. But the temper of the times and his own deep-principled convictions about equality and human dignity simply wouldn't allow him to do that.

In the run up to the young Cassius Clay's heavyweight title fight against Sonny Liston, he was training in Florida and invited Malcolm X and his family down to be his personal guests at the training camp. Indeed, Malcolm X was his guest at ringside at the fight. This was at the very time when Malcolm X had been suspended by Elijah Muhammad from full membership of the Nation of Islam and had been barred from making any public statements, allegedly because his statement after John F Kennedy's assassination – which was that it was a case of the chicken coming home to roost – had been damaging to the organisation and offensive to many Americans and he needed to learn humility. As we know from Malcolm's autobiography, which was published after his death, this is a time in which he was in absolute inner torment about his long-time loyalty to Elijah Muhammad and his growing sense that he was corrupt, autocratic and offered no meaningful political way forward for black people, who were facing racist violence.

So at this very moment when Malcolm X is undergoing a profound political, social and religious upheaval, he's spending a lot of time in the company of the young Cassius Clay, during which time I think it's simply inconceivable that they did not discuss these issues. And then, immediately after the fight, Cassius Clay announces his allegiance to the Nation of Islam with Malcolm X at his side. Within a week, they're in New York City, touring the United Nations building, Harlem and Times Square, doing the sorts of things that no black sportsperson had ever thought about doing before and causing a serious commotion.

But at this moment, Malcolm X was actually resolving to break with the Nation of Islam, and within a fortnight of Muhammad Ali standing up with Malcolm X at his side and announcing that he was a supporter of them, two things had happened: Malcolm X actually left the Nation of Islam publicly and was vitriolically denounced by Elijah Muhammad and other Nation of Islam supporters; and the young Cassius Clay was renamed Muhammad Ali by Elijah Muhammad, severed contacts with Malcolm X and became a loyalist for Elijah Muhammad.

It's my belief that we'll never know for certain everything that happened in that short space of time, maybe 20 days. It was a time of extraordinary commotion in the inner lives of a number of major, political public figures. It's a very disturbing period. There was a great deal of violence and threats of violence against Malcolm and his followers. There was also an attempt to burn down Muhammad Ali's apartment by persons unknown.

Now, trying to extricate the real truth from all of this is probably impossible, but there are some things that it's fair to conclude. For instance, Muhammad Ali was profoundly influenced by Malcolm X, whose teachings – and particularly his internationalist vision of the place of African-Americans – stayed with Ali throughout his career and, indeed, has done to the present time, and shaped his response to the draft. It also shaped his decision to fight in the Third World, most famously in Kinshasa. And it shaped his way of expressing himself. Muhammad Ali often used some of the homilies and allegories and arguments about white racism that Malcolm X had used.

But why, then, did he then not go with Malcolm? I think it was because

Malcolm was asking something that was very scary for Ali. Part of it could have been that he was frightened of the consequences of breaking from the Nation of Islam. Indeed, for some people, those consequences did prove pretty severe. But I think that the main reason was that Muhammad Ali felt at home in the Nation of Islam and its religious and cultural approach and that he felt challenged and uncomfortable by Malcolm's increasingly and explicitly political approach. He didn't feel that he could really sustain that. I think that Malcolm was asking a great deal of him, and although in the end Ali ended up defying the draft by becoming a global spokesperson for a global cause, at this stage – 1964/65 – that was not what Ali wanted.

To bring the story up to the conclusion, in 1975 Elijah Muhammad died and his son, Wallace Muhammad, became the leader of the Nation of Islam. An advisory council was constituted to give the new leader counsel and among its members was Muhammad Ali, Minister Louis Farrakhan and a number of other eminent thinkers.

Within a year of his father's death, Wallace Muhammad had changed the Nation of Islam beyond all recognition. He had abandoned the explicitly anti-white "white devil" theory; he had abandoned all the science-fiction elements; he had reverted to orthodox Islam; he had allowed white people to come to the meetings and had, ironically, abandoned the anti-American side of the organisation's ideology and announced that, from that point on, people should not only vote but be prepared to serve in the armed services.

Muhammad Ali was actually delighted by all this. By this time, of course, the war in Vietnam was over. By this time, all of the movements of the '60s had receded. It was a different era. And, of course, Ali always got on fine with white people. He was always prepared to defend the Nation of Islam's anti-white rhetoric, but he was someone who, in his own life, was a non-racist without question.

But not everyone was happy with that, notably Louis Farrakhan. He was very unhappy that the Nation of Islam had abandoned its black nationalist content, and so, in the late '70s, he set up a new organisation, which he also called the Nation of Islam, after the old organisation changed its name. And that is the organisation we now know as the Nation of Islam and which

Farrakhan has led with considerable success over many decades since then. But Muhammad Ali has never been part of that second organisation and, although he has always been friendly to Louis Farrakhan, he has always kept his distance. Since the mid '70s, he has been a very devout and very sincere and very committed but very orthodox Muslim.

The FBI under J Edgar Hoover also took a great deal of interest in Muhammad Ali's movements. The FBI was not only absolutely obsessed with surveillance and harassment of the left – and particularly anyone who could be called a communist – but it had always been obsessed with what Hoover regarded as black nationalism. In fact, Hoover had been wire-tapping, harassing and investigating Elijah Muhammad since the 1930s. He'd cut his teeth by prosecuting Marcus Garvey, and he built the FBI into what we would now call an institutionally racist organisation. There were no black agents allowed under Hoover, but that proved to be a problem, as it's rather difficult to infiltrate black nationalist groups with white agents, so he had to pay ghetto informants, some of whom were drug dealers. Much of the information they garnered was extraordinarily inaccurate.

However, thanks to the FBI and, more importantly, to the freedom of information provisions in America, the civil rights movement and the black freedom struggle of the 1960s are probably the best-documented movements of resistance in human history, because the people who took part in them didn't keep notes of all their conversations, but the FBI did. And among other things, thanks to the FBI we have the record of a wonderful telephone conversation between Muhammad Ali and Martin Luther King, where Ali says to King, "You're really great and what you are doing, brother, is fantastic. But, man, don't let them whities get you. They're after you." And King expresses his admiration for Ali.

Now, the FBI always hated Malcolm X, and it had been following him and compiling dossiers on him since the late '50s, but it was when the young Cassius Clay started meeting with Malcolm X that he first entered into the FBI's files. Then, of course, when he was publicly a member of the Nation of Islam – and, even worse, an opponent of the Vietnam War – the harassment and the surveillance was non-stop and probably remained so right up until the mid '70s, after Hoover died and the FBI was finally slightly reformed.

I used to stay up to watch late-night television talk shows on which Muhammad Ali would appear, and so the government was spending taxpayers' money on making transcripts of Ali's discussions with Dick Cavett, Johnny Carson and that kind of absurdity. And when Ali's trial for draft evasion took place, there were things in his FBI file that ranged from things like anonymous letters, anonymous racist abuse written by the FBI, which they solemnly pasted into the Muhammad Ali file. There was also records of all kinds of private conversations, and these are of huge historical interest now, but it's shocking that the FBI thought that this was appropriate. And, of course, it has to be said that all the presidents – including John F Kennedy, Lyndon Johnson and Richard Nixon – knew that something like this was going on, and they all found it appropriate.

Nowadays, of course, we have Martin Luther King day and public monuments named after not just him but even Malcolm X, and the civil rights movement has been institutionalised as part of American history. The dogged and bitter resistance that it met among the white establishment has been forgotten. In as early as 1964, there was a massive white backlash – which is the name the media gave it – to the civil rights movement running right across both the North and the South, most famously in George Wallace's primary presidential primary campaign in 1964, where he was getting 30% more of the Democratic primary vote in Northern states. This alerted politicians – particularly those of George Bush Senior's and Ronald Reagan's generation – that the most reliable political or electoral card for the Republicans to play was the race card, was to capitalise on white resentment of the very modest advances that black people had been able to make.

So what happened in the 1960s was not some triumphant march of reason and goodwill and harmony in which intolerance and prejudice simply disappeared. Far from it. Every advance made by black people, every attempt to get the most minimal civil, political or economic rights, was met with the most bitter and unusually violent resistance. And so, internally, the dynamic of the civil rights movement was a complicated one. It wasn't as people look at it now, as one of infinite hope and naïve aspirations; on the contrary, it was definitely, on the one side, one of expanding hopes and aspirations for black community and for black individuals but, on the other side, increasing frustration within the American system which simply refused to respond to reasonable appeals.

And so what you get in the later '60s is the growth of Black Power and the growth of black militancy. However, this was not a repudiation of the civil rights movement, although it took the form of it at the time; it was the logical conclusion to draw from the fact that white America had refused to bow to the entirely reasonable and moderate demands of the civil rights movement, so it seemed to the people who were involved in it at the time.

You have to remember that Martin Luther King was absolutely loathed by most white people until long after he was dead. I know that's an uncomfortable fact for America to deal with to this day, but it's demonstrable. And, of course, never mind Martin Luther King; there was also Malcolm X and Muhammad Ali, a brash young black man who didn't feel that he had to justify himself in white terms. That was just completely outside their ability to comprehend.

When Ali was banned from fighting in the United States, in the years 1966 and '67, he fought several times abroad, including twice in London. It's ironic that, by banning him from fighting at home, the American establishment actually helped him build a global fanbase which stood him in very good stead throughout the years in which he faced legal and financial persecution. That was a fantastic lever for Muhammad Ali against the American establishment.

In 1966, he came to Britain and he famously fought Henry Cooper at the Arsenal stadium in Highbury and made fairly short work of him, as he did with most of his opponents in those days. Of course, Britain wasn't directly involved in the Vietnam War at that time. The labour government of Harold Wilson was giving some support at that time, but it was a more remote issue, and so Ali found that the British press were a good deal more sympathetic or at least more reasonable than the American media.

But, more significantly, when he came over here, he made a point of meeting representatives of the new generation of black and Asian militant young people, people who had either come to Britain as young people themselves, along with their parents, or been born here and didn't feel that they should be grateful just to have a home in Britain, that they should be treated as equals. Famously, he met Michael X, the most notorious Black Power spokesperson in Britain at that time. With Michael X and other militant young black people, he toured the black communities of Notting Hill and Brixton and very much gave the Muhammad Ali seal of approval to the rising tide of black consciousness in Britain's inner cities.

Ali was one of a series of visitors from America in those years who brought with them the ideals and the language and the style of the African-American freedom struggle, and that was hugely significant for the black and Asian communities in Britain, which in the mid '60s were just establishing themselves here. Mid-'60s Britain saw the birth of the term "Paki bashing" and saw extensive physical attacks by white racists – some of them organised in fascist groups but, frankly, most of them not – against Asian people, who were routinely dubbed as "Pakis". And, in that context, for the heavyweight champion of the world to be coming to Britain and to be a Muslim, a *fighting* Muslim, someone whom you most definitely could not take out to the back of the bus stand and kick around and think no one would care – that was an incredible psychological boost obviously for the Muslim communities and, indeed, for all of the communities of colour, because he brought with him not just the Nation of Islam but also the whole of American black experience.

In 1964, Martin Luther King came to Britain and met with some of the leaders of the black community who were just then beginning to build the first organisations – the Campaign Against Racial Discrimination and others – and attempting to advance the lives of the black community. In 1965, Malcolm X had visited and been warmly received, by the students at Oxford University, among other places. In 1966, Muhammad Ali visited. In 1967, Stokely Carmichael – who later changed his name to Kwame Ture and was one of the major spokespersons for Black Power – came here and was promptly deported by the Labour Home Secretary, Roy Jenkins, who is usually misrepresented in British history as a great liberal but who clearly could not tolerate an aggressive, outspoken black militant in the country at the time.

So Ali was easily the most famous of all these people because, of course, he wasn't a political activist; he wasn't a political ideologist; he was the world heavyweight champion, and that was something that reached into every working-class community of whatever colour. One upshot of this was that, throughout his period of exile, he enjoyed huge popular support in Britain and across Western Europe, Asia and Africa. In 1967 and '68, there were demonstrations in Britain against the Vietnam War at which leaflets were given out saying, "Defend Muhammad Ali!" There were a lot of draft resistors in the war, but none of them remotely as famous as Muhammad Ali. Outside the United States, if you asked people, "Who is the American most closely associated with opposition to American policy in Vietnam?" overwhelmingly the answer would be, "Muhammad Ali."

One of the many amazing facts about Muhammad Ali is that the first thing he chose to do when he won the world heavyweight championship in 1964 was to go to Africa. At this time, no black sportsperson and certainly no white sportsperson from North America had ever even noticed the existence of the continent. No less thought of actually visiting it. This visit was actually Malcolm X's idea, and it was he who initially organised it by introducing Ali to some of the reps of the newly independent African nations in the United Nations building in New York. However, Malcolm broke with the Nation of Islam and so wasn't on the scene when Ali actually did go to Africa with a small number of people from the Nation of Islam.

It was amazing. This guy was the world heavyweight champion and this was the first time a major African-American sports star had visited Africa, yet no American media covered the trip at all. There was not one TV camera. Ultimately, *Sports Illustrated* published quite an interesting article about it, but that was several months later.

Muhammad went to Ghana, the first post-colonial nation in Africa. Its leader was Kwame Nkrumah, who was a great ideologist about Africanism and someone who had actually spent many years in the US and so knew a great deal about the traditions of American-based black nationalism. Kwame Nkrumah was the first head of state to shake Muhammad Ali's hand. It's hard to believe that now, when there isn't a politician in the world who wouldn't give his or her right arm for a photo op with Muhammad Ali, that for ten years – from 1964 to 1974 – no American president or head of state would dare to be seen with Muhammad Ali.

But it wasn't just meeting the famous and the great national liberation leaders – not only Nkrumah but he also met Nasser in Egypt; what was more important was that, for the first time, Ali came into contact with the African masses, with the poor people of colour who make up the majority of the human race, as much now as in his time, but which most Americans have no contact with. And he was overwhelmed by this. Here were tens of thousands of poor people chanting his name – "Muhammad Ali, Muhammad Ali, you are the king of the world" – and first of all it made him realise how important his new name was. It's been said by people who know Ali that it was in Africa that he really became committed to the new name and became prepared to fight for it back in America, because he could see how important it was.

What was happening was that there was a new generation of Africans who had lived through European colonialism and were just in this period beginning to emerge as independent citizens. Most of Africa was still under European domination at this time. And what they found was that they were emerging into a Cold War era where they were abused playthings between the US and the Soviet Union. And here was Muhammad Ali, an African-American who had defied the American establishment, who had embraced his African patrimony and had given himself an Islamic name. And, of course, West Africa is heavily Islamic.

Now, the ordinary people of Ghana didn't have televisions at that time, and most of them didn't speak English but they knew what it meant. It meant that something new and important had come into the world and that they had a new ally in the US, in the advanced world, that they hadn't been aware of before. Their emotional response had a huge impact on Ali, and ever since then he has been an absolute sucker for walking tours in Third World city streets. I suppose that anyone who is greeted with the kind of warmth and love that he is greeted with would feel the same way. He can't resist it.

In fact, when his passport was finally returned to him in 1971, when his conviction was quashed, the first thing he said was, "Man, I can go to those places now and see all those amazing people on the streets. Then I'll know I'm free again." So what was important for him wasn't just going to rich hotels in Third World cities; it was going to all the cities of the world and interacting with ordinary people. I think that is quite genuine in Ali. And it goes beyond any intellectual ideological thing. It was a deeply emotional thing. I think Ali had a great need to be loved and he had a great deal of love to share out, and to be surrounded by African children in a marketplace was just glorious for him.

His second trip to Africa was in October 1974 for the Rumble In The Jungle, which was fought in Kinshasa, in what was then called Zaire and has now reverted to its proper name of the Congo. One of the amazing things about this trip was that this time, of course, every media outlet in the world was present. In 1974, Muhammad Ali couldn't go anywhere in Africa without having the TV cameras on him. It's precisely ten years after his first visit to Africa, but neither Ali nor the media chose ever to mention the fact that he had been there before, that he actually knew a great deal about Africa. It was a kind of informal conspiracy among them. Instead, he played up his naïve wonderment card, because he had a point to make. He was going around saying to the white reporters, "Look at these Africans! They drive cars, they fly planes, they have running water. Man, most of them speak two or three languages. That's more than you do." He wanted to be a champion of his people and a champion of Africa, and he saw himself as an African. But in the course of that, he decided to eliminate from history the truth, that he had already been there but the white media didn't know it. And that's classic Ali. He did play fast and loose with historical facts, but he did it because he had certain points he wanted to make.

Now, there's another irony in his second visit to Africa. On the first visit, he had met Kwame Nkrumah, and he had been one of the sponsors of the second visit. In fact, for him, Muhammad Ali was one of a number of great African American spokespersons.

Mobutu Sese Seko – who was the dictator of Zaire at that time and was the principal person who staged the Rumble In The Jungle – had very different reasons for wanting Muhammad Ali there. Ali came to Africa on his second visit not at the invitation of a great leader of African independence but at the invitation and sponsorship of one of the most brutal killers of the 20th century, a man who used black identity to murder thousands of black people, to plunder black countries and to generally destroy civil society in the heart of sub-Saharan Africa. And so Muhammad Ali played a tragic role in bolstering one of the most nightmarish regimes of the 20th century.

Whether he was aware of this or not is an interesting question. He was certainly more than happy to play a leading role in what was being promoted as a great all-black African-American partnership between Africans and between African-Americans. That is a beautiful and noble ideal, and I think Ali really subscribed to it. The problem was that the African side of the partnership was being represented by Mobutu Sese Seko and the African-American side of the partnership was being represented by Don King, and so the interests that were actually furthered by the Rumble In The Jungle I think were not the interests that Muhammad Ali really had hoped, ie the ordinary people in both continents. But there was an amazing moment shortly before the fight when Muhammad Ali turned to the camera and said, "I ain't fighting for money or fame; I'm fighting for poor people all over the world. I am fighting for the moms on welfare. I am fighting for drug addicts and winos. I am fighting for anyone who can't get a fair break. I am a fighter for Allah. I wish Patrice Lumumba was here to see me."

Now, Patrice Lumumba had been murdered 13 years before by Mobutu Sese Seko, along with help from the CIA and Belgian mercenaries. The person who had told Muhammad Ali about Patrice Lumumba and his great vision of an independent Africa was Malcolm X, who had met Lumumba before he was murdered and had described him as the greatest African ever to walk the face of the Earth. So, all these years later, and despite pressure from both the Nation of Islam and the American establishment and the general pressure on Ali to get along and be the loveable rogue that he quite liked being, and despite all that he remembered, at this key moment in his life and career the shadow of Patrice Lumumba was over him, a name that most Americans don't know but a name that was known in Africa and a name that you could not mention publicly in Zaire at that time, because his murderer was the dictator.

So it was a very complicated but a very beautiful and inspiring moment at the

Rumble In The Jungle. Any of us who had followed Muhammad Ali through all his trials and tribulations, who had felt that his causes were our causes, we felt vindicated and boosted. Maybe only for a few moments, but I remember the feeling and it was glorious that Muhammad, now in his mid 30s, could come from all those years of persecution and exile and reclaim the world heavyweight championship before the eyes of the world but in front of an African audience. It really was one of the most glorious moments of sport, and all the contradictions of it – the role of Don King, the role of Mobutu – cannot take anything away from the immense symbolic drama of the beauty of the moment. Sometimes beauty comes with ugliness, after all, and if Muhammad Ali's career isn't about that then I don't know what it is about.

Then, of course, he visited Newcastle. As far as I know, there are only two black men who have enjoyed the honour of massive public civic receptions in the north-east of England. The first was Paul Robeson and the second was Muhammad Ali. These two guys have some very interesting things in common. Firstly, of course, both were incredibly bold, confident, brave black people who would not allow themselves to be defined by the American white establishment. They were also black people with an internationalist vision. In Robeson's case, of course, this was much more intellectually developed than Muhammad Ali's. They were both also incredibly good looking, charismatic in person and immensely charming when they chose to be.

Now, even to this day, the black population on Tyneside isn't huge, and there is a huge amount of racism there, but these guys reached out to the Geordie working class in a very special way, and they were seen as icons of the underdog. You could relate to that not only in the basis of the colour of your skin but also where you were in the class hierarchy, and of course the north-east is a place which has a very strong working-class consciousness and very much a consciousness that they were different from the rest of the country, particularly those toffs down in London, and so they could embrace people from an entirely different culture. I think they spoke the same language. To me, this is beautiful, because it's about the spirit of internationalism and a mutual recognition among people who have experienced oppression. They have something in common. Also, of course, there was an element of individual masculine heroism and charisma, which shouldn't be underplayed. But what an amazing tribute to both of those guys, and what an amazing statement! After all, Robeson was a major political activist and a major intellectual, a person who gave political speeches. Muhammad Ali actually tried very hard not to do that, and mostly did not do it, but nor was he merely a boxer.

They both demonstrated the way in which popular culture had come into collision with the politics of resistance and had found an echo among a population that had a very different historical experience. It's part of the same phenomenon whereby you can go to almost anywhere in the world and you will find people who are not linked in any way to Africa-America but whose whole world and emotional view has been shaped by African-American music – soul music – or, similarly, to Caribbean music – reggae. Reggae is probably one of the most popular musical idioms in the world for people who can only barely understand the patois, but there is a mutual recognition, a language of the oppressed that ironically enough gets transmitted by the commercial mechanism of popular culture – film, sports and music, etc. Ironically enough, these act as conveyor belts for subversion, and I guess one of the most effective users of that conveyor belt must be Muhammad Ali.

Of course, one of the keys to Muhammad's personality is that he was untroubled by intellectual contradiction. For instance, one minute he's meeting with Colonel Ghadaffi, the next with President Ford. He really didn't feel that it was his job to connect the dots. He felt that it was his job to speak out against injustice and generally meet with and be polite to anyone who would talk to him. Ali's point of view about Gerald Ford and Ghadaffi was, "Yeah, I'll meet them, same as I'll meet the guy down the street," and anyone who has actually watched Ali interact with people knows that there really is no difference in the way he interacts with anonymous, ordinary people and the way he interacts with the rich and famous. He is always ebullient and, apart from the very damaging impact of the illness from which he now suffers, always very outgoing.

Throughout most of his career, Ali was much more respected and admired abroad than he was in his native land. He had built a massive fanbase abroad long before the majority of white Americans where prepared to regard him as any kind of acceptable, no less an admirable, figure. When he

MIKE MARQUSEE

was prosecuted for draft evasion and his title was taken away from him, there were protests in Karachi, in Akra, in Ghana and in Cairo, as well as in London and Paris. There was one in Guyana which was led by Cheddi Jagan, who subsequently became the President. I think that tells you how much global resonance Ali already had back in 1967, even before he did all the amazing things he did in his second career.

Since writing *Redemption Song*, the scale of Ali's global stature has really been brought home to me, not least by something that happened to me when I was watching a cricket match in Sri Lanka. As people who know that watch cricket matches, there are a lot of long hours and plenty of time to have chats with the people next to you, and the guy who was sitting next to me was a Sri Lankan who worked in a bank there. He asked me what I did, and is said, "I'm a writer."

"Oh? What do you write about?"

"I've just written a book about Muhammad Ali," I said.

"Oh," he said. "He's Sri Lankan."

I was a little embarrassed, because I thought, "Oh God, he doesn't know what I'm talking about. There must be some other Muhammad Ali." So I said, "No no no. Muhammad Ali the boxer."

"Yes, yes," he said. "Muhammad Ali the heavyweight champion. He's Sri Lankan."

Now I decided that he wasn't confused. He was mad. "No no no. I think you'll find that he was an African-American."

At that point, the guy smiled very broadly at me, having completely trapped me. He said, "Ah yes, but in the 1970s our government awarded him honorary citizenship in tribute to his contribution to world peace and equal rights." There aren't too many boxers who can say that about themselves. I was incredibly moved by this story, and I've had similar points made to me in many different countries and cultures.

The moment that Cassius Clay became Muhammad Ali, the moment that the American heavyweight champion declared himself to be a follower of Islam, albeit a very unorthodox follower of Islam, that was headline news in every country with a significant Muslim population all over the world – Indonesia, Pakistan, Nigeria, etc. It was hugely significant because, although we now live in an era in which Islamic self-assertion – sometimes in a fundamentalist form but also in many other forms – has become commonplace, this wasn't true in the '60s. One of the reasons why people really loved Muhammad Ali around the world was that many hundreds of millions of Muslims who suddenly felt that they had a place in Western consciousness, where before they had none. However, that was also a contradiction from the beginning, because people were also very aware that what the Nation of Islam taught was not what they learned in their local mosque. Ali mostly played down the unorthodox elements of the Nation's teaching, and when he went to Egypt and other Islamic countries he just got into the flow of it and was happy to be a typical Muslim. And this was well before he had formally converted to orthodox Islam. So I think that one of Muhammad Ali's many achievements is helping to introduce the Islamic presence into North America specifically and, broadly, European or Western culture at that time.

The third time that Muhammad Ali visited Africa was in 1979 and 1980, when his boxing career had come to a conclusion – for that time, at least. Whereas in 1964 he had gone completely off his own bat and in defiance of the American establishment and in 1974 he had gone as a great champion of anti-American global sentiment, in late 1979/1980 he went for the first time as the official ambassador for the United States government, in particular for President Carter. His mission there was to win African support for the proposed American boycott of the 1980 Olympics, which were to be staged in Moscow. This was to be America's retaliation for the Soviet invasion of Afghanistan, and I think Ali was dragged into this partly because, as a Muslim, he had strong objections – and understandable objections, in my view – to the invasion and partly because by this time he was no longer a member of the Nation of Islam. The organisation had changed. He was no longer explicitly a black nationalist, and he was quite keen – in his usual, emotionally guided way – to be loved by and reconciled with the American establishment.

After weathering a storm on the ropes, Ali hits George Foreman with a hard right hand on his way to regaining the title in Zaire, 1974.

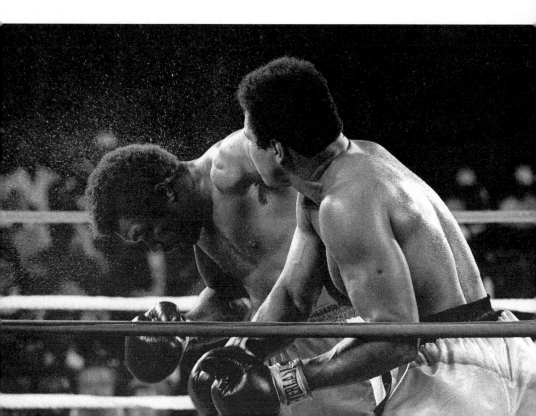

Ali avoids a left hand from Smokin' Joe during their brutal fight for the championship in Manila, 1975.

Leading a rally in support of jailed boxer Rubin "Hurricane" Carter in Newark, New Jersey, 1975.

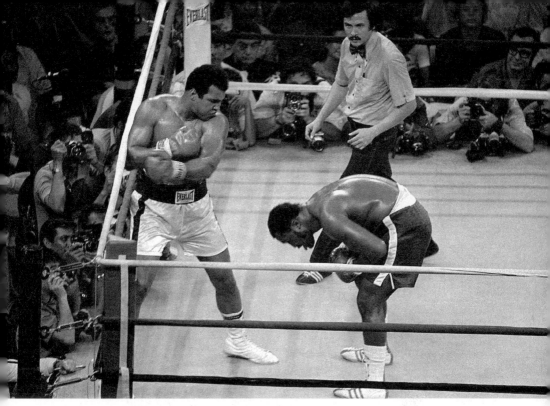

A tired Joe Frazier is battered in the Thrilla In Manila, October 1975.

A record third title is regained against Leon Spinks at the New Orleans Superdome, September 1978.

However, the trip was a total disaster because Ali found that the people who had loved him so much in Africa now looked to him and said, "You have betrayed your race," which is something that no one had ever dared to say to Muhammad Ali before. They said to him, "You don't know what you're talking about. You've just become a Cold War pawn." And, frankly, that is what he had become through his naïveté and his own good intentions. But good intentions aren't enough in politics, and he got this one profoundly wrong and was very wounded by it. In fact, at one press conference, it got quite bad and people who knew a lot more about the nefarious games that the American State Department was playing in Africa were saying, "How can you be part of this?" And he was very shaken. He came out and said, "OK, maybe I'm wrong. I'm not a traitor to you. I love Africa. Maybe I've got this wrong." At that point, his State Department minder closed the conference and whisked him away.

That pretty much killed off Ali's hopes that he could become some kind of official American ambassador. Ironically, I think he really hoped that, at the conclusion of his glittering boxing career, he would be taken up by the American establishment and be allowed to pursue a peace-making role. But it soon became clear to him that there was no way that he could play this role, given the reality of Cold War politics. And one of the tragic consequences of this botched third trip to Africa, was that he went back to America and decided to fight again for money and, in the following fight, was completely humiliated. Worse than that, he sustained some of the physical damage from which he now suffers.

Of course, he always had "the Ali industry" to fall back on. That started to gain momentum the moment in the mid '70s when he reclaimed his heavyweight title, when the anti-war movement had ended with the end of the war, when the black liberation movement had receded because it had come up against some very difficult obstacles, and the initial impetus of the civil rights movement and the Black Power movement had been lost. Ali suddenly found himself no longer at the head of a complex series of social movements but instead just another celebrity. My own belief is that the symbolic moment that started the ball rolling came shortly after the Rumble In The Jungle. It wasn't so much the handshake with President Ford at the White House, although that's pretty symbolic, but even more so was the time when he posed for Andy Warhol to do a silk-screen print of him and thus entered Warhol's galaxy of stars – James Dean, Marilyn Monroe and so on. I think that that was the beginning of the commercialised, corporate Ali industry.

At this point, Ali was ironically an icon of resistance, and that was his power. That's why people wanted Muhammad Ali's picture up on the wall. Now, he became something that was extremely profitable, as is the way with a number of similar icons. From that point on, all kinds of people cashed in on Muhammad Ali. Quite often, Ali himself wasn't one of them, and everyone who knows him will confirm that his management of the money was hopeless and that other people made far more money off Muhammad Ali than Muhammad Ali ever did.

But then things reached a second phase. Ali of course became very ill in the 1980s and, I think, very confused. He divorced, remarried yet again and found his way to becoming a devout Muslim, rejecting his womanising past. He established an arm's-length relationship with the Nation of Islam, which had very much controlled his life up until then. But it was really in the early 1990s – as the causes and the conflicts with which Ali was associated receded into a more distant past, and especially with Thomas Hauser's wonderful oral history of Muhammad Ali – that the Ali industry went through a second rebirth. And that climaxed, of course, in the 1996 Olympics at Atlanta, when Ali was chosen by corporate America to be the final link in the torch-lighting ceremony.

I don't deny that that was a very moving moment, but it was staged for the benefit of a number of large multinational corporations who wanted to use Ali's image of global respectability to sell their products and also to sell America to the world. But then he was actually given a new copy of the Olympic gold medal that he had first won in 1960 but which he had flung into the Ohio River in protest – a very personal, private protest – against Jim Crow, against the fact that he went back to his home town with his gold medal around his neck and still couldn't get served a cheeseburger in his local restaurant.

But the guy who awarded him the new medal was one Antonio Samaranch, who I think it's fair to say represented all the worst elements in the sporting establishment. He was a very close associate of General Francisco Franco, who was a fascist, and through his whole career had done his best to resist everything that Muhammad Ali stood for. But I guess this is part of the triumph of the guy, that he forces even the Samaranches of this world to embrace him.

It's kind of forgotten now but one of the many things that the very young Cassius Clay that unnerved the media was that he called himself pretty. Before he had established any connection with the Nation of Islam, and long before he was a politically controversial figure, he unnerved people because of the rather outrageous way that he presented himself to the public. He made jokes. He was anything but solid in a world which was used to sportsmen saying nothing but solemn banalities. Suddenly, here was a guy who was saying, "Ain't I pretty? Ain't I beautiful? You ever seen such smooth skin as mine?" Up until that point, the word *pretty* was a word that was used almost exclusively to refer to feminine beauty, a kind of passive or decorative kind of beauty – women or girls were pretty; men were handsome. But now here was a black heavyweight boxer saying he was pretty. It was one of many things he did that just stunned people and made them rethink all kinds of associations.

That was the feminine side of Ali – his love of joking and teasing, his self-mockery, his refusal ever to take himself too seriously, his softness. This was a guy who outside the ring was the most gentle person and who was physically comfortable with children. He loved to cuddle and kiss them. Again, that wasn't something that macho, superstar athletes were supposed to do. I was born in 1953, so I was a very young boy at the time, and that made a huge impact on me, before I knew what the Nation of Islam was. In fact, it prepared me for that, and I vividly remember reading in the headlines that Cassius Clay was seen at this meeting with Malcolm X and thinking, "Well, they think that's really bad, but wow!" The ground was prepared for Cassius Clay to break the stereotype, and he did it first by upsetting a lot of people's ideas of masculinity.

I think that this is something that Ali had in common with Malcolm X. These days, Muhammad Ali and Malcolm X are held forth as two great icons of black patriarchy and black masculinity by some sections of the black community in the US, including quite a few of the people in the hip-hop world, and I can see what they're getting at, but I think it's important to remember that both guys actually made friends and influenced people on the basis of another side of their personalities – the jokey side, the intimate side. These were both people who really loved and needed friendship and were good at it. They were capable of giving themselves to people and loved to make fun of themselves. They didn't need to bully the people around them. Just the opposite, in fact.

I don't think Ali himself ever had any messianic delusions, though. There's no doubt that he always loved an audience, whether it was a TV show, a boxing ring, a street corner in Harlem or a bowling alley. To this day, if he walks through an airport, people surround him and he stops and he is happy. I don't think that's a bad thing. In fact, I think it's quite charming. It really depends on what you do with that feeling, and he has done something quite democratic. That's the main point. From the very beginning, he was pretty wary of the role he was playing. I mean, he loved it and he enjoyed it and he felt he had to do it, but he knew that he didn't have any worked-out strategy for people. Particularly between 1967 and 1970, during his ban from boxing, he went around America speaking to colleges, both black and white, and he would bring his audience into that. He would say not just "I should be the heavyweight champion of the world because I won it in the ring" but "I should be the heavyweight champion of the world because it's unfair to you that they impose an imposter on you. Who do you think should be the heavyweight champion of the world?" And of course people would answer, "Muhammad Ali," and he would lead them in this wonderful call and response, straight out of the traditions of the black Church.

Ali was probably more famous than anyone but a handful of individuals of the 20th century, and his approach to his mass following was profoundly different from that of most politicians, say, or frankly almost any religious leader in that he felt strongly accountable to them. He was very aware that he was there because he was a famous boxer, and that made him humble. And so one of the key messages about Ali is that the guy who called himself "the greatest", who invented the art of modern *braggadocio* in sport, was a genuinely humble person. Everyone who has interacted with him one-on-one confirms that at every level, and I think that's why he kept on the straight and narrow. That's why – with a few exceptions, and they are serious exceptions – he did mostly stick to his sense of social responsibility and of what was just and what he was obliged to do because of his ideals, because these people paid good money to see him fight and without them he would be nothing. And, given what fame and celebrity has become since Muhammad Ali's time, I think that's one of the most important lessons to learn from him. In a way, he was one of the first major mass-media, global media celebrities, but he was very different from the people who followed him.

One of his great achievements was that he liberated the earning potential of black sports performers. He wasn't the only one – the baseball player Curt Flood is probably the most immediately significant, but Flood himself has said clearly that he was inspired by Muhammad Ali. So nowadays, particularly in the US, sports stars from the African-American community are making mind-blowing sums of money, sums that are greater than the entire gross domestic product of whole African nations. The paradox of this is that, in doing so, they have grown further and further away from the communities they come from, and that means it's harder and harder for them to play a representative role in any meaningful way.

I'm not sure we could see another Muhammad Ali now. I don't want to disrespect Michael Jordan or Tiger Woods, but they cannot be compared to Muhammad Ali. First, they have not been prepared to make any sacrifices for the communities they come from. Muhammad Ali was prepared to go to jail. Muhammad Ali was prepared to give up every penny he owned. He was prepared to be reviled and hated because he believed in a certain principle and because he believed he had to be accountable to the poor, black community from which he came. I don't see much of that ethos any more in the black sports stars of today. I don't blame them for that because, after all, I don't see much of it in the white sports stars either, and I think that this is a degree of racial hypocrisy that sometimes enters into this debate.

I suppose what you say about Michael Jordan is that he's no better than all the rest of them, but I do think it's a shame because sport is, by its nature, a popular thing. Contrary to what some people believe, it wasn't originally created by the corporations to sell products; it was created by working people all over the world as a pastime and a recreation. If they hadn't done that, if there hadn't been tens of thousands of young black people going into gymnasiums generation after generation, there would be no world boxing industry or football or baseball or cricket. And so, when these guys make huge amounts of money from it, I do think that they have an obligation to be more like Muhammad Ali, to have more of a sense of accountability to the people who put them there.

Second, the incredible affluence of a small number of African-American sporting superstars gives an incredibly false picture of America. In the old days, baseball was exclusively white until 1947, when Jackie Robinson broke the colour bar. The argument was that major-league baseball didn't really represent America. OK, but now look at basketball, which is dominated by young black men who are millionaires. What picture of America does that give? What remote relationship does that have with the demography of the US? It's a lie about the US, because it implies that there is economic equality there, and I'm sorry but any statistical measure confirms that that is just not true.

Somebody once spoke about Ali as being a barometer for the times, and I agree with that enormously. In fact, one of the reasons that I wanted to write a book about him was precisely because I thought that he was such a fantastic barometer for so many of the pressures and tendencies of his times, in both good and bad ways. If you follow his career, you can find the impact of first the civil rights movement and then the impact of black nationalism and the more militant Black Power things. You find decisively the impact of the global anti-war movement. You can follow the course of Islamic fundamentalism through his career. You can follow the whole history of the corporatisation of leisure, sport and popular culture. You can follow the changing self-image of Americans through Ali – it's partial, most of the time, but nonetheless there. And how many figures can you say that about? But you have to see that that's not because he was an empty vessel into which all these things just poured; you can only become that kind of representative figure – however conflicted and contradictory – if you are yourself active.

It's an important point, that Ali became representative because he took risks; because he took stands based on principle, whether people agreed with them or not; because he made things happen as well as having things happen to him. There is a chemistry between the psychology of the individual and the times in which they live. Neither can be understood without the other. And that is certainly true in the case of Muhammad Ali.

Ultimately, the greatest lesson of Muhammad Ali's life and career is his rejection of a narrow American national identity in favour of a personal identity that crosses all borders on a map, that sees the individual as part of a global community that is both diverse but also united in its essential humanity. Ali not only talked about that; he was willing to put his body and soul on the line for it. There are a lot of reasons why Muhammad Ali is the most popular sporting figure of the past 50 years, without a doubt, but I think the main one is that solidarity was more that just a word to him. He practiced it. That's why, when he beat up George Foreman in the ring, many millions of people who really didn't care very much about boxing felt a share in his triumph, felt that he was standing up for them and, in his victory, got a passing moment's relief from some of the pressures they lived under.

There's no doubt that Ali is a hero, but I think we have to remember that all heroes are flawed. Certainly, all heroes who are going to be of any use to the rest of us ought to be flawed, because otherwise we could never hope to emulate them. To me, the heroism of Ali isn't that he got it all right. Far from it – he made some serious errors of judgement in his life, and he admits that now. The beauty is that, despite the terrible pressures on him at certain key moments in his life – which happened to be key moments of our own shared history – he resisted temptation and stood up for some very basic principles, and nothing can take that away from him today. That's what makes him a hero still today. Recently, in an article he wrote in *Newsweek*, he said, "The most important thing I ever did was refuse to go to Vietnam." Now, that is a realistic self-assessment. That makes him a hero, because he still hasn't repudiated it. There were quite a few people who took heroic stands in the Vietnam War who don't want to talk about it any more, but Ali is still happy to. At the same time, he bears no grudges to the people who criticised him back then, and I applaud him for that. I'm not sure I would be capable of that degree of forgiveness, but it's genuine in his case.

Joe Martin Jr

Son Of Muhammad Ali's First Boxing Coach

A long time ago, they used to have a little fair in Louisville every year and the kids came and got free ice cream and candy. Ali and his friends parked their bikes out front and came in to get their free candy and popcorn and ice cream, and when they went back out, someone had stolen his bike. So he went to the man on the desk and he wanted to report it to the police, but the guy at the desk advised him to go downstairs to the boxing gym, where my father was a police officer. After he reported it to Dad, he was still crying a little bit, and he said, "When I find out who stole my bike I'm gonna whup him." But Dad stopped him: "Do you know how to fight?" And Ali said, "No, but I'm gonna whup him anyway." So Dad said, "Why don't you start coming to the gym and learn how to fight before you go out picking on someone to whup." So the next time, he was there, and they continued from there on.

We had a show on TV in Louisville called *Tomorrow's Champions*, and everybody watched it, three amateur boxing matches over 30 minutes every Saturday from 6pm to 6.30pm. Of course, that's where I wanted to be, on TV. A lot of people had TVs by this time. So everybody got to know us as kids, and that was great for us.

I knew him back when he was Cassius Clay. He was just like one of the other guys. He wasn't a loudmouth. We all had to be polite around my dad, but we all were just good buddies. He was always very fast, even then, and nobody could catch him, nobody could hit him. And then he worked up to his reputation as he grew older. He almost didn't go to the Olympics, 'cause he was afraid of aeroplanes, but Dad talked him into it: "You won't be heavyweight champ unless you go to the Olympics." He finally decided to go, but he was scared to death. In fact, when they got on the plane, he had a parachute on and got down on the floor of the plane and started praying. People thought he was joking, but he wasn't. He was that scared.

Muhammad never forgot my dad. He called him all the time. He used to call my mother too. She liked Muhammad. He would kid around and hug with Mum, but always very respectable. His manners were beyond what people expected of him.

When my father ran for sheriff here in Jefferson County, Muhammad came in and put on an exhibition boxing match to raise funds for the campaign and made speeches for Dad.

When he fought George Foreman, that was a tremendous fight. And I listened to the radio when he won the championship the first time, and that was impressive too, you know. The most emotional fight was his last fight in Vegas, where he fought Larry Holmes. He had called and invited Dad, Mom, myself and my wife. I talked to him about 30 minutes before the fight. He said, "Joe, I wanna win. I wanna win!" There we were in ringside seats waiting for him to win. And it was really disappointing that he didn't. I felt real sad for him personally at that point.

Mark McCormack

Head Of IMG

I'm not a great connoisseur of prize fighting, but I'd certainly heard of Cassius Clay, the brash young boxer, in the early '60s. One day I got a call from the Louisville Sponsoring Group, who were financing this young man. They wanted to know if I'd like to join them and help with the commercial and the marketing aspects of it. But fighting wasn't something I was involved in at the time, and the whole profession was somewhat tainted. I decided to decline.

Then, in the early '70s, of course, when he came back after having his licence taken away from him and the famous Ali-Frazier fight, suddenly this brash, young kid became a world icon, a world personality, and obviously the marketers of products around the world were anxious to be associated with him. However, from the standpoint of my company, once again boxing was considered a dirty sport, permeated by criminal elements, and I just didn't want to get involved in it.

But then, one day in around 1978, I got a call from a very well-known banker named Bob Aboud, who was chairman of one of the leading banks in Chicago and a huge fight fan in general but an Ali fan in particular. He said to me, "You know, I don't want this young man to end up like Joe Louis. I've turned the bank's legal department and trust department over to him free of charge to help him with his legal and financial problems. I want to get arms around all that, and I thought you might be interested in coming in and talking to us about handling the out-of-the-ring activities and marketing."

So I went to Chicago and had a very productive meeting with Bob and his staff, and that led to an association with Ali in the late '70s. The company's subsequent relationship with Ali was certainly unique. He had an entourage of people, a lot of advisors around the world hanging onto him and trying to get a piece of everything he was doing, and we weren't welcomed into the group very enthusiastically by a lot of them, so it wasn't an easy relationship. But we did a lot of good things for him, a lot of marketing for his farewell tour.

He was a unique and very exciting personality. You'd say to him, "Don't sign anything until we've had a chance to look at it," and he'd say, "Oh, I won't sign a thing. You don't have to worry about that." And then he'd go down in the elevator from the meeting and sign something in the elevator. He was pretty tough in that way.

He told me once when I met him in the late '70s in our London offices, "I could take you to places in this world where they would kill you, but I could put up my hand and say, 'Stop, he's a good man,' and they wouldn't." So he was certainly aware of the impact that he had in many places in the world.

My own feeling about Ali is that he's a microcosm of our society in the last half of the 20th century. His career and mine have run parallel, in time. He was a young, brash kid and then became a draft dodger and the public despised him. From there, he suddenly became a world icon, a comeback person, and everybody was rooting for him. And now he's facing old age and the problems of dealing with it.

Hugh McIlvanney

Journalist

Boxing is a sport in which two men try and batter each other senseless. No matter how you dress it up, the basic objective in boxing is to render the opponent unconscious. It's the only sport in which that is the imperative. Therefore, when people try to dilute it, they are very much fighting a losing battle. Motive, not statistics, will always separate boxing from other sports. You can say that more people are killed in motorcycle racing, that more people are killed in mountaineering, but in neither of these two activities is it the fundamental objective to knock the other guy out. Anybody who embraces boxing must embrace the implications of that motive.

Muhammad won a lot of fights with a lot of graceful movement. He bewildered and confused his opponents. But with serious opponents, if he could take them out in 35 seconds, that's what he would want to do. Of course, he prolonged certain fights for his own purposes, but only when he felt absolutely safe. He wasn't inclined to prolong fights with Joe Frazier or George Foreman; those fights were prolonged because he had no alternative. But he was a professional fighter, and all the beauty of his performances shouldn't obscure that.

I don't think that boxing really needed Ali. I think, though, that any sport would always welcome him. He's the greatest figure in the history of organised sport. But when people talk about the circus element in professional boxing now, it's mainly heavily contrived showbiz approach. Of course Muhammad had a huge inclination to behave in a way that suggested showbiz values, but it was a spontaneous showmanship or, even if not entirely spontaneous, it nevertheless had wit and style and it came from him. That's the essential point. What I find appalling and just boring beyond tolerance now is the sort of showbusiness nonsense that we get associated with someone like Naseem Hamed and, to some extent, Lennox Lewis, with these ludicrous entrances and the smoke and explosions. Usually you find that, after the entrance, the whole thing goes downhill. The performance isn't so good. Of course, Muhammad made some quite wild entrances – in the first fight against Henry Cooper, for example, he came in wearing a crown and robes, but that was just a crown he'd found backstage at the Palladium that he thought he could have a bit of fun with. That's a lot different from the production numbers these days, which are mainly devised by television people. It's not simply the fact that they're outrageous; they're just so boring.

And of course now people try to massage the personalities of certain fighters. Now we return to the little featherweight that tries to make out that he's a fascinating character. They're constantly making comparisons with Ali, and it's madness. Naseem Hamed compares with Muhammad Ali the way a speak-your-weight machine does with Woody Allen. It's just pathetic to talk about him that way.

Take Chris Eubank. He's another master of the genre. But I must admit that, occasionally, when he was performing with the jodhpurs and the riding crop, it was very difficult to keep a smile off your face. There was a wee bit of fun about it. But with certain others, when they attempt to do what they perceive as their Ali number, you just emit a terrible groan and your heart falls into your shoes.

The fact is that Ali is unique, and anybody who says he's not has a very peculiar view of human behaviour. I also think that we underestimate just how extraordinary he was. He didn't merely bring excitement and entertainment to audiences and to everybody he encountered; he brought a sense of joy. And he reinvented himself every morning, so it wasn't unusual that he also invented ways of fighting. In some ways, he was an eternal amateur. He never did obey the orthodoxies of the ring, even those that perhaps he should have obeyed because they were a basis of self-preservation. For a start, his head was often in strange places – he went outside hooks instead of going inside them, as the old tutors would have advised. But he had such athleticism, such elasticity of torso and limb, that he was able to do magical things in the ring to violate a lot of the orthodoxies to his own profit. It's been pointed out that the great American sports writer AJ Liebling – of whom I am a huge admirer – always found it difficult to relate to Ali. Of course, that was when Liebling was mainly writing about the very early phase of Ali's life. But even more important than his professional life is the simple fact that, no matter what Liebling has written about boxing and other matters, he never did tune into Muhammad's aesthetic, either inside the ring or outside it. But I think that, as Muhammad's career went on, Liebling probably would have taken to him much more, had he lived.

In around 1963/64, there were some who objected to the way he boxed, but without a doubt, the main basis of the prejudice against him was that he was provocative about American values. And of course, when he came out and not only refused to be drafted but denounced the war in Vietnam, there was tremendous hostility towards him. Even in the first fight with Joe Frazier, in 1970, once Frazier got to him there were ringside sports writers saying, "Kill the son of a bitch! Take his head off!" So there was already evidence of a division appearing. Later, everybody saw the point about Muhammad and there was, if not entirely universal love of him, then there was very widespread love of him. But at that first fight, there was a horrible, hostile prejudice against him, even amongst blacks. I remember the black maid in my hotel saying, "The bigmouth got shut good," and she followed it with a smile that was an invitation to dance on a grave. But in fact, losing the first fight to Frazier made Ali bigger than ever, because the heroism of his performance, the grace of how he handled defeat. It left no option to any reasonable person but to accept that this was somebody utterly exceptional in fundamental ways, apart from the very obvious sense of entertainment and excitement that he brought to the game.

But it's a great sadness that Joe has never really seen Ali in that light. Joe remains very bitter, even though, after that first fight, Muhammad was lavish in his praise of Joe Frazier. He always said that Joe was a true adversary. And just before the Foreman fight in Zaire in '74 I spent more than two hours with Ali, and he managed to work in a tribute to Frazier. Then again, after that savage third fight, he was still full of praise for Joe. But Joe's absolutely immersed forever in this bitterness, it seems. There seems no likelihood that he will come out of what is a very bitter attitude towards Muhammad.

I first met Ali when he came over to fight Henry Cooper in the first of their two fights in 1963. Then I went to Muhammad's fight with Floyd Patterson in November 1965, in Las Vegas, and I had quite a close contact with him there. But when I really got properly close to him was in May 1966, just before Cooper fought him for the title at Highbury. I went over to Miami and spent a week over there with Muhammad, and I was the only journalist around him at that time, and so I was on my own with him for quite a while. I'd reported on him for some years before that meeting, but that was something very special for me. It was without doubt the first time that I'd had the sort of access to him, and I started to seek – and gain – that kind of access quite strenuously after that.

In Miami in '66, I had suspected that there was a dreadful superficiality about the reporting of Muhammad, that it was all "Gassius Cassius". He was known for his lip, but I just knew that there is a hell of a lot more than that, and the main result of the time I spent with him there was a glorious confirmation of that suspicion. It also brought home to me that his humour was much richer and much more satisfying and much more genuine that had been conveyed by the printing of his doggerel and the reporting of the wild vaunting that was central to his act. That was there, of course, but I realised very quickly that there was no point in reporting Muhammad by walking up to him with a clipboard because you just got the stage performance.

There was a celebrated Italian journalist and novelist there at the time who thought that, because of the Italian entrée, she would get some special treatment from Muhammad. She went in to ask him questions and told me afterwards, "It's hopeless. Every time I try to give him my list of questions, there are children crawling all over him and he's doing other things." Now, most of us would think that was pretty interesting, but she wanted this formalised interview, and of course that was pointless with Muhammad. I think that people were very disappointed when a lot of people in my scufflers' trade continued to repeat the old stuff over and over again, when in fact there was more. It wasn't only that the truth was more complex; it was also more entertaining, more colourful. I always felt that the way to cover Muhammad was to hang around him, eavesdrop on his life and observe and then give him a little nudge here and there, but never to approach him frontally for these pronouncements, because then most of what you got was a lot of nonsense.

Of course, people were obviously interested in his personal life. In some way, it was perhaps contradictory – for instance, his involvement with the Nation of Islam and his sex life. Those two themes were particularly interesting, and of course I was interested in both. Former *Sports Illustrated* journalist Mark Kram suggests in his book *The Ghosts Of Manila* that he was just a puppet for the Nation of Islam. Now, he was exploited on all levels, because he was very useful to Elijah Muhammad and to Herbert Muhammad and to everybody concerned with the Black Muslims, in that he gave them a visibility and created the impression that they were a serious power in black politics and in general politics in the US. He represented an advantage that they couldn't have without him. He was also a bridge, a very powerful proselytising tool for Muslims. But they gave him a great deal, too, because he always had a great hunger to be a world figure, but the heavyweight title wasn't quite enough. So when the Muslims gave the impression that he had a validity and an influence beyond sport, that suited his dreams of himself. They didn't go out and gather him into the fold and then forget about him; they made use of him. They exploited him.

After the Liston fight in 1964, he said he would retire and become Mayor of New York. I heard him make that kind of statement many times. I remember being driven by him in Chicago in his Rolls-Royce convertible with a friend of mine, photographer Chris Smith, and he was talking about what he could do if he ran for President. He was just fantasising about how everybody else would just drop out of the race and it would be a walkover. And I remember talking to him before he fought to regain the title from

Leon Spinks, when he was training in New Orleans, and he was fantasising about the fight, giving a commentary. *But this is impossible, Ali.* So he goes through all the fight and then comes to the climax, where he's beaten Spinks. It's unbelievable. He said, "And then I go and pick up my briefcase, get in my Lear jet and go off to see a president somewhere." He always had that kind of nonsense that he was gonna be a world figure.

It also brings us to the issue of what impact he really had on say the civil rights movement. In terms of practical political influence, it would perhaps be hard to quantify the influence that Muhammad had. I wouldn't presume to speak for black people in America when it comes to how important Muhammad was, but all of us know that, if there is a movement such as the civil rights movement or a crusade for emancipation and betterment of a group of people, heroic figures are essential. Of course, the men and women who work behind the scenes and do the day-in/day-out sweaty labour of the battle, they get it done in the end; but clearly, somebody who had the symbolic impact of Muhammad, who imparted pride and self-belief into so many people, if he didn't have a big effect, then I find it hard to imagine what kind of figure outside professional politics would.

In the political context, of course, Muhammad was preaching segregation, and he had to be regarded by many people as a divisive influence, particularly during his period with the Nation of Islam. But for me, the ultimate impact of Muhammad was as a demonstration of the magical propensities of human beings. He was just a great joyful manifestation of how wonderful the human spirit and the human body of can be. It wasn't excitement that he created; it was joy. That's a pretty extravagant gift.

It's no surprise that that kind of celebrity status is tied in with overt sexuality. There's plenty of evidence to suggest that great sportsmen can be fond of sexual action. But I also think that a lot of stories are told that have very little foundation and truth. Early on in Muhammad's career, these black characters around the entourage were saying, "He gets 'em, we fucks 'em," which is very much the opposite of what is suggested by those who insist that he was never out of the sack. Well, that was obviously nonsense, too. There were even people trying to suggest that he was gay at one stage. I remember talking to Angelo Dundee about that and Angelo saying,

"Nothing could be more crazy." I think he was just a very healthy, big guy. He was beautiful, after all, and he was heavyweight champion of the world and a very exciting figure in society in general. And he was quite randy. But I don't think there was any need to regard it as much more than that. I don't think his record would necessarily outstrip Warren Beatty's, for example.

I went to report on the court hearing in Houston, Texas, when he was trying to get his passport so that he could go out of the country to fight during his three-and-a-half-year exile. People say he wouldn't go to Vietnam. Well, maybe he would have been sent to Vietnam and maybe he wouldn't. Joe Louis didn't have hazardous service when he was in the US Army. But afterwards, we were in the hotel coffee shop and Muhammad was telling jokes, very good jokes, with brilliant timing. I mean, the allegations that he was of low intelligence was just so ludicrous that it shouldn't be dignified with a response. Of course we know his literacy level was very low, but he had a remarkable intelligence. He could carry several sort of fairly complicated ideas in his head at one time. And a very simple rebuttal of those allegations of his intelligence was the way he could tell these complicated jokes.

Of course, his licence to fight was taken away within a month in Britain. Britain was the first country to revoke it. It's part of the pattern of what is laughingly called the governing of professional boxing. The governing bodies tend to co-operate as much as possible and, to be fair, the British Boxing Board of Control had a much better record than most organisations in trying to fight against a fragmentation of the control of boxing. But, although many of us would have been much happier if everybody on the board had stood out against it, I don't think we're entitled to be too judgmental. I don't think that was necessarily a declaration of bigotry.

The thing about Ali was that he dreamed a conclusion and then made it a reality. To me, that was the most magical aspect of his whole career. It was almost like what we're told about the vaunting in the mediaeval mead hall, when, if somebody said he was gonna do something, he had to do it or he was finished. Muhammad was a bit like that. Most of the apparently wild utterances were addressed to himself, obviously. Most of the time he was psyching himself up. But it was beyond what would normally be regarded as a self-psyching manoeuvre. It was a demand that he was placing on himself, a demand that he believed when nobody else did.

In Zaire, for instance, a lot of people tell you they had a good idea he'd beat Foreman. But people who say that just aren't talking sense, because by that time his legs had gone. When he came back after three and a half years out of the game, he'd lost the leg speed, he was available to be hit in the head by moderate heavyweights. Now, Joe Frazier was liable to get to him, but the guy you thought was bound to get to him with calamitous results was Foreman, who had this great wrecking ball of a right hand. And Foreman had not only beaten Ken Norton but had frightened the wits out of him. I saw that fight in Caracas, Venezuela, and although Joe was the truest adversary for Ali, perhaps the most awkward was Norton, because Norton knew how he wasn't a great puncher, so he would take more chances and he had this sort of strange spidery style that could give Ali difficulties at all times. But George frightened Norton in the first round, then knocked him kicking in the second round. People were wondering, "When that right hand hits Muhammad, what's gonna happen?" When I was in Zaire, most of his camp were terrified.

Muhammad was the only one that had absolute faith. Angelo claimed to do so, and he would give you a lot of technical reasons why he would win, some of which made good sense. But they all left out what was going to happen when that big right hand hit Ali in the head. Well, of course, Muhammad went in and we had the rope-a-dope legend coming alive in that fight and some real nonsense was being talked about there and in that great documentary *When We Were Kings*. In that film, Norman Mailer said that Muhammad had contrived this rope strategy, rope-a-dope, but when I spoke to him in his villa on the same day as that victory, Muhammad acknowledged categorically that he had no option but to go to the ropes. He said, "I've tried dancing around George. There's just too much of him. I'll exhaust myself." I said, "Let's get to the ropes while we've still got the wind to do it and let him blast his ass off. Then we'll see what happens." But the nerve needed to do that is beyond belief, but that was Muhammad. He had this flawless diamond of a nerve that never let him down.

And of course he did it with such skill, leaning back over the ropes and making George miss. But George didn't miss with all of them. He hit him with some terrible blows. I was watching the first few rounds virtually through my fingers. In the third round, George straightened his left hand and hit him full in the face, and he just took it and came through it. Nobody in the history of boxing ever took a punch better than Muhammad Ali. Sadly, there's a price to be paid for that, and his condition now is the direct result of physical trauma of the brainstem. People talk about Parkinson's disease, but it's not; it's Parkinson's *syndrome*, which can have several causes. The specific cause in Muhammad's case is physical trauma of the brainstem.

For most of my adult life, I've been ambivalent about boxing. While it's there, I find it quite irresistible, but if it were abolished tomorrow, I'd have great difficulty joining in an outcry of protest, because I do think it's extremely hard to justify the violence in the sport, because, as I said, it contains the motive to destroy your opponent, or at least to knock him out – what the Mexicans call the "little death". When you are observing from the safety of the ringside an activity in which the object is to knock someone unconscious, you've got to ask yourself questions.

Of course there are all kinds of arguments that can be made on behalf of boxing. The first is that they're consenting adults. Are we entitled to play God and say, "You're not going to do it"? I mean, you can get governments wanting to ban boxing, and yet they're not so keen to ban nuclear weapons, and they wouldn't dream of imposing more severe speed limits because there's too much of a lobby. There is so much hypocrisy about it, but that doesn't let those of us who follow boxing off the hook. Like I say, I'm ambivalent. If I was asked if I wanted my son to box, I'd have to say no. And that, I realise, is to some extent a declaration of a hypocritical attitude on my part, and I can only own up to that. But I don't have a bloodlust for boxing. I just find it utterly enthralling, the repository of genuine nobility and heroic action. I admire great fighters and I'm moved by them, utterly moved.

I remember the crowd at Ali's comeback fight in Atlanta, when he fought Jerry Quarry after being out for three and a half years. That was one of the most amazing crowds I've ever seen at a prizefight. Black America chose to put on the style that night, and it was a dazzling occasion. Perhaps it was because it was mainly the black America of the street, rather than the black

America of legislative assemblies and the politics of the civil right's movement, but you could say that the blacks in America have had more chance to express themselves through being very lively and very cool in the streets than they have through legislative assembly. So it was an amazing, very thrilling occasion. And Ali just cut Jerry Quarry to ribbons. He realised that his legs were very poor and went in and punched him, ensuring that blood flowed and that it wouldn't last very long.

But inevitably, there's an alarming violence in boxing crowds. They're voyeuristic. They're often inclined to want destruction rather than grace and technique. But you find that crowds at all sporting events are filled with values that you wouldn't be too keen to identify with them. When I go to a football match, as a paying spectator, it's frightening. Even going on the tube to Wembley can be frightening. But at most boxing games, the tickets are very expensive, so most of the people have spent a lot of money to get there.

When it came to reporting Ali, I was always conscious of covering the activities of a figure who transcended the normal limitations of sport. On the other hand, I think it would be very dangerous for any journalist to start imagining that he was doing more than covering a boxing match. Of course you should be aware of the world beyond the ropes, of the world beyond the touchline. If you're not, you shouldn't be in the job. You should be willing to bring in the implications and the other issues when they're relevant. But I think that it would be disastrous to have a portentous sense of how important your coverage will be and would reflect a not very intelligent view of your function.

When I went to the US to report the first fight with Frazier, it was Ali's third fight after his three-and-a-half-year exile, after fighting Jerry Quarry in October and Oscar Bonavena at the beginning of December. The point is that, just slightly more than four months after coming back at the end of three and a half years of idleness, he was fighting Joe Frazier at Madison Square Garden. I mean, that is unbelievable. He should have taken a year before taking on somebody as desperately formidable as Joe Frazier. When I went to that fight, I felt that it was more than just a championship 15-rounder. I felt that Muhammad had spent much of his life convincing himself that he was addressing the world and always trying to give himself a bigger and a bigger stage. Then he found himself on an extraordinarily big stage, because this was without doubt the most publicised fight in history at that time, and it was clearly the richest – they split $5 million, which sounds like bus fares now, but it was a great deal of money then – and there was still a hell of a lot of people who wanted to see him get the most brutal comeuppance. I think that was the watershed fight, because he certainly came out of it bigger than he went into it. Before, I didn't fancy him to win. I thought no man had ever worked harder to promote his own funeral, given Joe's condition.

After Muhammad had lost the points decision to Frazier at that fight, there was a wonderful scene around the New Yorker Hotel, a huge throng of people in the lobby, all kinds of people, little girls – white girls, black girls – wanting to touch him. But it wasn't like the sort of excitement that would be stirred up by a pop star; there was an extra *resonance* to this. As he came out of there, he was like the Pied Piper, taking them out of Eighth Avenue into 34th Street. Then he takes them to where he has this camper van so he can drive to the home he had in New Jersey at the time, but there's this swirl of humanity following him and all this fuss being made of him. I remember some guy said, "All that for a beaten fighter." And there was a great big red-haired guy next to him and he spun on this fellow and said, "He won't lose next time." The emotional identification with Muhammad was marvellous. I felt it, too. And then Muhammad got in his van thing and he started to drive away, and he gave this little wave almost like the Queen Mother. I wrote a wee line at the time: "He waved like royalty. How else would he wave?" That's what we all felt, all of us who were standing there.

I believe absolutely that there is a huge depth of warmth and humanity in him. I know that the way he had spoken about Frazier, for example, just could not be sincere. After the Manila fight, he wasn't gonna come to the press conference. But when he heard that Joe had come to the press conference, with this swelling around his eyes pressing against the dark glasses, he said, "Get me up." He couldn't even put his shoes on. He turned up in his white boxing socks, being held up. And what he said there wasn't the doggerel. There was none of the shouting about how great he was. Most of it was about Frazier.

At that fight, he took terrible punishment, because you had the collision of two remarkable wills. You had these two men who could really fight and who knew how to inflict damage but were also willing to take an incredible, almost intolerable amount of damage. I was so happy when the fight ended. I would have been happy enough if it had ended earlier. That's possibly where I might be considered a betrayer of the cause in boxing, although I'm just as angry as anybody else when there's a premature stoppage when you know it's inflicting an injustice. But I find it hard to get too worked up about early stoppages, and that wasn't an early one. Joe was very angry and wanted to fight on, but it would have been terrible. He'd gone by then and Muhammad was dredging strength up from a place that can only be an absolute mystery to most of us.

The truth is that, most of the time, I was so enthralled by what was going on. The other important thing about that fight was that they were both well past their best. When I saw Sugar Ray Leonard fight Thomas Hearns in Vegas – one of the best fights I've ever seen – that fight fluctuated. There were stages when you thought one man would win and other stages when you thought the other guy would win. But those were two men at the peak of their powers. But there was something especially poignant about Manila because both men were definitely past it. Muhammad's prime was behind him when he came back in 1970. His highest level of performance would probably be Cleveland Williams late in 1966 or how he was working in '67. But still, he moved like a welterweight then. That's why I think that, when people talk about him being the greatest heavyweight of all time, if he hadn't lost those years, if he had gone on say in about a couple of more years, even in '67 I'd have backed him against any heavyweight that ever lived. If his career had gone normally, I think by '69 they might have had to impose a handicap system.

Arthur Mercante

Retired Boxing Referee

I wanna talk to you about what it's like on the day of a fight. Take the Ali-Frazier fight. They had seven referees in *The New York Daily News* who were eligible to referee this particular fight. At about four o'clock in the afternoon – very, very late in the afternoon – my wife received a message that I was to report to Madison Square Garden at six o'clock. When I arrived there, I didn't know which fight they were going to give me, because they had a few other referees. But they say, "Arthur you'll be the referee for the big fight," and I got the goosepimples, of course. Then, when I entered the ring, Johnny Adie was the ring announcer, and he introduced Jack Dempsey and Gene Tunney. All the celebrities were there. Frank Sinatra was the photographer for the event. Burt Lancaster, the movie actor, was broadcasting. And it was just the greatest sporting event of all time, actually. Ali proved to be a very valiant fighter. As I recall, in the 15th round, when he went down, I got to "one, two..." and was just about to say three and he was up. He took a tremendous left hook from Joe Frazier. And I also recollect that, in about the last 30 or 45 seconds of the 15th round, Ali came on as fresh as could be. A very great athlete.

What stood out about Ali's technique was that he was a heavyweight but fought like a lightweight. He was very, very dextrous; he was very, very light on his feet; and he was very, very quick with his hands. It was a very, very unusual talent.

You might not see this on the TV, but when I was in the ring with him, he was quite talkative. I believe it was maybe the eighth or ninth round that he was talking and jabbering, and I just said to him, "Stop talking." And I remembering him saying to Frazier, "You know, you're in here with God tonight." And Frazier responded, very quickly, "Well, if you're God, you're in the wrong place tonight." After that, they were jabbering, but they didn't mean anything. There was no cursing at all. It was just, "If that's the best you've got man, I'm going to take you out." Stuff like that.

I'm not sure that I was aware of the ongoing bad feeling between Ali and Frazier, but Ali was very cruel to Joe, calling him an Uncle Tom and calling him the ugliest nigger ever around, and he was very, very rough. So I kind of felt sorry for Joe, but as it turned out he knocked him down and it went to a decision. I thought then that it was going to be all cleared up, but it seems to be that it still exists, because Jo Frazier's daughter Jacqui and Ali's daughter Laila have fought before, and I kind of think they still remember. Jacqui still remembers how Ali treated her father, and that's why she was desperately trying to knock out Laila. That night, the crowd were rooting for the underdog, Frazier.

Of course, that wasn't the only fight of Ali's I refereed. I also did Ali-Patterson in 1973, I believe, and Ali-Norton in 1976, in the Yankee Stadium. He was a great fighter in each fight. In fact, he was great right up 'til the time he fought Frazier for the third time, in Manila. On the whole, though, I will say that old-timers like myself and a lot of the the Dundees and the Clancys and the Douvas really have selected Joe Louis as the number one fighter. Ali would be number two, but Joe Louis was a great, great heavyweight. He had a beautiful body, he threw vicious punches within a five- to six-inch range.

As a referee, though, the whole thing about Ali the political man, Ali the man who refused to go to Vietnam, Ali the man in the Nation of Islam, I honestly blocked all of that out. It was very, very political. I tried not to get involved with any of the write-ups at all, because I was scoring then, so I wanted a clear mind. I didn't want to get involved with any of the political discussions. I just remember entering the ring and blocking myself out just like I was wearing horse blinders, not even listening to the crowd and not even looking around to see all of the actresses there. And I was proud of myself for being able to do that, because it was a such a great night that I wanted to see everybody in the audience. I wanted to pick out the actors and the actresses. But I stayed focused.

That night was the greatest sporting event in history. If I were to ask any ten people today where they were when President Kennedy was assassinated, they'd know. I know where I was. Everybody seems to know where they were. This fight is getting to be the same way. People will remember where they were the night of 8 March 1971. "Oh, I know where I was that night." The Ali-Frazier fight has taken on that focus.

Of course, when you're in the ring yourself, you can actually hear the punches. You feel the slosh when a punch is thrown because they're all perspiring and the sweat is flying out in the air. You feel the impact. But of course, my method of refereeing is to remain very close to the ropes. You have to be in pretty good shape to be a referee and just stay out of the picture.

Something a lot of people don't know about is that, in the tenth round, when I broke Ali and Frazier to a brushstroke-type motion, Ali floats right back, but Frazier keeps moving in like a bull. I had my pinky finger extended and poked him in the eye. Fortunately, my nails were cut short. Joe turns around to his manager and he says, "I've got two men beating up on me in this ring!" He was about ready to go back to his corner to sit down, but I pulled him back into the fight. Thank God I did that, because if Frazier had gone back and sat down and he said, "I can't continue, I can't see, the referee hit me," he would have lost the fight on a technical knockout, and I would have been in the greatest controversy ever, because it was the referee who caused this fighter to retire.

Actually, Ali could have won that fight, because he gave two rounds away. He leaned up against the ropes and was taking enormous punishment inside and all over, and if he had fought like he did in the earlier rounds, he really could have won that fight.

During the '60s and '70s, Ali created an awful lot of interest in boxing. There's no question about it. But today, there doesn't seem to be that much interest in the heavyweight division. It seems now that all of the interest is in the welterweights and the middleweights. That's where it is now. But Ali did have an impact, and a lot of young folks admired him and went into boxing because he was the hero.

At one point in his boxing career, though, Ali was much hated. Then he resurrected that, and now of course he's loved by everybody and is classified him as the athlete of all times. But he was quite a rebel rouser. He could incite a riot because he was so volatile and dynamic, and he could get a crowd of people to go anywhere he liked, in any direction. But, of course, a lot of people feel very sorry for him, too, to see him today. I often say that a head wasn't made to take vicious blows like that.

He really should have gone before the Holmes fight in Las Vegas, his last fight. Holmes was always his sparring partner, and then they fought. He had lost it all then. He should have retired right after the Frazier fight, the Thrilla In Manila.

When I look back to the '60s and '70s, you can see that Ali created a moment which – partly because of politics, partly because of satellite television, partly because of the increasing impact of sport – will never be repeated. It was just an extraordinary moment that he symbolises. He's a very unusual personality. Very respectful. Whenever he sees me, he utters, "Oh, ma ref," and he'll kiss me on both sides, Italian style. And I love him myself. When he was known as Cassius Clay, I was a technical director for a picture called *Requiem For A Heavyweight*, with Jackie Gleason, Mickey Rooney, Julie Harris and Anthony Quinn, and if I recall, Jackie Gleason wanted to be known as the greatest and he had a chair with "The Greatest" on it. Then Ali came down a few days later and challenged him to that title and he put his chair next to Gleason's and it said, "I'M THE GREATEST", in capital letters. He's an amazing personality, really.

Kevin Mitchell

Journalist

Muhammad Ali is an exceptional human, a magnificent athlete, probably the finest boxer there ever was, a magnificent personality. And yet in many ways, he was a pawn.

He said and did things that no one else could say or do because of the position he was in, and it wasn't his fault that events ran out of his control. He was essential to them, but he didn't really create them. The Vietnam War – which he didn't really know a hell of a lot about; the connection with the Nation of Islam; Joe Frazier; the white, liberal intelligentsia who were pulling for him as a token of what they believed in; the establishment, who didn't like him because he'd changed his name and they didn't understand Islam; and at the centre of all this is this complex ego who let himself down many times, most specifically with Malcolm X, whom he pretty much abandoned. That was a pretty ugly episode in his life and I think he felt guilty about that, if you believe the statements he made after Malcolm X was gunned down.

Later on, things got worse. There was all sorts of manipulation, friends and enemies around him. He didn't trust a lot of people, but he had to trust somebody. And also he liked to have fun. He liked people like Bundini Brown around him. He liked laughing. That's why he liked Don King in many ways, because they were both performers. When I saw them together in New York recently, it was a revelation to see them interact. Don King has done some things to Ali that were easily described as reprehensible, but Ali forgave him and they met up. King walks into the room and they hit it off straight away, laughing, going back over their history, as they call it, or "my history", as Don King calls it – he wants to run the whole show. But there was a rapport there that was all based on fun. It was like two kids having a good time, and that was a lot of Ali's make up. He was a big kid, which I don't think a lot of people could accept. They wanted him to be responsible and grown up all the time, and that doesn't happen very often. He wasn't a statesman, as he tried to pretend he was; he didn't understand the intricacies of politics; he was cajoled into campaigning for some quite rigidly right-wing politicians in America whom he didn't really understand. He was sent off to help the boycott of the Moscow Olympics – he didn't really understand that, either.

But throughout his career, in his boxing, it wasn't just that he was a great fighter; he looked great, too. He very much had a vision of himself in the ring. A lot of boxers have that, but the thing about Ali is that he could deliver it. He could talk, he could dance, he could joke about what was happening with the ringside reporters – which he famously did with Richard Dunn, when he told the TV people to get the ads on because he didn't think he could hold this guy up much longer. He combined a great deal of luck and an amazing talent to box with an incredible beauty. When he beat George Foreman in Zaire, he didn't throw the last, finishing punch because he didn't want to spoil the picture, because Foreman was falling in front of him and it looked great. Ali skipped away like a ballet dancer, and that was exactly the way he wanted it to be. And when he stood over an opponent, he stood in a brilliantly vertical line, with his arms held up as if he was some sort of god. There aren't too many that you have ever seen able to be that self-contained under pressure in a boxing ring. Most men disintegrate under pressure, in one way or another, yet Ali hardly ever did. Towards the end, it didn't really count, because there wasn't much of him left, but even then, he was defiant and he did things that he should not have done – like fighting Larry Holmes – perhaps against his own better judgement and against the advice of others.

Like most people of my age, I first came across Ali on the radio in the '60s. My family were very interested in boxing, and we used to talk boxing at home a lot. Joe Louis was a hero of my father's. When Ali fought Liston, that was just an incredible event in our lives. We would all sit around, my dad and my mother as well, because Ali – or Clay as was – was more than a fighter; he was a huge star. And also boxing was very much more mainstream then than it is now. It was an event that everybody talked about. We all talked about it the next day at school and we'd go down to the gym and pretend to be Ali. I was Ali for about five years.

Ali was a very easy word to get your head round, too. Three little letters. No one ever called him Muhammad Ali; it was always Ali. You only had to say, "Ali." There were no other Alis. Most modern boxers today will tell you that he was the man who inspired them in the first place, because he just looked fantastic. Nobody moved as fluently, and for a big man – 14 and a half to 15 stone, over six foot tall and handsome with it – he was the perfect picture. He was a movie director's dream of how a fighter should look in a ring. He wasn't ugly – he didn't have a nose spread all over his face. He didn't look like Rocky Balboa or "the Raging Bull" or any of those squat, uglier fighters. He was smooth. People wanted to be like him. And when you watched kids boxing in those days, they'd always box with their hands down, trying to be fancy and then getting clobbered.

But Ali had the same inner toughness that just about any boxer has to have. Very few boxers would survive purely on the gifts of their fancy boxing; they have to have a fortitude that goes beyond all of that. They have to dig deep, when it stops being pretty and it gets really rough. Ali had very many hard fights towards the end of his career and a lot of hard sparring. Like most boxers, he knew pain, but he could handle pain. He was comfortable with pain. Heavyweight boxers have to calibrate how much pain they can absorb and still win the contest. It varies from fighter to fighter, depending on how good they are. Ali used to do that. He used to calculate how he would win. The rope-a-dope technique was about absorbing pain.

You also have to have a viciousness about you, and as kind a man as he was and is, as much as he likes children and as much as he cares about people generally, like any professional boxer, if he saw an opening, and if he wanted to, he would finish the fight as ruthlessly as he could.

There were three famous instances when he protracted the agony – against Floyd Patterson the second time, against Cleveland Williams and against Ernie Terrell. In his view he was punishing them for sins that were committed outside the ring. He'd use boxing to punish his opponents, to make a statement. They were unusual fights in that regard.

In other respects, he backed off, like when he fought Bob Foster, who was much lighter than him, motioning to the referee, "Stop this. I don't want to hit him any more. There's no point." So there were those little kindnesses. And when he fought Richard Dunn, there are many anecdotes about that fight. The referee at the time didn't get paid his full wage and Ali gave him the difference in cash on the plane on the way back to London. He was very generous with his spirit. In the ring, there isn't a lot of room for generosity, and for all that Mark Kram says that Ali was stupid or easily led or unintelligent, he had a fighter's intelligence that said, "Finish him. Hurt your man. Get him out of here."

It's an interesting dilemma that fighters have. They have to look after their bodies because they have to keep them a certain size and shape. With heavyweights, the weight is not such a factor, but they still have to be in good condition. Their hands, particularly, have to be able to endure a lot of pain. All fighters suffer from bad hand injuries, almost without exception, because they're not made for hitting.

Ali sometimes would be in terrific shape, would train extremely hard. That's part of the regime – you become addicted to the monotony of it. And Ali had his moments when he didn't train as hard as at other times. Then, as he got older, his body started letting him down – his reflexes were slower, his movement wasn't quite as fluid or as sharp or as responsive as he wanted it to be. And he then had to kid himself that he could still do it. That's what boxers do – they lie to each other and themselves all the time. He would say, "Yeah, I can still do it. I'm still the greatest." And he knew, deep down, that he wasn't. And on the occasions that he was delivered up to hospital, after a hard fight, he would then lie to himself again that these things weren't happening to him. He would lie to himself when his Parkinson's syndrome started to kick in. He would lie about his treatment.

He lies to himself now. He will pretend that he's much better than he is, sometimes. He's not supposed to eat sweets and chocolates, but there's a story that, when he came over to accept the BBC's award for Sportsman Of The Millennium and he came over with Lonnie, when they were in the BBC complex, he detached himself from Lonnie for a minute when he saw a chocolate-vending machine and rushed across and got a chocolate bar out. Lonnie heard it clunk into the tray and rushed around the corner, but she couldn't get to him in time to stop him eating the chocolate bar. So that's the little boy in him – he's constantly being naughty, and as a grown man, as a professional fighter, he was quite often undisciplined.

He was an intrinsically narcissistic man, but I don't think his self-love stopped him risking pain or getting hit. He fought the way he did because that was the most effective way for him to fight. He knew that he was quicker than any other heavyweight, living or dead. Nobody else ever moved like that. And he was a scientist in the ring. He could analyse the strengths and weaknesses of his own boxing game and that of others, so that, when he fought Liston, for instance, in the very first round of the first fight he hardly lands a punch. It's the most brilliant piece of boxing. He draws all the fight out of Liston in three minutes, just about, and it laid the foundation for the rest of the fight. Liston was hitting air and Ali was moving like a god. There was no way that Liston could touch him. But obviously, you can't got through your entire boxing career like that, and years later, when he slowed down a bit, he planted his feet when he fought Frazier for the first time. He was asked at the time, "Do you think you could have beaten Joe a few years earlier, before your inactivity?" and he said, "No. I wouldn't have been strong enough." So he changed his style of boxing. He moved less, or he moved less frenetically. He used the ropes a lot more. He was a master of space, like the great Cuban amateurs – he knew exactly how to box off a ring. All of a sudden, his opponent would be in a corner he didn't want to be in, or he would come after him and Ali would leave himself an escape route. There were very few as good at that as Ali.

Ali would map out a fight, as would any fighter, automatically. They know the length of the rounds. They know where they are most of the time, in relation to the corners and the ropes. It's just that Ali was better at it than anyone that's ever been. His knowledge of the geography of a ring was unmatched. All of a sudden, he wasn't there, and then his opponent would charge at him, say, or swing a left or a right and miss, and all of a sudden he's swung around on the ropes and Ali's pecking away at him and moving away again. And he would use the canvas to draw people on. He would create space and he would stand in the middle of the ring and draw people towards him, and then they'd find that they'd ended up in a cul de sac, and he'd peck away at them.

He also had a tremendous ability of ragging people about, doing illegal things. He had about three different jabs where he would flick the glove illegally in the other guy's face to make him blink and then hit him, just to annoy him. And then sometimes he would plant his feet and really let a thunderbolt go where previously he'd just tapped him, with almost the same sort of punch. It's a bit like a fast bowler who's got two bouncers, a quick one and a very quick one. Ali was a master of all these little tricks.

Also, he could hit from either shoulder with equal facility. He didn't have to arrange himself side-on; he could box square-on, which you're told not to do, because you can't get leverage. He very rarely boxed on the inside; he would tangle the guy up and frustrate him and hold his arms and then push him off and jab him, because he knew that his speed was what kept him in front of the other guy. He used all of these tricks better than most people you could ever think of in the history of boxing.

He was very good at conserving his considerable energies. He had tremendous stamina. As much as Frazier, who was a bull of a man who used to train extremely hard. As much as Marciano, or any of those energy fighters. He had as much stamina as they did, because he lasted the distance with these people, but he would expend less because of his accuracy – he would make Frazier miss three hooks out of five or six and take the other two or three on his gloves, nullifying the effect of that particular rally. And in the meantime, he would just flick him with a couple of jabs and a right cross, maybe, for better scoring effect, and then move away, and he would have expended less energy. So he was a master at keeping his strength. But even he had to go really deep in the well against Frazier in Manila, because he was ready to quit a couple of times then, once at the end of the eleventh round and then at the end of the 14th. He'd really taken Joe to the cleaners then, but there wasn't much left of Ali, either. Joe says that Eddie Futch pulled him out against his will, which is a reason for a lot of the animosity between Frazier and Ali, but I'm not sure how true that is because, when you look at it on tape, Joe was pretty much gone. If they'd gone out again, I don't know what would have happened. But Ali was terrific at marshalling every single resource that he had, all his strength, his confidence, his magic. The way he used to impose his will on another fighter and create something out of nothing, as he did against Oscar Bonavena.

And of course the Ali industry is pretty huge now. There are something like 57 Ali books and a couple of films and documentaries. All that probably started the moment he reported his bike stolen, when he was twelve years of age, because people recognised then that he was something special. I've often wondered where that bike is now, and if the guy who stole it realises that, if he turned up on a chat show, he'd be enormously famous. But people have taken legitimate pieces of tat and genuine books, shorts that he wore or he didn't wear, robes that he was alleged to have worn, all sorts of things, and these are all circulating all over the place as part of the Ali industry. I personally wonder why people want things like that. Maybe it's something that brings them closer to the man himself. And I wonder if they take whatever they've bought out at night and look at it or never even think about it again. I'm not sure what it is. But they go for tremendous prices, and Ali himself has always been very cavalier about it, which goes against the grain of the image of him as a manipulative miner of his own talent. I don't think he's ever really done that very well. Now he gets paid an enormous amount of money for personal appearances, but that is pay-back time, I think, after a long time off the scene, and also he loves the limelight.

The estimate of how much money Ali generated or earned or that came his way is pretty hard to determine. He used to write it all down, all his purses, and then stopped. Various people will tell you that the Nation of Islam took him for a ride, and I'm pretty sure there's some truth in that, but it's the same with most big-name boxers – people feed off them. They certainly fed off Ali, there's no two ways about that, like a lot of other people did. As to whether he generated millions or billions or tens of millions of dollars, these figures are almost academic, in a way. Certainly, you could say that there were undreamed-of sums from the day he signed up with the twelve businessmen of the Louisville Sponsoring Group. I don't think he ever imagined that this much money would swirl around him. I'm sure he has given away or lost quite a lot of it.

And today, the sums that fighters now earn – which are measured in the millions, usually, for the really big fights, especially the heavyweight fights – you could make the argument that Ali started it, but those sorts of sums do go back a little further than that. Mainly, though, the money didn't end up with the fighters – well, not those sorts of sums, anyway. But it was a million-dollar thing as long as a hundred or so years ago, with the likes of Tex Rickard and Doc Kearns, the early great promoters and managers and shysters. These were guys who could generate millions – for themselves, quite often. So the money has always been there. I guess it's only come to the fighters in those huge sums, though, in the modern era.

But even now, they still get ripped off. Don King, for instance, he's everybody's punchbag, and rightly so, in many cases, especially for those fighters who've sued him over their contracts down the years. But some fighters would say, "I don't care if Don King gets $3 million and I get $1 million – that's $1 million I never would have got, because whoever else promoted the fight might not have been able to generate that interest." The fighter might have ended up with half a million.

But boxers don't have the same morality about money as a lot of other people. They don't really look at the fine print. There's a lot of short-termers in boxing. The wonder of Ali is that he did go on so long. But then, at the end of his career, when his earning power was diminishing, he was thrust back into the fight factory to earn more money in the only way that he really felt comfortable, in the ring. Subsequently, he's become a big earner away from the ring.

But Don King and Cassius Clay, as he was then, came together partly through Don King's good fortune and partly through Don King's astuteness. And the key link is the '50s R&B and rock 'n' singer Lloyd Price, who occasionally used to sing in Don King's bar in Cleveland. Ali met Lloyd when he came to Louisville, back when Ali was a teenager, and the young Cassius Clay asked for his autograph. They got to know each other, because Lloyd was the sort of guy who'd remember a loud young kid like this.

Later on, when King moved out of the numbers racket and into boxing promotion, with Lloyd by his side quite often, he knew that Ali was someone that he should go to in order to make money. Ali was initially a little reticent about all of that, as he was about a lot of things until he was convinced, and then he got aboard the whole Don King bandwagon.

It all came together in Zaire in 1974, when King persuaded both George Foreman and Muhammad Ali that each had signed for the fight, and in the end they *did* sign. Lloyd Price was there as well. He organised the music. It was a sort of extravaganza, a celebration of black music in Africa, with a lot of the big names of the day performing, and that bond that was forged between King and Ali at such a momentous sporting moment in the 20th century was very strong, and they carried it on, not always very smoothly. There were other people chipping away at Ali as well, trying to get exclusive rights to him, but that's where it was forged really. It was through the Rumble In The Jungle that they became almost this fractious double act, two people who'd made boxing extremely exciting in the second part of the 20th century.

But the argument about whether or not Don King forced Ali to fight too long is a pretty short one, because it's unlikely that King would ever say to Ali, "No, I don't want you to go out and make millions of dollars for me." For his part, Ali found the Rumble In The Jungle a very, very hard fight, even though he knocked out George Foreman. Then he went on to the Thrilla In Manila, which was probably the most horrendous fight that I've ever seen, between two committed heavyweights who disliked each other intensely. That was the time when anybody around Ali would have said, "You've really pushed the boat out this time. Call a halt." But Ali wouldn't listen. Ali still had ten more fights after that.

Fighters quite often will not listen – Barry McGuigan said a very true thing once: "Fighters are the first people to know when to stop and the last people to admit it." Deep down, Ali would have known – as King would have done, Angelo Dundee, Ferdie Pacheco, Bundini Brown – that he should probably have stopped after Zaire, and certainly after Manila.

To illustrate the enduring legend of Ali's name, those three little letters, I went to Cairo to see Chris Eubank in a pretty farcical fight there some time ago, so farcical I can't remember who the opponent was, an Argentine who weighed considerably less than Chris did, so it wasn't a competitive fight. Going from the hotel to the venue took me across Cairo, which is a huge city, and we got lost. We were in the middle of nowhere and it looked like we were going to miss the fight. I tried to explain to the taxi driver that it was boxing, and he didn't really know what I was talking about. I used all sorts of words, like "stadium", and then I said, "Ali," and he said, "Oh, Muhammad Ali." He then knew that it was boxing we were looking for. Nothing else registered in this taxi driver's mind about the sport of boxing other than those three letters.

The latest debate about Ali and what he actually meant, what he was, is a fascinating argument, because he is such an interesting and charismatic character, and if he wasn't, we wouldn't be talking about him. I think sometimes even Ali doesn't really know the true extent of his nature, because he's so many things in one person. In one way, he's not very complicated. He's quite intuitive. He says and does things that just come out. In other ways, though, it's alleged that he's been programmed by the Nation of Islam over a period of time to spout what they wanted him to say, and there's a measure of truth in that as well. And, of course, no doubt he's been manipulated by various promoters and managers and whatever. But essentially, Ali rose above all of this, because he's a consummate performer, one of the great actors. Even now, in his stillness, when you can only hear a whisper of the man, he's still an amazing presence. When I met him recently, it was just wonderful – if that's not the wrong word – to see him just sitting there with his shirt undone, being quite normal and lazy and fat in a hotel room, just having finished his dinner. But there was something that came off him. And then he went into his old routine and told three of the oldest jokes that he has, because he felt compelled to perform for us total strangers. He felt it was almost a duty to entertain us, and also it give him a sense of self-worth that he could still do it. He does it now with little magic tricks and jokes, and he makes you laugh and he makes you feel good. Essentially, whatever the criticism about Ali, his motives or his naïveté, that's what he's all about. He's this wonderful, warm presence – maybe despite himself, but that's what he is.

Leroy Neiman

Artist

I first met Ali in 1962 when he fought against Billy Daniels at St Nick's in New York. At that point, he'd been an Olympic champion, he'd won half a dozen or more fights, and this was his first New York appearance as a professional, although he had fought in the Garden, as a Golden Glover. A friend of mine, Jack Dreeze, was doing a television commentary at St Nick's arena, and he takes me to this room and leaves me alone with this kid, this beautiful, honey-coloured young guy – about 19 or something – sitting on a rubbing table.

So here I am alone in this room with this kid. I didn't know that much about him. All I knew is that he was really some specimen. My mission to go over there was to draw, so I started drawing and he seemed to like it. I worked on the drawing for a while, and then he said, "I want to draw." So he takes the piece of paper, takes my pen and he makes this drawing. First he draws this rocket. Then he draws what I assume is his profile, then he draws a twin-tail Cadillac – at least, I think that that's what it was supposed to be. He had a red Cadillac at the time. Anyway, I was pretty impressed.

Just when he was just finishing off, some guy's head comes around the door

– "Get in the ring, kid. You're on." And this kid says, "Hold it. Just a minute." And he finishes the drawing. Then he slowly gets up and Angelo Dundee comes into the room and they walk to the ring.

So my initial introduction was Ali as an artist. I saw him draw before I saw him perform that night, when he won a reasonably shaky fight. He looked okay but he didn't look great. I've got another drawings that Ali did in 1984 in Chicago, one of his relatives, a kid, about twelve years old, and it shows real artistic development, more detail. But it shows the same rocket. Now, that is '62 to '84. That's 22 years later. I bet you if he had to do a drawing right now, he'd draw a rocket! I'm sure it was a self-portrait. He definitely saw himself as a rocket.

After that fight, our relationship developed. He had another fight at the Garden with Doug Jones, which was another close fight. He didn't look all that great. But while he was training down in Miami, he did a drawing just before the Liston fight, his prediction of the fight: "I told you I was going to stop Liston in eight." This was quite a remarkable experience. So then it became the thing that before a fight, we'd get together and do his prediction drawing.

I've got one of the second Liston fight, too, in 1964. He did that drawing in Boston and then had a hernia operation. It shows the judges, the whole crowd looking sad. Everybody's sad. He's knocking out Liston again. Me and my assistant at that time, Linda, we're the only two happy people in the crowd.

But the remarkable thing about these drawings is that, at this point, I fully realise that the strong artistic aspect of Ali was the fact that he could finish the drawing. He would stay with it. Total concentration. He was a closer. Anybody can start a sketch and make a suggestion, but artists, we fancy ourselves doing suggestive drawings with very little detail. But to be able to finish a drawing or a painting is still a sign of a student, that there's something special in his head there.

Back in those days, it was much easier to get down to a fight. Today, there's more mystique involved. Everything's big time today. I would imagine that getting next to a heavyweight champion today would be as difficult as getting next to Tiger Woods. I mean, I spent all of Tyson's career with him, but nobody at the moment interests me. When you've hung out with Ali and Tyson, it's pretty hard to find a new act, 'cause the contrast between two men is just so spectacular, so positive. They're both so effective. They so much demand the public's attention, their approval or disapproval. Ali would go up and down the public opinion, depending on what his position was.

Muhammad had an entourage. All the great heavyweights have hangers-on and loafers and drifters and admirers, a whole cross-section of the lesser-respected society hanging around in the fight game, and Ali was no exception. But still, in any one of these entourages, there was always an inner circle. There was probably a half a dozen people that were really close to him. They could go wherever they wanted. The camp consisted of Angelo Dundee, his trainer; a doctor; a masseur; and then, later, when he opened his camp in New Jersey, he added Gene Kilroy, who ran the place. Over the period, there were about ten people that were notable. And then there were a few sports writers that got close to him.

I was at all of Ali's fights, and it was always pandemonium. Ali was always hysterical, always putting himself in the forefront to be noticed. If he needed a holler, he'd holler. If he needed to act up, he'd act up. Sometimes he'd sulk and pout and lay back, depending on how he felt.

The atmosphere around the first Liston fight was strange. Liston had to be beaten. He was a villain. He'd been in prison, on major charges of burglary and mugging. Ali was a golden boy out of the Olympics. Such a contrast between the two. But Ali won that first fight under strange circumstances. And then, by the time of the second fight, the President of the time, Johnson, sent word that he wished for Liston to beat Ali, who was now a Muslim.

I was sitting in the third row in the first and second fights. Then, in the other fights, I got to the first row, and then eventually I got to hang in the corner with him, down to the ring. In the corner, you always have to kneel. You can't sit. And his corner was always pure bedlam. Sugar Ray Robinson started this dancing in the corner and making flashy moves, and Ali, of course, was a student of Sugar Ray Robinson. Robinson was his idol. So he went one step further. But then, when he became a Muslim, he'd pray in his corner, and that would pull the whole thing down and focus attention on him. The opponent was always in a hurry to fight, but Ali was pulling himself together before going out there and going to work.

After they took the title away from him, Ali spent a lot of time around New York. But then, when he came back in 1970, his first fight was with Jerry Quarry in Atlanta, and that was a big, big affair. I've got a picture of his from that fight, where he's walking away from Quarry. It's a pretty fine drawing. He put in the aisles and everything.

I've got one of the fight after that, too, when he came back to New York and fought Oscar Bonavena, the Argentine heavyweight, in December 1970. He knocked him out in the 15th round and the place just went crazy, so he added all these colours. Started out with the brown magic marker and then he'd add these colours. There are a lot of black faces looking at the ringside, because Ali brought the black Americans down from the gallery to the ringside – they spent their money to see him fight, after all.

There's one of the 1975 Frazier fight, too, one that he never finished, and that's more brutal, both stylistically and in terms of content. There's a little blood-letting going on in that one. He and Frazier had such hard fights.

But he was always such a performer. When he was arriving to a big venue, he'd get out of the car and there was always mobs of people, and he would try and give autographs to everyone. Once we'd gone through that and got him in the building, he'd go silent. He'd swagger into the room, kind of slow, looking around, not talking. And then other people would be buzzing around, people introducing him and all kinds of buzz going on. And then Ali would start talking, very slowly, very politely, and he'd slowly rev up. He'd get going more and then more, and then he'd start shouting, getting loud. Then he'd start raising hell and criticising things. After that, it was the mayhem. He'd go out, leave his room raving. This worked-up character would leave the room with a whole bunch of people following him out the door.

He was like that in training, too. He'd come to the gym for a workout, he'd step in the ring and he'd shadow-box, move around. The guys would fool around with his bandages or his gloves but he'd keep his head bowed. Then he'd start pecking around, going through all of his wizardry. And then he'd start talking while he was cuffing. He'd get himself worked up and he'd go over to the corner, and pretty soon he'd start talking to the people in the audience. Then, of course, he'd start raising hell and making predictions, and he'd start knocking his sparring partner. He'd get himself worked up to a rage over nothing. It was just great. And the sports writers would sit back and take notes. It was all a performance. We didn't know what it meant.

And then, in the morning, we'd get up for his road work. He'd wear these great big weighted paratrooper shoes. We'd usually get a car and come, too, which would take him a little distance before he'd start running. And sometimes the car wouldn't be there, and then he'd recruit the attention of a dog: "Get the dog over here. I want to talk to you dog." Then he starts mumbling to the dog, and then pretty soon he'd start getting a little louder and telling the dog things. All he needed was one person, you know? Road work in the morning was a performance. Then, after the road work, we'd go back to the hotel and he'd stretch out on the bed for about a half hour and he'd just talk. Anything off the top of his head. Sports writers would be taking notes, and he had them going all the time.

But he didn't talk all the time. He worked hard. He worked himself up, but that's the way he fought. He'd come out in the first round and feel the guy around. He didn't come on to knock the guy out – he wasn't that kind of a fighter. Then he'd start peppering the guy, and then pretty soon he started cuffing him and then he started spinning him around. He'd try to make the guy look a little monkeyish, get him a little off balance, and then he'd start to take over.

I'd been around the fight game before I met Ali, when I lived in Chicago. I did a lot of great fighters and ordinary people. I chose boxing because it's a one-on-one sport, like the art game – you do it by yourself. The guys giving you instructions can't work on your canvas, but they can tell you things, if they want to give you some tips. Same with the fight game – they can say all they want in the corner, and then, when the bell rings, you go out there and you're on your own.

I've got some pictures from later on in his career, when he was slowing. I've got one from '87. At that time, he starts sitting around like a Buddha. There's one I did at a friar roast and he's sitting at a desk, and he just falls asleep. I don't want to draw him that way, so I don't draw him any more.   Was he the greatest? Greatest of what? I think he only took himself seriously when the bell rang. But now he's not going to speak. The question is, what does he hear? And how much does he want you to understand what he says? When we were in Washington recently, he received an award and he made a short speech, two or three minutes long, very coherent. If the occasion's big enough, he'll come through.

Ferdie Pacheco

Ali's Fight Doctor

Ali was a primary thinker. Primary thinking is what you do if you put your hand on a stove and it's hot. Your primary thought is to get your hand off there and don't ever do that again. Primary thought records it on your brain. Don't put your hand on the stove. If you're hungry, eat. If the steak is good, eat that again. Basically Ali's not given to introspective, intelligent thought, in the way that you examine all different views on what's gonna happen to you if this happens or that happens; this is bad, this is good. None of that figures.

He applied this way of thinking to his personal life as well as through his boxing life. He had very good people around him in boxing, like Angelo. Angelo is very, very good. But Ali wouldn't have listened. Everything he did was primary thinking on his part. If so-and-so isn't hurting me, I can lean on the ropes a bit. We didn't think like that. We didn't get on a drawing board. We were *there*.

Oh we trained for it – to get off the ropes, to not let George Foreman catch us on the ropes and pummel us. "This guy can't budge. He can't hurt me." And he couldn't. "The ropes are loose. I can get away from him." That's the way it goes. And Ali won all those rounds that he was supposed to be losing because, in between all that leaning back and forth, he was killing George. He was hitting him with shots that would've knocked anyone out, but you didn't see it because you were so worried about him. We were used to seeing George knock out Joe Frazier. He knocked him around like he was a little kid. Knocked him out – *pshhhh!* One round.

When you're used to seeing that, you think, "Hey, he's gonna hit Ali. Ali's gonna go down and not get up. So you got that apprehension: "My god, this is not the right thing to do." But he had that primary thinking. He didn't have to explain it to us, didn't have to justify it to the corner. "Shut up, I know what I'm doing." That's all he said.

Of course, back in the '60s he was mixed up in all that Martin Luther King business. But what is now distasteful and politically unfavourable to say is to recognise that there was an extremely low level of opinion of blacks up to the '50s and '60s. To give you a little demonstration, I knew a pharmacy that stocked 32 different kinds of cream to lighten up your skin. There was also great prejudice from the black people about the colour brown you were, from African black all the way up to white.

The prevailing, overall thought was that black was bad. "Those people are ugly. They got nappy hair. They got big lips. They got flat noses. They got big asses. Black's bad. You should try to look white if you can." Every ad that you saw in every magazine had models that looked white, with their hair straightened out. Everything was white. They were wearing white clothes. They were looking white. I mean, every girl Ali was attracted to was more white than black. He's way more white than black. His mother was way more white than black. It's not easy to accept today, but blacks were considered subhuman. It's a hard, hard word to say. A hard word for *me* to say. But that's what they were. In the South, especially, where Ali's from. He comes along and, by dint of his athletic ability, his graciousness, his friendliness, his personality and this incredible good-looking body and face, he says to the camera, "Life is beautiful. I'm better looking than anybody in Hollywood. And I'm black."

But he could be worried about being black, too. Later on, he got the idea that black was ugly, that you had to get away from black. Not just be white, because you can't do anything about being black. It's an impossible dilemma. If you're black, what's the only solution? To be proud of who you are. I had an office in the black section for 20 years. For 20 years I'd see these guys that were trying to look white. Man, sod that. If you can't change it, be proud of it. I mean, if I had an orange growing out of my ear, and I couldn't change it, goddamn, I'd be proud of the orange. I'd say, "Look at me, I got an orange! You don't have an orange." You turn it in your favour. That's what Ali did.

But millions of blacks were not proud or happy to be black. They gave themselves over to the white people, because everything they saw was white. But Ali says in a childish way, "You don't see any black doves. And did you ever seen any black soap?" Until then, in all those magazines like *Life*, all the advertisements were white. There was maybe one black person, an Uncle Tom or Aunt Jemima person. A slave. Ali came along and everything changed. *Ebony* and *Jet* magazine started up and everyone became apostles of "beauty for blacks". They all came out of the woodwork. They'd never put on white make-up, never fixed their hair, never felt proud of their bodies. Black girls got the goddamn best bodies you ever seen in your life, but they used to hide them. Now, all of a sudden, the cameras and Hollywood and television's full of gorgeous black girls. Where'd they come from? Ali brought them out. He said, "Trust me, you're beautiful."

Wherever he went in his limousine, he would stop on street corners – even in the rain, in the snow – where there were beautiful women, going off to work in the factory or waiting for a bus. He'd get out and kiss every one like they were Rita Horne, no matter how ugly they were. Every one. And he'd say something nice to them: "You're looking fine today. You tired? Well, you look good, though." Some little ray of sunshine. A heavyweight champion had stopped the car, got out and said something nice to you. He'd help you fix a flat tyre. I've seen him do that. He's a people person.

He's not a heavy drinker, of course. He himself decided not to. That was a Muslim thing. They were taking him for money and they were giving him an identity that he didn't have before. He went to a Baptist church with his mother, I think. The blacks sat in the back. That's no kind of church. His church said, "Black is best. And the whites are devils." That fitted his purposes for the time, and so they hit it off. They needed each other. The Muslims got a lot out of Ali and Ali got a lot out of the Muslims.

Even the Vietnam thing turned out to be in his favour. He didn't think about that. He didn't think for one minute that that was going to happen to him. They even took his name away from him. And the Muslims, of all people, threw him out when the well ran dry. Yet he stuck with them. He came back. But when he came back, he was a different Ali. When he came back, he was a Muslim but not exactly a Black Muslim. He saw that they were just were people, not gods. Greedy, capricious murderers. He became a Muslim in the sense that there were so many million Muslims around the country. He'd go to Arabia and get $1,000 a day for being with a sheik. One guy gives him a million a day if he'll go through Ramadan with him.

But I have seen him accomplish miracles. I don't mean miracles in the ring. Forget about that. He just was able to out-think, out-wit, out-hurt, out-take punishment. There's no fighter like him in the history. No person like him. A guy called me and said, "You think Michael Jordan is as a big as Ali?" I said, "Are you joking? Is that a serious question? You a real journalist? You can go into the middle of India, Tasmania, South America, wherever, but everybody knows Ali. Everybody, everywhere." We'd go up to Indian villages and guys would come out with posters and books. I don't know where they got them. I've seen my book on Ali in India.

He fulfilled the grammatic requirement for greatness. The fact that he has a crippling disease now makes the end of his life dramatic and tragic and fulfils every quality you need for the dramatic. And on top of that, he's handling the disease just as good as he did boxing. The guy's milking the disease! He's sick, there's no question about it, but he just will not go under. He's saying to everybody that's got a bad disease, "Don't stop and feel sorry for yourself. Make a reservation in Disneyland. Go someplace. You're not dying; you're sick. Get going!" I think that's a colossal boost for the human race.

Blacks in general, though, a lot of them cut like hell in the ring. The prevailing thought for many years was that black people have a lot of melanin in their skin, which is kind of rubbery thing. They don't have a parchment-like skin Englishman do or people who live in a country where there is no sun. The guys from Africa or South America hardly cut up, because of that melanin. Also because they have great rounded ridges in their skulls that protect the eyes, whereas whites have more sharp ridges. In Ali's cases, these were factors. He only got cut once that I know. I sewed him up. It was a tiny cut. He just didn't get hit enough. He was always ducking and diving and holding his hands up. So it's a combination of everything – his incredible boxing skills and the configuration of his skull.

I remember some guy charged him $15,000 dollars to pump out like his body was a piece of machinery. And then this guy gave him a series of stuff like milkshakes to drink, stuff that nobody could drink. It's was like plastic. Ali took one and downed it manfully, said, "Don't worry. I'll use this." As soon as the guy left and he'd paid him his money, he threw everything up.

And then he became associated with Malcolm X. I mean, it wasn't anything he did. People came around him and they tried to recruit him. It's very easy to do, because Ali opens up to everybody. "You're my man. I'll be right there." So, when these political people came by, it looked like they were recruiting him easy. It was, "Come on by. I'd like to talk to you about something." "Yes, I'll help you with that." Malcolm X got suckered in worse than anybody, because Ali he just seemed like he just took them in like a brother. So Malcolm was like, "Oh boy, I'm in with this guy. I'm gonna talk him into coming with me and leaving Herbert." And Jesse Jackson was the same kind of thing. He was in Ali's dressing room, after being with us for training, and he just got the feeling that Ali and him were one. This was a new era. I remember saying to him, "Whatever you do, don't go back after the fight. Get lost. Just ease on up and send him a wire congratulating him and so forth and save yourself some trouble. You not going to get this guy. You're going to get dead, you and your family." Whether he would admit that now or not, he's probably forgot the whole thing. But Jesse Jackson was a very charismatic, important person to the black race and he didn't need Ali. He had his own charisma.

Could he have done anything else to help? No. I don't think he knew that they were fucked. I don't think he had a clue that they were going to kill Malcolm X. What could he have done even if they wanted to? Gone and said, "Don't kill him"?

But here was no pressure on Angelo Dundee and me, as whites on the scene. We served our functions. We didn't care what they were doing. We had our guy to take care of. I wouldn't try and be part of their scene. I didn't want to be any part of the Muslim part of his life. And Angelo is a very innocent man. He still is today. All he knew was to pay attention to what he knew, which was boxing. He didn't even know Ali had turned Muslim. He didn't even know what a Muslim was! He's just a very simple, clean-living, wonderful man. Doesn't see any bad in anything, just sees boxing. So we were not part of their scene. We were not a big threat to them. We didn't want to take him over. We didn't want to change his ways. We didn't want talk about his religion, his marriage, his attitude: "Do what you want to do. Just call me when the bell rings." We were out of the way and he needed us, and he knew it.

A lot of people wonder what it's like in the ring. That's what these guys train for every day. They toughen their bodies for that. I mean if some guy hits me a shot in the kidneys, I'll be out for a week, if not six weeks. But, if I've been training and get hit there every day, four, five, six or ten times, it no longer hurts. Your abdominal wall and your musculature is so trained. A punch in the right place just knocks you over. Not to a boxer. Ali has an iron, ridged board on his abdomen. That's training. That's why fighters lose fights when they don't train. They begin to feel the punches they didn't before. Training is the key to boxing. If you don't train, you can't fight.

But why is boxing so intriguing to the world at large? Because boxers are sub-divided by weights. Being a successful boxers is not dependent on your size, except for the heavyweights. There is a weight limit to you. And so you're fighting a guy your size. You don't have to worry about getting in with a guy that out-weighs you 20 pounds and is going to beat you into the ground. It's talent that counts, not size. Every other sport, you have no weight restrictions. If you're playing a very tall tennis player that can volley right down your throat and you're a little short guy from Indonesia, you're screwed.

The truth is that Ali is an icon. Since the beginning of time, we've had heroes and knights. There was always one man who rose above the crowd to become something everybody would like to be and is therefore a superhuman, someone you can worship without having to think you've got

Getting back into shape at Caesar's Palace before his fourth attempt at regaining the heavyweight championship against Larry Holmes, Las Vegas, September 1980.

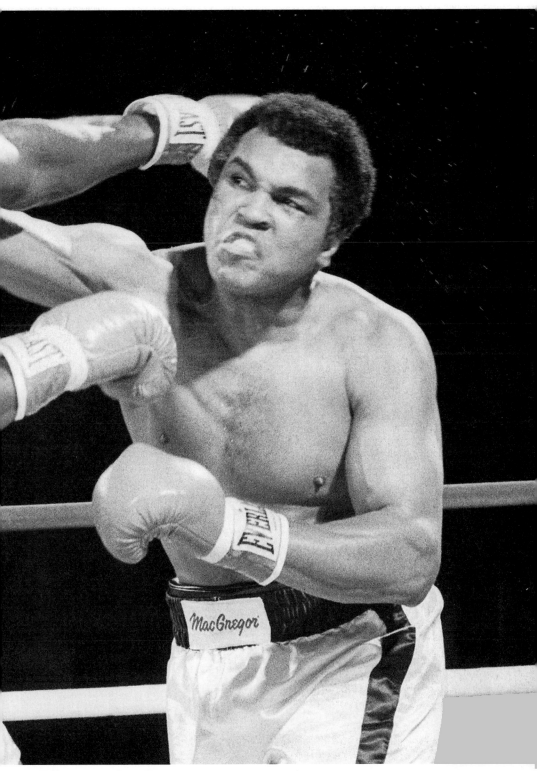

Ali misses a right hand in his ill-fated comeback against Larry Holmes, 1980.

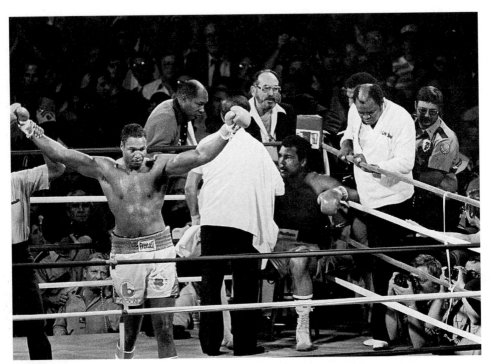

The end of the line: Ali is a sad figure, unable to answer the bell for the eleventh round, while Larry Holmes celebrates, Las Vegas, October 1980.

Addressing a news conference before his final fight against Trevor Berbick, September 1981. Ali lost the fight and retired for good shortly after.

to copy him. Take Joe Louis, a very nice man on the outside. Hero, patriot, representative. Sugar Ray Robinson was a big hero, also. He was a draft-dodger, a slacker, a con artist, a thief, and yet he became huge because of his athletic skill. And because he was beautiful.

These days, though, it's all about what happens in the media. You're getting television starting to explode with satellite transmissions, etc. And the media focuses on the heavyweight championship because it's perfect television. Two men get into the ring, and you can see who wins. Ali started all that with Africa and Manila. Imagine a fight like that now, with Ali and George Foreman in their prime. It's an incredible waterfall of money and exposure, the world over.

There's nothing like that kind of excitement in any other sporting event. It's something electric. You know something crazy is going to happen. Some guy has his ear bit. Well, that's really crazy, but it's a heavyweight championship fight and anything can happen. Ali gave you all that, plus entertainment, the fight and the lead-up to the fight. He defused the violence of it, or at least defused the danger of it. It's like two kids playing: "OK, so we're going to go play tennis today." Sure. We're just going to go box and try to kill each other. But it didn't seem like that on Ali's part. Joe Frazier and Foreman, they're all huffing and puffing and steaming. That made him even more charming. "We're just going to have a good time. We're just going to play a little."

And the public needs that. The public needs one guy. The more aspects of his personality and character are suitable to the audience, the bigger he becomes. Ali is suitable in looks and personality. He's seductive to women. People fall over in front of him. He is modest, in spite of the rhetoric, and he lives a modest life. Left to his own devices, he'd have a black shirt, black pair of pants and black boots. He doesn't need a suit. He's just a normal guy. He doesn't mind getting in a jeep. He's got a bunch of Rolls-Royces, but he'd just as soon get in a jeep. And on top of that, he's this fearsome warrior. Perfect casting.

Living in Miami, he was great with the Cubans. Remember, we had Cuban heroes. We had Cuban boxing champions that were teaching Ali. Luis

Rodriguez taught him how to jab and how to move. Cassius Clay used to carry Luis' bags into the fight so he could get in free, so he didn't have to buy a ticket. All the Cubans knew him and they all loved him. We'd go into a Cuban area and eat Cuban food and he just knew all about everything. He was like a child who liked everything.

I left after the Shavers fight. By that time, it was evident to others, not just me, that he was falling apart. A New York doctor showed me that he was losing blood after the fight. Stacks of the cells that filter the blood were going out. It means that blood is going straight from blood to urine. There's nothing to filter it through these cells that lie in the glomerulus. Then you're talking about kidney disease, which cripples you and you end up in a dialyser. You can see the progression. All you have to do is just put on the tape of Ali at the Frazier fight and the press conference; then put on the tape of the next press conference in Africa; then put on the tape of Spinks, diminishing to where he was slow beyond belief, compared to this rapid-mouth, funny guy. He was deliberate and slow, slurring, walking different, taking all kinds of punches. Everything you could possibly write as a criterion of brain damage, he had: thickening and slurring of his speech, inability to walk straight, inability to move straight – he couldn't have run five miles.

But he kept going, because he is the very embodiment of the word "champion". A champion doesn't think he can be beaten. That's why he's in there in round twelve beating up on you. He doesn't think he can lose, and he doesn't see that he's slower. He thinks he looks the same. Looks in the mirror, looks pretty good. "Say, Ali, looking good." Plus, he had the people that had built him into a business and needed him to fight to continue to live. All these hangers-on that he had, these 30 or 40 guys. He quits, they're out of work. Everybody wants him to continue. I didn't give in to them, 'cause I didn't get paid. I never took a dime off the guy – I never took a dime off any fighter – so I could walk away. I've always been very independent. I made my own money.

At the beginning, Ali was just another one of my fighters. Tending fighters was my main hobby. It was what I did to relieve the tedium of practising medicine in a tenement black ghetto and an exiled Cuban society. Those years were very grim. In black society, with the level of poverty that I worked in, there was tragedy every day, and the Cubans compounded it. I needed something to get away, and there was nothing better than boxing. But a great deal of that has to do with ego. There's something magnificent about going up in a corner with a well-known fighter like Ali or Rodriguez or Fernandez or Willie Pep or Willie Pastrano or any of those guys. You're standing there and you're part of their team. There's only three of you. You are third of the brain power that's behind this guy fighting for the title, and that's a huge rush. And you know you can be an integral part of it. You can be the difference between winning and losing.

At the time, though, I was just a doctor. I wasn't a painter. I wasn't a writer. I hadn't done anything important but become a doctor. So a little sugar came my way. It is unvarnished ego. Like I say, you're a part of it. Once you become part of boxing, you can understand why people stay. It's heady stuff to be in there, all the drama that goes on before and after fights. You travel all over the world and you meet everybody – presidents, the Queen of England, the President of the Philippines.

One day, in England, I was at this banquet, speaking to a bunch of people. I got up and I said, "You know, I've gone through twelve years of college education and five degrees. I'm a pharmacist. I'm a doctor. I do really important work in a ghetto with hundreds of people. And the only thing I'm really known for is something I don't do anything for: being Muhammad Ali's doctor. Being Muhammad Ali's doctor is roughly like being a gynaecologist to the Queen of England – you don't get to see much, but you get a lot of publicity." There was a stunned silence. Now that I've stepped in shit, I might as well finish it. I said, "By the way, can you imagine the Queen in stirrups, draped? Which end would you bow to? Your royal highness? Your royal butt? Which way would you go, you know?"

My responsibilities were, first of all, to be there during Ali's training period to make sure every little thing got taken care of, whether it was a cold or a rib fracture or separation of a rib. Then, if he was all well and in perfect shape, I'd numb his hands before he started punching, because his hands were very sore, after being off for three years. There were injections in his hands. After that, I worked in the corner, carrying buckets and swabbing him down and trying to stay out of the way.

His corner was unusual and he didn't need anybody to talk to him. He knew what he was going to do. But really, I didn't have anything to say to him. How was I, a doctor, going to tell the greatest fighter in the world what to do? He didn't need my opinion, and he didn't need Angelo's, either. Angelo would say something, he'd just go right over his head, or he'd say, "Shut up, Angelo. I know what I'm doing." The most we could do was tell him whether he won or lost a round. And Ali would argue with you. You'd come in, "I think you won that round." He'd say, "No. I lost it. The guy hit me four shots before it came to the bell." And he would almost always be right. We would keep a running count as to whether he was ahead or behind. That was pretty much it. The two injuries he had while I was with him – one was a broken jaw – he ignored. I wanted to stop, but he chose to keep on. That was a political decision. The other injury, the cut, that was nothing.

When you see Ali fighting, he keeps his head high so he can see what's going on. He had a God-given radar which told him where the punches are coming from, but he needed his eyes for that. The eyes are important – you need that to see where the punches are coming from – but he also had this speed and the intelligence to avoid almost anything you threw at him. If Ali doesn't want you to hit him, you don't hit him the whole fight. That's why his head is up, you don't hit his head. The other thing is, Ali has an inordinate span of vision. He could not only see what was coming from where, but he could see what everybody is doing ringside. He could tell you who's sitting next to who, who just ordered a Coke, who did this, who did that. He was incredible. You couldn't surprise him with a punch, unless it was exhaustion or he was in the middle of winging blow to blow, like when he was knocked down in the last round of the Frazier fight. That was just a lucky punch, thrown at the same time he was throwing a punch.

That fight was close. It would have been maybe a draw. It was too soon. He wasn't ready for it. I said to him, "This guy's body is ready for this. He's a machine. He doesn't stop. He keeps coming to the body, and you ain't going to knock him out." So we're looking at a twelve-armed body beating. I didn't think our guy was ready for that.

Foreman was different, though. He had size on his side. He was huge, cumbersome, and he punched down very, very hard. If you stand still in front of him and crouch down, you're going to get hit in the back of the head and everywhere else. He'd bounce you off the canvas like a ball. He would have done the same thing to Tyson.

Sister Imogene Perrin

Spalding University Archivist

I am the Sister of Charity of Nazareth, Kentucky, and I maintain a special collection at Spalding University archives that involves a very special relationship between Muhammad Ali and the people who work at the university, which began as Nazareth College. These archives tell a story of two buildings and two people who played a role in the beginning of Muhammad Ali's boxing career. Muhammad Ali had his first job here and began his boxing training in a building that was across the street from the college. At the time, he was under the training of a man named Joe Martin, a policeman who was interesting in saving the people out on the streets who had nothing to do, so he began a boxing program and other types of educational programs for them. Cassius Clay would work at the college in the afternoons. Sister James Ellen would save him part of her lunch each day and he would take one item of food. Then he would walk over to the gym where he practised. It was during these years that he moved into high school, when he worked for one year at Spalding University as an after-school cleaner. He cleaned and he also was a messenger, helping to carry heavy materials from one part of the building to another. He received 60¢ an hour and I believed he worked from 3.30pm until 5.30pm each day. Then he went for practice across the street, at the gym.

There were several librarians who worked here in this one room at the college. When Cassius Clay served as a page here, when he thought that everybody was occupied with other work, he would take that time to do shadow boxing. He would dance through the stacks for quite a period of time. Also, on one occasion he was found asleep on the table. He didn't lose his job over this, but a sign went up on the table that said, "Cassius Clay slept here," and last year two basketball players came dashing over from the gym and they said, "Show us the table where Cassius Clay slept!" I told them they were 40 years too late, because this isn't the same building and these aren't the same tables and so forth.

It was here that he made friends with Sister James Ellen. This became a friendship that lasted for 40 years. She followed every fight and sent him repeated letters of congratulations and invitations to return to Nazareth College for a visit. It was Sister Ellen who collected all the material that she could find regarding Muhammad Ali.

We secured all of the articles that Sister Ellen collected, and this is now our present collection – scrapbooks, magazine articles, correspondence with Muhammad Ali. In total, the collection includes three scrapbooks that are finished, one that is in the process of completion that that will be volume four, which includes numerous magazine articles and a prayer book that was given to Cassius and then somehow was passed onto us. And then we have correspondences, a couple of biographies and some personal things that I keep separated from the rest of the collection. We also have some ephemera – a menu from a dinner that he and some of the sisters attended, autographed, "To Sister James Ellen, my old boss. Muhammad Ali, man of God, 10 September 1979."

I suppose that some people might find it slightly unusual for Catholic nuns to be so supportive of a boxer. It's true that it is a violent sport, but it has been characteristic of the Sisters of Charity of Nazareth that we continue to support out students when they leave school. There are lots of people that we have supported who have succeeded in different capacities, and they have supported us through the years, too, so this was not an unusual relationship in that sense.

John Ramsey

Friend Of Muhammad Ali

Muhammad Ali was the Elvis of sports, bigger than the event itself. Hanging with Muhammad is hanging with royalty. He has an aura about him – for adults and children alike – a magnetism, and he still holds it, despite his health issues.

For me, he was ahead of his time. How many other athletes before him talked trash? – "I'm gonna beat you in this round. I'm gonna take care of you. Better get on the TV early, 'cause I'm gonna take care of this man. I don't like him"? That was the first time we'd been exposed to someone who knew how to build a demand and knew how to work his opponent in his favour. He combined being controversial with being a handsome, good-looking man, who lived the life we'd all love to live.

My favourite film is *The Greatest*. It shows a lot of the inner Muhammad and his motivation for fighting and his mindset. What I find amazing about it is that some of the things that he says in the movie still hold true in America today, about the way the African-American people have been belittled, how they need to stand up for themselves and get away from drugs. If you watch some of that old film from the '60s, you can see that Muhammad was angry and agitated by the press.

He does like to be provocative, though. He still likes to do that. He does it to me all the time! He'll put me in a situation, like we're packed in an elevator and Muhammad will say, "Someone called me a nigger," and you can see he's laughing. I think it's his way of breaking the tension. Muhammad's the only guy who can get away with that, and everyone knows that it's innocent.

There's no question he's had a huge political and social impact. He's always been against war, and he stood up for what he believed in even though they told him, "We'll have you and Joe Louis. You'll go through basic training—" which, for a boxer, would have been easy "—but we're gonna have you go through the camps and entertain the troops. We'll cut a deal with you. You'll never see the front line." But Muhammad wouldn't do it. He has never compromised his position. Never.

But really, his boxing was just an avenue he went down to become famous so that he could really show what he's made of. I believe that, and Muhammad has told me that himself. He's said that what motivated him to win the championship the third time was that he knew that, if he lost, he wouldn't have the same platform as if he won. It wasn't ego; it wasn't that he wanted to prove that he was the greatest boxer; but it gave him a channel to communicate. He now feels that the first 20 years of his boxing career were preparation for what has been the next 20 years of more spiritual work. I think he has a calling . I don't wanna go as far as to say that Muhammad is a prophet, but it's close. I believe that he does talk to God and has a personal relationship with Him. He had a bigger calling than just being a famous boxer, and he's used that to his advantage and to the good of everyone.

That's not to say he's a good judge of character, though. There were a lot of people in his entourage who just were not worthy, a lot of hangers-on. There have been people who have taken Muhammad for large amounts of money, and he still will hire them, even though he knows they did it. He forgives. He accepts the sinners.

I wasn't at the '96 Olympics when he lit the torch. I watched him on TV, crying and shaking. I was singing out loud, "You deserve that! You deserve that! You deserve that!" I was so proud of him. It felt like America was finally saying, "Hey, listen, we've got a hero here and he's alive and willing, and he wants to see you." Back when we had the PGA championships, I asked him what meant more to him, the replacement gold medal they gave him or lighting the torch, and he said lighting the torch. He told me he actually slept with that torch and was up all night, excited about it. It felt to me like it was confirmation of something he wasn't sure of, that people love him and embrace him; that, as controversial as he was, we respect the fact that he stood up for what he believes.

When I first became aware of him, like most men of my age it was because of the athleticism, the great boxer, and the fact that we were both from Louisville. My parents divorced when I was young and I embraced Muhammad as a role model. I wanted to be just like him, the first and the biggest. That combination enabled him to speak his mind. So at a very young age, I was into the athlete; but then, after meeting him, I couldn't have cared less if he boxed or not.

I asked Muhammad once what he thought was his best sporting moment, and he always refers to the Frazier fights as his best fights. Frazier brought out the best in him. That was the classic conflict, there, and I think he's very proud of winning those fights.

What made Muhammad such a great fighter is the fact that he could adapt. Most fighters have one style; Muhammad at one time was a dancer, then he would play on his feet and box, then it was rope-a-dope. And he could adapt his style in the psychological games, too. So yeah, if you asked him, he'd say Frazier. Frazier brought out all of his ability, psychological and physical, and Muhammad knows that. That's his mark in history, as far as boxing is concerned.

When I met him, it was at the end of his career and I was at a party. I was scared to death. I remember I was talking to someone in his entourage and he say, "Hey, you better go on up to the champ, 'cause if champ says leave, we leave." But I was really afraid, so I leaned up next to Muhammad, wearing this tuxedo, and I said, "Well, Muhammad, you could be the greatest heavyweight of all time." I was trying to be funny. He was so nice.

He sat down with me and we talked about fights. "Write down your address," he said. "I'll come and see you sometime." Yeah, right. But I wrote it down and he puts it in his pocket.

Two or three weeks later, he's back in town from Louisville, seeing his mum. He drives over to my place in a Rolls-Royce, knocks on the door and said, "Call all your friends. Tell them the greatest is here. Come on over." So I've got a bunch of guys watching old fight films with Muhammad. And he was so accommodating.

He knows that I don't want anything from him but his time, and I love being around him. But he calls the shots. He's the boss. If he wants to go and see kids in the hospital and doesn't want any cameras, we just do it. He always wants to make people happy, and that's genuine. He doesn't want any media attention; he just wants to do it because it makes him feel good.

But he loves that moment of surprise when he's knocking on your door. I've seen that a lot. We'll be in traffic sometime, just driving, and we'll pull up alongside somebody and Muhammad'll grab the horn. When the guy looks over, you can see him go, "Oh my god! Muhammad Ali!" All of a sudden, everyone's jumping out of cars and he's giving autographs and police are coming and we've got to move on.

I also think that he's is interested in all people. He gets a thrill from meeting someone who is so interested in him, and who can blame him?

Some people claim they're people of the faith and compassionate, but then you see them in the headlines the next day for some misdemeanour. Muhammad, though, he's always been right there. He's not gonna kill anyone, but to prove what he believes in, Muhammad could really go to battle.

Some people point out the hypocrisy of his faith. He's saying, "I want my wife to wear the long clothes and not to be sexually alluring when she goes out," and yet he's having girlfriends and illegitimate children. Muhammad would admit that he has his flaws, but the difference between Muhammad and the athletes of today is that, any woman who had children by Muhammad, he took care of them. You never see him in court for that. You never see him getting sued. He faced up to it. We've talked about this before and maybe now Muhammad would say he wished he hadn't done that. He'd say, "Don't do anything you wouldn't do in front of your mother, because God sees everything."

He has a good sense for people who are really into him. To this day, whenever people are around him, he'll pick the one who is the most intimidated and afraid and he picks them out and embraces them. A lot of that stems from when he was younger and he was shunned by Sugar Ray Leonard when he waited for him outside his gym for an autograph. He told me once, "I'll never forget how I felt. I felt *this* big. I will never make someone feel that way again." And I've never seen him do it. I can't tell you how many dinners we've been to and been the last people there, giving out autographs while they're cleaning up. I can't tell you how many flights I've missed because Muhammad says, "Let's wait for another hour or two, make sure everybody's happy." He knows how much it means to people to meet him. He knows it's an important moment in their life, and he wants it to exceed expectations. And it always does. When I travel with him, I'm always hoping for the best, and he always exceeds it.

Once I was in Australia with him, watching a fight. It was like a rock concert. The crowd was awesome. They snuck us backstage, no formal announcement or nothing but news trickles through the crowd that Muhammad's there. There's all this noise, Muhammad's waving to everybody. After the fight Muhammad goes up to the kid that wins and congratulates him and embraces him and everyone gets their photo op and everyone's happy. Then Muhammad leans over to me and he says he wants to see the loser. So we go into a locker room with the kid who lost, and he's the saddest guy in the world. Muhammad walks over to him, hugs him and messes with him and says: "You did good. You did all right." We left him the happiest kid in the world. No one thought about the loser but Muhammad. I didn't and I think I'm a nice guy.

He wants to show people in America that Muslims are nice, God-fearing people. And he once pointed out to me, if someone hijacks a plane, he's a Muslim hijacker, or a Muslim terrorist. But when someone robs a bank, they don't say Christian bank robber.

But, you know, for Ali religion is like a body of water; it's all from the source it just branches into rivers and the like. I think part of his mission is to show people tolerance of all religions and colours, and I think he does that every day.

Dick Schaap

Broadcaster / Journalist

In 1960 I had some friends on the United States Olympic team who said to me, "You've got to meet this kid, Cassius Clay. You've never met anyone like him." So I did and I took him, and three of his team mates – Wilbert McClure, Eddie Crook and a fellow named Campbell – out to dinner at Sugar Ray Robinson's restaurant in Harlem, on the corner of 125th Street and Seventh Avenue. When we were in the cab, he said, "I am the greatest."

"Yeah, sure kid," I said.

"Don't pay any attention to that," Wilbert McClure said. "That's just the way he is."

I showed Cassius Clay, as he was then, his first black nationalist that night. There was a guy on a soapbox preaching "Buy black, buy goods from black merchants" – quite mild stuff, but Clay was taken aback by it. He had never seen that in Louisville.

"How can they get away with that?"

"Easily enough," I said.

I introduced him to Sugar Ray Robinson that night, too, and he was all excited. He loved Sugar Ray's flashy car and flashy clothes, flashy smile. At that time it was his ambition to grow up to be another Sugar Ray Robinson. Of course, he grew up to be a lot more.

He was using the Olympic village, which wasn't that big a place, but there were people from all over the world and he loved meeting them. Growing up in Louisville, Kentucky in the 1940s and '50s as he did, even Chicago is a different world, so obviously Rome was even more so. He was immensely popular in the village. He went around taking photographs of everybody and giving people pictures. Many of the Iron Curtain countries tried to get him to talk against the United States, but he wouldn't do it. At that time he was what you would call a patriot, although when he later became involved in the Muslim movement he had his own criticisms of the United States. But at that time, he was very much a defender of it. He was carefree, he was in love with life, and there was no bitterness then. He was a very different person.

When he returned from Rome I met him at the airport. This was 1960, the airport's name was Idlewild and his name was Cassius Clay – within five years both he and the airport had changed their names. One to Muhammad Ali, the other to JFK. I could have gotten terrific odds betting on that to happen. He had a suite in the Waldorf Towers, paid for by a wealthy aluminum company who wanted to sign him up, and I took him to dinner at a place called The Bull And The Bear. I ordered him a steak dinner and he ate the whole meal, before asking if he could have another. And he ate it all, another whole dinner, from beginning to end.

Then we went out on the town, starting in Times Square. He was amazed that everywhere we went, people recognised him. Of course, the fact that he was wearing his Olympic blazer, with the letters "USA" about eight inches high, helped. Plus he was wearing his gold medal around his neck! He had not, at that point, taken it off, even sleeping on his back for two days, which was not his style, because he was afraid that if he slept any other way he'd cut himself on the metal. He thoroughly enjoyed the recognition, though. We went into a penny arcade, where you can print up phoney newspapers, and he had a newspaper printed up with the headline "Clay Signs To Fight Patterson" which was sort of a dream for him at the time, but it did turn out to be prophetic.

I then took him to Birdland, which was the jazz capital of the world at one time. We went up to the bar and he ordered a coke and said, "Put one drop of whisky in it" – he wanted to be able to say he had a drink at Birdland. That's the only time I ever saw him drink, and it was only one drop. We went up to Harlem, where people recognised him, and we went down to Greenwich Village because he wanted to see what a beatnik looked like. I showed him, but I don't think he was overly impressed. We had a great tour of the city and ended up, at three o'clock in the morning, going back to his suite in the Waldorf Towers where he wanted me to look at all the pictures he had taken in Rome. That took another two hours and I said to him, "Cassius, you're going to have to come out to New Jersey tomorrow and explain to my wife why I didn't get home."

"You mean your wife knows who I am, too?"

He was just beautiful.

I went down to Louisville when he was getting ready for his first professional fight and we had a great time together there. My love for him was intensified one time when we were driving down the main street. We stopped for a traffic light, and saw a very pretty young woman, who happened to be white, standing on a corner. "Boy, she's pretty," I said. Eighteen-year-old Cassius Clay grabbed my shoulder and said, "You crazy man! You could get electrocuted for that, a Jew looking at a white girl in Kentucky."

I knew then that I had never met anybody quite like this.

In Louisville in 1960, he and I could not eat together in a "white restaurant" downtown. We could eat together in a restaurant in the black section of town, but not in the white section. I had encountered this in other places – I'd been covering sports, getting to know a lot of black athletes and these things came up. I took a young fighter named Jose Torres, who later wrote a book about Ali, out to dinner in New York, in the late 1950s. We went to a well-known German restaurant and were told there'd be a wait for a table. Based on experience, I assumed it was because I was with a Puerto Rican, but about 30 seconds later, all the waiters and all the people in the kitchen came pouring out and all of them were Puerto Rican. They all recognised Jose, yelling "Joselito, Joselito, Joselito!" A few minutes later we had a table.

Malcolm X is one of the most charismatic human beings I ever met and, at the time, Cassius Clay was quite malleable. I'm only half kidding when I say that if I'd tried really hard to convert him to Judaism, I think I could have done it at that point. But Malcolm X got there first with stronger material. It was very easy to be swayed by Malcolm X. I didn't join the Nation of Islam but I surely came under the spell of his charisma. I don't think it was Elijah Muhammad who converted Clay, it was Malcolm X.

He was looking for something to hold onto and he liked what he was told, he liked the people who were around him, he liked the principles. Of course, the principles of any religion tend to be good; it's only the practices that sometimes tend to be bad. He liked all of that and he took it quite seriously. He was not an educated person but he had great native wit, great native intelligence and a smartness to him that went far beyond his education.

In 1969, I had a TV show and we always had one athlete and one showbusiness guest. This week we had George Segal, the actor, and Muhammad Ali. Segal began talking about a movie he had just made with Barbra Streisand, describing a nude scene that they did in it. Ali stood up and started to walk off the set, so I said, "What's the matter?"

"You know I'm a minister," he said. "I can't listen to stuff like that."

We calmed him down, changed the subject and he stayed and finished the show. Afterwards I said to him, "I'm sorry, I didn't mean to get you upset."

"I've got to talk like that. You know, the CIA's watching, the FBI's watching they're all watching." So he knew part of it was a game, although I do think he had an honest belief in the principles of Islam.

Malcolm X and Cassius Clay were close, but not for a very long period. It wasn't very long after Malcolm brought Cassius into the Nation of Islam that he was expelled because of his comment about the chickens coming home to roost, after the assassination of John F Kennedy. Why that remark in particular triggered the reaction of the Black Muslim movement, I've never quite been able to figure out. There were certainly far harsher things said by Malcolm and Elijah Muhammad and other people. But he was sent to Coventry and therefore wasn't allowed to have contact with someone like Ali/Clay. I think his would have been a very good influence if it had continued but, of course, he was assassinated soon thereafter.

Some people blamed Ali indirectly for the assassination. Actually, it wasn't so much blaming him, but there were a lot of strange things that happened around Ali. There were a lot of people who died under strange circumstances who were involved with him in one way or another, including a woman – an attorney – who drowned in three inches of water. I only vaguely remember the details, but there was a theory that this was to keep him in line. I have nothing to substantiate that theory but I certainly heard it.

When he took his stand against the war, it made him more of a hero to us. When you realised that he was going to be suspended from his profession and lose millions and millions of dollars for taking a theological stand, you had to admire him. Many of us who were young and left-leaning were opposed to the war anyway, so we applauded him. Of course, afterwards a lot of those feelings were vindicated when more and more people came to realise that the war was not exactly America's greatest hour.

Ali is a great influence but there have been so many people along the way who have influenced him at various times. The one constant, at least in the last 30 years, has been Howard Bingham. I don't think he ever set out to shape Ali; he just set out to be a friend. Angelo Dundee had an influence, too, but only within the ring. He did not try to exercise any influence beyond boxing and he probably would not have been able to. He was a great guy and a great trainer and a great student of his sport, but nobody has ever said that Angelo was a diplomat or a statesman or anything like that – that's not his field.

Ultimately, I think, the greatest influence on Ali has been Lonnie Ali. I think she does an unbelievable job of it. Partly because of Muhammad's condition, she has to be more of a shaper, but she's terrific, the best part of his life. She knows how difficult it is to get him to draw back. I was hosting a golf tournament at which he was my guest of honour and there were hundreds of people engulfing him as soon as he arrived, posing for pictures with him, signing autographs. We had a room where he could rest, but Lonnie said, "No, no he loves this, don't take him away from this. This is why he's here. This is what he feeds off, what he lives on." And he does light up. Even though his powers of speech and movement are impaired, the light in his eyes is as bright as ever.

Most people enjoy their celebrity up to the point where it interferes with their life. Ali doesn't mind when it interferes with his life – that's all part of it. When he was living in Cherry Hill, New Jersey, tourists would come up to the little cul-de-sac that he lived on, and stop and point and say, "There's Muhammad Ali's house." And he'd come out and invite them in. It drove his wife Belinda crazy, but he'd have strangers marching into the house so that he could show them where the champ lived. He was the champ in every way.

I was in Manila covering the fight there and it was very early in the morning – around six o'clock. I was in Ali's suite with my *Today Show* camera crew and Angelo. I was interviewing Muhammad when Belinda arrived at the airport from the United States, having read all the reports in the newspaper that he was going around accompanied by a woman named Veronica – who obviously was not Belinda. She walked in at the middle of the interview and he excused himself and they went behind closed doors. There were very loud sounds coming out, typical husband-and-wife sounds when they're not in total agreement, so Angelo said, "Why don't we go get a cup of coffee?" He always has had good advice, so we had a cup of coffee and, when we came back, it was calm. Ali sat down after a few minutes, regained his composure and his sense of humour and finished the interview.

I really didn't know Veronica, I'd only met her a few times, but I liked Belinda a lot. I remember being at their house in New Jersey when, as soon as Ali left the house, she put on music and smoked a cigarette and didn't have to pretend to obey all the Muslim laws. She was a nice person and she really loved him I thought. I don't think she was just using him as so many people have done over the years.

I don't think Ali would be different today. He was unique in his own time and he would be unique in this time. There wasn't anyone else like him when he was at his prime. There's no one even close to being like him today. He is a walking carnival. If you had the opportunity to follow him for 24 hours, you would stay with him for 24 hours. For 20 of those hours, nothing exciting might happen; but four hours are going to be the greatest four hours of your life.

Athletes then were not as open as Ali was. He did not hide things, he brought reporters into his room the day of a fight. He invited you to go out with him at night as he walked around the streets. He loved having people around him. His book was one of the worst-selling books of all time because there was nothing to reveal. He had always opened up about himself, so the book was filled with everything that everybody already knew and nobody bought it. Ali likes people; he's not afraid of them. If you had to have one adjective to describe most athletes today, it would be "wary" – they are wary of everybody. You say hello and they want to know what it means. Ali took hello to be a friendly greeting when it was intended to be a friendly greeting. He just really loved people. He loved the cameras, he loved the spotlight, he loved children, he loved winking at pretty women. There was no facet of his life that he didn't love including the fighting. And he was so good at every facet.

I hate the sport of boxing. I just think it's barbaric and I don't think it should be allowed. But I love the people who are in it, there are so many interesting characters. Ali brought people to boxing who otherwise might have stayed away, no question about it; I wish they had stayed away. Since he has left the active scene, more and more people have recognised how barren the world of boxing is. Now, the only people who are totally absorbed by the sport, in the US at least, are the Spanish/American population because they're the group that's on top now, and people who want to watch the violence of Mike Tyson, to see if he's as big an animal as they think he is.

People say there is a cruel side to Muhammad Ali. I think he was cruel with his words, in talking about Floyd Patterson and Joe Frazier at various times. I wish that he would have modified some of that, particularly towards Patterson whom I knew really well and whom I liked. But it would be very hard to be heavyweight champion of the world without having some kind of strong, destructive streak in you somewhere. Ali was not a saint, he's not perfect, he's probably indulged – except for drinking – in most of the vices known to man. But the love that he gives to the world and the love that the world gives back to him, that's what his identification is, not the fact that he was cruel to Floyd Patterson and Joe Frazier. Yes, he may have been, but that's not what defines him.

I watched the Rumble In The Jungle fight at Madison Square Garden, in a luxury box owned by a friend of mine. There were about 20 of us in the box – 19 caucasians and one black man. He was the only one who thought Ali was going to win. Most of the rest of us wanted Ali to win but we were afraid that he was going to be destroyed by this indestructible man called George Foreman.

He should have ended it after that. Metaphorically, I felt that he should have been frozen in ice and taken over to nearby Mount Kilimanjaro and preserved there, like Hemingway's leopard, for all time. I thought that would have been the perfect end, the greatest triumph of his career, beating George Foreman, the most spectacular show and this rope-a-dope technique which the world had never seen before. He should have quit then, just as I feel that Michael Jordan should not come back after ending his career on a perfect note. Strangely enough, he did not diminish his image or his legend, even with the fights that he lost later on, and that's remarkable. Even slowed by Parkinson's, his image is not diminished at all. If anything he's probably a little more loved each year. There are people who do pity him, but I think those are people who've never been with him.

In 1975, I was the editor of *Sport* magazine and we had chosen Muhammad Ali unanimously as our Man Of The Year on the basis of his victory over in Zaire. For our awards dinner, we had the singer Melba Moore, the writer George Plympton and the playwright Neil Simon coming. I also wanted a comedian, so I called Robert Kline's agent who told me that Kline would not be available. "But," she said, "I've got a young comic who's really terrific."

"Who?"

"Billy Crystal."

"Who's that?"

"Trust me, he's funny."

All I could think was, "You're an agent – how can I trust you?" but nevertheless I spoke to Billy on the phone and invited him to perform. I met him ten minutes before the dinner began. He was wearing one of the ugliest tuxedos I've ever seen in my life, with velvet collars and a bow-tie that even he said looked like a tarantula. We put him up on the dais with all these famous people, including Ali, and no one in the audience had any idea who this short Jewish kid from Long Island was. When it came for Billy to perform, as Master of Ceremonies, I stood up and said, "And now, one of Muhammad Ali's closest friends," and Billy stepped towards the microphone.

Ali looked at me like I was crazy – he had never seen Billy before. But Billy took the microphone and immediately launched into his Ali and Cosell routine which later became quite famous. Everybody tried to memorise it afterwards, but that night no one there had ever heard lines like "I'm so fast I can turn off the light and be in bed before the room gets dark". Ali fell out of his chair laughing, he and I just cracked up. And that was the start of a three-way friendship: Ali, Billy and me. I love the fact that Ali and Billy were pretty much unknown when I met them. They both would have made it without meeting me, of course, but it's still nice to have met them then.

I've covered sports for 50 years and there is no question that Ali is far and away the most significant, the most charismatic, the most charming person that I've met in sports. Nobody else is even in second place. If the Queen of England, the President of the United States, the Pope and Muhammad Ali walked down Fifth Avenue, a lot of people would say, "Who are those three people with Muhammad Ali?" He was definitely the most recognisable human being on earth and he probably still is.

Rod Steiger

Actor

Muhammad Ali is one of the few men I can think of who, never mind the money, put his *life* where his mouth was. This is a man who, because of his beliefs, denied the stupidity of the government by saying he wouldn't go to war, a man who always stuck up for what he believed – and that's more than a rarity.

I've always been – and this is a word that's become dishonoured – a progressive, like a liberal, in that I am against any form of prejudice. But something my country doesn't understand is that all people are not born equal. I'm not going to rush up to Toscanini and say, "Give me your baton, you don't know what the hell you're doing with the music." But I have the equal right to go up to him and make a jackass out of myself. There's a difference. And that's what a lot of people in America don't understand. I certainly am not going to tell Einstein about physics or anything, but I have the right to, if I want to look like a schmuck.

It's the same thing with Ali not going to Vietnam. I had four years in the service, so I disagree with what he has to say, but I'll defend to the death his right to say it. I have to admire a man sticking up for a principle, so long as the principle is not detrimental – if somebody stood up for what the Nazis believed in, then you'd have to say, "Wait a minute here." But this man was putting his honour on the line so you began to realise that this was not your ordinary pugilist.

After that I started getting a little serious about watching him and many times I was amazed at his cleverness in public. Like in fighting, he'd slip one question, another would come up. This man was incredibly bright. I don't know what the hell his IQ might have been, but when you think about when he did the "rope a dope", while everybody in the world was screaming, "What the hell's wrong with you? What are you doing?", that was smart. He took a chance in getting Foreman tired and, boy, he took a lot of blows which must have affected him years later. He was a great general in the ring. It looked like he was retreating but his retreat was the best attack.

He's very creative and he must see things in a total sense. He says, "Well, they're expecting this, so I'll make them think they're gonna get it, but they ain't." Vocabulary has very little to do with instinctive intelligence. I always tell the story of two men standing on a street corner. One is the intellectual, one is the man who is born with instinctive intelligence. They start to go across the street. The intellectual says, "Look at that. Look at what's coming towards us. A 20-ton truck carrying 480 tons of steel has an air-conditioned cab, two men drive it, one sleeps while the other drives…" and the other guy pushes him out of the way so they shouldn't get hit! Now who's smart there? And that was Ali. He didn't want to get hit.

I was in New York when he made his speech. It was amazing to see a man on a medium called "television" declare his absolute beliefs. To say, with about about 40 million people watching, "I am not a liar", took courage. Very few men could do that. I don't think I could. That was a heroic moment, because the guy's on television, he's very clever and he knows everything that's going on, and he uses the simplest language: "I'm not going". End of story. That example gave strength to the people – his own people. He demanded respect for what he believed.

When Ali won the world title, he then decided to become a member of the

Nation of Islam and he went public on that. My view on that was the same as the Vietnam issue. You have a right to believe in what you choose, as long as it doesn't hurt or damage another human being. I don't believe in any religion today, but I respect the person's right to believe. I think, though, you have to remember that a lot of those things are a human being's attempt to find a place where he is equal. And here was a group that said, "You're not only equal, you're better!" One can understand. In my opinion, you wind up with groups that give you support. That may not be too healthy for you, but you don't know at that moment, at least somebody says they respect you. Hitler managed to convince the Germans that if it hadn't been for the Jews, they would have won World War I. He got a scapegoat, and people followed.

Ali grew up in an America that was segregated, that was racist. When he won his gold medal, and as a black man was shouting, "I am the greatest", I took the view that here was one of the greatest showmen. This man could sell himself or sell you the Tower of London. He had this charm, this rapid mind and an insane insistence on being heard. Here was a guy who's a good boxer and very clever at getting your attention. The more attention he gets, the more people go to see the fight.

My film, *In The Heat Of The Night*, is about racism. My character, Gillespie, the sheriff, is brought together with Mr Poitier's character because they were both loners. They learned to respect each other through actions, which is the best way, not through discourse about prejudice. The sheriff realised, in another way of speaking, that this black guy was just as good a gun fighter as he was, so he began to look at him a little differently. "Well, this man is a man. I may not like him but I have to respect him. He sticks up for what he says." I always liked that about the picture.

The death of Martin Luther King was a terrible, crippling blow to a march towards true reality and communication between people. He was one of the leaders that were fighting against colour getting in the way of what is intelligence. A person who fights for freedom is instinctive. If you see a man being beaten up by people of another colour, something inside of you, unless you're off your mind, says, "That's not right. I don't like that. This is terrible." From there you can get into, if you want a fight, against why there are the differences in salaries, the differences in cities, the differences in education, the differences in schools and churches and things like that. In my country, the problem is – the problem in all big countries, I guess – apathy. You'd have to blow up the White House before Americans would finally say, "What's happening here? What is this?" Part of that is because each individual is busy 24 hours a day, trying to earn for his family, so you can't expect him to be a wizard at sociology. But he has some responsibility as long as he breathes. And to get his attention, a big thing has to happen. For instance, dropping the atomic bomb or the assassination of Kennedy.

The majority of people in society are basically "normal", and with Ali, they unconsciously realise they made a big mistake with this guy. In general, America loves Ali. But they are embarrassed, not because of him but because of their stupidity, because of how they thought of him before they found out this was indeed one of the most courageous and, in a sense, socially important men in the world. Nobody thinks of a boxer having social responsibility, but this man was a leader. He could walk into any nation in Africa and be the president the next morning!

He became an ambassador for his people. It happened because the press followed him everywhere, so he had global communication. If he went into a sewer, they were going go down and take a look. If he went to Africa, anywhere, they were there. The bad part of that was they did it because they could make money off him. But the good part was that he used it to reaffirm certain human beliefs that must not be forgotten.

I had empathy at all times with Ali, and after empathy it became respect, and after respect it became awe. After awe, it became "Jesus, he's got something I'll never have, that's for sure!" We all have beliefs, but there are very few of us who believe strongly enough when suddenly you have to put the beliefs into action. We can sit and bullshit ourselves in the coffee houses, talking about society and everything, but when somebody comes through the door and says, "All right, one of you has to come with us to prove you believe this," you'd have a hell of a time getting anybody out of that booth. But if Ali was sitting there, he'd say, "I'm here. What do you want?"

I am impressed and in awe of his physical abilities, of course, but this man, as far as I am concerned, is an example for my children, or anybody else's, especially if it's a young boy. This has nothing to do with colour. It has everything to do with honour, honesty, intelligence, desire, simpatico, compassion. He really is a gift to mankind at large, in the sense that if you watch him – watch his actions – and listen, he sets an example to the world. Now, the people who don't like black culture, good luck to them. This man spiritually represents the essence of honour that should exist in all of us.

If he was an actor, not a boxer, you would have said, "This man's the greatest improviser who ever walked the earth." He took the moment and could see it all in one – and himself in it – and then he found a way to improvise what would fit into that given moment. Which is like an actor doing a scene. As a moment comes in, he knows how to use it. I don't think in general his fight plan was ever the same. He had the guts to improvise in front of the world.

I didn't go to many fights. I'm one of these hypocrites who watched on television. I went to one fight and I saw a man – not Ali – with blood coming out of his mouth and his eye, and I thought, "This is inhuman." But if I sit at home, with my big TV set, I lie to myself. "Oh, this is okay, it's just a movie because it's on TV." All my great love of humanity disappears!

In my opinion, boxing is one of the dirtiest sports in the world and it's never really changed. There are ten thousand or more young men mangled each year that you never hear of, all trying to become boxers. Boxing is like bullfighting in the Latin world. So many poor, young men want to become famous and have a fortune. How many that you never hear about get gored or get knocked senseless in the ring? And how many cases have you heard where a brave world champion is suddenly broke, often because his manager was crooked and the woman who married him to be the wife of a world champion has divorced him and taken almost everything he had? We should have a home for boxers, or something.

I'll never forget seeing Joe Louis become the greeter at a Las Vegas hotel. That shouldn't be allowed because of all the things he did, and all the ways he showed his courage and strength. We sat and had a beer and he told me a wonderful story about when he was fighting Marciano. Marciano was incredibly strong and after the sixth or seventh round, Louis went back to his corner and said, "Well, he's not touching me. I'm blocking everything with my forearms." But they rang the bell for the next round and he couldn't lift up his arms. Marciano had broken all the little blood vessels, and that was it.

These days Ali has Parkinson's. I see that as a continuous purgatory that he does not deserve. Think of it like being inside a plastic, impregnable cylinder. Something comes through it and you say, "Oh yes!", but your words don't get out that fast and you can't understand it. "How come they can't hear? How come I can't answer as quick? My mind is answering quick. I can think, I can give the answer, so why can't I communicate it?" And yet Ali does not indulge himself. He does not whip you up about self-pity. He doesn't say, "My God, how can they take a great artist like me and do that to me?"

I watched the opening ceremony at the Atlanta Olympics and I said, "Dear God – if there is a god – let him get up to the top of the steps. Let him be able to light the torch." That sums him up in a nutshell. He climbed the steps and all his life, he has lit the torch. You've got to take your hat off. So, thank you Muhammad. You're indeed a man.

I've written this poem. I hope that it reaches him:

Some you took in three,
Some you took in one,
Some you took in six or seven
You despatched to boxers' heaven,
But this was all with body and fist.
If you were paid attention to the strength of your mind
And your ability to resist
Insults, frauds, "yes" men
And the prejudice of the world.
Few would realise you were indeed a poet in action,
In spirit,
In determination
A leader for all men.
All.
You proved that you can get knocked down but

You can get up again.
You are truly a warrior of wisdom
Ali – bum-bay-ai, Ali, bum-bay-ai, Ali, bum-bay-ai.

Bert Sugar

Journalist / Boxing Historian

The first prominent black heavy weight champion was Jack Johnson. Johnson crossed every more the white establishment had down set for blacks. He was his own man and he flaunted it. He dated and married white women, he raced cars and he opened his own cafe in Chicago that catered to none of society's ethics or mores. Jack Johnson rubbed the white man's nose in his own rules. As such, he was sort of an outcast, even from many of the members of the black community. He didn't want this kind of symbol representation. And after he was defeated, in 1915, it was 22 years before another black man fought for the heavyweight championship because of the vestiges and heritage that Johnson had left. That man was Joe Louis, who was basically taught by his handlers not to do any of the things that Jack Johnson had done. "Don't have your picture taken with a white woman. Don't gloat over a fallen opponent. And, incidentally, don't eat watermelon." That was his favourite fruit, of course, because it reinforced the stereotype. He was the new champion and the new man and the new representative. In point of fact, in his second Schmelling fight, he was adopted by both blacks and whites in America as their champion, because he was fighting in a fight that was pitting democracy against totalitarianism, represented by Max Schmelling of Germany, so he became everybody's champion. That was almost the lineage of black champions after Louis – Ezzard Charles, Jersey Joe Walcott. It became a kind of currency. There was an exception in Rocky Marciano, and then Ingemar Johansson, but it really became a black man's championship.

So Louis is very much a hero for blacks. Maya Angelou wrote, "A black woman's son is heavyweight champion of the world." That was meaningful. To the whites, it became a secondary. They adopted him because he represented America. Also, not incidentally, Joe Louis did it with dignity, which was that old canard that the establishment had about knowing your place. Joe Louis represented both sides and himself well.

What you've got is Joe Louis, who retires in 1951 – or is retired by Marciano – to '60, when Clay wins the light-heavyweight championship at the Rome Olympics and turns pro. I won't say it's a sea-change, but it's a change in society. There's a change in integration which is now going full force. There are people like Stokely Carmichael and others on the scene and saying, "Black is beautiful." Schools are becoming integrated in the South. So it's not the same thing you're looking at, when Clay comes along, as you would've seen in the hey-day and the after-day of Joe Louis. And some writers of the old school couldn't adapt or accept.

So here comes Cassius Marcellus Clay, a totally different kind of athlete – outspoken, hardly with the dignity of a Joe Louis, hardly accepting his place, which is what blacks were supposed to do. Here was Cassius Marcellus Clay, a braggart at best, at worst a spinner of poor doggerel, beating his chest and beating the basic precepts of every writer who covered him. Clay did nothing, nothing that basically fitted with any of the preconditions that people had thought. You know, it's nice to have a quiet Jersey Joe Walcott, a quiet Ezzard Charles or a quieter Joe Louis. Now you've got somebody giving the bombast, calling himself the greatest. Himself! He dubbed himself. He took his own gloves and dubbed himself the greatest.

He was full of fire and fury. Nobody knew what to do with him. They were almost hoping against hope that he would have had somebody's glove shoved down his throat, and he was fighting a fight that nobody knew in the heavyweight division. His fight for a six-foot-three fighter was that of a welterweight or lightweight – fast. And he didn't do anything any boxer should. His hands are down, he doesn't bob and weave, he pulls straight back – that's a no-no – and he doesn't have a jab, so they don't know what the hell to look for. There's no comparable definition of his boxing style, of how he presents himself. It wasn't comparable to anything they'd seen before. In fact, I can almost trace the current playground habit of dissin' somebody, street-talking to their face, to what Cassius Marcellus Clay did in 1960. So he was part of this, which was something nobody understood, least of all the old-time writers.

Sonny Liston, though, was every man's vision of black society and white of a goon. Sonny Liston had been a union enforcer. Sonny Liston had been in jail. Sonny Liston – at least to listen to his public utterances – was unschooled, illiterate. And that wasn't just the white community; it was the black community, too. The National Association for the Advancement of Coloured People's Roy Wilkins did not want Sonny Liston as a challenger for Floyd Patterson, telling Floyd, "Don't take him." John F Kennedy did not want Floyd to risk his title against him and go into the "wrong hands". Not that Sonny Liston wasn't a smart man to himself or close people, but the utterances he gave were that of exactly everyone's worst dream – the defiler of morals, the defiler of our land, the defiler of everyone's white daughter. He did not exactly come in under flying colours. And yet, when he fought Cassius Clay for the first time, there was an irony to it. And the irony was that Clay was so unpopular that people were actually rooting for the convict: "Stuff a glove down his throat." That was the irony of their first fight, in Miami.

And something happened just before the fight that made the match even worse, box office-wise. Malcolm X was on the scene, and there were rumours that Clay was involved with the Nation of Islam. Rumours were flying in Miami that Cassius Clay was being proselytised by the Black Muslims. One of its spokespersons, Malcolm X, was seen at the site all the time and, even worse, Clay he had threatened to pull out of the fight, telling the promoter, Bill McDonnell, "I'm out, if you don't let me talk about my religious affiliation and my interest, if you continue to have me denounce the Muslims." Threatening to pull out didn't help sales. Even worse, it pushed those writers who couldn't understand what he was doing into a fairly fervent atmosphere with the Nation of Islam, the members of the Muslim Church, the Black Muslim religion, all standing around looking like enforcers. The whole atmosphere was such that, even though there were a few people who were charmed by him, his personality, they were not charmed by what they foresaw or thought they did in his association with the Church that was preaching that white men are devils. Add them all together and you've got Cassius Clay then, on the cusp of becoming as unpopular as anybody and of making Sonny Liston ironically popular for the first time.

And, of course, Clay chose to align himself with the Nation of Islam, as opposed to Martin Luther King's more liberal group, the civil rights Movement. But then, he was young at the time of that, 1964. He was 22 years of age – impressionable, given the direction – and I think Malcolm X talked to him sincerely and seriously, one to one, and was able to charm him. And Clay/Ali accepted it. It was all new thinking to him. And if Ali ever did anything, it was to adopt people's thinking and make it his own with his own spin. He was very impressionable, and in whatever way this made sense to him – I'm not going to judge – and that's why he joined the Nation of Islam.

At that time, although the rumours were flying around, most people didn't give him a hope in hell, including Liston. Liston had pronounced, "It's going to take me one round to find that young whippersnapper and a second round to despatch him, and I'll step over his body." Clay was a seven-one underdog, and I think, of the 38 writers at ringside, only three picked him, and two did because some horse running that afternoon had had a similar name. So he wasn't given much of a chance. You have to remember, Sonny Liston was viewed as invincible. In his last two fights, he had knocked up Floyd Patterson in two minutes six and two minutes ten and had a long string of one-round knockouts. I think he lost once to Marty Marshall and had his jaw broken in that fight and came back then to knock out Marshall. The word attached to Liston was "invincible". Invincible! So there was this theory that Clay was going to be lucky to walk out with his life, let alone the title.

There was a rumour at the time that Liston bagged that fight because he owned 50 per cent of a company with the Nilon brothers and he had options on Clay's next fight. No, I don't think that Liston "bagged" or "took a dive" in that fight for two reasons. One, I think he was surprised, right from the introductions. No, I take that back. I think Liston was surprised from the weigh-in. He had never come across anybody like Clay before. Clay came into that weigh-in with Drew Bundini Brown chanting, "Float like a butterfly, sting like a bee." If Liston was afraid of anything, he was afraid of crazy people, and here was Clay on the very afternoon of the fight that night jumping up and down so much so that they took his blood pressure and were ready to call off the fight. They took it an hour later and it was normal. It was one of his mercurial rises and falls in his whole metabolism as well as his mood.

Add to that the fact that Sonny Liston had always intimidated his opponents. He would come out to the instructions at the centre of the ring by the referee with towels underneath his robe so that he looked even more humungous, bigger than he was. All of a sudden, he's standing in the middle of the ring, for the first time in his life he is facing a man taller than he is. And you can see that he never stood up face to face with Clay before. Then he tries for two rounds with a very long left – and he had a lethal left jab – to catch him, and Clay was nowhere. Then he resorted to one of his old tricks, something he had used in the Eddie Machen fight and the Zora Folley fight, when both of them complained that there was stinging in their eyes. And in the fourth and into the fifth rounds, there was Clay completely blinded, going on instinct, and it was the only time that Liston was able to lay in, and yet Clay was fast enough to get out of corners until his eyes cleared and blurred and teared and he could see.

Put them all together, I just think that, by the time he retired, Liston had tried everything he could to win and just said, "Oh, the hell with it." At that point, yes, it might have occurred to him, "I have a return-bout contract," but I don't think that did anything to help him. This was the first time in the history of the heavyweight division – going back to John L Sullivan in 1892 – that a champion had retired on a stool, with one exception: Jess Willard, in 1919, who had been pummelled to the canvas seven times by Dempsey and had a broken jaw and a broken set of ribs. In Liston's case, he now started blaming it on his left shoulder, which was the only one he ever threw a punch with. He didn't know what the hell to blame it on. But he knew he couldn't catch Clay. His eyes were puffed, his face was puffed and he had pulled out of his bag the trick that had always worked for him, and it didn't.

After the fight Clay announced that he was involved with the Nation of Islam, and that night he called himself Cassius X. Then, the next day, he made an announcement – he was now Muhammad Ali. Elijah Muhammad gave him the name. He was reborn in the Nation of Islam, and the muslims had a victory here. They had now in their fold a heavyweight champion of the world. They had attached their hopes and their dreams to him and bet on him, if not with money then at least with the anticipation that one of their flock would be the heavyweight champion of the world. At that point, they were a struggling little group, and this gave them, if not acceptance – and it did not – then at least notoriety and somehow, some way, some more headlines. But the sports writers didn't accept it any more than the public did.

Personally, I didn't care one way or the other. I figured everybody else had changed their name. Papa Leo was a Pep. Marciagno was a Marciano. Fine. I didn't care. I didn't have any precepts and preconditions. He was a heavyweight champion. In fact, I put his name on the cover of my magazine, the first writer ever to do so, and promptly misspelled it. Did not know it was *ad*. I put *ed* and *Muhammad*. It was all new to us. But he had the right to call himself whatever he wanted.

That wasn't the problem, though. It wasn't what he was calling himself; it was what he represented to most people, particularly the older generation. And one must always consider that the older generation is not only the older generation; they're the ones in command, because they've lived long enough. And they were horrified, particularly in the writing industry. They'd grown up with Joe Louis who "knew his place" and had seen it in Floyd Patterson and Joe Walcott and Ezzard Charles. Now they have someone who not only doesn't seem to know his place; he doesn't seem to know his religion or name or anything that coincides with their beliefs. If that's not frightening, it's so out of the ordinary that, in effect, it is distasteful. So that's how they started writing about him.

One of the best examples of how unpopular he was, I guess, was the fight venue for the next Liston fight which was up in Lewiston, Maine – not the original venue, I might add. The rematch was to have been in Boston but, during the week before the scheduled rematch, Clay had a hernia operation – Clay/Ali now, but still called Clay, because that's what it said on the posters. So the fight is not only postponed but somehow, some way, somewhere, the Massachusetts Boxing Commission decides the fight cannot be held in Boston, because they have a rule in their books that said that a boxer cannot be the promoter of his own fight, and that's what Liston was, in conjunction with the Nilon brothers. So the same promoter, Sam Silverman, having had the fight that was postponed in the fall, now starts searching for another site and winds up in Saint Dominic's Ice Arena in Lewiston, Maine, of all places. And Liston was the favourite in that fight, too.

Shortly after the first Liston fight, Ali went on a trip to Africa with Herbert Muhammad and various other members of the Nation of Islam. At that point, he became more than a fighter. He was the world heavyweight champion, and those were the days that there *was* one world heavyweight champion. There weren't these fractionated alphabet-soup WBA, WCBS, who cares that somebody's got a belt. He was the *the world champion*. Therefore, he is given accord. Mated with that is the fact that he's now travelling around the world on what is his version of a goodwill tour, sort of spreading his name and his fame. That exposed him to more than just the United States, the boxing fan. It was the first step, halting though it was, towards Muhammad Ali becoming a worldwide figure. Some people think that this unnerved the establishment, but I think the establishment was already unnerved. I mean, at a given point, you're out of nerves. I mean, there's a *reductio ad absurdium* where you come down to zero nerves. They were already so upset with Ali that a trip to Africa made no nevermind.

The one person who was unnerved, though, was Sonny Liston, especially in the second fight, the famous fight. That fight in Lewiston, Maine, was strange, and for many reasons, not the least of which was because, as you came in, you were searched for weapons. And there were all kinds of rumours – the mob was out to get Ali, because it was well known that some of Liston's camp was associated with the mob; the Black Muslims were out to get Liston. Every writer who went in there was looking for a place underneath their desk to die. It was not a pleasant place to be, beside the fact that it was an ice rink in February, with the ring and all the flooring laid over the ice rink and your nose running like hell. Put it all together and what an evening – an evening that has never been explained.

Yes, I saw the punch. Yes, I saw Liston's foot go up. Yes, I saw Liston go down. Yes, I saw Ali standing over Liston like the avenging Angel of Death, hollering, "Get up!" Yes, I saw a confused and bemused Jersey Joe walk out as the referee tugged at Ali and gave no count. Finally, Ali goes away, Liston gets up and they start fighting again. Liston's hurt but he's fighting, taking more than he's getting. At this point, Nat Fleischer, the editor of *Ring* magazine, calls Joe Walcott over and they're talking with Walcott's head out of the ring. There's a fight going on in the opposite corner that he's supposed to be refereeing. Fleischer is telling Walcott that Liston was down for more than ten seconds, which he was, but there was never a count. Walcott just comes walking back, separates the two, raises Ali's arm. The timekeeper says, "One minute," and it was obviously more than almost two minutes. Nothing about that whole damn things rings true or rings at all. But I did see a punch, and I saw Liston go down legitimately. After that, I don't what the hell happened.

Funny thing about Sonny Liston. When I met him, I said, "Sonny, how old are you?" He said, "33." I said, "A lot of people say you're 38." "My mama says I'm 33. Are you calling my mama a liar?" I said, "Sonny, don't try to outmanoeuvre me. I'll outmanoeuvre you," and he walked away, going, "Crazy white kid." But nobody knew Liston's age. He was a question mark throughout. But the punch I saw was Liston leaning in because he had to reach to get to Ali, who was so fast and just moved against the ropes, and Ali crossing his right over a long left that was left hanging out there. That's something that the people behind Ali on that side of the ring didn't see. All they saw was Liston going down and something like that from Ali, whose hand speed is extremely fast – I don't think that's a secret.

So now, almost four decades later, there are people who didn't see the punch who call it a fake. The people on this side of the ring saw the punch and *they* don't call it a fake. I mean, this is similar to the fact that, in 1971 for the Ali–Frazier fight, all the close-circuit locals were sold out, so in the Chicago Arena they established a screen and sold seats behind it. And there's still people there today in Chicago who swear it was a right hand by Frazier that knocked down Ali when it was a left, because they were seeing it over a screen. So it all depends on how you saw it and where you saw it – which, as a comparison, is not unlike the life of Muhammad Ali.

After the second Sonny Liston fight, boxing was in a pretty weary way. The general opinion was that maybe the fight was fixed, that there was something fishy going on. But then, throughout boxing at the end of the '50s, boxing was on its downers in every division. The champions were long and obtuse, the Archie Moores were over 40, there was very little young blood coming into the game. It really was in dire straits, on a life-support system. The writers covering it, who had seen down cycles and up cycles – because boxing has them like anything else – were looking for someone new, but they were looking for someone new within the concepts and confines and boundaries of what they knew. This is what happens when you're on the beat 40 years. These are your preconceptions of what a boxer should be. They'd never seen a boxer full of all this piss and vinegar, bragging, trying to out-psych his opponents, delivering on his promises, even, and then changing religions. And so fast! He did everything wrong for a heavyweight. I mean, his was a welterweight style.

So all of this was mind-shattering. You couldn't fit it in with your preconceptions. Then, along with Ali came a whole new breed of writers – young writers, thankfully – who grew up in a different society, so they had different standards. I'm talking about the Lipsytes, the Merchants, and Ziegels and the Schechters. Hopefully I'm in there, too, but I'm not including myself. This is a whole new breed of writer who has watched the civil rights Movement, maybe even marched in Mississippi, and they're watching this, and this is just a reflection a society that the older writer had no part of and didn't understand. To them, Ali was more understandable than he was to the older writers.

I could see the change. I had a better grip on it than I had a voice to express it, but I saw it. I had seen it coming. I didn't know in what form, what manifestation it would occur, but Ali was certainly as good a banner-carrier as anybody. Plus, he had the World Championship under one arm while he carried the banner with the other. The only problem was that, to many people, he was carrying two banners: the new black man and the Black Muslim flags. So sometimes they got intertwined. Even when you were with him, you weren't sure which way he was carrying you and the banners.

Of course, not all of his fights were like the Liston fight. There were some horseshit opponents in there. The Lion of Flanders, for crying out loud, Jean-Pierre Coopman. Hardly a great symbolic fight. The only thing that happened is that Ali leaned over to a CBS cameramen between the first and second rounds and said, "You guys have got some trouble. I can't carry him."

Then, in the Floyd Patterson fight and, ultimately, in the Ernie Terrell fight, where they had stripped a portion of the WBA title from him, in both those fights, Ali is showing a side we never saw before, and that was *cruelty*. He was hitting both of those men, Patterson and then, later, Terrell, and punctuating each punch with, "What's my name? What's my name?" Because they had called him Clay, not Ali. It was a cruel Ali, and we tend to sweep that under the rug that there was a cruel Ali in there. And that was a little disturbing, because we didn't want to see this side. It's supposed to be a sweet science. It's a civilised sport, barbaric though it is, legalised assault and all. There's got to be some niceties to it, and this wasn't nice.

This was highlighted at the time, obviously because Ali was such a controversial figure. I mean, because there have been dirty fighters in the past. Dirty, but still, not cruel. Dempsey would pick up his man after he'd knocked him out. I mean, he was a dirty fighter to win, but he was not a dirty fighter to punctuate a point. He hit you. He wasn't talking to you. Fritzie Zivic led with his thumb. You know, there were all kinds of things, but that's within the confines of the ring. That doesn't carry extra territorial weight. With that "what's my name" business, we've been told that boxers express themselves with their hands. He was expressing himself every whichway he could. This is why I say the whole aspect of trash-talking which has now become commonplace in sports goes back to Ali. It was there but we tended to ignore it, because we got caught up in that legend that started building around Ali, that he was all powerful and all wonderful. Like any man, he had warts, but we tended to overlook this.

After he beat Patterson he had troubles with the Draft Board. He was required for the Vietnam War, after being adjudged 4F. I mean, he was a man that graduated 313 of a class of 323 at central high school in Louisville, and he had failed his mental test. Now, all of a sudden, in need of more men for the Vietnamese conflict, the Louisville draft board goes back and makes him 1A. Ali, in a very cute remark, said, "I don't understand how I got so smart so quick." But they said that he was now eligible and he appealed, to no avail.

At that time, he was at his peak, and some reporter came to him and asked something about his being reclassified as 1A and he said, "I ain't got no quarrel with them Vietcong," which made headlines all over the world and also cost him his licence in the state of Illinois, where he was supposed to fight Terrell. So much for free speech. But at that point, he was becoming dubbed as a draft dodger, even before he failed to step forward for the draft. In fact, he then had to move fights to Canada, to anywhere else. Muhammad Ali was becoming an unpopular figure.

At that magic moment in time, there was a fervour over the Vietnamese War: "Should we pull out, or should we go in?" Lyndon Johnson was sending more troops over. We were divided down the middle, young versus old. Young wanted to pull out, old wanted to go in and bomb them, win the war. We had never lost a war. Personally, I didn't think it was a wise action to be in there, but I had no strong feelings either way, until they beat up the people in Chicago in 1968. That was too over-the-top for me. But that's after Ali was defrocked.

In other words, I was not in lockstep with him. I was somewhere in the proverbial back of the bus, just learning that the wheels were turning. But Ali was in the vanguard of this anti-war movement, which won him a lot of support, particularly from Martin Luther King, from the black community and from the young white community, too. But that's not to be confused with what we then called the hard-hat mentality – the workers, the union people, the veterans. So there was a major conflict going on socially in the United States, and Ali was viewed – and I'm not sure it didn't help him in terms of his later popularity – as one of the leaders of the anti-war movement, though at the time I couldn't see how he thought it would help him. It was merely the reflection of abuse of the Black Muslims.

But he dealt with all that very well, and especially the fights with George Chuvalo, which itself wasn't a great fight. All it proved was that Chuvalo's best punch was a left jaw with a right glove. What the hell did that prove?

During that period, the best fight Ali had was Cleveland Williams. It was the first time he showed one-punch-knockout power. So when I wrote my book *The 100 Greatest Boxers Of All Time*, I rated him Number Ten, because he did not have one-punch-knockout power which you would expect from heavyweight champions – Louis, Dempsey, Sullivan, whomsoever. That was his greatest fight as a heavyweight champion. He decimated Cleveland Williams with almost every right hand he threw. He did not have to spend his time running around the ring. He did not have to wear a man down pitty-patting him or stop him on cuts or stop him standing up. He laid him straight out. He exhibited punching power I'd never seen before or since in one fight.

Shortly after that, after the Zora Folley fight – which was a great fight for him, one punch coming over the top, knocking him down and out – his titles were taken away when he failed to step forward for the draft in Houston. March 1967, that was. New York, Madison Square Garden. Within three months, the call came up for him to report to the Induction Center in Houston, Texas. They transferred his papers to where he was then living, and when they called for him to step forward to accept the draft, he did not. He was promptly arrested, and within 24 hours those clowns in clowns' clothing who call themselves the boxing authority had stripped him of his title without the use of due process, without the use of reflection, without anything. They just stripped him in that fervour that is always pro-nationalistic, pro-American, pro-whatever in hell you want to call it, and for the next three years Muhammad Ali had to scrimp for a living. He's in a play called *Buck White*, he makes a college tour and people give him money, one of whom is Joe Frazier. But things are not easy for a man who is denied a passport to fight overseas, who is denied the right to fight in the US, who basically has his living taken away from him because of this conscientious objectorship to the draft – which, not incidentally, reflected the Muslims' view.

During this period, we'd sit and talk with Ali. He was quite open at this time. He was an excellent speaker, and he could shape his speech to any audience, whether it was to a black audience in Howard University or to a white audience at Pace, but it was always Ali. He would talk to his black audience about being black and how society calls the white cake Angel Food and the black cake Devil Food. And he'd make all these wonderful references. He was a great spokesperson. He was the orator that you would hear in any great oration, and he could tailor his speeches to any crowd.

These days, I get the feeling that it was more the Nation of Islam that caused him to make that stand. I think Ali *did* care, but I think that, with his predilections and thinking, it was not dictated to him so much as the constant rote reminders that gave him that approach to it. I think it was more the Islamic training and teaching than Ali *per se*. But it was brave and courageous, no matter for what reason he did it. There's no question about it. I am not nay-saying or gainsaying the fact that it was courageous; I'm just wondering how much of it was his decision and how much of it was, as he said it, "the learned decision of the Black Muslims". But whatever it was, it was courageous.

During the period that he was away, in around '68 or '69, the Nation of Islam actually turned their back on him. They were softening their hard edges. White people were no longer the blue-eyed devils. I don't know if they were also becoming more centrist or if it was because of the arguments with Malcolm X, but they were trying to position themselves. But whatever was happening, Ali was becoming more acceptable and accepted and they were becoming more acceptable and accepted, so you were getting both.

I supported him during that period, I suppose, not because of religious preferences but because he was standing up for something that I had then come to believe in. I hadn't at the time, admittedly so, but it was just becoming more of a morass over Vietnam, and now that Lyndon Johnson had started, Richard Nixon was escalating things into Cambodia. It was just a mess. Nothing was happening, our kids were getting killed and it was just silly. And Ali, at least, was the most visible protester with that silence of not stepping forward, sort of a Martin Luther Kingism, and so I had to support him. A lot of people did.

Eventually, though, we got some sort of severance of the two distinct sides. I think that was fuelled by the 1968 riots at the Democratic Convention. The deaths at Kent State by the National Guard repositioned people's thinking, so that there was no middle ground any more. It was either A or C, and B didn't exist. That all came to the moment of 8 March 1971, when the two camps basically adopted one or other of the battlers. The warriors represented them as much as they represented themselves.

There's a wonderful story about Ali. In his comeback fight in October of 1970 at the Hyatt, Ali has now come back, to great acclaim, particularly from the younger black audience, which has stuck to his ribs. Part of this is because of his stance, part of which is because of his courage to speak out as a black man and part of which is that he went out to college campuses and they were one with him. So they've all flocked to Atlanta, Georgia, in white ermine coats with matching white hats – and those were just the men! The women were in their hot pants. And Ali, after shaking as many hands and signing as many autographs as he could – and he never turned down a request – goes in one of those bullet-like bubble elevators up to his floor, leaving the people on the first floor waving at him like he was a god ascending. It was the most unbelievable, surreal sight I have ever seen. There was just something about it. He's waving, and it's almost like a ray of light is beaming down on them as they're waving up at him. I mean, Rousseau could have painted it. Now he had the touch of the people, which is why he was now on his comeback, campaigning as the people's champion.

The whole of the black vanguard were there, really. Coretta Scott King had a meeting with him. Bill Cosby was there. Diana Ross. It was a coming-out party for Muhammad Ali, and he did not come back against a patsy by-the-by; he came back against Jerry Quarry, who was the only man who would meet him. Ali and Jerry got death threats. Jerry told me, "They threatened to shoot me when I did road work," 'cause the Governor at the time in Georgia was a guy named Lester Maddox. He had owned a restaurant and used a pick-axe handle to chase away blacks. Ali was told on the day of the fight by a writer that the fight would be in Atlanta and that the Governor had vacated the state house. The writer said, "This is a maudlin day for the state of Georgia."

Ali said, "Maudlin? What does that mean?"

"Black days," said the writer.

Ali said, "It sure is a black day."

The first Frazier fight, though, on that day, the whole of New York seemed to have come to a standstill. It was a build-up of one of the greatest publicity campaigns in the history of publicity campaigns. You had two undefeated heavyweight champions fighting in the then-mecca of boxing, Madison Square Garden, in the biggest city in the world of communications. You'll never have that again. Their pictures have been on the front of *Life* magazine, of every magazine. They made commercials. They were the first two athletes to ever be guaranteed $2.5 million dollars apiece. And they both represented different camps in the war/anti-war countertops.

People flocked in from all over. Not only was Madison Square Garden sold out in one day, but every close-circuit ticket locale around the country was sold out in one day. This was a much-anticipated fight, because Ali had fought Quarry and then he had fought Oscar Bonavena. In fact, he was the only man to knock out Bonavena. That fight was held on 7 December 1970, the anniversary of Pearl Harbor, and people were out protesting that they had picked that date of all dates to have the fight. Then it comes down a Supreme Court decision between that fight and the Frazier fight, eight to nothing, saying that he had been a conscientious objector to the draft and that therefore he was now adjudicated to be in the right, so the people coming to the fight were on both sides but mainly Ali supporters. But the gamblers and betters had installed Joe Frazier as a seven-to-five favourite.

Even I thought Frazier was going to win. I had seen rust in Ali. Three years takes a lot out of a man, and in the two fights he had won he didn't do the wonderful dancing he once had; he was doing rope-a-dopes, leaning on ropes, and he didn't have the speed that he'd had in his prime. Frazier was a younger man – remember he won the gold medal in the '64 Olympics and had been active. Ali had not been active. So I thought that Frazier would win, but I was caught up in the entire hoopla. I mean, it was just hoopla. You'd go into the arena after you'd watched the fashion parade going in and there was Frank Sinatra taking pictures for *Life* magazine and Burt Lancaster doing the close circuitry. Everybody was a celebrity of some sort. There was industry, entertainment and sports people packing the house. You never heard a word from the announcer. It was just a roar. It was a cavern of roars. Here comes Ali down the aisle first, all red, with red tassels on his shoes. Then here comes Frazier, green brocade, waves of roars and no choir master to wave it off. It just kept building and building. And the fight acquitted the build-up. Ebbs and flows. For two rounds, Frazier couldn't get near Ali, just pops at him, and he kept closing and closing and closing, the area between them ever closer, and his pre-fight prediction that I'm a small piece of leather but well put together was holding true. Meanwhile, Ali had written down, "This might shock and amaze you, but I'm going to beat Joe Frazier." They had even gone to the point of having him predict it on television for the close-circuit broadcast right before the fight, as if that was all he had on his mind.

The whole thing was a combination of showbusiness and sports. But in effect, this whole thing transcended sports, because basically it was a fight between two sides, the supporters and the dissenters from the Vietnamese War. I brought a guest to that fight, Gene Fullmer, the former middleweight champion of the world. He also had in tow Jose Padez and Floyd Patterson, but I was sitting next to Gene, who was against Ali because of his anti-war stance.

After the fight, I chanced to go back into Ali's dressing room, and he was sitting there, straight up on the dressing room table, a towel over his head, his face looking bloated as if he'd just eaten a whole bag full of walnuts unshelled and a crowd around him looking as if they had just been at a wake. There was one woman's head hugging him almost on his lap, crying, and it was Diana Ross. That's how much he meant. For the next two days after the fight, Ali was taken to a hospital. Frazier was taken to a hospital. Rumours abounded that Frazier was dead, although I don't know if the rumours would have touched Ali. But just like the stone that hit water, the rumours kept growing and growing and with them, too, the legend of Muhammad Ali, who had given everything he had and more in a losing cause and didn't complain and didn't alibi and didn't make up any excuses. The winner in that fight became the loser. The loser in that fight became the winner.

After the Frazier fight, he announced his own sort of tour. This wasn't "bum of the month"; he's fighting legitimate foes. In fact, he's fighting better fighters than Frazier is, who is fighting with the Terry Daniels and the Ron Standers. He's fighting with the Buster Mathises and the Jimmy Ellises, former champions, and then he's fighting Ken Norton, winning the NABF championship – the North American Boxing Federation, a minor-league championship – on the way, and he gets his jaw broken by Norton and beaten, although nobody knows what round it was in. But again Ali had shown courage, because it's known that he broke his jaw. We know it had happened to Sonny Liston, but we all thought he was a brute and he could take it. We are now witnessing Ali taking it, and suffering through with it with nary a complaint. This feeds again the image of his greatness.

But still, all things considered, after he beats Frazier the second time and Norton the second time, when he's matched up against George Foreman in the Rumble In The Jungle, we fear for his very life. We've adopted him, particularly the new generation, those who we would call "intellectuals" – I have no idea what that word means – the Mailers and the Plymptons and the Schulbergs along with the beat writers, etc. And everyone expected that the best he could do was get out with his life, and yet he goes over to Zaire and he captivates the crowd and wins them over with his effervescence, his charisma, and they're shouting in Zaire's language, 'Ali! Kill him! Ali Bomaye!" For Foreman they had nothing; for Ali, they had everything.

Albeit once postponed, the fight finally gets on in the middle of the night over in Kinshasa, and Ali does it, and he does it in a way that is not Ali, this dancing master that we know. Now he goes against the ropes, and round after round he's taking Foreman's heaviest blows to the arms with the occasional one getting through while Angelo Dundee and Drew Bundini Brown screaming, "Get off the ropes!" He hasn't let them in on what he's doing. And he punctuates the end of each round with a little volley and flurry just to let Foreman know he's there. This goes on for four or five rounds, and you can see Foreman like that water hose going down, down, down. Ali's shouting, "Is that as hard as you can hit?" and Foreman tries harder but goes down, down, down, until the eighth round, when Ali puts together a series of punches punctuated by a right that spins Foreman around. He walks to his corner, and Ali was, again, heavyweight champion of the world.

Ali got such a great support from the African people, though, and that was maybe because he'd been to Africa before, so he identified with it as the land of his kinfolk. And it was also his charismatic, out-on-the-street everyday demeanour, interfacing with them, chanting with them like a little child. First it was the children he won over, then it was the adults, then it was everybody. At that time, George Foreman was doing his best imitation of Sonny Liston, so you almost had a re-do of Ali–Liston. He was stoically sealed away, almost under house arrest, because he had threatened after the postponement and the cut under his eye to leave the country. He was isolated, and Ali was working the crowd as only an Ali can. Ali knew how to work a crowd. He was on his highest pitch, I think, and his best performance in Zaire.

Some people think that his stand against the draft in the '60s gained him support in Africa, but I personally don't think they gave a shit. That was our war. I think they cared that he visited their continent. That made him a man of the world, and I think he played off that. I don't think he made one mention of Vietnam on the streets of Kinshasa, because I don't think it would have resonated with him.

After the Foreman-Ali fight, the Ali roadshow took off and became global. He went to Kampala, he went to Germany, he went everywhere. He was, after all, the champion of the world. He goes to London to fight Henry Cooper and he's walking down the street with a bowler and a cane and and cars were stopping, people were jumping out. All of a sudden, Ali had become a personality. He was no longer a boxer. He was not yet a world leader, but he was a world personality and that's a second step. During that period, I remember Ingemar Johansson saying, "My sister could beat him." Then I saw Ingemar Johansson's sister.

So he's now this global superstar. He's this charismatic, good-looking fighter, obviously a magician in the ring. His popularity also had a political edge to it as well, although I don't know if that carried. I mean, you're giving a lot of credit to people, particularly in Zaire, who are of the street. They were busy trying to live hand to mouth, from what I remember. I mean, world politics? Those people were worried about where their next piece of bread was coming from.

At that point, though, I think Muhammad Ali was on the cusp of becoming the most popular man in the world. Not a statesman, but a personality. He could play that. And that's what people were responding to, his showmanship, his effervescence, his ability to relate to people. He's had crowds of thousands thinking he was the only one. That was Ali. But politically, you think they gave a shit over there about the Vietnamese War? There are no Vietnamese restaurants in Zaire.

The third Frazier–Ali fight, the Manila fight, I missed that one. Unfortunately, he brought the wrong wife to that one. Ferdinand Marcos was always referring to Belinda, his second wife, as his "Mrs Ali". Belinda was a karate champion. You didn't screw with Belinda. I liked her, but she was some tough lady. I remember one time I was standing at a press conference with Ali after his comeback and every woman in the world was approaching him. Belinda was there, and he was giving me their room numbers! I had a set of room numbers and I was wondering, "What is this white man doing with about 40 room numbers of black women?" I'm just standing there going, "How am I doing?" It's a good thing he wasn't a woman, 'cause he'd always be in the family way. He couldn't say no. He had offers like you wouldn't believe.

Anyway, for the fight in Manila, I think he didn't train as rigorously as he should have. I think he underestimated Joe Frazier. He didn't think Joe had anything, which is one of the reasons he took the fight. Joe had a champion's heart, no matter where and when he was. He gave it to Ali in those middle rounds, and he lost again, as he did in the first fight. (Their second fight was a non-fight, for no championships, after Frazier lost his championship to Foreman.) But he came on, raked Ali's body for about four rounds with the most bodacious, brutal punches I have ever seen thrown to a body constantly. And Ali was there, but you can almost hear Ali going *oomph, oomph.*

Then Ali turned it around to the point where he closed Frazier's eye in the 14th. Frazier was a blind man groping for him, and Eddie Futch stopped it between rounds, an act of compassion rare to boxing. Ali could barely get off his stool to acknowledge that he had won, and then he collapsed. So the winner was on the ground and the loser was arguing with his managers and trainer: "Why did you stop it?" It was a weird sight. This fight, as Ali said afterwards, was the closest thing to death he had ever suffered. It was for Joe Frazier, too.

After that, neither were the same again. It could have been the ravages of this one fight or other fights, it could have been the ravages of age, but whatever it was, neither fighter was the same again. Ali went home with a couple more defences at Jimmy Young and Earnie Shavers. Earnie Shavers could knock a brick wall down. He hit Ali almost to the point where his head was spinning around like Michael Keaton's in *Beetlejuice*. But Ali had done enough to win a 15-round decision. Even so, it was clear that Ali was over the hill times three and that he couldn't find his prime in his rear view mirror. To that end, you knew his career was coming to closure.

But even as his career was coming to a close, something funny was happening: his stock on the world radar screen was going up and up and up, because there was an appreciation now beginning to build – not of this boxer whose skills were diminishing but of this man of the world. Not political, almost social. Socially, he was becoming accepted as a man who... Fill in the blank yourself. And so this was far more than boxing. Books were being written about Ali – I was guilty of that or not guilty, as the case may be – and each book climbed upon the shoulders of the previous book to further reinforce and build to the mortar of the word his greatness, not just in the ring but overall. In the late '70s, Ali was being viewed as something more than a fighter. Much more. He stood up for minorities, he had taken a stance against the government, and he was his own person now. He'd come back from almost a self-imposed exile. Yes, the government had a heavy hand in it, but he had the choice. And then he faced up to the government and sacrificed three years of his prime earning power for a belief that's almost Gandhi-esque. That's what the people were beginning to understand about Muhammad Ali. But it ain't political. You go to a guy in the street in Zaire – can they tell you there are the Democrats or Republicans in the White House in America or what Tory or Labourite is in 10 Downing? It's a sociological thing. They knew he was one of us. We're a minority, he's a minority. He's his own man. Most of us aren't.

He shouldn't have gone on, though. After Leon Spinks, you could see he had nothing. He did beat him again, but only because Leon was so flighty. When asked in the press conference after the rematch in '79, "What happened, Leon?" he said, "My mind wasn't on the fight." As if he was in New Orleans to catch a bus or something. I never understood that. But you can tell that Ali had nothing; he was doing it on fumes and memory. I think he fought Larry Holmes because of Don King's persuasiveness and money. Don King oversold him and took his money. I think he fought Trevor Berbick because of money, money and money. Sometimes you fight for money, sometimes you fight because you miss the roar of the crowd, sometimes the combination of all, and for Ali I think it was because he thought he was Ali the invincible.

Whatever it was, those fights took something from him, the accumulation of all those punches. I ain't no apologist for boxing. I don't blame it for everything, and I don't think that all of Ali's physical troubles today are boxing related – some are Parkinson's syndrome – but I will tell you that getting hit in the head does not help an ingrowing toenail. Those last fights sped him on his merry way to the where he is today. And the shame of it is that we all remember him growing up, and rather than looking at ourselves in the mirror and see how old we've become, we look at Ali and say, "Look how old he looks." But this happens to all of us. We pity him. We didn't want to see him get old. But when he was asked, "Do you regret where you are now?" he said, "If I hadn't boxed, I'd still be a sign painter in Louisville." He doesn't regret it. I don't know why we do.

When it came towards the end of his career, when I was at Greenside, I felt that I'd seen the end of so many fighters. It was like a personal tragedy. I felt very bad that I was watching a man in decline trying to exhibit the skills and needing the skills that he had in his prime and they weren't there. When I watched Larry Holmes beat him, I felt like Santa Claus was dead. Muhammad Ali's career was, too. There were no more miracles left. It was all over.

Then, during the '80s, the boxing world turned their back on him because he was a bad advert. People misunderstood what his illness was. He was our hero and our youth, and our youth was gone. To so many people, this was a tragedy, and they ignored him because he was a bad memory of what we were and a bad reminder of our ageing. If we didn't see him and

Ali is supported by the Reverend Jesse Jackson before being hospitalised because of Parkinson's syndrome, New York, 1984.

Performing a magic trick at his home in Los Angeles, 1984.

Ali and Nelson Mandela – two of the world's greatest heroes – meet in Los Angeles, 1990.

The signature of one of the most famous names in the world, Louisville, February 2000.

Ali comes home: Louisville honours its most famous son, February 2000.

Ali and fourth wife, Lonnie, Louisville, February 2000.

"I'm still pretty": Ali in Louisville, February 2000.

didn't think about him, we weren't older; we were still as vibrant as we were when he was Cassius Clay. He was the sport's most valuable player and he was exiting, and so it was like we were exiting. We wanted to believe that our youth was still with us, and to see the man who epitomises that youth grow old... No. No thank you.

When he was picked to carry the Olympic torch, though, the Ali industry was in full swing. It was a secret as to whom would be lighting the torch at the end in Atlanta. Everybody thought it was going to be Evander Holyfield, who was an Atlantan, a hometowner. Only a handful of people knew it was Ali. A rumour started a day and half earlier, but still nobody knew. The roar of that crowd seeing Ali – shaking visibly even from the stands way back there, let alone the cameras way up here – was heartening. Here was a hero. That, with the Olympics being a world event, officially confirmed that he was a hero for the world. The only dissenting voice was that of Joe Frazier, who had never forgiven him for having called him an Uncle Tom and a gorilla before that first fight, and he said that Ali should have fallen into the flame. The rest of us thought it was wonderful, and yet the rest of us knew what Joe was talking about. That is the other side of Ali that nobody talks about, the fact that Ali can be a cruel person, that Ali can be, for all his gregariousness and laughing, even at the height of his career, a callous and uncaring person. But having said that, with all his warts, he's a world hero and shall be remembered for all time as such.

These days, though I think he's something of a hand-me-down hero. I don't think that the youngsters today understand exactly what he stood for, or even where Vietnam is, but I think enough stories have been handed down about Muhammad Ali, from father to son or father to daughter or however it works, to make him a hero for all times, and someone who will stand up and be counted as a hero. Also, I think that we tend to make heroes more so out of martyred people, whether it's John Kennedy or John Lennon or whomsoever. And in his own way, from the ravages from his infirmities, Ali is martyred as well, having given his all twice to his profession, once by not standing forward for the draft and twice now for suffering Parkinson's syndrome, exacerbated by punches. He is martyred. Put them all together and you've got a hero for the ages.

I don't know if we'll see his like again. Who am I to say? Each generation has a new hero and new standards. But by the standards of the generation I grew up with, there will never be another Muhammad Ali. Let the next generation have their own.

Ernie Terrell

Former WBA Heavyweight Champion

I first met Ali when he was Cassius Clay and we were both competing in the Golden Gloves, the Tournament of Champions at the Chicago Stadium. He was an amateur then. I had won it the previous year and I was pro this year. That was about 1958, I think. We were both very young at the time.

We were the same weight – he was a light heavyweight – but I never thought about looking at him as a possible opponent in the future. There were people there from all over the country, and he said to them, "Everybody who weighs 175 pounds, stand up." And guys from all over the country start standing up, guys from as far west as California, from Denver, from all across the United States. He said, "I just want you all to know one thing. You know who's going to win this? It's going to be me." And then he sat down. He was the same bigmouth then as he was when he turned pro.

Then, when he turned pro, we became friends. We got to know each other. Of course, I knew who he was, because I had met earlier, but when he turned pro, after he won the Olympics and all that stuff, he was rising fast and I was on the rise myself. I sparred with him down in Miami a couple of times. We just got in the ring and boxed a few rounds. And it turned out pretty good.

After that, we fought on the same show a couple times, maybe. He would fight somebody and I would fight somebody the same show. And we'd drive back together. He lived in Louisville, Kentucky, and he needed some help to get back to Louisville. I had a plane ticket but I drove back to Louisville from Miami with him, 'cause he was going to do it by himself. We talked, and everything was all right. We were comrades.

I fought Ali in 1967. Well, the fight was supposed to be a couple of years before then, I think. We were scheduled to fight in Chicago but the fight was thrown out of Chicago because of some unpatriotic statement that Ali made – "Them Vietcong, they ain't done nothing to me," or something. So they used that as an excuse to throw it out. And when they did that, because I was a WBA champion and he was the recognised champion at the time, he went over to London and fought with Henry Cooper and I fought George Chuvalo and Doug Jones. Then we got together for the fight in 1967 in Houston, Texas, at the Astrodome. I was anxious to fight him. I was just trying to get my recognition as a champion, so I defended the title twice and I was ready to defend it again against Muhammad Ali. He won a 15-round decision.

Ali, of course, was associated with the Nation of Islam. I didn't really understand that at the time, to tell you the truth about it. The Nation of Islam was painted as a subversive group. They was really talked bad by the press, and I thought it would hurt his career. I thought it would hurt anybody's career to be associated with that group. As it turned out, that was probably the thing that propelled his career to such heights, because he so controversially embraced his religion, even though it wasn't popular. He was against the war, too, even though it wasn't popular. So in all, it helped to build his "Ali-ism".

That fight now is quite an infamous fight. When it was time for me to fight Ali, he called me and invited me to an office in a small nightclub. We went into the office and he says to me, "I'm gonna fight you next."

"All right," I said. "That's great. Let's get it on."

"No. I've got to get 50 per cent. How much do you want?"

"I've got to get 50 per cent, too," I said. "I'm champion."

He laughed and then says, "OK, we'll work that out later. But let's figure a way how to get the money."

"What are you saying?"

"Don't make no mistake," he said. "I'm going to knock your head off when I get in the ring."

"That's what I'm going to do to you, too," I said. "You're going to get the same thing."

And he said, "I'm gonna figure out something to call you. I don't know what, but I'll work it out. I'll call you something."

"OK."

So that's how we started with the promotion. We met to sign at a press conference with the boxing commissioners and everybody there. This is for the fight that got thrown out of Chicago. The promoter says to me, "You have to train in Chicago at least two weeks ahead of the fight in order to sell the fight. Is that alright with you?"

"It's all right with me if it's alright with Clay," I said.

"Muhammad," says Ali.

"Well, Muhammad, then."

"Why do you call me Clay?" he says. "Why do you call me Clay when everybody's calling me Muhammad?"

I said, "Well, man, look, you told me in May it was Muhammad when I met you, but I just got used to Clay."

"I ain't told you nothing," he says. "You're just an old Uncle Tom." And he pushed me and we started wrestling, and I thought that was the beginning of the promotion.

But it just turned sour from there. It kept on as it built up all the way after the fight got thrown out and all the way to the next one. He called me an Uncle Tom and he pushed me and stuff like that. But he takes things too far.

People have talked about Ali always had the psychological edge, that he would control a fight mentally, he would make the other guy, it's like he could almost get into his head, but that didn't affect me during the fight. What affected me was a scheme he pulled. When that fight finally made it to Houston, Texas, I'm leaving my hotel room and I get a call. All of my trainers have to run out. They said, "You stay here." So I stayed there.

Then, after they got on the elevator and went downstairs, there was a knock on my door. I opened my door and there was about 30 girls there who pushed themselves into my room. Then they went through turning over my stuff. They took my mouthpiece and dumped it out, took my gym clothes – my training clothing – and just dumped it out. And they were saying, "Mr Terrell, you're not big enough to beat Ali." They were talking all this crazy stuff and all my help was gone. But at least when my people came back, they ran out. But my mouthpiece was laying on my bed there and I didn't know whether they'd put something in it. This was the day before the fight, and I didn't have time to get a new one. That little crazy stunt was the only thing that was on my mind about the fight.

I had a great chance to win that fight. I was bigger than Ali at that point. But during the second round of the fight, we got caught in a headlock and he took his thumb and he poked it in my eye. And my eye sits like it's an egg – that's what the doctors explained it to me. His thumb pushed the eye down through a bony substance that sits under the eye, and the muscles that turn the eye got caught in that bone and the eye just stayed straight. It wouldn't turn. I would see one guy over there and one guy over here whenever he moved around. It looked like I was fighting two Alis. So I had to change to a peek-a-boo style in order to go through with the fight. I kept thinking that somehow my eye was gonna be all right, but it never was. I had to go to the hospital and they worked on the eye and they took it out of the bone, and later on it could turn again. During the rest of the fight, it was a real handicap. I couldn't really fight my style.

So Ali could be a dirty fighter, a ruthless fighter, when he had to be. People would say this is sour grapes, but it happened. I really wanted another chance at Ali, because I felt like I had the style to beat him, but we never had a second fight. He got barred right after that fight. He fought Zora Folley and he didn't fight any more for a year and a half. I didn't have any interest in fighting those men, so I retired that year. When he started back, I started trying to make a comeback and didn't make it.

But I don't really have anything against him personally. I don't think he did those nutty things himself; somebody he was working with got him to do it, trying to get an advantage in some kind of way. When he was fighting Liston, he did a lot of that kind of stuff himself, but later he just had some people come round and aggravate you, so you needed to have bodyguards around that could handle that. You'd have to have your people representing you, protecting you.

They formed an amateur boxing tournament in Louisville named for him that people have to go through to qualify for the Olympics. I went there to support him - he had done some things to support me. The fight is over now.

In the end, circumstances create opportunities for all kind of things. Whether it turned him into a villain or a good guy, people wanted to see him get beat or beat somebody. He's just a guy that seems to be fortunate, except for the Parkinson's. That's really a terrible thing, to see him with that. I hate to see a guy of his stature the way he is now. He does the best he can with it, I'm sure, but that's a devastating thing to have.

Ali's had a very fast style. As far as being a complete, full-rounded boxer...well, he wasn't that, but you didn't need that then. But he needed that speed when he got older, and he didn't have it. There wasn't that much to look for from Ali. He had a quick jab, a quick right, not much of a left hook – he would throw a left hook in combination – and that's about it. You didn't have to worry about a body punch with him. He might jab you down there, but he was not a body puncher. But he was great with whatever he had, and he had great speed. His greatest asset was his speed, because he would run and jump out of the way of the mistakes he would make. But he could have stayed on a long time like Archie Moore, who didn't get a break until he was an old man.

But when Ali's speed left him, he started getting hit with those hard punches. He had a terrific chin, and he could take 'em, but over the years it just tolls up, and he got hit with some terrible shots off some heavy hitters. When he was in his prime, when he was there with me and other people – Williams and Sonny Liston – this guy had reflexes like you would not believe. I mean, he would lean out of the way and jump around, jump out of the way. It was maybe unorthodox for some people, but it worked for him. But when he slowed down, people hit him with some hard punches.

But as far as the other stuff, he could go to some places and make a difference because he was a Muslim and people like Ghadaffi would talk to him when they wouldn't talk to the head of state. He did whatever he could do with that to benefit the United States. If Ali was able to provide that, that's great.

Jose Torres

Journalist / Former World Light-Heavyweight Champion

In terms of his style of fighting, Ali did everything wrong. But it all turned out right. He is the greatest fighter in the history of boxing because he took risks. He would consciously, purposefully do something that is physically wrong to show the world that boxing was more of a psychological than a physical debate.

For example, he never threw a punch below the jaw. I became champion with a body punch, and a lot of fighters become winners with that, but Ali never punched to the body. He would pull back to evade punches. It's like, if a train comes towards you, you move to one side or you move to the other to avoid being hit. If you move backwards without getting off the track, the train will catch up with you and kill you, unless you're Muhammad Ali. He believed in the magic of men in the ring and he would not get caught by the train.

When he got old, he began to get hit, but he'd get up and do the same thing over and over until he demoralised his opponent. But he knew *where* to punch and where to connect. That was the trick. He'd hit you mostly when you were not looking, and that's the punch that knocked you out, because you cannot prepare for the impact. He was an artist in the ring, and he put all those things together to become such a super heavyweight champion.

But he is also intelligent and you have to be very intelligent to know the right moment to punch and where to connect, and he knew. A trainer cannot teach you that. A manager cannot teach you that. That is something that you learn from experience. And in the case of Muhammad Ali, when he set himself to become the heavyweight champion of the world, he knew unconsciously that he had to know everything that goes with champions. He discovered all that on his way up and he began to apply it.

When Ali announced that he had embraced the Nation of Islam, he became more than just a boxer, and I admire him for that. I admire him as a fighter and as a human being, and I applauded his move to be so controversial and his independence. He did what he did in spite of the fact that half of the people used to come to his fights to see him lose, and every time he won – and won, and won. Sometimes I disagreed with some of his specifics, but I was a friend of him all the time, because he was doing what he thought was right.

I mean, this was very new. There'd been sportsmen before who had been controversial, like Jack Johnson, but he'd pretty much stood alone, whereas Ali was a part of an organisation which was a threat to the establishment. It was like when I became a boxer, when I was also involved with the politics of Puerto Rico and I began to write many books. I became very close to people like Norman Mailer, Bud Schulberg and Pete Hammill. In fact, 95 per cent of all my books belonged to Pete Hammill. I was amused and inspired by these people. As a matter of fact, I was writing even when I was training, in the late '50s. I didn't dream to be a champion.

But Ali didn't inspire me to think about myself as a sportsman and a Puerto Rican, so much as he inspired me in the ring. When he used to insult his opponent, I realised that he was beginning to work on his opposition as soon as he signed his contract, not when the bell rang. By insulting these guys, he was either making them mad or intimidating them, which are two out-of-control emotions. The defeat of a fighter went beyond the punches. Before fighting Joe Frazier, he said, "When Frazier was born, he wasn't the first to cry; his mother cried, because he was so ugly." And then he said, "He looked like a gorilla." That was a little bit too much, but he got his point across, and Frazier was mad. And when they went in the ring, Frazier was out of control, from the emotional point of view, and Ali used that as a weapon. He was a master – hands down, chin up in the air, pulling back from punches, punching to the head and winning fights, and winning fights, and winning fights. He was like a miracle.

Then, in 1965, he boxed a brother of mine by the name of Floyd Patterson, and that was when Ali started to show his cruelty in the ring. I was a little concerned, because Patterson was one of the best fighters I had ever seen in my life before that. I used to box with him every day for over a year, and he taught me a lot, taught me that size had no relevance – it wasn't how big you were but how good you were. And then Ali got in the ring with him and appeared to punish Floyd to the limit without knocking him out. He not only gave that impression there in the fight, but he said after the fight that he wanted to punish him. I'm not sure if he was very honest when he was saying that, but it appeared that way to me. And he was proud of doing that. He said, "I punished him because of what he said about me. He didn't want to call me my real name, which is Muhammad Ali. He wanted to call me Cassius Clay, so I punished him and punished him and punished him before I finished him off."

A couple of years after that, the US establishment took Ali's title away and he was sentenced to five years in jail and fined $10,000. He didn't go to jail but he lost three years of his career, and I was one of the guys who supported him during that period and asked for the decision to be overturned. But he was very controversial. I think he was the most controversial athlete in the history of our hemisphere. He was a master at creating controversy. It wasn't all because he was trying to do that; it just happened that way.

I remember that he told me one time that he had a lot of respect for the black people of Puerto Rico. He said, "You guys had to be tough. You were created by jumping off the ship." "When they were bringing slaves from Africa to America, they went by the Caribbean and you used to see land 20 miles away and jump overboard. The guys who survived would have to be tough, so I consider you a tough Puerto Rican Afro-American." Then, later on, of course, I heard a different version form a historian from Puerto Rico, who said that we're the children of the queens and kings from Africa. And now I can't figure out which I like better! But Ali made sense.

Puerto Rico was where Christopher Columbus discovered the New World. When the Spanish went to Puerto Rico, they went specifically to kill all the Indians there, to eradicate a whole community, a whole country. And today, the Puerto Ricans honour the name of that killer, Christopher Columbus, on a principal avenue.

Juan Leon, too. He founded the oldest town in the United States, St Augustine, in Florida. The Indians said that there was a fountain of youth there, that you drank the water and you became young again. Leon went there when he was getting old, and started killing the Indians in Florida. Then one Indian put a poisonous arrow in his shoulder. They took him to Cuba and tried to save his life, but he died.

But the point I'm making here is how history can be messed up by those small situations that become a denominator for all the guys who become heroes. This guy Juan Leon became famous by being a no-good bastard, by killing and eradicating people. Muhammad Ali's moment was saved by Angelo Dundee, an Italian. A white man. He saved his moment in 1964 when he wouldn't let him give up on the Liston fight and Muhammad Ali becomes a superhero.

I look at Ali as the guy who taught the world that boxing is character and intelligence. To me, that's an incredible lesson, and I love him for it. I was there when he came back in 1971, before Jerry Quarry, and the black vanguard were *en masse* in Atlanta to welcome him back. The Governor of Alabama, a man by the name of Wallace, was still against him. He had the reputation of being a racist. I remember going to a press conference and somebody asking Muhammad Ali, "Governor Wallace says that, on the day of the fight, it will be a black day for this state." And Muhammad says, "Oh yes, it's going to be a very black day. You're going to see more blacks than ever in the history of Atlanta!" I'll never forget that.

But that was an interesting fight. There were blacks there from all over the country, high-class blacks all dressed up, because there were lots of restaurants where they would not allow you in without a tie. There were more celebrities in that fight than ever before, especially black celebrities – artists and actors and singers. And it was wonderful. The New York media were flabbergasted by the experience. Ali opened many doors. He was an important figure. Of course, he was also used by the federal government to placate some problems in Muslim countries. He was sent over there to represent the United States.

There was a lot of racism in America at the end of the '50s and early '60s. Anyone who was not caucasian had some contact with racism. Racism on the east side of America – New York, Pennsylvania, New Jersey – was more subtle than the racism in the South. I experienced it myself in the army. I had a sergeant who used to wake me up in the morning by calling me a spik, and then he used to call a friend of mine, who used to sleep next to me "Nigger." I thought that was a nice nickname, until someone told me that was racial slur against the black Americans. When I found out that it was wrong, I decided to stop this guy without warning and I hit him. I broke his jaw and a rib, sent him to the hospital. After that, I was court-martialled, but because I was very close to the post-commander and I was a fighter, they just accused me of disobeying an order and I paid a $50 fine. But that sergeant didn't mess around with me ever again.

Ali saw his mother being refused water at a luncheonette when he was young. And then, when he came back from Rome as Olympic champion, he was still banned from going into a restaurant.

As a boxer Ali was respected by most Americans, including caucasians. I think that they were aware that he was a champion, and by considering him a champion he's therefore better than the others, including caucasian fighters. I also believe that all Americans respected Jack Johnson and Joe Louis, because America believed that boxing was strictly a physical sport, and it's OK for a black man to have the muscle and the strength of a white man but not the intellect. Jack Johnson was accused of transporting white women from one state to another, and he was tried and punished, but he was still respected as a champion because people were not aware that, in order for you to be a champion, you also have to be better than the others intellectually.

When I became involved in the politics of this country, I was always in the habit of looking at the human and civil rights of people. I hated racists, for example. I hated people who abused the poor and the blacks and the Latinos, but I didn't hate caucasian people. I used to argue about this with Ali. I remember one time I said to him, "Ali, if a little caucasian baby is born, you call him a little devil because of the colour of his skin. I disagree with that. This racism is taught, and you're teaching the kids from the beginning that they shouldn't like others because of the colour of their skin."

So he says, "Well, the reason why a white baby is a devil is because they come from the mother and the father, who are also devils, so what do you expect? It's like, two tigers get together and a little tiger comes out. Two devils get together and a little devil comes out."

But Ali really loved kids of all colours – white kids, brown kids, black kids, all kids – so I never felt that he was wholeheartedly racist. He was just forced by circumstances to talk that way.

After he was taken to court in '67, I supported him, because I felt that it was such a shame that the best boxer we ever had should be considered an outcast. When his title was taken away, Bud Schulberg, George Plympton and I were a part of a group that were trying to get the decision overturned. Our picture was on the cover of *Esquire* magazine. We were there to attract the attention of the American public to the fact that here we have this superhuman being, Muhammad Ali, who was dissenting to the way that the system was reacting to him. And the system was awful. It was so awful that, eventually, the Supreme Court decided that Muhammad Ali was right and that the government was wrong. To me, that was a victory for humanity, not a victory for Muhammad Ali.

After all, the United States is a very political country. The people get involved in all kinds of protest. Although many white people agreed with Muhammad Ali, he was considered anti-caucasian because of his religion so they were not with him. Years later, when the Supreme Court decided that he was right, those who were originally against him became even more severely against him, because they *knew* that it was not right, that he wouldn't serve his country. They felt that he did not consider the United States his country – he was a Black Muslim.

All of this came about because Angelo Dundee refused to allow his fighter to quit. Muhammad Ali would have been irrelevant to this country if he had quit that time. People would not pay attention to him. They would not be attracted to him. The fact that he was forced to go out and fight, that created a new history in Muhammad Ali, and it was a very positive one.

I was there for the first Frazier fight at Madison Square Garden, too. The thing I remember most of that fight was an incredible left hook that Ali was hit with. That was Frazier's best punch, and Ali took it on the jaw. Nobody takes that kind of punch and stays up. He could not get away from it, but was able to assimilate the impact of that punch. He goes down and I say, "That's it. The fight's over." But then he gets up again.

And of course, the other fight that they had, that was even tougher than the first one. When they interviewed Ali after that, they asked him, "What do you think about this fight?"

"This was the closer I have ever been to death."

I get goosebumps just talking about it. That is the most fitting definition of that feeling. Every champion has to go through that experience – feeling that he's dying. I went through that experience, too, when you decide, "No, I don't want to give up. If he's going to beat me, he'd better knock me out or kill me."

It was the same when Sonny Liston got knocked out by Ali in that second fight in Maine. I was there, too, broadcasting the fight in Spanish for New York. I spent an hour with Sonny Liston before the fight and I illustrated to him how he was going to beat Ali. "You have to use your jab," I said. "You have to put pressure with your jab. Forget about him being fast. Forget about him having a good jab. If he jabs you, move to the side and you jab him."

But when the fight began, he didn't do that. And I said, "Oh my goodness, he forgot my teaching!" But then, all of I sudden, I see Ali throw the first jab – *boom!* Sonny got hit with a right hand on the jaw. I said, "Oh my goodness, he did what I said, what I taught him to do, and he got hit with a perfect right-hand to the jaw. He's not going to get up after that." They counted him out.

Later, I go into Sonny's dressing room with my tape recorder and I say, "Sonny, did you see that punch?"

"No," he says. "I never saw the punch coming. And he hit me. He hit me hard."

"OK," I say. "Thank you." Then I walked out.

I went to a press conference later with Liston and Ali and people began to say that it was a phantom punch, that there wasn't a punch, and I became very doubtful myself, but the answer he gave me in the dressing room convinced me that I was right, that it was a perfect shot, a perfect right hand over the jab and around the jaw.

So people are saying, "Ali, lots of people are saying that that was a phantom punch because they didn't see the punch."

"Don't feel bad," says Ali. "Sonny was closer and he didn't see it either."

But that's it. Ali he had the right answer at the right moment for every question. He had that self-response physically. He threw the punch when he had to throw a punch. I remember him hitting Cleveland Williams with eight consecutive punches to the jaw and this guy collapsing like a huge building.

Eventually, of course, Ali got sick. Even at the end, some people went to see him getting beaten and were happy when he got knocked down by Frazier, when he was massacred by Larry Holmes. But even at that time, he was sick. In the '80s, I went to visit him during the Olympic games and saw him take a couple of pills. He tried to imply that they were vitamin pills but I knew what the pills were. "Those are not vitamin pills," I said. "Those pills are used by Parkinsonians." My father, who was a Parkinsonian for 27 years, was one of the first 15 people in the world to be tested with that pill, so I knew what it was. Ali was taking the drug when he fought Larry Holmes. This guy had Parkinson's and he was still fighting.

It was obvious he was sick when he fought Holmes. Even Larry Holmes himself – who is not the most generous person in the world – stopped punching at Ali because Ali was defenceless. But I never spoke about that. Even though I went there to cover the Olympics for *Penthouse* magazine, I never mentioned that experience I had with Ali.

I stopped boxing through boredom. I just got bored and wanted to do something else. Ali, though, carried on for a long time, partly because of the three years he'd spent away but also because Ali's name had begun to be spread all over the world in 1974 thanks to communication technology getting much better. It was easier for Madison Avenue to spread any situation all over the world, good or bad. And by then lots of people, white and black, were being represented by Ali. Maybe because of the global adulation I think people near him were also trying to persuade him to continue. He was pushed. If you were close to Ali, and you know that he had Parkinson's, to carry him to fight Larry Holmes was criminal. It was obvious he was sick. I saw him training for that fight, and I saw him fall into this habit of being unable to punch and of getting himself against the ropes. Then, he – and this is the magic of Ali – he created a notion in everyone, including his opponent, that when he went to the ropes it was to force those people to throw punches and out-punch themselves. That's what I look for, to get my opponent against the ropes, so I can punch freely, but Ali used to go there voluntarily.

This was the principle of rope-a-dope. When he was fighting Foreman, he would go to that position and Foreman would not approach him. He would wait for Ali to get off the ropes. I'd say, "What is this guy doing?" I wished and prayed for fighters to go against the rope so I could open up with a combination. This guy's doing that, but he gave the notion to the opposition that it was a trick, and because the guy thought it was a trick, he would not punch Ali when he was against the rope. Only Muhammad Ali could do that with the opposition.

Igor Vitisky

Former Russian Boxer

I was winner of the top category of young boxers in the USSR in 1973. Then, in 1978, I was champion of the Soviet Union. I was in a number of world championships after that, in a lot of fights against the US. Then, my biggest win was when I won against Teofilo Stephenson. I won against him twice, once in Cuba in 1973 and then in 1976, in a knockout match in Wilmington.

When Ali came to Moscow in 1976, everyone was excited and curious about the man. Where the fights took place, it was packed. Generally speaking, he had come as a boxer to promote boxing, as a promoter of peace. He met up with President Brezhnev when he was here, which was front-page news, even though he wasn't the first sporting figure to have met the General Secretary. I don't know what the ordinary people thought about it, but Ali was known in the Western press as being a freedom-fighter and an anti-war figure. When he lost his licence in America because of his protest against the Vietnam War, the Soviet people supported him.

When he came over to fight in 1978, the fights took place in the CSK Palace of Sport.* Of course, everyone was excited. Everyone wanted to see him, because it was the first time that a professional had fought with amateurs

* CSK = Tsentralny Sportivny Komitet Armii (Central Army Sports Committee).

in a showfight like that. There were six rounds. Zayev went on first for two rounds and then I was in the ring for the final two rounds. The crowd was mostly amateurs or professionals. Every boxer, every sportsman knew who Ali was, and of course everyone had come to watch him. There were even some American supporters in the crowd.

I felt pretty agitated that night. Fighting against such a top sportsperson is tough, as you can imagine. We hadn't really prepared ourselves – we were simply told that we were going to fight. My nerves were really on edge and I remember, when we were getting ready he burst into our changing room and called out to us, "I'll beat you all!" He was just trying to scare us!

He was a talented boxer, superb. That's how he remains in my memory. I don't think that meeting him was particularly significant in my career, but of course the fact that I met him, the memory that I have of him, that's something great.

Chuck Wepner

Former Heavyweight Contender

During the time I fought Muhammad Ali, I was ranked in the Top Ten in the world for almost 42 months. In them days, there was only one champion in each division, and there was twelve divisions. Now there are 96-106 champions.

I fought a guy named Terry Hinsky, who was George Foreman's "policeman". He's the guy you had to beat to get to George Foreman. I knocked him out in the eleventh round to earn a shot at George Foreman and the championship.

Anyway, to cut a long story short, later, Foreman fought Ali. Everybody thought he was going to destroy Ali, and Ali upset him, knocked him out in the seventh round. Don King, who was the promoter, promised me a shot at the title, said, "You're gonna be fighting Muhammad Ali instead of Foreman." I didn't believe him, but three months and a day later it broke in the New York news that Chuck Wepner was gonna be fighting Muhammad Ali for the championship of the world.

That fight took place on 24 March 1975. There was a lot of pre-fight publicity.

They really did it up good. Like I said, Don King was the promoter, and King does everything big. That fight was the only time in a 20-year career of boxing that I got to train full time. For all my other fights, I used to wake up in the morning, do my road work, come home, take a shower, go to work all day, and then at night I'd go to the gym and train. And it was *hard*. I wasn't subsidised like a lot of these guys are. I didn't go to big training camps. I went to a little place called in Jersey City, and it was tough. But for that fight, I got to go with the campus. Seven weeks. Every day, there was some kind of newspaper or some kind of media people there, and it was great. I lived there for seven weeks, I slept there, I ate three meals a day, I did road work, I had my sparring partners. I got myself into great shape. It was probably the best seven weeks of my life and it allowed me to go to 15 rounds and to give Ali a good fight when nobody really expected it.

Meanwhile, the press were saying that Chuck Wepner was a big underdog and that it was a mismatch, that I had no chance, that Ali was too good. I mean, he just came off a knockout of George Foreman. So they just gave me no chance at all. I was 20-to-one underdog going 15 rounds with the great Muhammad Ali. The rest is history. Sylvester Stallone was watching the fight in a movie house in Philadelphia and it gave him the inspiration for *Rocky*: Stallone said, the night before the fight in *Rocky*, "Even if I don't win this fight, I just want to prove that I belong in there." That was one of my lines, and that's what it was all about, proving that I was better than the press gave me credit for.

We all know that Ali psyched out his opponents before a fight, all that mouthing off. People say you lost against Ali before you even stood in the ring because he'd already beaten you down psychologically, but that wasn't the case with me at all. First of all, Ali never gave me a name like he did everybody else, calling them "the Mummy", "the Gorilla", the this, the that. He never gave me a name, never said anything bad about me. As a matter of fact, Ali used to write poems about people, and I wrote two poems about Ali, called 'Goodbye Ali, Hello Chuck' and 'What's In A Word?'. That first one went, "And by March 25, there'll be a new champ, and his name will be Big Chuck." But the poems were actually extensive. Both of them were 20 or 30 lines long, and both of them were published in magazines. I thought they were pretty good, myself. A little bit maybe on the corny side, maybe, but as good or better than what Ali used to write. Half the stuff Ali used to put out I didn't even understand. Where he used to to make up little one-liners, I made up poems.

Ali didn't psych me out, though. Nobody every psyched me out. I was never scared, going into a fight. And he was so great in them days, before he got sick. He'd be throwing punches and moving around. At one time, on *The Mike Douglas Show*, he threw a punch at me and I slipped and threw a punch at him. We were on this raised platform, and he moved back and he almost fell off the platform. And Don King says, "Chuck, God forbid Ali hurt himself, because you'd blow a shot at the championship." He said, "Don't throw. Let him do all the shenanigans and stuff. Don't throw punches back at him. He's not going to hit you; he's just doing it to hype up the fight."

The fight, though, that was great. The media attention was even greater after the fight, after going 15 rounds, tapping him down. To this day, 26 years later, people still talk about the fight and say, "How ya doing, champ?" and "Great fight." A lot of guys can fight somebody and, if you don't do well, they forget your name in a couple of years; but when you fight Muhammad Ali and you go 15 rounds, you have him down, they make a movie about you.

Richard Williams

Father Of Venus And Serena Williams

When I grew up in Louisiana, back in the early '40s and the middle '50s, it was very difficult. Prejudice was one of the main traditions there, and most people had got so accustomed to it that I don't think a lot of people saw anything wrong with it. However, my mom did, so she taught me.

I didn't have much of a reaction. A lot of those who did have a reaction were killed. A lot of them were bombed. A lot of them were shot by the police. But by about 1954, when the first Act was passed, I was ready to respond. I was not going to ever call anyone "Mister" – regardless of who they was. So I got in a lot of trouble for that.

It was an unjust time. Unjust was education. Unjust was you couldn't drink out of certain fountains. It was the same when you went into a building to eat or even on public transportation. If it was raining, the black person had to get off the sidewalk and get in the mud. You might have on a new pair of shoes, but you had no rights whatsoever.

I began to develop a fear for what they called at that time the "caucasian race". My mom told me I couldn't have that type of fear. She said, "Even if they kill you, any day is a good day to die if you die for what's right. Always stand for what's right." That was in 1954 and '55, and then in '56 I began to make a major stand.

A good friend of mine, my only friend, was called Chilli Bowl. The white people, or the caucasian people, cut off both his hands and hung him from a tree. They said they were making an example that this would happen to the negroes that didn't say "yes, sir" or who stole from them. So I made it a point to steal everything they had. They had a black guy as their night watchman, named Mr Percy, who had his arm chopped off with an axe by them. I remember once he wanted to tell on me that I had stolen something from the white man. I told him I would whip his ass, and when I saw the white guy come out, I whipped him, too. From that point on my life was always in danger.

I first heard about Mr Muhammad Ali, called Cassius Clay, back in the '60s and I was aware who he was in '61. He didn't start doing a lot of talking until late '62 – and it was the first time I had seen a black man who had so much confidence in himself. I never thought he was bragging or boasting like most people say. It was just confidence – and if you've got confidence in what you can do, you are great. But this guy changed history for black people.

In 1963, when Muhammad Ali was to fight Sonny Liston, he couldn't get the fight so he went out at night to Liston's home, blowing his horn, saying "Come on out here, I'm going to beat you up, I want ya, I got to beat ya, I'm the greatest." He got Sonny Liston a little nervous there, so when Liston decided he would fight him, Muhammad Ali predicted the round he would knock him out. And this guy did everything he'd said he would do. He should never have won the fight, but he was out there, so confident that he broke down Liston's confidence. I was watching this fight in '63 at West Los Angeles, in a bar. I was very fortunate to be there because it cost you five dollars to get in!

I was so honoured to see Cassius Clay win because here was a black guy speaking the truth. That's not to say that a lot of blacks – like Dr King – during this time were not speaking the truth. But here was a guy saying who he was, what he was about to do and doing it. My confidence came in, and he gave me courage to believe that I could accomplish anything, like he did in '63.

In 1964, I went back to school because I had seen Muhammad Ali. I had stopped school in the eleventh grade, but I went back and I graduated. The following year, in 1965, I went to LA City School of Business and 18 months later I got a business degree. Then I went to an electronics school for almost two years and got qualifications in engineering. And all because of Muhammad Ali.

He helped me also to understand the importance of family and what family should stand for. The value of family is like a bicycle chain. If one link in that chain breaks down, a bike will not function correctly. And, for the first time, watching Muhammad Ali made me understand that the major university I was hoping to get into – like UCLA or Berkley – wasn't important any more. The major institution and college in the world is family, but that's what we do not have today, not only in the black race, every race. It was like Muhammad Ali was teaching me one on one when I looked at him box or when I looked at him talking. When he said, "I'm the greatest", I felt the same way.

In 1965, Muhammad Ali helped me to do something else that I never would have been able to. He came over to Santa Barbara, and I was in a silk and wool suit, because that's what was going on during that time. He said, "You know, black brothers are dressing like pimps." And I said, "Hell, I don't need that suit now!"

In 1966 Muhammad Ali was doing a presentation and I was able to get about two metres from him. I asked him a question: "Do you mean everything you say?"

"Brother, if you just try half of the things I say, you'll be all right."

And he was right – I am all right!

In 1966 Ali decided he wasn't going to go to Vietnam. I viewed it that he was telling the truth, because everything he was saying was coming from Elijah

Muhammad. And he told me that if I believed half of the things that he'd say I would be okay. And I believed it when he said, "I'm a black person, the Vietnamese are brown people. We do not have anything against each other. A black man shouldn't be out there killing when he's being killed here in America by another race. Why would we have a war over there with those people, when we have a war in the south of America?"

What was interesting in the war that we had in the south, is that no one was seeing it but us. Everyone else kept saying it was okay. I don't think that Muhammad Ali should have been in Vietnam. I don't think any black man should have been. The government had been against black people for 400 years, so Muhammad Ali was just opening up doors that had been closed. Ninety per cent of all the black people in America, I felt, believed in what Muhammad Ali was doing. The ones that didn't were what we called "aristocrat black people" – they went to white schools and learned white history, and naturally some of them were brainwashed.

A lot of the white people believed him. But all black people, in my opinion – at least 90% of them – they definitely did. The reason they believed in him was because they had been in the united forces – the army, the marines and so on – before Muhammad Ali was there. When a lot of the soldiers got out of their corps, they had to go back to the back door way of life. Pee behind trees, get beat up by the police, watch their wife and kids get raped. So Muhammad Ali took the right step by making a stand. It taught me one of the most valuable lessons in the world: one person can make a difference.

He joined the Nation of Islam after that 1963 fight. I believe that the Muslim has the only way that's right for black people and brown people around the world, because they teach you how to eat correctly. Black people don't know what they are supposed to eat or when they are supposed to eat. Every race in the world knows what they are supposed to eat except for black people. The Chinese have their food, the Mexicans have their food, Cubans have their food – but where is the black man's food?

I never became a Muslim but if I was going to be a religious person that's exactly what I would be, because any other race has been infiltrated by other races. Black people need their own way of worshipping the true god.

If it was able to help people like Malcolm X and Muhammad Ali, what makes people think it wouldn't help me? I believe that it's the only truth and it's the truth that every black person should be involved in. That's what helped Muhammad Ali so much, that he was able to take that truth and go marching on and help millions of other people of my colour.

When Muhammad Ali decided to become a Muslim, it helped me to understand that, as a group, people are extremely strong, but as an individual, you are not. If it wasn't for Muhammad Ali a lot of things would have never changed.

Elijah Muhammad was the leader and spiritual government behind the Muslim organisation and I believe in all his messages, even though he is dead. He was the one who helped a lot of black people to stop drinking, get off drugs, grow their own food, have their own books. They were saying that, because we've been doing all this work for you for nothing always, now we'll separate ourselves, we'll get our own Nation of Islam and we'll produce our own things. That's when other races decided that – *gosh* – these people are prejudiced. We weren't. We were simply saying, "We're not going to be beaten up by you any more. We're not going to let you rape us any more. We're not going to allow you to work us for 50 cents all day any more. We're going to start our own thing." And I think that is exactly what black people should do to this day.

I really feel that every black person throughout the whole world, whether it's in Manila, in Africa, England or America, has been given something to be extremely proud of by Muhammad Ali. Not just Richard Williams and the Williams family. Muhammad Ali has stood up and made a difference. If you wish to make the same difference in your lives, go back and look at Muhammad Ali's life and, I guarantee, your life will never be the same.

There was a white lady who used to come to every fight Mr Muhammad Ali had. Finally, before he had the second fight with Mr Joe Frazier, Muhammad leaned over the ropes and said, "I just want to shake your hand. Who are you?"

"I come to every fight you have because I want to be there when you lose," she said.

He looked at her, smiled, and said, "You know, I'd like to be there when I lose, too."

But this guy just didn't believe he could lose. When he had the second fight, Muhammad Ali knew he had experience. He knew he had the best feet, he knew he had the best hands. And, for once in his life, not only did he have America behind him – which didn't make that much difference – but he had the world behind him, too. So he did what he was supposed to do, and he did that famous thing that no one had ever done before. Wow! I could feel the chill going all over me and, for the first time, I wanted to be just like he was. Muhammad Ali.

He had a huge impact on other sports. Richard Williams brought big money to tennis, but Muhammad Ali brought a lot of money to everything else. There were guys out there playing almost for peanuts, but he had people like Carl Lewis – a track runner, a young kid out of Santa Monica – beginning to believe that he could make money, and Wilt Chamberlain making a hundred thousand dollars in basketball. No one was making money in any sport 'til he raised the level of it, and he should be given credit for this.

Certainly, there was no one making money in tennis. A lot of players who were professional couldn't accept money sometimes, so they had to try and play another way. But he changed everything in every sport.

Venus met Muhammad Ali at an awards ceremony once. I wasn't there. She came back home, so excited, and said, "Dad…"

"Venus, Venus, take it easy!"

"You know who I met? I met the greatest fighter in the world, Muhammad Ali. I met him, Dad. And I got a picture with him!"

That picture is in her room to this day.

Ian Wooldridge

Journalist

When I first saw Cassius Clay, he was in the 1960 Olympics in Rome, and of course no one knew what to expect. They'd never heard of him, didn't know who he was. He was then a light heavyweight and he got into the final against this very experienced Pole who'd had well over 300 fights, and there was this gangling kid of 18 coming with his fists dangling down to his knees. He waited to the third round and then he really clobbered this Pole. You realised then that you'd seen something big. Of course, you couldn't tell what was going to happen for the rest of his career, but you knew you'd seen something strange. It was an extraordinary evening. Some went away saying, "Well, he's got no future at all. How can he?" But he had nine minutes to prove himself to the world and of course he took three minutes to do it. But even then, you couldn't imagine what was going to come from this. It was like his personality, which was so unusual.

I was there as a general reporter, covering the cycling and the athletics for my column, and I just dropped into the boxing. I didn't even know he was going to fight, and I didn't know his name. Of course, he didn't keep that name very long. But I was shocked with the way he dealt with people. For example, just before he fought Henry Cooper, there was this braggart giving out this appalling doggerel verse – "I'll knock him over in five," which, in fact, he did – and you thought, "I've never seen anyone like this." But he was never unkind. He didn't do the mean things that go on in boxing today. There was no eye-staring going on. He just knew who he was and he just gave himself to you. And he never asked for money. Now, when you get exclusive interviews, all these guys want money, but money never occurred to him.

One appreciated that his was a new style of boxing, and that you'd never seen anything like it before. But it was all part of that boxing business. Creating publicity for a fight, that just came to him naturally. Whereas now fighters get together with all sorts of gimmicks, punches thrown in streets, Ali didn't need to do any of this. He was just his own man. And in England, when he got a little bit better known, he did a vaudeville act in London for a week at the Victoria Palace. He was hugely loved.

Before the Henry Cooper fight in '63, obviously all the sentiment was for Henry. He was probably the most loved sportsman we ever had, him and Lester Piggott. A lot of people took offence that Ali was going on about what he was going to do to him, but it was good copy – he got huge space in the press. In the end, though, it was just, "Here's another American braggart. I hope Henry knocks his head off." Which he didn't.

In the fight itself, I thought it was all over after three rounds, because Henry was bleeding appallingly from one of his eyebrows. Blood was pouring all down his face. I thought that, after three rounds, God, they'd have to stop this, but they didn't. Then, of course, in the fourth, Henry comes out and hits him, clobbers him with his left and knocks him over. I thought at the time that that was the first time that Ali – Clay as he then was – had ever been knocked out. But then, in the fifth, he knocked Henry out, exactly as he had predicted in his poem. Henry was in a bad state, and mercifully they stopped the fight. But then, afterwards came the story that there had been this gap at the end of the fourth round, after Clay had gone down, and that, instead of ten seconds it went on and on – "What's going on here?" I wouldn't like to say how long it was, but sitting at the ringside you thought, "My God, old Henry is back on the trail again." I would guess that it was 30 to 40 seconds that the fight had been held up. You thought, "There's something very strange going on here." And of course Clay's glove had become unstitched.

His fight against Foreman, the Rumble In The Jungle – my God, what a mess-up that was. We went down to Kinshasa in Zaire and had to go out to this other town, another 60 or 70 miles away, where they'd actually built a village for them. So we got down there, got settled in, and then blow me but Foreman had damaged his eye. We came back to London and then went back down again a couple of weeks before the fight. This time, it *did* take off, but during that fortnight a lot of British reporters got to know Ali well, because he had a villa there which was open house. There was no question of an interview or anything. You just wandered in the house. As long as you didn't smoke on the premises. You'd come in, sit down, have a beer and he'd chat for half an hour, telling amazing stories. He was interested in the occult and outer space. He'd describe his latest journey to Saturn. He just loved getting on with people. And some of the great publicity there came about through these conversations. But he talked mostly with British reporters, because it was a very difficult time for him in the States. He was really, really knocked over there, after he'd become Muhammad Ali, changed his religion and refused to fight in Vietnam. He came here, though, and nobody gave a damn, so he took to British reporters. Many of us, he wouldn't know our names, but he always knew you by sight. Remarkable. He was a lovely person. Quite a few friendships began at that time.

I think the two British journalists that Ali would have known best were Harry Carpenter, the commentator for the BBC, and Reg Gutteridge for ITV. One year, Ali was being interviewed by Harry at the BBC and, at the end of the interview, he said, "How's Reg?" And Harry said, "Well, he's not too well, actually. He's in hospital." Then Ali said, "Let's go." They got a cab, walked into the hospital in Hammersmith late in the evening and Ali said, "I want to see Reg." They took him straight up to the ward, and there was Reg Gutteridge, lying in bed, and there was the great Ali, standing over him.

One day, I was approached by a guy called Charlie Perkins, who had once been a professional footballer in England. He said, "Can you get me in to see Ali?" Now, Charlie was the leader of the Aboriginal movement in Australia, and what he wanted to do was to get Ali to go down and speak on their behalf, and Ali said, "Sure." But he wouldn't go down to Australia – he wouldn't get involved in that – but he put Charlie Perkins and his mate on the payroll and paid their air fares back to Australia.

The Foreman fight, though, the evening of that fight was one of the most hysterical I've ever known, because in fact it was early in the morning in Zaire. You weren't sure how the communications were going to work. Everyone was nervous, all 600 reporters at the ringside. Were the communications going to be OK? By this time, everyone was so het up that they didn't realise that Angelo Dundee had gone into the ring. He was going around to the corner posts and slackening off the top ropes. No one picked it up at the time!

The odds were very much on Foreman. He was this huge rock of a man. You couldn't imagine anyone knocking him over, even Ali. And for the first five or six rounds, Foreman couldn't get at Ali's head. Now we suddenly realised why the top rope had been slackened. Ali was leaning right back, keeping his head out of range. And he had such a strong body. Foreman was pummelling him all the time, but he couldn't get at his head. And of course, when it came to the eighth round, Foreman came out with this punch, Ali straightened up and *bang!* The man mountain was over. But, like I say, the problem was communications. In fact, I lost the phone for 40 minutes.

Kinshasa was right in the middle of Zaire, a very poverty-stricken country. But while we were there, the British Embassy or the British Consulate gave a cocktail party for us. There was a very nice little chap there, and he said, "You'll be OK. There won't be any thieving going on in the streets. They hung 'em all in the square the other day." He said that, if you went down there, the bodies were hanging from the trees.

Ali fought Joe Bugner twice. Bugner was very much a journeyman boxer. Occasionally, Ali would take these fights just to keep the funds coming in. The first one was in Las Vegas in '73. It went 15 rounds and it was quite undistinguished. Ali won on points, rather obviously, and that was the end of that. The second one was in Kuala Lumpur, again an exotic setting, and the thing I remember about that occasion was the size of the entourage Ali had. There were 44 people in his camp. He only needed about six or seven, but then there were hangers-on, there were relatives and there were relatives of relatives. There were people there who had fallen on hard times. And they were all buzzing around this hotel shopping complex, getting jewellery and clothes and whacking it all on Ali's credit cards. I remember thinking, "This is disgusting."

I suppose a lot of people thought it was rather strange, though, to find Joe Bugner in the same ring as Muhammad Ali, but Ali took quite a few of these fights in between. He had to earn some cash. He was getting rid of it fast, either being ripped off or spending it. And I think quite a few of those fights were pretty average fights. I'm not suggesting he didn't try to win, but I saw both of the Bugner fights and they both went 15 rounds, and one felt that they might have ended a little bit earlier.

Then, the Larry Holmes fight in Las Vegas in 1980, that was one of the worst things I've ever seen in any kind of sport. Ali was now past his best. The fight was stopped in eleven rounds. He was tired and he was gone and suddenly Holmes opened up on him. In those last three rounds, he must have hit him in the head at least 20 times, really big punches, two of which would lay me out, if not kill me. But Ali's pride was such that he would not go down. I don't know how he stayed there, and such was the terrible bloodlust in the atmosphere that the referee wouldn't stop it, either. It should have been stopped. Personally, I believe that's when Ali's health went. It was simply terrible to watch.

The next morning, at about eleven o'clock, Don King came in and said, "You've just seen the great Ali. He will recapture the heavyweight crown of the world." And you thought, "My God this man should never go anywhere near a ring again." But, tragically he did. He didn't need to, because he had a contract with the American agent Mark McCormack which guaranteed him a million dollars a year for publicity, provided he didn't get back in the ring. But Ali was so caught up in the whole cacophony of the thing that he went back in for another two or three fights. All it did was worsen his health. I never saw him even remotely fit again. It was terrible.

Among the many sportsmen I've met over quite a few years, Ali was the most passionate about people. He just loved people. As long as you were reasonably polite to him, you were greeted as a friend. One or two people do this – Arnold Palmer is another one – but it didn't worry who you were, what nationality you were, he would come up and he'd put his arm around your shoulder. He was much more relaxed than other people. And he never signed business deals. He didn't want to sell himself for cash. I am sure he got fees for big things he did, but it wouldn't have occurred to him to actually want money from these people. There's not many sportsmen like that in the world.

Since 1999, I've only met him twice. I went over to New York simply to interview him in his private house. I walked in and he got up and shuffled across the room and bear-hugged me. Lonnie, his lovely fourth wife, she did all the chatting for him, but he was suffering from narcolepsy, and every five minutes his head is down. He's asleep. Then he'd jerk up and try and say something else.

The only other time I saw him recently was when my newspaper, *The Daily Mail*, gave a dinner for him in the Savoy, and I sat next to him. That was about a couple of hours long, and the same thing happened – the old narcolepsy was there and he was going down and down. Towards the end, though, he woke up. I was making some notes and he picked up my pen and started doing some doodles on the tablecloth, muttering, "Skyscraper thing, skyscraper, airplane," in this sort of whisper. Well, that was the end of it. They whipped the tablecloth off the table and auctioned it for charity for £1,300, and Ali loved that. There he was, this man in terribly frail health, supporting people even in his sickness. Remarkable.

Appendix I – Mike Fox

President / CEO Muhammad Ali Center

I can't think of anyone from this or the last century who is the equal of Muhammad Ali. He is singularly the most recognised person on the face of the Earth at this moment, and I think that speaks volumes. There is no one else who could be his equal in terms of being a carrier of messages that could help change individuals' lives, as well as society in general. And Muhammad recognises this unique power that his maker gave to him. He wants the Center to be his legacy and carry on far beyond his time.

At the Center, there are going to be some major multimedia experiences that we would wish for all visitors to participate in. Certainly film will be a very significant component of the experience, but the environment that we'll be creating for a particular media experience will be just as important as the media presentation itself. For instance, we're creating a theatre where you feel as though you are literally in the ring with him and a virtual-reality opportunity to make you feel as though you're there with Muhammad, experiencing the excitement and drama of having thousands of people cheering you. We'll certainly have many interactive components where you can communicate, in a sense, with Muhammad Ali – video screens, for instance – and hope that people leave feeling that their experience of the Center is but a beginning of a relationship with the Center and, through us, with Muhammad. We'll encourage them to communicate their thoughts about particular themes that may be presented and point out opportunities for us to be able to respond to their thinking. We're interested particularly in providing opportunities for young people.

We also have plans to form a partnership with regional, national and even international organisations that are in harmony with the mission of the Center. For instance, the United Nations will have a very strong relationship with the Centre, and in terms of human rights and issues of humanitarianism or children's issues, there will be opportunities for us engage in collaborative programming. The UN thinks of the Center as a kind of venue from which they can share with a broader public much more of what they are learning across the globe.

Locally, we're very fortunate to have the highly respected University of Louisville. The university's relationship with the Center is formalised, and they have created an institute of peacemaking and conflict resolution, so we can foresee that the Center will be the place for which many of the programs under the auspices of this partnership will be offered for the benefit of the general public, because we have specialised groups around the country and beyond. So there will be training programs for different groups across the country and far beyond, helping people to have a better understanding of how to prevent conflict in the first place, as well as how to manage it when necessary. There will also be opportunities to actually negotiate and mediate conflict.

We've also have formed a partnership with an organisation called Shine, which is a young adults' organisation that aims to reach out to millions of young adults and make them think about their own lives and teach them to respond in a non-conflicting way to societal circumstances. So we intend to collaborate and to truly partner with these organisations that are themselves doing some significant things in the development of individuals.

I know that Lonnie hopes that the centre will be a very receptive institution for anyone, whatever their own objectives, but she wants to make certain that, when leave the centre, they have truly received the messages that we hope to provide them with and get much more than their preconceived ideas of what they might experience within the Center. So, if people come here to see the wonderful fights that Muhammad was involved in, they won't be able to experience those. We will have many of those moments captured so that visitors won't be disappointed, and we'll have an archive, too, as well the opportunity to give those kinds of visitors everything they want to experience about that particular sport, but the mission of the Center is much more than that. We people – whether they have a real affinity for the sport or not – to fully appreciate the storyline, the message of the Center, and we want that message to affect their lives in very positive ways. The Center is there so that people can share Muhammad's legacy and his ideals.

For people who aren't into boxing, though, there will be plenty for them, and plenty for other people with other interests that are leaning toward different aspects of Muhammad's life. It's not to be looked on as a boxing museum – as Muhammad himself says, his boxing career was just a vehicle for him to do what he's been doing for these last 30-plus years. It's a place where people can come and feel as though they have that same potential that he had to become great in their own lives.

We've had some high-profile support from corporations and individuals, including people like Billy Crystal and Robin Williams, and we continue to cultivate that interest amongst others that we hope will show similar support for what we're doing. Today, we're finding from both the individual benefactor and the corporate sector a better understanding of what the Center's goals truly are. They're beginning to recognise the significance of what the Center can become. But they have had to be convinced that it's not a place to honour and glorify Muhammad; it's a place to continue the work that Muhammad's has started, to reach millions and millions of people, even more than the number he's reaching now, spending 200 days of the year on the road, touching people's lives.

I would hope that, for the people of Louisville, the Center would be a place that they respect, honour and pride – respect for one of their own; honour for a place where one can acknowledge someone who has had an international effect on people's lives; and pride for them, because they will undoubtedly be the ones whom will be the greatest beneficiaries to have such a place here in their own community.

I believe that this is the culmination of the dream that Ali has dedicated himself to, and I hope that he is an active participant in the Center for a long time to come. This is his goal and something about which he is terribly excited. Hopefully, he'll play an active role, individually receiving our guests every day and having a relationship with them.

We look at the Center as an international organisation, because of his recognition all over the globe, and there'll be every opportunity for those who can't get here to interact with the Center, via our website and publications and programming that we'll be able to offer globally in an outreach manner. They'll be able to feel as though they are participants within the Center.

We're currently at the design development stage, both of the facility itself, architecturally, and of the exhibitions and public programs we'll be offering visitors, so from this stage we need to identify supporters to help fund the Center. Our goal is $60 million for the construction of the actual facility itself and an additional $20 million for an endowment fund to provide money for general operations and special programming opportunities. We're about halfway to our goal of reaching the $60 million mark, and our hope is to obtain the rest by the end of the first quarter of 2002, start construction very soon thereafter and to open at the end of 2003.

In a sense, it's surprising that nothing like this has been attempted before, but I think that any opportunities Ali had in the past to consider similar options were certainly things that he was right to reject until the right time and the right place were determined. This is the right time and it is the right place, because this is Ali's home, so it's a full circle. Here, we can begin the story of Muhammad in his home community.

We're going to have a very strong, dynamic exhibition component at the Center that will hopefully inspire an appreciation for having conviction in one's life, as Muhammad has done, and to be courageous and to really stand up for one's own beliefs. We'll be encouraging visitors at times to feel what it must have been like for Muhammad to make some difficult choices, such as when he chose not to fight in Vietnam and had to deal with the public's response. We want visitors to feel how he must have felt, so you'll be in a chamber where you'll experience the same confrontation that he felt, so you'll gain an appreciation of his strength and courage and what it meant to be faced with that period of difficulty and then have an opportunity to apply that to your own life.

Appendix II

Muhammad Ali Personal Archive

Cassius Clay / Louisville Sponsoring Group contract, October 1960.

Affidavit and Certificate of Counsel for contract, October 1960.

Louisville Sponsoring Group, 1960.

Contract amendment, 1960.

Broadcast rights agreement, February 1963.

BBC broadcast rights agreement, March 1963.

Clay / Cooper contract, April 1963.

Letter of intent, September 1963

Clay / Liston contract, November 1963.

Certificate of Incorporation, February 1964.

Ali / Liston fight agreement, July 1964.

Boxing licence application, May 1965.

Manager's licence application, May 1965

Unsigned Liston contract, May 1965.

Broadcast rights permission, September 1965.

Ali / Patterson / Terrell agreement, November 1965.

Register of fight receipts, 1960-66.

Payment, January 1966.

Louisville Selective Service correspondence, July 1966.

Request to travel, July 1966.

Travel permit, July 1966.

CONTRACT

THIS CONTRACT made and entered into at Louisville, Jefferson County, Kentucky on this 26th day of _October_, 1960, by and between THE LOUISVILLE SPONSORING GROUP of Louisville, Jefferson County, Kentucky (hereinafter referred to as "The Group", which is a group composed of individuals listed on Exhibit A which is attached hereto and made a part hereof, and known by all parties to this Contract) party of the First Part, and CASSIUS M. CLAY, Jr., (Born January 30, 1942), Eighteen (18) years of age, (hereinafter referred to as the "Athlete"), and CASSIUS M. CLAY, Sr., his father, and ODESSA L. CLAY, his mother, both of Louisville, Jefferson County, Kentucky, parties of the second part.

WHEREAS, the Athlete is Eighteen (18) years of age and does not otherwise have a legal guardian residing in this State or elsewhere; and

WHEREAS, his father, CASSIUS M. CLAY, Sr., and his mother, ODESSA L. CLAY, are his natural guardians in law and fact; and

WHEREAS, the Athlete and his father and mother have been advised, counseled and represented throughout the negotiations culminating in this contract by qualified and competent legal counsel of their choosing who have fully discussed and explained the contents hereof to the Athlete and both his parents; and

WHEREAS, both the Athlete and his father and mother and each of them have the utmost faith and respect for the members of the Group, and each of them, to further the purposes of this Contract so that it will be mutually advantageous to all, they, the Athlete, the parties of the second part, and each of them by affixing their signatures hereto approve and agree to the terms of this Contract, individually and as

This page onwards: the full contract between Cassius Clay and his management team, the Louisville Sponsoring Group, October 1960.

guardians of the Athlete, as hereinafter provided:

W I T N E S S E T H:

For and in consideration of the terms and conditions of this Contract and of the promises of the Group to the amount of compensation as herein set forth, the Athlete and the Parties of the Second Part, agree and are hereby firmly bound to the following terms, and hereby grant to the Group the following rights or options:

1. The Group engages the Athlete, and the Athlete agrees, for the period of time or any extension thereof, as set forth in this Contract, to render services solely and exclusively for the Group in such boxing contests, exhibitions of boxing, training exercises, personal appearances, motion pictures, television and radio appearances, commercial product endorsements, and any other commercial and promotional activities of any and every nature and description whatsoever, subject to the approval of the Athlete, which approval shall not be unreasonably withheld, whenever reasonably required by the Group in the United States and foreign countries as the Group may from time to time direct.

2. (a) In consideration of and as compensation for the Athlete executing this Contract and in agreeing to the performance of all services required hereunder and in further consideration of the other terms and conditions provided herein and agreed to by the Athlete and the parties of the second part, the Group agrees to compensate the Athlete at the rate of Nine Thousand ($9,000) Dollars per year for each of the first two (2) years (being the first two (2) twelve (12) month periods) constituting the initial term of this Contract, such compensation to be paid to the Athlete as provided in Paragraph 3 hereof.

2. (b)   In addition to the foregoing agreed compensation, the Group agrees to pay to the Athlete, and the Athlete
agrees to accept, subject to provisions of Paragraph 5 hereof
and except as provided in Paragraph 4 hereof, the sum of Fifty
(50) per cent of all sums of money derived or earned and paid
for the services of the Athlete of any nature and description
whatsoever that the Athlete may render under this Contract.
At present the Athlete is committed to the performance of two
professional boxing exhibitions with William H. King Enterprises, Inc., which commitments were made prior to the execution of this contract, and, therefore, no portion of the remuneration earned by the Athlete from these performances shall
be considered money earned and paid under this contract.

2. (c)   It is further agreed between the Athlete
and the Group, that the Group shall receive the remaining
Fifty (50) per cent, except as herein provided in Paragraph 4,
of such sums of money derived or earned and paid to the Athlete
under this Contract.

2. (d)   It is agreed that the Group, not the Athlete,
shall pay for all expenses of management, training, traveling,
promotion, and all other necessary and proper business expenses
incurred by or on behalf of the Athlete, in the furtherance of
this Contract.   All decisions as to the proper location, cost,
and duration of such training, or any other decision relating
thereto, shall rest solely and exclusively in the discretion of
the Group or their representatives, subject, however, to the consent of the Athlete who specifically agrees that such consent
shall not be unreasonably withheld.

3. It is further agreed by the Group that the agreed fixed compensation to be paid to the Athlete as provided in Paragraph (2)(a) hereof shall be paid to the Athlete, Ten Thousand Dollars ($10,000.00) during the calendar year 1960, at the time of execution of this Contract or at such other time as the Athlete may direct, and the balance ($8,000.00) shall be paid to the Athlete during the initial term of this contract, as hereinafter provided in Paragraph 4, on a monthly basis in equal monthly payments commencing on January 1, 1961. At the end of the initial term as hereinafter provided, these monthly payments shall cease and any further compensation to the Athlete shall be governed exclusively by the provisions of Paragraphs 2 and 4 hereof, however, the Group agrees that the compensation to the Athlete during any extended 12 month term under the contract shall not, in any such extended 12 month term, be less than $4,000.00.

4. This contract shall have a fixed minimum initial term of twenty-four (24) months from the date of execution. After this initial term of the Contract, the Group may, at its sole and exclusive option, extend the term of this Contract and all of its provisions for the term of 12 months, and shall have the continuing option to so extend the Contract for one additional 12 month term thereafter. Further, the Group shall have at its sole and exclusive option, the unlimited right to extend the term of the Contract for two additional terms of 12 months each, (the fifth and sixth 12 month periods respectively) provided, however, that the Athlete shall be entitled to receive in each of these fifth and sixth 12 month terms the sum of 60% of all sums of money

- 4 -

derived or earned and paid for the services of the Athlete under this Contract and the Group shall be entitled to receive the remaining 40%. Except for the changes in interest as provided for in the preceding sentence for the last two 12 month terms, all provisions of the Contract shall remain the same during the extended option periods.

Under the Contract, after the initial fixed 24 month term, the Group has four (4) separate options to extend the duration of the Contract for four (4) additional 12 month terms under the conditions and provisions set forth herein. If at the end of the last option period hereinabove provided for, the Athlete and the Group have not further extended this Contract by mutual consent or negotiated and entered into a new Contract, then the Athlete agrees that he will not enter into any contract, agreement or commercial arrangement with any other person, persons, groups, associations, organizations, partnerships or corporations until he has presented such good faith and valid proposal which he would intend to enter into to the Group. The Group shall then have ten (10) days to accept the terms of this proposal or to refuse it. If the Group accepts these terms, then the Athlete agrees to enter into a contract with the Group based upon the terms of such good faith proposal.

Group shall give notice of its intention to exercise its options herein to the Athlete within thirty (30) days prior to the expiration of the initial term or any extended 12 month term of the Contract. Should the Group fail to exercise its options as provided herein to extend the Contract, this Contract shall terminate on the last day of the initial term or any extended option period.

5.   It is agreed by the Athlete and required by the Group that at least fifteen (15) per cent of the monies which would otherwise be paid to the Athlete under the 50% or 60% compensation provisions of this Contract, as provided for in Paragraph 2 hereof, must be set over on behalf of the Athlete into a Trust to be created for the Athlete's sole benefit, and that such monies shall be accumulated and invested (with any income becoming corpus) until the Athlete reaches thirty-five (35) years of age or permanently retires from boxing, whichever occurs first, at which time income from the Trust shall be paid to the Athlete pursuant to Trust terms to be agreed upon between the Group and the Athlete. Final disposition of the corpus in such Trust shall be pursuant to the Trust terms to be agreed upon between the Group and the Athlete.

The Trust contemplated by this contract shall have co-trustees, one being Alberta Jones, Attorney for Cassius M. Clay, Jr., and the other a corporate trustee having minimum assets of One Million Dollars. Cassius M. Clay, Sr. and Odessa L. Clay, the parents of the Athlete, shall serve as an advisory group to the co-trustees with regard to the investment of funds which may be transferred into the trust pursuant to the terms of this Contract.

The Athlete hereby authorizes and empowers the Group to collect, accept and receipt for all monies, checks, drafts

- 6 -

or money orders which may be due and payable to the Athlete for services rendered or fees earned under this Contract, and the Athlete agrees to endorse his name to any such checks, drafts, or money orders whenever necessary and authorizes and empowers the Group to withdraw therefrom the percentage due the Group pursuant to this Contract, together with the amount to be placed in Trust for the Athlete's benefit pursuant to the terms of this Contract, and to pay over the balance to the Athlete. The Athlete does hereby appoint the Group as his attorneys in fact for the aforesaid purposes, it being understood that in regard to handling of such funds the Group, and the members thereof, occupy a position of trust and confidence in relation to the Athlete, and the Athlete shall be entitled to a statement showing receipts and disbursements as promptly as such statement can be prepared after receipt of any income paid to the Athlete for services under this contract. The Athlete further agrees to execute sufficient powers of attorney to carry forth the purposes of this paragraph.

6. The Group agrees to use its best efforts to secure remunerative boxing contests, exhibitions, personal appearances, and other endeavors of any and every nature whatsoever for the Athlete. The Group shall have the exclusive right to carry on all negotiations for all contracts made in the furtherance of the purposes of this Contract.

7. The Athlete agrees to perform and render his services conscientiously and to the full limit of his ability in carrying out each and every agreement, contract, or commitment of any and every nature and description whatsoever entered into on his behalf by the Group, subject however to the Athlete's prior approval of such agreement, contracts, or commitments as

-7-

provided for in Paragraph 1.

8. The Athlete agrees that he will not, during the
life of this Contract, take part in any boxing contests, exhibitions, or personal appearances of any nature or description
whatsoever, or perform or otherwise exercise his talent in any
manner or place, except as directed by the Group, and shall not
allow his name, photographs, likeness or biography to be used
in any commercial or charitable endeavor, enterprise or under-
taking, or any other endeavor whatsoever, or enter into any commercial or charitable contract, commitment, or agreements without first obtaining the permission of the Group to do so, and
such permission shall not be unreasonably withheld.

If the Athlete shall be offered employment in some
field of endeavor which has no connection to the type of services which are contemplated to be performed by him under the
terms of this contract, then with the approval of the Group,
which approval will not be unreasonably withheld, the Athlete
may accept such employment and wages or salary received from
such employment shall not constitute remuneration to the Athlete
earned or paid under this Contract.

9. The Athlete shall perform all training exercises
as the Group or its representative shall reasonably require,
and shall proceed and travel by such means of conveyance that will
provide the Athlete's presence when and where required by the Group
for the purposes of this Contract.

10 This Contract shall not be assignable by any of the
parties except, that if the Group as presently constituted is
reorganized into a corporation, partnership or association, with
the present members of the Group being the sole stockholders,

-8-

partners, or members of such resulting corporation, partnership or association, then, and in that event, this Contract may be assigned to such resulting organization without the consent of the Athlete. There shall be no change in the membership of the Group as presently constituted without the consent of the Athlete, which consent shall not be unreasonably withheld, nor shall there be any change of stockholders, partners, or members of any succeeding corporation, partnership, or association, without the consent of the Athlete, which consent shall not be unreasonably withheld. Further, except as provided in Paragraph 11 below, no member of the Group shall sell, or devise by will or otherwise his Group interest or any part thereof to any other persons, groups, corporations, partnerships or association except other present Group members, without the consent of the Athlete, which consent shall not be unreasonably withheld.

11. Notwithstanding the provisions of Paragraph 10 hereof, the Group shall have the right to select and propose to the Athlete an appropriate and skilled person or persons to act as manager and/or trainer for the Athlete. If such person or persons is approved by the Athlete, and such approval shall not be unreasonably withheld, then the Group shall have the exclusive right to negotiate with such person or persons and assign to such manager and/or trainer such portion of the Group's interest under this contract which the Group, in its sole discretion, shall deem proper and to negotiate and enter into such agreement with said manager and/or trainer as the Group, in its sole discretion, shall deem reasonable and prudent to assure the best services of said manager and/or trainer to the Athlete and the Group. Any such

interest assigned to a manager and/or trainer shall not be assignable by such manager and/or trainer to any other person, persons or groups without consent of the Athlete and the Group.

12.   The Group and the Athlete agree that any royalties, rents or revenues of any kind or description whatsoever that may accrue at some later time subsequent to the termination of this Contract, which arise out of the performance by the Athlete of his duties under and during the effective period of this Contract, shall be divided equally, fifty (50) per cent to the Athlete and fifty (50) per cent to the Group.

13.   The Athlete agrees to conduct himself with due regard to public morals, as such public morals would be determined by a reasonably prudent member of society, and agrees that he will not do or commit any act or thing that will tend to degrade him in society or bring him into public hatred, contempt, scorn, or ridicule, or that will tend to shock, insult, or offend the community, or ridicule public morals or decency, and that he will not do or commit any act or thing that will tend to injure his capacity to at all times fully comply with and perform all of the terms and conditions of this Contract, or which will tend to injure his physical or mental qualities. The Group may at its option, upon thirty (30) days written notice to the Athlete, cancel this Contract for breach of the provisions of this paragraph.

14.   If the Athlete is injured in the performance of any of his properly authorized duties or services under this Contract or any extensions thereof, and by reason of such injuries, he can no longer perform his duties and services as contemplated by this Contract, then the Group agrees that it will fulfill whatever re-

maining financial commitment it may have to the Athlete under
this Contract until the end of the Contract term in which the
injury occurred.

15. All of the parties to this Contract are aware
that the Athlete is presently under twenty-one (21) years of
age. This Contract is entered into with full understanding
of all parties, in good faith, that the Athlete, upon arriving
at twenty-one (21) years of age, shall re-execute and/or ratify
this Contract. If upon reaching twenty-one (21) years of age
the Athlete shall fail to re-execute and/or ratify this Contract, the Athlete and the parties of the second part hereby
acknowledge a moral obligation to the Group to refund in full
the initial payment of Ten Thousand Dollars ($10,000.00) made
to the Athlete at the time of the execution of this Contract.
If this Contract is given validity by a Court of competent jurisdiction, thereby making it legally impossible for the Athlete
to repudiate this Contract, then the provisions of Paragraph
15 shall be null and void.

16. It is mutually agreed by and between the parties
hereto that the services to be rendered by the Athlete are
special, unique and extraordinary, and that this Contract shall
be subject to all of the applicable rules and regulations of any
State Board of Athletic Control in any State in which Athlete
may perform his services, reference thereto being expressly made.

17. The Group may require the Athlete to move from
Kentucky and establish his residence in California for the purpose of management and training, it being presently contemplated
by the parties that the manager and/or trainer will be located in
the State of California. Should the Athlete by reason of his

-11-

change of residence to California, as may be required by the Group, thereby incur additional tax liability exacted by the State of California over and above the California tax liability that he might have incurred by working in California, but being a resident of Kentucky, then for the initial term of this Contract, the Group agrees to reimburse the Athlete for any such California taxes which he would have otherwise not incurred had he retained his residence in Kentucky.

18. Patrick Calhoun, Jr. is the authorized agent of the Group for the purpose of signing this Contract on the Group's behalf. Sufficient formal authorization and acknowledgement of his capacity as the Group's agent will be supplied to the Athlete and the parties of the second part as soon as practicable. Further, the Group shall make known to the Athlete as soon as reasonably possible after the execution of this Contract, a member of the Group who shall be the Group's duly authorized agent for the purpose of consulting, advising and directing the Athlete and to carry out all the powers granted to the Group under the terms of this Contract.

19. It is specifically agreed that this Contract contains all of the terms, conditions and promises of the parties hereto in the premises and that no modification or waiver thereof of any provision shall be valid or binding unless in writing, executed by the parties hereto.

It is agreed that if any provisions of this Contract be held void or unenforceable, the other provisions hereof shall nevertheless continue to be and remain in full force and effect.

IN WITNESS WHEREOF, the parties hereto have set their

hands to triplicate originals hereof the day and year first above written.

WITNESSES:

Rudolph Valentieno, Clay

[signature]

THE LOUISVILLE SPONSORING GROUP

By *Patrick Calhoun*
Authorized Agent and
Representative

WITNESSES:

Gordon B. Davidson

H. Wendell Cherry

Cassius M. Clay JR.
Cassius M. Clay, Jr.
ATHLETE

Cassius M. Clay
Cassius M. Clay, Sr.

Odessa L. Clay
Odessa L. Clay

PARTIES OF SECOND PART

-13-

AFFIDAVIT AND CERTIFICATE OF COUNSEL

The affiants, ALBERTA O. JONES and GORDON B. DAVIDSON after being duly sworn according to law state:

The undersigned counsel are both duly licensed attorneys and counsellors at law admitted to practice before the highest court of the Commonwealth of Kentucky and both are presently engaged in the active practice of law in Louisville, Kentucky.

ALBERTA O. JONES states that she was employed by Mr. and Mrs. Cassius M. Clay, Sr., and Cassius M. Clay, Jr., to represent them in all matters connected with the professional career of Cassius M. Clay, Jr., age eighteen (18) years, and that she has so represented them in the lengthy and involved negotiations culminating in the contract between her said clients and the Louisville Sponsoring Group, and further she states that she has fully advised her clients regarding each and every provision of said contract and that she believes that they fully understand said contract and the provisions thereof.

GORDON B. DAVIDSON states that he represented The Louisville Sponsoring Group in negotiating the Contract between that Group and Cassius M. Clay, Jr., and his parents and that the minor, Cassius M. Clay, Jr. was at all times capably represented in said negotiations by ALBERTA O. JONES.

Both of the undersigned counsel state that the Contract was entered into by all parties hereto freely and without duress or coercion and with full and complete knowledge of all pertinent facts; and both counsel state that they feel that the subject contract is fair and equitable in all regards and to the best interests

This page and next: the affidavit and Certificate of Counsel for parties representing Cassius Clay in his contract with the Louisville Sponsoring Group, October 1960.

of the minor, Cassius M. Clay, Jr.

Alberta O. Jones, Attorney
2300 West Broadway
Louisville, Kentucky

Gordon B. Davidson
Gordon B. Davidson
300 Marion E. Taylor Building
Louisville, Kentucky

STATE OF KENTUCKY)
              : SS
COUNTY OF JEFFERSON)

      Subscribed and sworn to before me, a Notary Public in
and for the State and County aforesaid, by ALBERTA O. JONES and
GORDON B. DAVIDSON, at Louisville, Jefferson County, Kentucky, on
this 26th day of October, 1960.

      My commission expires: _May 22, 1962_

                      Martha D. Jones
                     Notary Public _Jefferson Co, Ky_

(SEAL)

LOUISVILLE SPONSORING GROUP

PATRICK CALHOUN, JR.
Retired, Chairman of the Board, American Commercial Barge Line, Jeffersonville, Indiana. Home: Goshen, Kentucky

WILLIAM S. CUTCHINS
President, Brown-Williamson Tobacco Company Louisville, Kentucky

W. L. LYONS BROWN, SR.
Chairman of the Board, Brown-Forman Distillers Corporation, Louisville, Kentucky

VERTNER D. SMITH, SR.
Chairman of the Board, Vertner Smith Company, Louisville, Kentucky

ARCHIBALD MCG. FOSTER
Vice-President, Ted Bates Advertising Company New York City, New York

WILLIAM FAVERSHAM, JR.
Vice-President, Brown-Forman Distillers Corporation, Louisville, Kentucky

ELBERT GARY SUTCLIFFE
Farmer - Home: Harrods Creek, Kentucky

JAMES ROSS TODD
W. L. Lyons & Company, Louisville, Kentucky

GEORGE W. NORTON, IV.
Executive, WAVE, Inc., Louisville, Kentucky

ROBERT WORTH BINGHAM
Assistant Managing Editor, Louisville Times Louisville, Kentucky

Members of the Louisville Sponsoring Group, 1960.

FIRST ENDORSEMENT

FIRST ENDORSEMENT to Contract dated the 26th day of October, 1960 between the Louisville Sponsoring Group, Cassius M. Clay, Jr. and others, it is hereby agreed between the parties that the last figure of $4,000.00 contained in Paragraph 3 of the aforesaid agreement should read and be changed to $6,000.00.

Witnesses:

Rudolph Valentino Clay

[signature]

THE LOUISVILLE SPONSORING GROUP

By _Patrick Calhoun_

Authorized Agent and Representative

Witnesses:

Gordon B. Davidson

H. Wendell Cherry

Cassius M. Clay, Jr.

Cassius M. Clay, Jr.

Cassius M. Clay, Sr.

Cassius M. Clay, Sr.

Odessa L. Clay

Odessa L. Clay

PARTIES OF SECOND PART

Contract amendment, 1960.

MADISON SQUARE GARDEN BOXING, INC.

304 WEST 50TH STREET

NEW YORK 19. N. Y.

February 27, 1963

Mr. Cassius Clay
c/o William Faversham
Brown-Forman Distillers
Louisville, Kentucky

Dear Mr. Clay:

As you know we have entered into an agreement dated
February 8, 1963 with William King wherein we granted to Mr. King
the right and license to transmit and exhibit and to license others
to exhibit a closed circuit television transmission of your forthcoming bout with Doug Jones on March 13, 1963.

For the sale of such rights to Mr. King we charged a price
of 50% of the receipts received by Mr. King from his exploitation
of the rights less certain expenses as set forth in our agreement
with him. We hereby agree to pay to you, after deducting the gross
receipts tax payable to the State of New York, 30% of the payment
made to us by Mr. King in accordance with said agreement.

Would you and your licensed manager please sign this letter
in the space provided below to indicate that this letter correctly
represents our agreement.

Very truly yours,

MADISON SQUARE GARDEN BOXING, INC.

By _Harry Markson_
Harry Markson

ACCEPTED AND AGREED TO:

cc _Cassius Clay_
wf _William Faversham_

00106

Broadcast rights agreement – for the Clay v Doug Jones fight – between Clay, his management and
Madison Square Garden, February 1963.

MADISON SQUARE GARDEN BOXING, INC.

304 WEST 50TH STREET

NEW YORK 19, N. Y.

March 7, 1963

Mr. Cassius Clay
c/o Mr. William Faversham
Brown-Forman Distillers
Louisville, Kentucky

Dear Mr. Clay:

In connection with your forthcoming bout with Doug Jones in Madison Square Garden, Lester Malitz has advised us that he has conveyed to the British Broadcasting Company for $2,000 the right to show a delayed telecast of the bout.

We are writing to advise that you will receive 30% of all sums paid to us by Mr. Malitz after the deduction of expenses, commissions, and the 5% tax payable to the New York State Athletic Commission by reason of such sale to BBC. In the event other ancillary rights to the bout are sold, you will be paid, after the deduction of such expenses, commissions and the deduction of such 5% tax, 30% of all sums paid to us by reason of such sales.

Very truly yours,

MADISON SQUARE GARDEN BOXING,
INC.

By _Harry Markson_

00104

Notification of the rights for the BBC to broadcast non-live coverage of the Clay v Jones fight, March 1963.

BRITISH BOXING BOARD OF CONTROL (1929)

PROMOTER AND BOXER

Ramilies Bldgs
Hills Place
London W1, England

ARTICLES OF AGREEMENT

(For the use of Members of the B.B.B. of C. only)

Where alternatives appear in italics they must all except one be struck out.

An Agreement made this 19th day of April, 1963 between

JACK SOLOMONS of London

(hereinafter called the Promoter) of the one part

and CASSIUS CLAY of America

(hereinafter called the Boxer) of the other part

All blank spaces must be completed before signature.

WHEREBY IT IS AGREED THAT:

1. The Boxer shall appear and box at Wembley Stadium, England on the *afternoon/evening* of 18th June 1963 in a contest of Ten rounds of 3 minutes each round against HENRY COOPER of England

or such substitute Boxer (hereinafter called the opponent Boxer) as hereinafter provided in accordance with the Boxing Rules of the B.B.B. of C.

2. The Boxer shall weigh-in at ─ stone ─ lb. at 1 a.m./p.m. at the appointed place on the date of the contest. If overweight the Boxer shall be allowed one hour to make the agreed weight. If he is then overweight he shall pay a weight forfeit to the opponent Boxer of £ ─ .

3. The Promoter shall provide in his agreement with the opponent Boxer that the opponent Boxer shall weigh-in at .. stone .. lb. (under similar conditions to the Boxer) and if overweight the opponent Boxer shall pay a weight forfeit to the Boxer of £ ─ .

4. The Promoter shall be responsible for the collection and payment of weight forfeits. The payment of forfeit money as above shall in no way prevent the Board or Area Council taking any action they deem necessary under REGULATIONS 15 and 22.

5. If the opponent Boxer shall be not more than lb. above the stipulated weight, the Boxer will box him and shall be paid the agreed weight forfeit.

6. In the event of the Boxer failing to appear and box or to weigh-in as provided above (except under circumstances set out under Clause 15A of this Agreement), in consequence of which the contest does not take place, he shall pay to the Promoter the sum of £ 1,000 damages and any such additional amount as may be assessed by the Board or Area Council after being satisfied that such additional damages have been incurred.

7. In the event of the Promoter failing to supply a duly qualified opponent he shall pay to the Boxer £ 1,000, damages and any such additional amount that may be assessed by the Board or Area Council after being satisfied that such additional damages have been incurred. FIFTY THOUSAND of TWENTYSEVENANDHALF PERCENT

8. In consideration for boxing as above the Promoter shall pay to the Boxer the sum of £50,000 or 27½ per cent. of the Gross Receipts if he wins the said contest. £50,000 or 27½ per cent. of the Gross Receipts if he loses, and £50,000, or 27½ per cent. of the Gross Receipts if the said contest is drawn. For the purpose of this Agreement it is agreed that Gross Receipts do not include Entertainment Tax, and any fee payable in respect of Broadcast, Television or Film(s). PLUS FIVE EDITION.

8B. The Promoter shall deduct such sum as may be payable in accordance with REGULATION 20, PARAGRAPH 38 (A) and (B) of the B.B.B. of C. REGULATIONS and shall forthwith pay to the B.B.B. of C. the moneys so deducted.

9. In the event of an Agreement being entered into for the said contest to be Broadcast or Televised, whether by the B.B.C. or any other person, firm or corporation, either in Great Britain or elsewhere, the Promoter shall pay to the Boxer 23½ per cent. of the fee or fees so received. In the event of the contest being filmed 23½ per cent. of the fee 30% shall be paid to the Boxer. Fees in respect of Broadcast, Television or Film(s) shall be treated as being separate and apart from the purse money mentioned in Clause 8.

In cases of Television or Broadcast of boxing contests where the fee is paid for a period of time as distinct from a specific contest 47½ per cent. of the fee is to be divided among the Boxers concerned in the Broadcast or Television. In the event of any dispute arising from the allocation of such fees the sum payable to the Boxers shall be forwarded by the Promoter within twenty-four hours of receipt, to the Board or Area Council concerned, who shall decide in their absolute discretion as to the allocation.

10. The Boxer shall on the signing of this Agreement deposit the sum of £ with the Board or Area Council as a guarantee of his appearance and his compliance with the conditions. In the event of the contest taking place, the sum deposited shall be returned to the Boxer.

11. The Referee shall be appointed by the Board or Area Council of the B.B.B. of C.

12. The Boxer shall not box publicly or in any Boxing Booth before 18th June days before the date of the contest without the consent in writing of the Promoter.

13. The Boxer, within eight hours of the contest, shall be certified in a fit condition to box by a duly qualified Medical Officer appointed by the Promoter, or, if called upon to do so by the Board, Area Council or the Promoter at any time by a Medical Officer appointed by the Board or an Area Council.

14. The Boxer shall from the date hereof until the contest conform in all respects to the reasonable arrangements made by the Promoter for, or in any way concerning, the contest, and shall not be guilty of any act or conduct calculated or which might reasonably be expected to render him unfit to carry out the terms of this Contract in all respects and will carry out all reasonable requirements of the Promoter which are put forward for the success of the contest and the fitness of the Boxer.

NOTE.—Promoters, Managers and Boxers should particularly note lines 4 and 5 of the first paragraph of Clause 9.

This page and next: promoter Jack Solomons' contract with Clay to fight Henry Cooper at Wembley Stadium, April 1963.

15A. IN THE EVENT OF THE BOXER BEING DECLARED MEDICALLY UNFIT TO FULFIL THIS ENGAGEMENT HE SHALL IMMEDIATELY NOTIFY THE PROMOTER. THE BOXER AGREES NOT TO ENTER INTO ANY OTHER AGREEMENT, OTHER THAN THOSE REPORTED TO THE PROMOTER BEFORE THE TIME OF SUCH UNFITNESS, BEFORE HE HAS FULFILLED THIS CONTRACT, SUBJECT AS HEREINAFTER PROVIDED.

15B. The Boxer shall notify the Promoter in writing within seven days after being certified fit.

15C. The Promoter after being so notified shall offer in writing within seven days a date for the contest contracted for herein which shall take place at the first reasonable opportunity. In the event of the parties being unable to agree on the date the Board or Area Council, whose decision shall be final, shall decide.

15D. In the event of the contest not being fulfilled within twenty-eight days of reporting shall prevent the Boxer from entering into an agreement to box before the date agreed for the fulfilment of this Contract, subject always to there being no contravention of Clause 12 of the re-arranged contest.

15E. In the event of the Promoter not giving a date to the Boxer in accordance with the above provisions the deposit shall be returned to the Boxer and thereafter each party shall be at liberty to enter into such other arrangements as he may desire and this Contract shall be considered at an end.

15F. If, however, the Boxer's unfitness is caused by his own misconduct, such misconduct shall be reported to, and dealt with, by the Board or Area Council.

16. In the event of the said   COOPER   being unable to appear through any cause whatever the Boxer agrees to box a substitute of *similar skill* to be mutually agreed upon. If parties are unable to mutually agree on a suitable substitute the Board or Area Council, whose decision shall be final, shall select an opponent.

17. Representatives of the Board, Area Council and the Promoter shall have access to witness the training of the Boxer at any time after the signing of these Articles.

18. The Boxer shall be at the place of contest on 18th June/63   at 6.30   o'clock.

19.   Seconds are allowed free admission with the Boxer, and should the Boxer be working on percentage he is entitled to bring   extra persons to look after his financial interests.

20. In the event of the venue of the contest being in the open air and the tournament is postponed owing to weather conditions, such as fog, rain, etc., the Promoter shall pay to the Boxer such reasonable expenses as may be agreed or as failing agreement the Board or Area may decide.

21. After all deposits have been repaid this Contract shall be null and void in the event of the stated venue being not available by reason of strikes, Queen's enemies, *force majeure*, or by order of any authorised authority, and in the event of any decision of the B.B.B. of C. affecting the contest or any of the parties concerned therewith, causing it to be impossible to hold the contest.

22. In case any dispute shall arise as to any matter arising under or out of this Contract, and whether the Contract has been abandoned, rescinded or determined by forfeiture or otherwise, and whether the claims arise under the Contract or from the breach, recission or abandonment thereof, it shall be referred for decision to the Board or Area Council.

AS WITNESS WHEREOF the parties herein mentioned have hereunto set their hands the day and year first before written.

Witness..

Promoter's Signature......................................

Witness..

Boxer's or Authorised Manager's Signature............................

Witness..

Guardian's Signature ....

OPTION CLAUSE

The Boxer agrees to grant the Promoter an option of two further contests under the same terms and conditions, both to take place within seven weeks of the *Contest* provided for at Clause 1, provided :—

(a) The Option is taken up by the Promoter within two days of the *Contest* at Clause 1.

(b) The first *such further Contest* shall take place within three weeks of the *original Contest*.

(c) The Promoter must within two days after the first *such further* contest fix the date of the second optional contest.

(d) The opponent in both such further contests shall be mutually agreed upon. In the event of the parties being unable to reach agreement the matter shall be referred to the Board or Area Council, whose decision shall be final.

(e) In the event of the option being taken up and the money received being a " percentage " sum, the Boxer agrees not to box elsewhere until this Contract is fulfilled.

(f) In the event of the money received being a "fixed" sum, the option on the Boxer's services shall only apply within 50 miles of the City or Town of the Original Contest. (Distance to be taken from A.B.C. Railway Guide.)

Boxer's or Authorised Manager's Signature. ....   Witness ....

NO SIGNATURE—NO OPTION

Guardian's Signature ....

DETAILS OF ENGAGEMENTS ALREADY ARRANGED (SEE CLAUSE 15A)

Date of Contest	Promoter	Opponent	Remarks

WPC 20755

September 19, 1963

Mr. Harry Markson
Madison Square Garden
New York City, New York

Dear Mr. Markson:

I hereby agree to fight the winner of the
Chavalo - De John fight in Louisville on November 8,
1963, under the promotion of William H. King under
terms which Bill King, the Louisville Sponsoring
Group and I have mutually agreed upon.

Very truly yours,

Cassius M. Clay, Jr.

Gordon B. Davidson
Attorney for Louisville
Sponsoring Group

A letter of intent to fight, September 1963

16. It is specifically agreed by all parties hereto that any and all actions for the breach of this Agreement shall be brought in, and only in, the County of Delaware and the State of Pennsylvania; to that end Clay, Liston and LSG hereby designate the Secretary of the Commonwealth of Pennsylvania as their agent for service of process upon them.

IN WITNESS WHEREOF, the parties hereto have set their hands and seals this 5th day of November, 1963.

_____ (SEAL)
Charles Liston

_____ (SEAL)
Cassius Clay

INTER-CONTINENTAL PROMOTIONS, INC.

By: _____

Attest: _____
                              Secretary

LOUISVILLE SPONSORING GROUP

By: _____
         William Faversham

Signature page of Clay / Liston contract, November 1963.

STATE OF NEW YORK,
COUNTY OF **NEW YORK**   } ss.:

On this   *3rd* day of   **February,**   19 **64** , *before me personally came*

EDWARD W. JACKO, JR.

to me known to be the person described in and who executed the foregoing certificate of incorporation and
he   thereupon (severally) duly acknowledged to me that   he   executed the same.

JAWN A. SANDIFER
Notary Public, State of New York
No. 31-97-16
Qualified in New York County
Term Expires March 30, 1964

Certificate of Incorporation

of

CASSIUS CLAY ENTERPRISES, INC.

under Section 402 of the Business Corporation Law
of the State of New York

Filed By:

EDWARD W. JACKO, JR.,
Attorney at Law
Office and Post Office Address

271 West 125th Street
New York, New York 10027

Filed: State of New York
Department of State
Albany, N.Y. Feb 4, 1964

Cassius Clay Enterprises' Certificate of Incorporation, February 1964.

A G R E E M E N T

THIS AGREEMENT made this fourteenth day of September, 1964, by and between CASSIUS CLAY, also known as Muhammad Ali, of Louisville, Kentucky, the present Heavyweight Boxing Champion of the World, and CHARLES LISTON, also known as Charles Sonny Liston, of Denver, Colorado, the Challenger for the said title.

WHEREAS, the said Clay by a contract dated July 27, 1964 has agreed to defend his title against the said Liston on November 16, 1964, at Boston, Massachusetts; and

WHEREAS, the said Liston by a contract dated July 27, 1964 agrees to engage in a boxing match for the said title;

NOW, THEREFORE, it is agreed by and between the parties as follows:

1. The winner of the said title bout agrees, in or within six (6) months, to execute a written contract with one of the then first four rated contenders as listed by the World's Boxing Association, whereby said winner agrees to defend his title against one of the four aforementioned rated contenders.

2. In order to insure the performance of the provisions and conditions contained in this agreement, the parties hereto agree and consent to the withholding of Fifty Thousand Dollars ($50,000.00) from the winner's purse by the Massachusetts Boxing Commission; and it is further agreed that upon a willful breach of the said provisions and/or conditions by the winner, the aforementioned Fifty Thousand Dollars ($50,000.00) shall be forfeited to the Commonwealth of Massachusetts. *as liquidated damages to be retained by the Commonwealth*

IN WITNESS WHEREOF, we have hereunto and to another instrument of like tenor set our hands and seals the day, month and year first above written.

Cassius Clay
CASSIUS CLAY
Muhammad Ali
also known as Muhammad Ali
Charles Liston
CHARLES LISTON
Charles Sonny Liston
also known as Charles Sonny Liston

Fight agreement between Muhammad Ali and Sonny Liston, July 1964.

State of Maine

MAINE STATE BOXING COMMISSION

Fee $6.00

Application for License as Professional Boxer

City or town .....Lewiston,..Me.......May..89..65....

I hereby make............first...........application for license to act as professional boxer at boxing and sparring
first or second

matches or exhibitions.

Real name ....Cassius Clay... Assumed name ...Muhammed Ali........................

Residence ....Miami,..Florida...
               (Street and Number)   (City or Town)

Nationality .....Negro... Business or occupation ....Boxer.........................

Name of Employer ......I am an independent contractor..

Business Address ....Louisville Sponsoring Group, Louisville, Ky......... Tel. No. .581-1881.
                      (Street and Number)   (City or Town)

Physical condition ......Excellent..

Experience as professional boxer:—

....Presently the heavyweight champion of the world...

....

Name of Manager ...Angelo Dundee....................................... Address ....

How long since your last bout? ...Last bout was on February 25, 1964.......

I refer for recommendation as to ability and character to (At least two must be given) :—

Name	City or Town	Street and Number	Occupation
Garland D. Cherry	Chester, Pa.	5th & Welsh Sts.	Lawyer
Robert A. Nilon	Ridley Park, Pa.	21 Sellers Ave/	Concessionaire, caterer, and sports promoter.

Personal Description of Applicant

Date of Birth .... Where born ....

Height .... feet .... inches Weight .... pounds

Complexion .... Color of eyes .... Color of hair ....

Distinguishing Marks ....

Signature of Applicant ....

This License was................granted   Print Last Name Here..

Date ....

License No. ....

Expires ....

Recent Photograph Must be
Attached to This Application

Clay's application to the Maine State Boxing Commission for a professional boxer's licence, May 1965.

State of Maine

MAINE STATE BOXING COMMISSION

FEE $5.00

Application for License as Manager

City or town Lewiston, Maine May 8 19 65

(Date)

I hereby make application for a license to act as manager at boxing and sparring matches or exhibitions.

Real name Angelo Dundee .... Assumed name ...... not applicable

Residence .... Tel. No. ....

(Street and Number) (City or Town)

Nationality .... Business or occupation Boxing Manager

Name of Employer ....

Business Address .... Tel No. ....

(Street and Number) (City or Town)

Physical condition Excellent

Experience as manager: —

....

....

....

How long since you last officiated? ....

I refer for recommendation as to ability and character to (At least two must be given): —

Name	City or Town	Street and Number	Occupation
Garland D. Cherry	Chester, Pa.	5th & Welsh Sts.	Lawyer
Robert Nilon	Ridley Park, Pa.	21 Sellers Ave.	Concessionaire, caterer, and sports promoter.

Personal Description of Applicant

Date of Birth .... Where born ....

Height .... feet .... inches Weight .... pounds

Complexion .... Color of eyes .... Color of hair ....

Distinguishing Marks ....

Signature of Applicant ....

Print last name here ....

This License was .... granted

Date ....

Expires ....

License No. ....

Angelo Dundee's application to the Maine State Boxing Commission for a manager's licence, May 1965

CONTRACT

(Form of Contract Approved by the Maine State Boxing Commission)

THIS AGREEMENT made and entered into this **eighth** day of **May** , 19 **65** between **XX Intercontinental Prom., Inc** Club of the City or Town of **Lewiston** and State of Maine, a duly licensed Boxing Club under the laws of the State of Maine, party of the first part and **Cassius Clay** of the City or Town of **Louisville** and State of **Kentucky** a duly licensed Boxer, License No. , under the Laws of the State of Maine, party of the second part;

WITNESSETH: That said party of the second part hereby agrees to enter into a Boxing Match before said club, either indoors or outdoors, in said City or Town of **Lewiston, Maine** , on the **25th** day of **May** A.D. 19 **05** for **15** rounds, to a decision, with **Charles Liston** of the City or Town of **Denver** and State of **Colorado** , as his opponent, at a weight not over **heavy-wt.** pounds, **12** hours before said contest, on the official scales of said club, for which match the party of the first part agrees to pay, after said contest, and the party of the second part agrees to accept as in full for all his claims and demands for and on account of the performance by him of this contract the sum of XXXXXXXXXXXXXXX XX **30** **none** per cent of the gross receipts of the house less the Federal and State tax and expenses as follows:

none, except: (nothing herein contained shall affect the contractual arrangement heretofore entered into between this party hereto and/or their agreement heretofore entered into... said contract being dated July 27, 1964)

IT IS UNDERSTOOD AND AGREED that said contest shall be with gloves to be furnished by the party of the first part, and shall be conducted in all respects in conformity with the laws of the State of Maine and the Rules and Regulations adopted by the Maine State Boxing Commission, which are hereby made a part of this agreement. The Referee, Judges and other officials for and necessary to the proper conduct of said contest shall be persons duly licensed by the Maine State Boxing Commission, and assigned to act as such.

The party of the second part hereby agrees to deposit with the party of the first part, cash, certified check or accepted draft for the sum of **none** dollars, as forfeit money, to guarantee his appearance, his making the weight as above agreed and for his performance of this contract in all other respects.

If said party of the second part shall fail to appear or make the weight agreed upon, or if said party is not in physical condition and should fail to pass the required examination by a duly licensed physician, then said forfeit money may at the discretion of the State Boxing Commission be forfeited to the party of the first part and under these circumstances the party of the first part will pay to **none** the other contestant in this match, or his duly authorized manager, at least 1/3 of his agreed purse as liquidated damages providing said contestant appears ready and able to fulfill his agreement or contract to box, unless said contestant shall have received notice from the party of the first part 24 hours in advance of the contest, for some valid reason, his services could not be used at the agreed place and time. If for any reason, other than the failure on the part of either of the two contestants to appear, the party of the first part does not fulfill this contract, the party of the first part shall then pay to the party of the second part an amount equal to said forfeit as liquidated damages, unless this match is cancelled by mutual consent and the approval of the State Boxing Commission.

IT IS UNDERSTOOD AND AGREED that the party of the second part shall personally report at the above named place for weighing and medical examination in accordance with the Rules and Regulations of the Maine State Boxing Commission, and shall report at the club not less than two hours before the time set for the contest, the default of which shall be a breach of this contract. It is also distinctly agreed that there shall be no other agreement for covering this contest than herein contained for weights or times for weighing in.

IT IS FURTHER AGREED that if said party of the second part enters into another contest prior to the one herein contracted for and is defeated, or in any other way does anything calculated to lessen his present value as an attraction, the party of the first part shall have the option to rescind and cancel this contract without further liability hereunder, provided such cancellation is approved by the Maine State Boxing Commission.

IT IS UNDERSTOOD AND AGREED that said party of the first part is to make all arrangements for said contest, and to provide a suitable place and proper facilities for the staging of said contest, and such conveniences and appliances as may be reasonably necessary shall be provided.

IT IS UNDERSTOOD AND AGREED that all parties to this contract hold licenses as provided for in the laws of the State of Maine governing boxing, and that no one shall be permitted to participate in said contest in any way who is not duly licensed.

IN WITNESS WHEREOF, the said parties hereto have hereunto set their hands and seals the day and year first above written.

In the presence of:

Intercontinental Promotions, Inc.

By

Boxer

In the presence of:

By

Angelo Dundee, Manager (L. S.)

This contract must be executed in triplicate, one copy to be filed with the Maine State Boxing Commission, State House, Augusta, Maine, and all the conditions herein mentioned are subject to the law and rules of said commission.

An unsigned contract to fight Liston, May 1965.

Mr. Jim Jacobs
The Big Fights, Inc.
9 East 40th Street
New York, New York 10016

Dear Jim:

You have told me that you are producing a motion picture
SPECIAL comparing and analyzing my brilliant boxing style with
that of Floyd Patterson, getting across the fact that "I float
like a butterfly and sting like a bee", and which will feature
films of my amateur and professional fights, as well as those
of Floyd Patterson's amateur and professional fights.

For good and valuable consideration, including a color
print of each of my boxing bouts with Sonny Liston, which
color prints are solely and exclusively for my own private
usage, and for no other purpose, receipt of which is
acknowledged, I hereby give you my permission, irrevocable
and without limitation, to use those motion pictures in
which I was a participant, plus interviews in which I took
part, for this SPECIAL, and also the right to advertise this
SPECIAL and use my name and photograph in connection with it.

I further give you permission to the unrestricted use
in all media and in perpetuity to films of all boxing bouts
in which I participated, including the color prints subjects
listed above.

Finally, I give you my permission for you to photograph
in color my upcoming fight with Floyd Patterson, and you
agree to furnish me with a color print of this fight at
no charge.

Muhammed Ali a.k.a. Cassius Clay

Date: Sept 9-1965

Permission from Ali for his words, fights and image to be used in a motion picture "special", September 1965.

WHEREAS, I, MUHAMMAD ALI, better-known-as-CASSIUS-CLAY, *M.A.*
am scheduled to meet FLOYD PATTERSON in a fifteen-round title
bout for the heavyweight championship of the World on November
22, 1965, in Las Vegas, and

WHEREAS, the World's Boxing Association, James E. Deskin,
President, has sanctioned said bout on condition that the
winner meet Ernie Terrell in a title bout within six months
after the November 22nd match (or six months from any postponed date thereof), *defend my world Heavyweight Championship*
M.A.   I hereby agree to meet said Terrell in a fifteen-round
title bout should I be the winner of the November 22nd bout, *against*
and in lieu thereof, I will pay to the World Boxing Association, *the Challenge*
or its designee, the penal sum of Fifty Thousand Dollars *of*
($50,000.00), provided all of the following conditions are met:

(1) Terrell must dismiss with prejudice his lawsuit now
pending against me and other defendants in Chicago no later
than 60 days after the fight between me and Patterson;

(2) The promoter, date and site of the bout are to be
selected by Louisville Sponsoring Group on ninety (90) days'
notice to Terrell in writing;

(3) The promoter of the ancillary rights is to be approved
by Louisville Sponsoring Group in writing, and any proposed
contract relating to such rights is to be approved by them
in writing;

(4) The percentage of the gates and ancillary rights to
be paid to me are to be satisfactory to me;

(5) The World Boxing Association and Louisville Sponsoring
Group and I must be satisfied that the managers, trainers, or
any persons, firms or corporations having any property interest
in Terrell, are free from any underworld connections or
contacts;

(continued)

This page and next: Ali's amended agreement "to defend my world heavyweight championship against the challenge of" Ernie Terrell – assuming he defeats Floyd Patterson, November 1965.

(6) Terrell and I must be in physical condition satisfactory to the World Boxing Association, and to the State Athletic Commissions having jurisdiction.

If any of these conditions are not met, this agreement shall be null and void.

WITNESS:

_____
MUHAMMAD ALI
(also known as Cassius Clay

Nov 21- 1965

Subscribed and sworn to before me
this_____day of November, 1965.

_____
Notary Public in and for Clark County,
State of Nevada

LOUISVILLE SPONSORING GROUP
ALI vs.

Date of Fight	Opponent	Location	Gross Receipts
** October 29, 1960	Tunney Hunsaker	Louisville	00 **
December 27, 1960	Herb Siler	Miami	$ 200.00
January 17, 1961	Donnie Fleeman	Louisville	913.25
April 19, 1961	Lamar Clark	Louisville	2,548.23
June 26, 1961	Duke Saledong	Las Vegas	1,500.00
July 22, 1961	Alonzo Johnson	Louisville	6,636.49
October 28, 1961	Alex Miteff	Louisville	5,644.46
November 25, 1961	Willie Besmanoff	Louisville	2,047.81
February 10, 1962	Sonny Banks	Madison Sq.	5,014.39
February 28, 1962	Don Warner	Miami	1,674.95
April 23, 1962	George Logan	Los Angeles	9,205.97
May 19, 1962	Billy Daniels	Madison Sq.	6,000.00
July 2, 1962	Alejandro Lavorante	Los Angeles	15,148.65
November 15, 1962	Archie Moore	Los Angeles	45,300.18
January 24, 1963	Charlie Powell	Pittsburgh	14,331.50
March 13, 1963	Doug Jones	Madison Sq.	57,668.10
June 8, 1963	Henry Cooper	London, England	56,097.69
February 25, 1964	Sonny Liston	Miami	464,594.58
May 25, 1965	Sonny Liston	Lewiston, Me.	361,819.44
November 22, 1965	Floyd Patterson	Las Vegas	300,077.98
March 29, 1966	George Chuvalo	Toronto, Canada	66,332.38
May 21, 1966	Henry Cooper	London, England	448,186.50
August 6, 1966	Brian London	London, England	290,411.25
September 10, 1966	Karl Mildenberger	Frankfurt, Germany	211,576.00

**This fight was contracted for <u>before</u> Ali's contract with the
Louisville Sponsoring Group even though it was actually held
after Ali signed with the Group, and the Group had no receipts
from that fight.**

The Louisville Sponsoring Group's register of fight receipts, 1960-66.

LOUISVILLE SPONSORING GROUP
LOUISVILLE, KENTUCKY

114047500

21-10
830

No. 1304

PAID
CITIZENS FIDELITY BANK & TRUST COMPANY

January 25 1966

PAY TO THE
ORDER OF   Cassius M. Clay, Jr.

$156,300.00

JAN 28 1966

---One Hundred Fifty-Six Thousand Three Hundred and no/100-------DOLLARS

LOUISVILLE KENTUCKY LOUISVILLE SPONSORING GROUP

FOR 1965 income taxes

CITIZENS FIDELITY
BANK & TRUST CO.
LOUISVILLE, KENTUCKY

AUTH.
SIG.

⑆0830⑈0010⑈ 004 358 3⑈   ⑈0015630000⑈

LOUISVILLE SPONSORING GROUP
LOUISVILLE, KENTUCKY

21-10
830

No. 1305

January 26,   19 66

PAY TO THE
ORDER OF Muhammad Ali

$ 38,926.41

PAID
CITIZENS FIDELITY BANK & TRUST COMPANY

JAN 28 1966

LOUISVILLE SPONSORING GROUP

----Thirty-Eight Thousand Nine Hundred Twenty-Six and 41/100----- DOLLARS

FOR

CITIZENS FIDELITY
BANK & TRUST CO.
LOUISVILLE, KENTUCKY

AUTH.
SIG.

⑆0830⑈0010⑈ 004 358 3⑈   ⑈00018926 41⑈

Payment from the Louisville Sponsoring Group made out to "Cassius Clay" on 25 January 1966 and the renamed "Muhammad Ali" the day after.

SELECTIVE SERVICE SYSTEM

Selective Service
Local Board No. 47
Room 106, VA Bldg.
1405 W. Broadway
Louisville, Ky. 40203

(LOCAL BOARD STAMP)

July 22, 1966

IN REPLY, REFER TO:

Mr. Cassius Marsellus Clay
46-10 15 Court
Miami, Florida

Dear Mr. Clay:

A Board meeting was held on July 21, 1966 and this letter is written by the direction of the Board Members of Local Board 47, Louisville, Ky.

All correspondence addressed to this Board shall be signed as the individual is registered, namely Cassius Clay. Any other correspondence will not be considered as coming from the registrant.

Yours truly,

Local Board 47

(Miss) M. Green
Clerk

Notification from the Louisville Selective Service board that only correspondence from "Cassius Clay" would be recognised, July 1966.

46-10 15 Court
Miami, Florida
July 7, 1966

Local Board No. 47
1405 West Broadway
Louisville, Kentucky 40203

Re: Request for permit to depart from the
United States.
Cassius M. Clay, No. - 15-47-42-127, a/k/a
Muhammad Ali

Gentlemen:

Request is herewith made to depart the United States for the period July 22,
1966 to August 15, 1966. I am to defend my World Heavyweight Championship in
London England on August 6, 1966 and expect to be in England during the entire
period I am abroad.

Arthur Grafton, Esquire, attorney for the Louisville Sponsoring Group is
authorized to receive the permit on my behalf when it has been issued.

Please be advised that I have also contracted to fight in Frankfurt, Germany
on September 10, 1966. When I return to this country in the middle of August, I
will make formal application for a permit to again leave the country to enable me
to defend my title in Germany.

I want to express my thanks to the entire Board, for having granted my two
previous permits.

Sincerely yours,

Muhammad Ali

MA/vn

Request to travel, July 1966.

Form approved.
Budget Bureau No. 33.R106.4.

July 22, 1966
(Date)

SELECTIVE SERVICE SYSTEM
PERMIT FOR REGISTRANT TO DEPART FROM THE UNITED STATES

1. NAME OF REGISTRANT			2. SELECTIVE SERVICE NO.			
Cassius	Marsellus	Clay	15	47	42	127
(First)	(Middle)	(Last)				

3. PRESENT ADDRESS

46-10 15 Court   Miami   Florida
(Number and Street)   (City or town)   (State)   (Zip Code)

4. CLASSIFICATION

1-A

5. PLACE OF BIRTH

Louisville   Ky.   USA
(City or town)   (State)   (Country)

6. DATE OF BIRTH

January 17, 1942

7. IF NONCITIZEN, ALIEN REGISTRATION NUMBER ....

8. IN HIS APPLICATION THE REGISTRANT GAVE THE FOLLOWING INFORMATION:

A. COUNTRIES TO BE VISITED   England

B. ORGANIZATIONS OR INDIVIDUALS REPRESENTED   Cassius Marsellus Clay

C. NATURE OF BUSINESS   Professional Boxing

The above-named registrant is hereby authorized to depart from the United States and to remain absent therefrom until ......August 8, 1966.......................
(Date)

M. Green
(Signature)

Clerk Bd 47 Louisville Ky
(Title)

NOTICE: Before leaving the United States, if an alien, secure a reentry permit, if necessary, from the Immigration and Naturalization Service, Department of Justice.

SSS Form 300 (Revised 1-29-65)   (Previous printings are obsolete)

& U.S. GOVERNMENT PRINTING OFFICE : 1965 OF—762-886

Travel permit, July 1966.

Index